Rome + C

Both of you were
great in the battle!

[signature]

A Courageous Cause

A Courageous Cause

A Personal Story of Modern Republicanism's Birth from 1956 to 1966 in Mississippi.

by Wirt A. Yerger, Jr.
with Joseph L. Maxwell, III

LifeStory Publishing

Published by LifeStory Publishing
P.O. Box 16428
Jackson, MS 39236-6428

First Edition

Library of Congress Control Number: 2010925552

Contents: v. 1. Biography v. 2. Non-fiction v. 3. History

ISBN: 978-0-9758988-7-1
         0-9758988-7-6

This book is dedicated to
the thousands of Mississippians
who had the courage to participate in
making a viable Republican Party
and two-party system in Mississippi.

Contents

Preface

by Joseph L. Maxwell, III

No one has told the full story of the birth of the modern Mississippi Republican Party. Wirt Yerger's story is that story, a narrative of sacrificial men and women dedicated to creating a brighter future versus clinging to a muddled past.

Historic scraps about the early new Republican movement in Mississippi often have been used as props in the historic—*and definitely heroic*—civil rights drama that happened at the same time that Wirt and his new conservative friends were laboring. Ironically, the bright clarity of the civil rights struggle may have led some to overlook, or perhaps sometimes to misinterpret, the modern GOP story in Mississippi.

I firmly believe Americans can never write or talk too much about the civil rights movement in Mississippi and the South. The bravery and sacrifice of so many to bring the possibility of equal treatment and opportunity to all Americans is a triumph of idealism over cynicism. Furthermore, anyone who might read this book in hopes of finding arguments against opening all opportunities to all people in the United States will be sorely disappointed. My African-American friends have waged an astounding "courageous cause," and nowhere was that more apparent than in the one-party State of Mississippi, where blacks endured unfathomable violence and scorn.

There was, however, a second remarkable movement during this same era, one that also combined bravery with idealism. I hope you will give it the benefit of your time and thought. It is another story of greatness; of a David slaying a Goliath; of a victory against tough odds. It has never been told in full. It deserves a full accounting, not only for history's sake, but also because amazing state and national achievements have not yet been fully set in context or understood. That is the goal of this book.

Wirt Yerger and his band of heroes combatted the same oppressive scoundrels—the old-line Mississippi Democrats—as did the state's civil rights leaders. Those Democrats spewed vitriol at blacks and at new Republicans. Mississippi's GOP pioneers did not suffer physical harm, segregated/substandard facilities, or death as did my black friends' parents, grandparents, etc. So in this sense the GOP leaders' plight did not equal and does not compare with that era's African-American heroes. These young, new Republican leaders did, however, put their careers and children's futures on the line. They faced threats and hatred. Both groups of idealists—the civil rights leadership and the new Republican leadership—faced ridicule. Both faced potential loss of business, friends, and reputation. Both freely chose a path of principle over stale pragmatism.

The new Republicans were true intellectual conservatives. They were Barry's boys (Goldwater, that is). Their ideals were not the old-line Democrats' New Deal, big-government ideals. Their view of what constituted a "conservative" was not the same as the view of old-line Mississippi Democrats, long fattened on good-old-boy power for decades.

What do you think of when you hear the word "conservative"? Sadly, a powerful racist group of old-line Democrats first claimed this word in Mississippi; in their hands, this word came to stand for all-or-nothing segregation and very little else.

But serious distinctions exist between the conservatism of old-line Democrats and Wirt Yerger's new Republican movement. Sometimes these distinctions have not been well-defined. This book, written in a narrative form and through Wirt's authoritative voice, may shed light on some false assumptions.

Without Wirt's young, idealistic team of true conservatives, the old-line Democrats' dark cloud of political scandal and half-baked conservatism may not have fallen as quickly as it did. It is as if there were two axes chopping at the tree of the old-line Democrats' racist power in Mississippi: one axe was the civil rights movement and the other was the new Republicans' movement. Both axes were sharp. They ripped at different sides of the old-line Democrats' racist tree. As a result the tree fell faster in the 1960s.

They did not consciously work together, to be sure. Yet the new Republicans and the state's civil rights leadership tore down the state's vicious, race-based one-party system, a system that had stuffed the pockets of old-line Democrats for so long. This book will show, among other things, that these new Republicans contributed to opening the door for people of all races and beliefs to vote their conscience in Mississippi and to pursue their ideals. First and foremost, Wirt's group constantly called for a two-party system for the state's voters. They trusted the state's voters to govern by the vote.

Many of these young Mississippi Republican men were from old Mississippi families. Wirt was a fifth-generation Mississippian. He easily could have dived into the established political scene and milked it as many others did. That scene, however, disgusted him.

Wirt and his compatriots began with no political power. If political power could be measured with negative numbers, then these new conservatives registered below zero. Mississippians in the 1950s and 1960s did not welcome new ideas. *A second party? That was unheard of!* Fresh ideas simply did not enter the political or social discourse. The natural pathways for such exchanges had been blocked for decades by the state's Democrat dictators.

In the 1950s Mississippi was almost un-American. It suffered under a regime that, in ways, now seems as oppressive as the Communist monster so feared by all Americans during that same time. The state had only one party, and with an accommodating state media, the old-line Democrats pumped out propaganda aimed at keeping a vice-grip on their power.

Wirt was, and remains, an iconoclast—ready to challenge the prevailing wisdom if necessary. He is a speeding tank of unyielding principles—impregnable and ready to outlast his enemy. With his friends he attacked the old-line, corrupt system. Wirt and his group advocated a real conservatism that they drew from reading intellectuals such as William F. Buckley and Russell Kirk. Theirs was an intellectually satisfying body of thought rooted in championing free enterprise, limited government, individual liberty, personal responsibility, and opposition to oppressive government systems. In this book, you will read many letters and memos that are being made public for the first time. You will read correspondence with top state and national figures. You will read heretofore confidential battle plans. All testify to the state GOP's intellectual and political integrity and wisdom in the face of harsh, irrational opposition.

Wirt and his new conservatives were sincere and gentlemanly; they sought a better future for all; and that is what they won.

But as the 1960s and 1970s waxed on, these new conservatives' accomplishments endured incredible revision and scrutiny by the same blunt national media that unfairly ripped Barry Goldwater to shreds during his 1964 race for the White House. Mississippi Republicans' founding story and accomplishments therefore were retold and re-interpreted mostly by those best described as less than sympathetic to honest conservatism, though surely most analyses have been sincere. Thus, the story of Mississippi's new conservatives has never been fully set in context.

Until now...

I prevailed upon Wirt to tell this story. He asked me only to write a family memoir. Once written, I felt so much more was yet to be told. Much of what Wirt recounted to me, I had never known. As I pilfered through libraries and archives, Wirt's stories lined up!

You owe it to yourself to read this book. You owe it to your children. You may agree with it or revile it, but I hope you will hear it. I have based our writing on Wirt's own amazing memory, along with hundreds of pages of archival research. I also have tried to set the story in the full context of its time. My opinion is that the only way truly to appreciate the realities of what Wirt and all Mississippians faced in the 1950s and 1960s is by viewing it through the news that they read and lived each day. Perhaps this approach might let us see and feel the unfolding drama afresh. So while this book draws from commendable scholarly works, it is largely rooted in first-hand journalistic accounts from that day, many terribly racist or biased but all representative of what people then actually read and processed daily. Some may say that this book includes too much about the issues of race and Communism. I don't believe it is possible to understand Wirt's and his team's efforts outside the context of these two issues. It would be like insisting a species of fish be studied but only out of water. To accomplish the book's goal of setting fresh context, I read the front page, and sometimes more, of every *Clarion-Ledger* newspaper from 1956 to 1966. This was, and still is, Mississippi's largest paper. It was the major paper of record in Mississippi at the time.

I have been humbled by this experience; perhaps you, too, will better appreciate that no period of history is populated exclusively with "obvious calls." I understand better how decent people could suffer from mushy thinking as they tried to mollify their own unsettled lives. I also understand that while many took no positive action during these difficult times, Wirt Yerger and his band of idealists did so with vigor.

If you are under the age of 60, you may be startled by some of what you read—it is often that ugly. Some portions of this book may offend you with dated language. It offended me. But it was in this context that new Mississippi Republicans waged a war against powerfully destructive ideas and words. Thus, we have tried neither to sanitize nor to over-play this era's cultural realities. Political heroes are heroes, political villains are villains. This book's tough stance on certain old-line Democrat Mississippi politicians, however, should not be understood as a measure of any indivdual's entire character, for that would be unfair and simplistic, and we ourselves would never stand up to such a slim standard.

Perhaps some of you will end this book angry or alarmed that you never knew some of the facts in this true story. Where were these stories in your school textbooks? By Chapter 9 you may not believe such events could occur. The narrative, however, is entirely factual, though it seems utterly outrageous. As one of my journalism mentors, nationally recognized historian Marvin Olasky, says: "Sensational facts, understated prose." This book's facts speak—even scream—for themselves. They need no enhancing.

Ultimately, I hope this book offers new, legitimate avenues by which to consider Mississippians' and Americans' complex identities. If this occurs, I will be grateful.

Joseph L. Maxwell, III
Jackson, Mississippi
2010

Acknowledgements

The author and writer thank our families and our friends, all of whom have offered interest and support throughout the writing of this book. We thank the great citizens of Mississippi. Thanks as well to the fine staffs of the Mississippi Department of Archives and of the Mississippi State University Special Collections Department.

Wirt A. Yerger, Jr.
Jackson, Mississippi

Joseph L. Maxwell, III
Jackson, Mississippi

A Courageous Cause

Champion belly-acher of Mississippi.

> — One of countless aspersions
> old-line Democrats threw
> at Wirt A. Yerger, Jr.

Yerger is probably the strongest voice in the Republican Party in the South.

> —Mike Goldwater,
> son of Barry Goldwater,
> to media in 1964

Introduction

Fielding Wright was sworn in as the 49th governor of Mississippi on January 19, 1948, accompanied by a 19-gun salute and the massive blast of a 105-millimeter Howitzer cannon over Jackson.

I, Wirt Adams Yerger, Jr., was an 18-year-old Jacksonian.

Wright told Mississippians: "Vital principles and eternal truths transcend party lines and the day is now at hand when determined action must be taken." He warned that the day might be coming for the South to break with the Democratic Party.[1]

The day did come when some of us led a "determined action" to break—once and for all—with the national *and state* Democratic Party. We founded the modern Republican Party in Mississippi—the ultimate break with old-line, racist Southern Democrats who didn't know whether they wanted to be liberal or conservative, but were vocally committed to keeping long-held, highly corrupted, power.

This book tells the story of our battle.

It is a largely-untold story behind the rise of today's outstanding Mississippi Republican leadership that now includes Gov. Haley Barbour, Sen. Thad Cochran, former Sen. Trent Lott, and hundreds of state and local office holders.

1

It is a story you deserve to hear. It may very well change how you think about Mississippi and about real conservatism.

It is a complex story because issues such as Communism and race and political power were involved at a fever-pitch level in those times. Too often, the reality of these forces and how they affected us have been glazed over. The fear and confusion of the 1950s and 1960s in the South are hard for anyone under 60 years of age to understand, much less those of us who lived through it.

Back in 1948, Wright actually felt that a split might soon be coming in his Mississippi Democratic Party due to the issue of racial integration. *But splitting political associations due to race was never the South's answer.* On the contrary, my own efforts in the 1950s and 1960s were geared toward promoting a new party based on *true conservative principles and establishing a two-party system* that offered all Mississippians a true political choice.

Saying that shifts in political alliances in our state in the 1950s and 1960s were due to any one issue is an over-simplification. This book will show that there were many issues that roused people such as me to press harder for a second party in Mississippi. The issues ranged from the right for every registered voter to have a say in their own political and cultural climate (an impossibility when only one party existed) to the need for a group of leaders to promote a real conservatism rooted in intellectual principles such as free enterprise and low taxes. The old-line Democrats were not for allowing a second party voice, nor were they for promoting economic progress via a strong free-enterprise system since their political hay was gathered amid the state's rural, agricultural economy.

Also, many of the old-line Democrats in Mississippi were corrupt and power-hungry, acting as if they were above the law. Increasingly sophisticated voters were tired of it and looking for a second-party option to this state party of demagogues who were wedded to a national party seeking to increase government size and to creating a welfare state.

This book will show how we new conservatives set out to

begin a second party in Mississippi that would champion real, fully-orbed conservatism. I will also explain my honest, conservative perspective, one often oversimplified when it comes to discussing Republicanism's founding in Mississippi and the South.

I will attempt to tell the whole story through my own life experiences, since I lived out the conservative revolution in Mississippi and America. This will include hundreds of stories and accounts about my compatriots, whose work deserves great attention. If you gain a better understanding of this sincere, intellectually viable philosophy of conservatism, then writing this book will have been worthwhile for me. This is because today we still face the same issues of real conservatism versus real liberalism and progressivism.

Even as this book goes to press in early 2010, a new movement is underway led by sincere liberals in America to make the federal government so large and to make so many dependent upon it that some even say it seems akin to socialism. As in the 1950s and 1960s, big government and small government advocates are facing off again, with the future of our nation in the balance. Conservatives, once again, look for a truly idealistic leader such as we found in Barry Goldwater. Everyone seems tired of polished pragmatic politicians.

This same interplay was occurring in the 1950s and 1960s when we true conservative Republicans pushed to take our place at the table in Mississippi and American politics.

In my mind, the Republican Party was the party dedicated to the liberty and ingenuity of the individual and to the idea that good government proceeds from the individual to Washington, D.C., not the other way around.

Barry Goldwater, the 1964 GOP presidential candidate, was a good friend of mine. He became our idealistic national Republican leader. Who will assume that mantle today? He once said: "The true conservative is not afraid of the future nor is he unalterably opposed to change. Conservatism is a body of ethical and social beliefs which suggest that we should apply the wisdom of the past to the problems of present and future.

Above all else the conservative is dedicated to the preservation of the dignity of the individual and freedom for all men."[2]

Such an approach, if allowed to blossom, means every individual is valued and has opportunity. Of course, like any movement, it may take a while, but it will happen.

This is a humane political philosophy that we championed, one that insists the best chance for each man's civil liberties is linked to smaller government and a strong two-party system.

Some assume that we mid-20th century Republicans were against civil rights; but our tiny Republican band really became a protagonist for giving all people in Mississippi a choice and a political voice. This book will show that the original Democrats in Mississippi were rabidly anti-choice when it came to voting, but then in the mid-1960s as we Republicans emerged to stay, they rapidly reshuffled their deck and rewrote their own history (with the help of some national media) to make it seem that they were the inclusive party.

A more nuanced and gutsy look at the realities of what transpired in the history of modern Republicanism in Mississippi may challenge us to think anew. I sincerely hope as well that it will call today's Republicans back to their greatness as a party of real conservatism.

Modern Mississippi Republicanism worked when it rose forth in 1956 in our state because it redefined "conservatism" from a backwater list of *"You can not"* and *"Don't"* statements to a list of hopeful *"You can!"* and *"Do!"* statements.

True conservatism's core principles include: limited government, low taxes, a strong free market, a strong national defense, opposition to Communism and totalitarianism, and solid laws that promote good, basic moral values.

This book tells countless personal and researched stories that show a much fuller reality of what real conservatism is and what we dealt with while founding our party.

To offer historic context, Chapter 1 goes back to my ancestors' struggles in the Civil War. No one chooses their ancestors. Mine—originally Whigs—make for interesting reading because by providence they were leaders in the South and in Mississippi. Their story helps set some historic context in Mississippi before my political years. We all know the harsh realities that drove the Civil War. This book therefore focuses only briefly on this period. But we need a backdrop so that we can understand how the modern Republican Party emerged.

Chapter 2 introduces you to the years 1952 to 1956, when political and social change were in the air. It offers necessary national context for understanding our ensuing Mississippi GOP battles. Real Republicanism was just a seed back then waiting to break open. Our state Democrats were becoming a mangled, dirty mess. Conditions were evolving that would necessitate creating a two-party system.

Chapter 3 tells of the creation of the official Mississippi Republican Party in 1956.

Chapters 4 through 12 proceed a year at a time—1957, 1958, 1959, etc.—unfolding the modern GOP's beginnings in Mississippi. It includes my progression from local, to state, to national influence in the Republican Party. It tells the stories, year by year, of many heroes and some villains. I hope you will feel a part of their battles.

Chapter 13 tells of my resignation in 1966.

Chapter 14 offers my thoughts on our state GOP's growth since 1966 and on the GOP's future. I offer these by reproducing a speech I gave to Mississippi Republicans in 2009.

The reader is invited now to explore a yet-untold story of the founding of real Republicanism in our state and of real conservatism nationally, and to continue his or her efforts to ensure responsible government.

As every schoolboy knows, the Republican name has been a stigma to Mississippi since the Civil War. The new party is out to create a new image. With it they are bringing a touch of freshness to the political scene. ... These boys are real dedicated. They may get there yet.

—U.S. Sen. Barry Goldwater (Ariz.) speaking in 1960 to the Mississippi Republican Convention

1

1880s-1950s

Ancestors, Strange Republicans, & the Need for Change

Our new Republican movement in the 1950s in Mississippi became necessary for philosophical and practical reasons, some of which you may not have been taught in school. These matters include strange Republicans such as Mississippian Perry Wilbon Howard and decades of racist Democrat domination. Understanding a bit of this history is vital. I'll offer it in the brief context of my own family tree so you can better appreciate why I, and others like me, started Mississippi's modern GOP.

My great, great grandfather was George Shall Yerger, a major player in pre-Civil War Mississippi. He moved to Mississippi from Tennessee, eventually settling in Jackson, where he built a mansion on the 700 block of North State Street. He owned plantations in Yazoo and Washington counties in Mississippi. When he died on a deer hunt at his Ivanhoe Plantation in Washington County, *The Jackson Daily News* announced, "HON. GEO. S. YERGER IS DEAD!" The paper further said:

The electric current never brought a sadder message to

the community. ... We can hardly realize that one whom we saw only a few days since in the strength and vigor of ripened manhood, moving about in our city, projecting and co-operating in new schemes for her prosperity, should be thus suddenly snatched forever from our midst.[1]

Jefferson Davis, president of the Confederate States of America, stated that "George Yerger had a methodical, well-trained mind and was quite successful in his profession. ... As one of the most prominent Whigs in Mississippi, Yerger was vitally interested in politics, although he never held public office."[2]

One of George's sons was William Swan, my great grandfather; he was a fine attorney and highly respected Confederate general. His good friend, Confederate Brigadier General Wirt Adams, eventually married William Swan's daughter, Sarah. William Swan Yerger and Wirt Adams helped defend Jackson during Ulysses S. Grant's Vicksburg Campaign and played vital roles in Jackson's rebuilding process after the Civil War. Many accounts exist of their efforts and close friendship.

After the Civil War, the United States Congress enacted Reconstruction, eventually dividing each Southern state into districts run by federal officers. Two political parties emerged in the state: white Democrats and a group of blacks and whites called the "Radical Republicans," which were devoted to enacting the federal government's dictates.

By the end of 1877, whites under the Democratic Party banner had regained every state office. Though the Reconstruction period was fading, the political landscape for the next 70 years was now in place, with the two major parties being: 1) white Democrats; and, 2) the "Radical Republicans," who also called themselves the "Black and Tans."

In 1924, a brilliant, young, blue-eyed African-American named Perry Wilbon Howard, Jr., took over leadership of the Black and Tans.[3] Decades later in the mid-1950s, Howard would become my first real political opponent. Born in 1877 and the son of former slaves, Howard was among a small group of African-Americans during the first half of the 20th century in Mississippi who gained political, economic, and social power amid the Radical Republican ranks.

Anyone reading this book must understand the work and influence of Perry Howard in order to understand the eventual emergence of a new truly conservative Republican force in Mississippi. Little, however, has been written of Howard, who by today's standards was a strange Republican. "In the small circle of successful black politicians, Perry Wilbon Howard, Jr. was one of the shrewdest and most enduring," claims University of Southern Mississippi historian Neil R. McMillen.[4] Adds McMillen: "During the 1920s national party officials reportedly thought the young Deep South lawyer to be 'the smartest negro in politics'. He was, many believed, a favorite of the Republican National Committee. Warren Gamaliel Harding made Howard his first-ever black appointment; this was as a special assistant to the attorney general and the 'highest paid negro in government service.'" After receiving that government appointment, Howard never again lived or voted in his home state. McMillen: "Yet for thirty-five years, from 1924 until a few years before his death in 1961 at the age of eighty-four, he served as Republican national committeeman from Mississippi." Howard would linger in the state's Republican apparatus into the late 1950s, but he lost all power in our party by 1960 and died in 1961.

During his days of power, Howard lived in the nation's capital, running his puppet Mississippi GOP from there. "An intelligent, congenial, articulate man of 'gentlemanly bearing and unfailing courtesy,' Howard was a conspicuous and useful token" to national Republican leadership.[5] He led the Black-and-Tan Republicans in our state, but did not live in the state. He took money from top national GOP officials who knew they were buying votes for themselves within Mississippi. One of Howard's political lieutenants from Mississippi's Warren County once admitted: "We proselytize these few Negroes to vote ... and, after pocketing the handouts from the party slush fund—and this is the only real purpose of our organization—we put our committee back in mothballs to await another presidential election."[6]

President Herbert Hoover publicly decried Howard's buying votes; nevertheless, in 1928 Hoover's campaign actually paid Howard's weekly expenses of $200, eventually totaling $4,000, to deliver Mississippi's 12 votes at the Republican convention.[7] In 1925, an FBI investigation of Howard said he "trafficked in Federal offices," selling postmaster positions via his patronage power for prices ranging from $500 to $1,500.[8] President Calvin Coolidge's officials reprimanded Howard, who feigned remorse; thus, Coolidge let Howard keep his positions as assistant attorney general and national committeeman.

As the years progressed, some liberal national leadership labeled Howard a sellout to his race. The National Association for the Advancement of Colored People had been founded in 1909. Though there were very few NAACP members in Mississippi prior to the 1960s, the organization's leaders were critical of Howard. Eventually NAACP national leader Walter White said, "There are Negroes like Perry Howard who for the sake of personal gain would knife every Negro in the country." Two more times, federal investigations probed Howard, who continued his patronage efforts. In July of 1928, he was indicted.[9]

At that time, a curious blend of constituencies suddenly mobilized in Howard's defense.

First, well-heeled white Mississippi Democrats seemed to have helped pay for Howard's legal defense, possibly wanting him to remain in power so that the make-believe Mississippi GOP would remain an ineffectual group. "A Republican party in Mississippi under the leadership of negroes offers no peril to white supremacy," explained Colonel Fred Sullens (a major Democrat force in Mississippi) in his *Jackson Daily News* column in March of 1929.[10] Sullens remained a powerful force into the 1950s, often berating me as our new group began to foster the growth of a truly valid Mississippi Republican Party in the mid-1950s.

Sullens was absolutely correct, however ignoble his observations may have been. For more than six decades leading up to the 1960s, not a single Mississippi official—local, county, or state—was a Republican; for, in reality, *there were no Republicans in the electorate.*

For decades in Mississippi every person who ran for office ran as a Democrat; thus there were no party primaries. Not a single candidate for any office came from any other party, nor could that even be imagined by the state's citizens. There was only Howard among Republicans, and he cared nothing for running GOP candidates within his state. He simply delivered puppet Republican delegates to the party's national convention every four years, directing them to vote for the highest bidder among the national Republican candidates for United States president.

A second phenomenon, however, suddenly occurred with respect to Perry Howard. National black liberals, the very ones who had once decried him, suddenly took Howard's side when they saw the national and Mississippi white establishment indicting Howard, who began claiming that he was being made "a martyr to the cause I represent, Negro leadership."[11]

Howard was indicted by state grand juries twice; each time, however, all-white juries in Mississippi did not convict him. The massive racist Democrat machine in Mississippi loved this fact, for they wanted Howard to continue running a weak Mississippi GOP. "The real psychology" of these trials, Major Sullens wrote, was that these juries wanted Howard free to maintain GOP power in the state, thus ensuring local Democrats a virtual dictatorship in Mississippi.[12]

President Herbert Hoover, however, began looking elsewhere for help to organize his GOP support in Mississippi. His former Mississippi puppet—and that was all Howard ever was to national Republicans—no longer seemed useful; he had been sullied.

In 1927, a new ineffectual faction of Mississippians caling themselves "Republicans" had begun asserting itself, led by white Picayune timber merchant, Lamont Rowlands, along with the former governor of Nebraska, George Lawson Sheldon, who had moved to Mississippi.[13] They called their group the "Lily White" faction, in contrast to Howard's "Black and Tans." When my own wing of Republicanism eventually began to emerge, we ultimately would have to defeat both the Lily Whites and the Black and Tans. We wanted no color label attached to our party's name and we felt that neither group was motivated by true philosophical conservatism.

Meanwhile, the nation at-large was being thrown into chaos.

On Oct. 29, 1929, the Great Depression had hit on Black Tuesday. It would take several years before most Mississippians felt its worst effects, but in the 1930s and 1940s several realities emerged: 1) both black and white Mississippians lost jobs and income (state unemployment in 1933 was at 25 percent); and, 2) President Franklin D. Roosevelt initiated a swirl of big-government federal programs including the Works Progress Administration, the Civilian Conservation Corps, and the Tennessee Valley Authority. Roosevelt's programs not only fomented massive growth in government, but they also created a massive new base of loyal Democrat voters among America's poor, both black and white, including those in Mississippi.

Howard continued to live in Washington, D.C., supported by the Northeastern GOP elite such as Nelson Rockefeller, who once paid Howard to deliver a token Mississippi GOP delegation to him. Howard even raised the ire of his brother-in-law, Sidney D. Redmond, supposed chairman of the flimsy pseudo-GOP state executive committee, who eventually called Howard "the greatest impediment conceivable to Negroes."[14]

Howard maintained that it was important to hold a realistic view of what blacks could expect in the South, adding that his method—that of cooperation with national white elites—was best. By 1950, Howard was 73 years old, World War II was over, and so was the Democrat administration of Roosevelt.

In 1952, Dwight Eisenhower was elected president as a

Republican. He could have won the election running as the candidate from either party, and he considered both parties before choosing the GOP. Eisenhower would hold the White House from 1953 to 1961.

During this period of the early-to-mid 1950s, several men, including myself, began to press our way into the state's factious and ineffective Mississippi Republican Party machinery. We began to challenge not only Howard's Black and Tans, but also Sheldon's newer movement, the Lily Whites.

Through the years that Perry Howard had ruled the puppet Black-and-Tan Republican party, I had been maturing from youth into manhood. A brief glimpse at those days follows.

• • •

Here is a quick summary of my family tree up to my birth.

My grandfather, Edward (1862-1943), was the only son of Civil War General William Swan Yerger (1833-1868). Edward's fourth child was Wirt Adams Yerger, Sr. (1901-1974), my father.

My father joined my grandfather's insurance business; then in 1928 he married Rivers Applewhite—my mother. One newspaper said their wedding was "an outstanding social event of Mississippi, and characterized by its distinctive elegance and beauty."[15] My parents honeymooned in Cuba, then moved into the Stillman Apartments on North State Street in Jackson.

On March 18, 1930, Mother delivered me at Jackson's Infirmary.

My early life moved along Jackson's North and North State streets, where all my grandparents lived. I was blessed with a stable family, two younger brothers, Swan (two years younger), Ivan (four years younger), and one sister, Rivers Gay, seven years my junior. We had cousins, grandparents, and friends galore with whom we played, talked, and, at times, wept, amid the rolling hills of mid-Mississippi.

In post-Depression days, my parents were "Ivory Soap" people, tight with their money. When we sat at the dinner table, Daddy rationed a pile of fried chicken as my eyes screamed with desire to eat the entire platter. You did not grab at food. You were *allocated*.

Accompanied by a host of friends, we Yerger brothers camped in the nearby Pearl River woods. We built lean-tos, spending nights on pine-straw beds. Our parents felt it was safe; those were different days. We played football in Mr. and Mrs. E.O. Spencer's large yard. (In the future, Spencer and I would team to defeat Perry Howard's Black-and-Tan Republican machine.) The Spencer boys—Doc, Sonny, and Bubba— were among the Yerger boys' best friends.

In the Spencer yard, I received the news about Pearl Harbor on a Sunday afternoon, Dec. 7, 1941. Mrs. Spencer had her radio on. She heard the report and rushed outside. ... *"The Japs just attacked Pearl Harbor!"*

Mother trained us to read newspapers and books. We listened to radio commentator H.V. Kaltenborn. Every day our newspaper was splattered with news of massive World War II battles and of those who were killed, wounded, missing, or captured.

Fascism, Nazism, and Communism—all three evils aroused patriotic zeal in me. Boy Scouts and my Christian faith further fed this. As a youth, I walked the aisle at Jackson's First Baptist Church and became a Christian without ever consulting my parents. They were not even there. Everybody welcomed me, shaking my hand. It was a very successful revival.

As a Boy Scout, I gained a strong sense of such principles as duty, honor, and country. I reached the rank of Eagle Scout, one of the accomplishments in life of which I am most proud. My troop participated in scrap-paper and tinfoil drives for the war effort. At Central High School in Jackson, I took ROTC three days a week and drilled on the high school's front lawn. We all felt we might soon go to fight the Nazis or Japanese. *I actually hoped so!*

One summer when I was twenty, I attended ROTC camp at Lowry Air Force Base in Denver, Colorado. There, I interacted with blacks of my age in an integrated system for the first time.

• • •

During my college days at Ole Miss, the nation's worried eyes were fixed on ever-expanding Communism. The media and many politicians, both Republicans and Democrats, and not just Joseph McCarthy, were now claiming that more and more American celebrities and government workers were actually Communist Party members.

Meanwhile, President Harry Truman was using executive orders to bulk up the federal government with expensive bureaucracy. A free democracy now seemed threatened both by the growth of Communism and by big-government spending.

Consider the following brief summary of world events that formed the backdrop upon which our modern Republican Party emerged. All of these events happened during my college days. Put yourself in the shoes of someone like me as I tried to process them and their potential effects on our country:

1948: In February the USSR (the Union of Soviet Socialist Republics) first jammed Voice of America broadcasts—effectively ending any democratic message into these lands; that same month, Soviet forces conquered Czechoslovakia, which joined Hungary, Romania, and East Germany as Soviet satellites; the Berlin Blockade began in June; responding to this Soviet aggression, Truman started a peacetime military draft; in July, Truman bypassed Congress and signed his executive order to desegregate the military; in August, the "Republic of Korea" was chartered (we soon would be fighting against Communism in the Korean War).

1949: In January, Truman announced his Fair Deal plan to expand Roosevelt's New Deal all the more; Peking (now called Beijing) was overtaken by the Communist Party of China; in March, the USSR deported 92,000 Estonians, Latvians, and Lithuanians, absorbing the countries; in June, the "Red Scare" began, as none other than the FBI reported that well-known celebrities including Helen Keller, Danny Kaye, and Edward G. Robinson were members of the Communist Party in the United

States; the U.S. withdrew from South Korea as promised, but the Soviets did not leave North Korea; in August, the USSR detonated its first atomic bomb; in October, the People's Republic of China, ruled by the Communist Party of China, began forcing its way further into Chinese territories.

1950: In January, Truman authorized work on a hydrogen bomb as a Soviet deterrent; in February, U.S. Senator Joseph McCarthy publicly claimed there were more than 200 Communists in the U.S. Department of State—and recent history has revealed there were, indeed, Communists there—not as many as McCarthy claimed, but not as few as many in today's popular culture still seek to purport; the young Vietcong attacked French forces in Indochina; Communist riots broke out in Paris; the USSR and People's Republic of China signed a mutual defense treaty; in March, German Klaus Fuchs was convicted of spying for the Soviets; the Soviets officially claimed to have the atom bomb; in June, North Korean Communist troops captured Seoul, sparking the Korean War; in September, West Germany ousted Communist officials; in October, the Communist Chinese invaded Tibet; 99.7 percent of voters in East Germany voted Communist; in late 1950, Communist Chinese troops entered North Korea; Truman warned he might drop an atom bomb on Korea.

1951: In January, Seoul was captured by Communist troops; the United Nations challenged China as an aggressor in the Korean War; in March, Ethel and Julius Rosenberg, declared members of the U.S. Communist Party, were convicted of spying for the Soviets and were sentenced to death; in April, Truman fired Gen. Douglas MacArthur, head of America's Pacific fleet.

1952: In May, East Germany claimed it would form its own army; in July, King Farouk of Egypt was toppled by a coup and many Americans feared Communists would take over the vital Suez Canal; in July, the Constitution of the People's Republic of Poland was ratified, making it a Communist Soviet satellite; in November, the first hydrogen bomb was successfully tested by the United States.

These were the alarming realities that college students faced as we graduated in the 1950s. There was a sense that America seemed under attack. In the South, many people began wondering if a sort of siege was occurring, not only by the Communists, but also by a growing federal government.

In essence, three great issues defined this era: the rise of Communism and the growth of the federal government were two of them, as the previous pages have illustrated. The last of the three great issues of that era, race relations, is often explained today as if it existed in a social and political vacuum; this, however, oversimplifies the massive matter. The fact is that experiencing the crippling effects of race relations in America during the 1950s and 1960s was much more complicated than often portrayed because the experience inevitably was entangled with the other two great challenges of that period. The issue of race in the 1950s and 1960s swirled amid a tempest of extreme fear of Communism and concern for our swelling federal government (Roosevelt and Truman style). The three together were just more than many people could handle.

Please understand that our main media sources in Mississippi in the 1950s—chief among them being *The Clarion-Ledger*, an old-line, hyper-racist state Democrat-controlled media organ—constantly reported that new "race agitators" were entering the South and were surely linked to an expanding Communist infiltration. Some of this proved true, some didn't, but it was hard for most to filter through what, and what not, to believe; and in the South, many people also viewed "race agitators" as somehow linked with socialistic efforts to win control of our federal government. Again, some of this was rooted in verifiable fact; some was overreaction.

When Dwight Eisenhower ran for president as a Republican in 1952, I was in Texas serving in the Air Force, where I helped supply B-36 bombers. I voted for him over Democrat Adlai Stevenson. Eisenhower's election put a Republican in the White House for the first time since Herbert Hoover in 1932. Everyone trusted Eisenhower though he was not classically conservative; his views came to be called "progressive conservatism" or, as he tried to label them, "Modern Republicanism."

Another man came onto the national political scene in 1952. Barry Goldwater was elected as one of Arizona's United States senators. For many of us, his emergence was much more important than Eisenhower's becoming president. Shortly thereafter, Russell Kirk in 1953 wrote a decisive book, *The Conservative Mind*. He showed that conservatism had a centuries-old history. He proposed a modern conservatism rooted in the thinking of the 18th century British Whig, Edmund Burke. This conservatism was based in a free-trade economy and limited government.

Kirk's book ignited William F. Buckley, someone I greatly admired. Already renowned as a young thinker, Buckley founded *The National Review* in 1955; its uncompromising conservatism quickly galvanized many of us. *The Nation* and *The New Republic* had long been champions of liberal politics.

From my military base in Texas, I read *The National Review*, watched the emergence of conservatives including Barry Goldwater, and saw Communism and big government grow. I watched the national news portray my home state as a one-party political doorstop for the national Democrats. Mississippi's white Democrat rule, with its convoluted form of racist conservatism, was hurting our citizens, a fact acknowledged by almost all liberals and conservatives today. Our state's national leadership—all Democrats—would sometimes vote one way at their national political convention or in the U.S. Congress (often backing the liberal policies of their po-

LOS ANGELES DAILY NEWS

William F. Buckley in 1954: Buckley's books and his magazine, *The National Review* (founded in 1955), became regular reading for Wirt and many young conservatives.

litical buddies); but when they returned home, they would advocate to our state's voters the exact opposite. They traded their national votes in exchange for keeping their raw power in Mississippi. This hypocrisy came to a head when national Democrat politicians ignored Southern Democrat politicians' voices in 1948 at their national convention. Average Mississippians began to see the truth for themselves.

I was becoming convinced Mississippi needed a real second party to resolve such hypocrisy. The portion of the Republican Party represented by Goldwater and Buckley looked better and better to me because it espoused the lofty, high-principled conservatism of Russell Kirk without the big-government baggage that our state's old-line Democrats' racist brand of conservatism carried.

In July 1945, Joseph Stalin, far left, Harry S. Truman, center, and Winston Churchhill, far right, joined against the Nazis. In August 1945, the U.S. dropped two atomic bombs in Japan, ushering in the nuclear age. Wirt was a youth who followed news closely. Truman's liberal social policies and Stalin's subversive Communist influence in the United States became two of Wirt's and the new Miss. GOP's life-long philosophical foes.

When my military service ended, I returned to Jackson at age 24 to work with my father in insurance. I married Mary Montague of Hattiesburg on June 6, 1956. We moved into a duplex on Gillespie Street in Jackson and over the years have been blessed with two wonderful sons and a lovely daughter, along with eight very special grandsons and two wonderful granddaughters.

At age 25, I attended the Royal Globe Insurance Company training program in New York City to improve myself.

And that is where my formal entry into Republican politics occurred.

• • •

In New York City in 1956, I met Charlie McWhorter, a Harvard Law School graduate. Charlie was president of the Young Republican Federation nationwide. My friend, Tom Crockett, was attending Harvard Law School and he referred me to him. Charlie was thrilled with my Republican interests. He knew the challenge that any sincere Republican effort in Mississippi would face against both Perry Howard's puppet Republicans and the state's massive Democrat powers. Charlie was a great friend and a very generous person. He subsequently invited me to the 1956 Young Republican Convention in Des Moines, Iowa.

To start a Young Republican chapter in Mississippi, I needed 40 signatures from state citizens. Some Kappa Alpha friends signed my petition, but many people were scared to sign, fearing it might hurt their businesses, which was a legitimate concern.

Soon I flew to Des Moines with my 40 signatures. I felt warmly welcomed by the Young Republicans, who treated me like a celebrity due to my youth and Mississippi roots. At the convention, I heard speeches from men including Californian John Rousselot, a leading conservative, and other like-minded citizens.

I was inspired to participate in a new life in politics. The new Mississippi GOP was in the works.

Wirt and brothers Ivan and Swan enjoyed visiting their Grandfather Apple-white's Hubbard's Well, a popular resort south of Jackson, Miss., known for medicinal springs. Wirt's father watches the horse.

Wirt with his mother.

Wirt with his Yerger grandparents.

JACKSON (MISS.) DA

COMPLETES COURSE

Lt. Wirt Adams Yerger, Jr., son of
Mr. and Mrs. Wirt Yerger, Jackson,
now stationed at Carswell Air Force
Base, Fort Worth, Texas, with the
19th Air Division, has just completed his indoctrination course at
Briggs Air Force Base, El Paso. Lt.
Yerger received his commission as
second lieutenant in the Air Corps
upon completion of ROTC and upon
graduation from the University of
Mississippi last June with the degree of business administration and
commerce. At the University he
was a member of Scabbard & Blade,
a military organization, belonged to
Kappa Alpha social fraternity, and
Phi Eta Sigma, Delta Sigma Pi and
Beta Gamma Sigma, honorary fra-
ternities.

When Wirt returned to Mississippi in his early twenties
from service in the Air Force,
he almost immediately committed himself to helping
bring about a new Republican Party in Mississippi. He
also married Mary Montague
of Hattiesburg, Mississippi.

A Republican was a contemptible, low-life person who should be avoided like the plague.

> —Carl Walters
> Mississippi journalist, 1956

The segregation-integration issue is so complex as to seem impossible of solution. It seems to me, ... only cool-headed and warm-hearted people, and not hot-headed and cold-hearted ones, can find, under God, the solution. No problem, not even this one, is too complex for Him.

> —Charles W. Horner
> Letter to the editor
> *The Clarion-Ledger*, 1956

"The judicial and verbal battle for segregation became synonymous with politics."

> —*The Clarion-Ledger,* 1956

2

1952-1956

NEW REPUBLICANS VS. DATED DEMOCRATS

In mid-April of 1962 in a Minnesota forest—cloistered from media and political pundits—a small band of about 15 GOP leaders gathered to answer one question: Could a true, classi - cal conservative win the Republican presidential nomination?

I was among this amazing set of men who met at Wone - wok, a getaway for Minnesota mining executives. It was a priv - ilege to be in such company, which included textile millionaire Roger Milliken of South Carolina, wealthy businessman Frank Whetstone of Montana, and New York City's F. Clifton White— a top conservative who disdained fellow New Yorker, Nelson Rockefeller. My roommate for the strategic weekend was William Rusher, publisher of The National Review.

What a time of conversation and fellowship among real patriots—one of the most invigorating experiences of my life! Every man was of a high caliber.

I flew into Minneapolis, Minnesota on April 13 and a private plane then shuttled me to the lodge. For an afternoon and evening, men arrived, all sensing a mission. Some of us knew each other only by reputation; we quickly bonded.

On Friday evening, Clif, who led our meetings, gave us a report that set the weekend's tone. He knew first-hand of the immense liberal Republican machine that Nelson Rockefeller already had assembled for his upcoming presidential contest. But Clif and the rest of us felt that the pieces were in place for a true conservative to win the GOP nomination.

We enjoyed relaxing after our initial Friday evening meeting. Hopes were high. Dress was casual. These were Barry Goldwater's men. These were my people. We all felt that to defeat incumbent presidentJohn F. Kennedy, our nationalGOP needed a man with Kennedy's passion, charisma, and speech-making ability. And this man needed a vision that was as optimistic as Kennedy's.

We believed we had found that man: Barry Goldwater.

• • •

But no Mississippian in 1952 could ever have imagined that a Mississippian in 1962 would be among 15 top GOP national leaders planning a strategy for a true conservative Republican to win the United States presidency.

I certainly could not have!

This is because Mississippi in the 1950s was an intractable one-party state, a fact that is surely equally as hard for many people under age 60 to imagine today.

But it was true. It was still the era of "Yellow Dog" Democrats, a term originally coined to describe a massive population who were set on voting Democrat no matter what.

Even as Soviet Communism's brand of single rule was striking fear of totalitarianism in us all, Mississippians lived under a virtual totalitarian Democrat vice grip. Our citizens had no real role in choosing their elected officials. Every candidate for local, county, or state office was a Democrat—every single one. None offered any new ideas. Our elected officials, therefore, did not have to hear, or respond to, the will of the people.

Our state's citizens were conditioned to think Republicans had only their worst interests at heart. "Republican" was a vulgar word. "A Republican was a contemptible, low-life person who should be avoided like the plague," wrote one major Mississippi journalist, Carl Walters.[1] Walters actually was more open to our Republican efforts than some.

Top state Democrats like state party chairman Bidwell Adam and U.S. Sen. Jim Eastland regularly denounced the idea of allowing a two-party system into our state. *Jackson Daily News* editor Fred Sullens warned that it would create competition and give black voters more power; and, in fact, our second party actually did give all Mississippians a real choice—eventually.

Old-line Democrat powerbrokers feared two things: 1) losing their absolute power; and 2) giving any minority (including Republicans or African-Americans) a decent chance to campaign for any sort of change to their good-old-boy system.

But when Dwight Eisenhower was elected president in 1952 as a Republican, it opened a new door. Mississippians love a war hero, and therefore a considerable 39.6 percent of Mississippians voted for Eisenhower. A chink now appeared in the state's Democrat armor. Mississippian E.O. Spencer—whom Eisenhower had chosen to lead his "Citizens for Eisenhower" committee in Mississippi due to Spencer's GOP sympathies—was viewed by Eisenhower's staff as someone who might help supplant Perry Howard in our state.

Spencer was the father of my old neighborhood friends. He led Mississippi's Citizens for Eisenhower (also called "Democrats for Eisenhower") in the 1952 and 1956 elections; each Southern state had such a group designed to pull Democrat voters over to Eisenhower without forcing them to become Republicans.

Eisenhower's election therefore helped open the state's political door for a small respectable group of new-thinking, business- and industry-minded conservatives. "When the dust [of the 1952 election] settled, it was apparent that a revolutionary event had taken place," stated political observer James Edward Cliatt.[2]

But few noticed it at that time.

After Eisenhower's 1952 election, Spencer traveled in March of 1953 to Washington to convince Republican National Committee Chairman Wesley Roberts that the national GOP should back a new Mississippi Republican Party leadership, not Perry Howard's Black and Tans. Eisenhower began giving Spencer state patronage rights that Howard had long held.

Howard and Spencer also battled over copyright issues to use the word "Republican" in Mississippi. A Fifth Circuit Court said no one could copyright "Republican," so Howard, Spencer, and any other group could use it.

• • •

None of this maneuvering in Mississippi was happening in a political vacuum. No political phenomenon is that clean. None can be understood merely as Democrat versus Republican or white versus black. That trivializes history and people. A recent fine book by Emory University historian Joseph Crespino, *In Search of Another Country: Mississippi and the Conservative Counterrevolution*, notes rightly that any such predictable account "reduces history to a morality tale, it ignores ongoing struggles for racial justice, and it oversimplifies white reaction to the civil rights movement."[3]

Crespino adds that some of the more popular theories regarding the growth of the Republican revolution in Mississippi, including the "Southern strategy," have "failed to appreciate the dramatic social and economic transformation of the American South in the second half of the twentieth century and the implications for the southern political ruling class ... a modern, industrially oriented urbanized (and suburbanized) business class that aggressively ... advocated a pro-corporate, antiunion politics of small government and low taxes, and increasingly came to identify with the Republican Party."[4]

The merits and value of the civil rights movement must continue to be commended and extensively documented for any and all readers and citizens; what has perhaps lacked sufficient consideration to date are some of the *true motivating forces* behind founding a new Republican state apparatus. We new Republicans passionately wanted a real, fully-orbed conservatism that was bigger than any single issue; old-line Democrats were not such conservatives, but rather they were attuned to Roosevelt's New Deal policies of bigger government as the best way to fight poverty; they favored increasing federal subsidies versus advancing free enterprise.

For these old-line Democrats, the word "conservative" was merely a convenient moniker to signal opposition to civil rights measures emerging out of Washington, D.C. Admittedly, we early new Mississippi Republicans at times allowed segregation in our party's platform, but we and the old-line Democrats were worlds apart in how we addressed this matter, as this book will show. And initially, at least, I had managed to keep segregation completely out of our state party's platform.

It is no secret that virtually all white native Mississippians at the time still supported segregation, even some who are now lauded as the state's most "progressive." For instance, former Mississippi Governor William Winter, who began and ended his political career as a Democrat, advanced that party's hard-line segregation stand as late as 1967. Again, Crespino's book sheds light on this subject: "Winter walked a narrow line on racial issues—too narrow for the taste of many Mississippi blacks. In the 1967 campaign [by Winter for Miss. governor], Winter did not shy away from the pieties of segregationist Mississippi. 'I was born a segregationist and raised a segregationist,' Winter told a Citizens' Council rally. 'I have always defended this position. I defend it now.' "[5] This was Winter's position in 1967, even after the deaths of civil rights martyrs Medgar Evers in 1963 and Michael Schwerner, James Chaney and Andrew Goodman in 1964.

But the classical conservatism that we early new Republicans favored had a bigger, loftier set of ideals offering enumerable benefits to all people, as was proved during Ronald Reagan's presidency.

• • •

Communism: This issue was where we new state Republicans and the old-line state Democrats shared ground. Our mutual concern for the Communist threat in the 1950s and 1960s has been regarded by some liberal thinkers, both past and present, as a comic tale—our pet excuse for opposing civil rights measures of the 1960s.

The fact is, however, that links between Soviet Communism and the civil rights movement are now indisputable, even if sometimes their presence was overblown in the mid-20th century as everyone grappled with the rapidly unfurling realities. Relatively new histories show that American Communists were actively associated with Soviet leaders, and that American Communists were clearly influencing the civil rights movement in America. The much-promoted notion that America's Communists were not influenced by the Soviets has been "pretty well laid to rest," states Arch Puddington writing in *The National Review*. "The question of American Communism's subservience to the Kremlin" is now indisputable, states Puddington.[6]

Several books have been written on this subject since the release of the Venona Papers, secret communiques that were exchanged between American Communist leaders and their Soviet counterparts during the Cold War. The papers were finally declassified in the mid-1990s by U.S. Sen. Daniel Patrick Moynihan's Commission on Protecting and Reducing Government Secrecy.

When opened for scholarly study, the files revealed "that the American [Communist] party relied on Moscow for financing almost from its inception; indeed, without the assistance of the Soviet Union, there is little chance that the American party could have survived," Puddington writes, adding, "The nature of American Communism was very much as anti-Communists charged: a puppet of the Soviet party whose leaders were selected by Moscow and dismissed by Moscow, whose policies were formulated in the Kremlin, and whose financial survival depended on Soviet largesse. Several hundred U.S. Government employees who were either party members or sympathizers engaged in espionage on behalf of the Kremlin during the war for reasons of ideological conviction."

Often dismissed as contrived in a conspiracy theory, American Communists nonetheless did do vital work within the civil rights movement, a fact that in no way discredits the movement. Writes Crespino, "Since the 1920s the Communist Party in the United States had been one of the most aggressive and outspoken advocates" for the civil rights movement.[7] In one famous early civil rights trial in Mississippi, the legal defense included a young, Bronx-born Communist associate, Bella Abzug, notes Crespino. "Radical elements were present within the [civil rights] movement in sufficient numbers to lend some credibility to the numerous and occasionally reckless charges," according to historian Neil R. McMillen of the University of Southern Mississippi.[8]

Filtering through such emotional issues was difficult for Mississippians in the 1950s and 1960s, much less for sophisticated scholars. "In the context of the early cold war, with American troops fighting Communists in Korea and Communist witch hunts taking place in Washington," notes Crespino, it might be understandable that some Mississippians concluded, rightly or wrongly, that "charges of southern racism by political radicals were merely a cover for an insidious assault on American political institutions."[9]

Communism's shadow always lurked in our minds.

In 1953:

1) Joseph Stalin died in March. Residents of the Magnolia State, like all Americans, now worried all the more about the Communist threat. What sort of tactics would a new Soviet leader take against the United States? Nikita Khrushchev finally emerged as the USSR's new general secretary.

2) Fidel Castro soon began attacks to overthrow Cuba,

bringing an official Communist presence even closer to our Southern shores.

3) And in November of 1953, Cambodia broke free of France, furthering Communist aggression there. On May 7, at the Battle of Dien Bien Phu, Vietcong crushed the French; the Vietnam War had begun.

Communism had all Americans on pins and needles; its effect was a bit like that of the encroachment of radical Islam during the last several years. Many Americans filtered their news through this lens of the Communist threat.

Our state's top newspaper, *The Clarion-Ledger,* daily published slivers of evidence that Communism was spreading, inevitably alarming the reading public. "It will end freedom as we have known it and bring upon us a system comparable to that now operating in Communist Russia and China."[10]

• • •

Mississippians were proud in 1955 as Elvis Presley hit the radio in Memphis for the first time; William Faulkner won the Nobel Prize for Literature for *A Fable;* and Tennessee Williams won the Pulitzer Prize for Drama for *Cat On a Hot Tin Roof.*

Such accomplishments gave us a boost in self-esteem as our state confronted rapidly destabilizing racial events, four of which in 1954 and 1955 threw Mississippi into a sad, ugly, media melee. Old-line Democrat state leaders responded to these events as if their only reason for future existence was to preserve segregation. Their political rantings exposed their brand of "conservatism" as little more than racial hatred.

The four events were:

First, the United States Supreme Court ruled in May of 1954 in Brown v. Board of Education of Topeka that segregated public schools were inherently unequal, priming the pump for a decade of desegregation battles not only in the South, but also in Chicago, Philadelphia, Boston, and elsewhere.

Second, Congress in 1955 passed the Interstate Commerce Act of 1955, making it illegal to segregate trains or buses in the South. Segregation had been at the core of our state's social fabric; national attention to the issue meant Mississippians were going to have to deal with it.

Third, Rosa Parks in December of 1955 refused to move to the back of a bus in Montgomery, Alabama, sparking the Montgomery bus segregation protests led by a relatively new civil rights voice, Martin Luther King, Jr.

And fourth, two Delta hooligans in August of 1955 kidnapped a young black Chicago youth, Emmett Till, who was visiting his Mississippi relatives; they beat him to a pulp, shot him, tied a cotton-gin fan to his neck using barbed wire, and dumped him in the Tallahatchie River, where the body was found three days later by local fishermen. Worse yet, the two perpetrators—J.W. Milam and Roy Bryant—were acquitted in late September of 1955 by an all-white, all-male jury.

Three months after this unthinkable act, in *Look* magazine the two men admitted killing Till. They lived just outside of Ruleville, Mississippi, the home of long-time United States Senator James O. Eastland (Dem.), who did not lift a finger to address the ugly, violent matter. Even the state's major paper, *The Clarion-Ledger,* whined editorially: "The NAACP [has] launched a nation-wide hate-Mississippi campaign."[11]

Race now became the state Democratic Party's chief political issue used increasingly to scare state voters away from our new party efforts; this vicious racial contempt had always been at their core, but now it became increasingly their bread-and-butter issue and our state's major newspaper was lockstep with them.

The Clarion-Ledger actually stated at that time: "The judicial and verbal battle for segregation became synonymous with politics."[12]

State residents desperately needed—but could not yet imagine the possibility of—another party that could articulate a bigger, better conservative philosophy. When I attended the national Young Republican meeting in 1956, I was able to secure an official charter for a Mississippi chapter. We became the last state in the Union to form a Young Republican group.[13] Upon returning, I quickly joined efforts with E.O. Spencer's "Citizens for Eisenhower" movement, composed mostly of disillusioned Democrats. Spencer wanted to transition them into Republicans.

This is when news about E.O. and me began appearing in the back pages of a begrudging state media.

• • •

At this time, we Republicans still took a massive backseat in the news compared to the daily hysterical chronicling by our state media of racial developments and the hyper-promotion of state Democrats.

For instance, the National Association for the Advancement of Colored People, the NAACP, was vocally present during the Till trial; the NAACP was not yet a behemoth, but it was gaining headway in Mississippi. In early 1956, it asked the National Democratic Party literally to oust all of Mississippi's U.S. congressmen from their seats in Congress as punishment for the Till issue. Rep. Jamie Whitten (D-Miss.) told a reporter that he was not fazed by the NAACP: "No one is surprised at this organization doing anything to agitate racial relations."[14]

But the ugliness of our state's real racial violence could not be ignored. When the *Look* magazine article appeared with photos of the murdered Till, a Michigan congressman insisted it be read into the *Congressional Record*.[15] Top NAACP leadership called Sen. James Eastland (Dem.) a "stinking albatross" around his national party's neck.[16]

The race issue was of such raw power at this time that this book must carefully note its progression alongside our party's growth from chapter to chapter. But this is not because our state's early new Republicans played to the race issue, *but rather it is because old-line state Democrats made it their only issue, doing everything in their power to keep both Republicans and blacks out of our state's politics.*

Here is the twisted irony: National Democrats in 1956 hung the "race-albatross"—rightfully—around the necks of Sen. James O. Eastland and Sen. John C. Stennis, as well as other old-line state Democrats; but then some of these same Democrats, starting in the late 1960s, cunningly tried to shift this stigma onto us state Republicans after we took some political power from them.

Only after the emergence of a powerful civil rights movement and a new Mississippi Republican Party in the mid-to-late 1960s and early 1970s did desperate Democrat politicians try to work with the very black voters they had once abhorred.

Let's be clear:

- The killers of Emmett Till were not new Republicans, but rather voting Mississippi Democrats;

- The killers of Michael Schwerner, Andrew Goodman and James Chaney in Neshoba County were Ku Klux Klan members such as Cecil Price, the county's deputy; he was a voting Democrat.

- The Mississippi governor who opposed James Meredith's entry into Ole Miss, during an embarrassing circus, was an old-line Mississippi Democrat.

- The man who shot Medgar Evers was not an early new Republican—no, he was a rabid, White Citizens' Council, voting Democrat named Byron De La Beckwith.

We early new Republicans were true, philosophical conservatives, mostly businessmen and women, choosing to spend our time in the 1950s and 1960s breaking the dated Democrats' vice-grip on our state's one-party system. All along, they played the race card to scare any and all voters away from us.

As this story unfolds you will see how these powerful state Democrats regularly warned Mississippians in the late 1950s and early 1960s that, if they voted Republican, and thus helped us create a two-party system in our state, blacks would have a bigger, real voice.

These Mississippi Democrats were fear-peddlers.

If we in the new state GOP had begun our efforts in order to oppose black progress, as most of today's liberal Democrats wish everyone to believe, then we never would have bothered starting our party at all, for the old-line Democrats were ingloriously galvanized in this very effort.

But we knew that new long-term leadership with fresh ideas was needed in Mississippi and nationally.

Fifty-five percent of Southern whites and 70 percent of Southern African-Americans in 1956 said they believed integration would come with or without marches, sit-ins or other shows of strength.[17]

The bigger question now was: *how would politicians and other leaders handle this shift in legal and social norms?*

Good men in our state were distraught at the enormity of the issue. "The segregation-integration issue is so complex as to seem impossible of solution," lamented Jacksonian Charles W. Horner in a citizen's letter to the editor of his newspaper. "It seems to me ... only cool-headed and warm-hearted people, and not hot-headed and cold-hearted ones can find, under God, the solution. No problem, not even this one, is too complex for Him."[18]

Horner's thoughts represented those of many Mississippians.

I believed then that articulating a true, philosophical conservatism could help us all. For that to happen, a true second party had to emerge in Mississippi. Everyone needed a political choice in our state. All our voters needed new freedom to express their convictions.

FINALLY: Wirt is awarded the official charter for Mississippi's Young Republican chapter, making Mississippi the last existing state to gain membership. This inserted Wirt into the thick of GOP state politics at the young age of 26.

FOREVER FOES: Once Wirt gained GOP power in Mississippi, he became the rhetorical target of long-time Miss. Democratic Party Chairman Bidwell Adam, pictured with Wirt. Bidwell Adam's vitriolic attacks often linked Wirt and state blacks together as Mississippi's twin enemies.

You have shown the Southerner what you can do and what you will do if necessary; give him a space in which to get his breath and assimilate the knowledge; to look about and see that 1) nobody is going to force integration on him from the outside; 2) that he himself faces an obsolescence in his own land which only he can cure; a moral contrition which not only must be cured but a physical condition which has got to be cured if he, the White Southerner, is to have any peace, is not to be faced with another legal process or maneuver every year, year after year, for the rest of his life.

—William Faulkner,
"Letter to the North"
Life magazine, Jan. 16, 1956

A motion soon arose for our new GOP organization to vote officially to back segregation. I killed the motion for two reasons: First, our new GOP was not, like our Democrat opposition, going to be a party known for just one issue, namely segregation; and, second, such a stand would have jeopardized us becoming recognized as the official Republican Party in Mississippi by national GOP leadership.

—Wirt Yerger,
regarding 1956 Miss.
GOP platform

May I suggest that you come back home, hang your coat and hat on a [Miss.] Democratic rack and join with the political forces of Democracy in administering a thorough repudiation of the [African-American] ... forces?

—Bidwell Adam,
Mississippi Democrat chairman
taunting new Miss. Republicans

3

1956

Miss. GOP Galvanizes in San Francisco

In 1956 four small GOP factions jostled for control of the tiny morsels of GOP presence in our state. We were fighting for the right to build a credible party that might one day speak up for real conservatism.

Four groups of Mississippians in some way called themselves Republicans in 1956.

The first group was E.O. Spencer's Citizens for Eisenhower, alternately called "Democrats for Eisenhower."

The second group was my Mississippi Young Republican organization. Spencer and I soon joined forces.

The third group was Perry Howard's Black and Tans. Most Democrats did not foresee Howard ever losing his stranglehold on the state's then-feeble GOP presence, thus they did not foresee any real Republican presence ever developing.

The fourth group was former-Nebraska governor George Sheldon's Lily Whites. They had been battling Howard's group, but had not made serious headway. But they were present in 1956 and wanted the right to carry the state's GOP banner.

All four groups wanted Eisenhower's approval as he began planning his presidential reelection campaign in 1956. By mid-February of 1956, Spencer had met in New York City with the National Citizens for Eisenhower, who asked him to lead once again our state's Citizens for Eisenhower movement in 1956.[1] At the time, there were only 400 members of Mississippi's Citizens for Eisenhower.[2]

As a sign of how meager the Republican presence was in Mississippi, Spencer's reappointment by the sitting U.S. president to a statewide position received only three paragraphs on *The Clarion-Ledger's* front page; by contrast, the Democrat state leaders' every thought and action daily commanded front-page coverage.

Spencer, not Howard, had handled patronage during Eisenhower's first term.[3] Now it was finally time to hold a true GOP state convention. The three groups represented by Spencer, Sheldon and me soon agreed to hold this unprecedented Republican state convention and there face off for state party control. Howard stayed away, planning to hold his own GOP gathering in May.

Spencer and I pulled together our own county precinct meetings—the first real Republican ones in decades—to elect our state convention delegates. We anticipated a real convention battle with Sheldon's Lily Whites, who also held some county precinct meetings for their group.[4] The GOP state convention was set for Thursday, March 21. Spencer and I documented all of our county delegates, because Sheldon's Lily Whites planned to fight us to the last delegate.

• • •

George Sheldon's son, Anson, was a heavy-set guy who lived in the Mississippi Delta. He looked like a party boss type. In March, the Lily Whites and the Spencer/Yerger group met for our state convention. There, Anson and I hooked horns.

Spencer and I displayed a verifiable slate of delegates selected from our state precinct meetings. But Anson waved a handful of would-be proxies, purporting that his delegates had been duly elected just like ours. A bitter fight ensued, filled with argument and debate.

Lester Wills, a Meridian attorney, helped our side, along with Ben Cameron of Meridian, who was later a federal judge. John Minor Wisdom, a New Orleans judge, was there for us, but he did not help much.

We held our executive committee meeting at the Walthall Hotel. There, I was elected GOP state chairman over Anson Sheldon by one vote—my own! If I hadn't voted for myself, I would not have been elected.

A motion soon arose for our new GOP organization to vote officially to back segregation. I killed it for two reasons: First, our new GOP was not, like our Democrat opposition, going to be a party known for just one issue, namely segregation; and, second, such a stand would have jeopardized us becoming recognized as the official Republican Party in Mississippi by national GOP leadership.

For the first time, Mississippi had two parties of real record, though it would be years before most anyone really would recognize this fact. The Mississippi Democratic Party stood squarely for segregation; the Mississippi Republican Party did not, in 1956, take a stand on the issue. Today many history books may lead you to believe it was the other way around. Our state delegates in some later election cycles did permit a segregation plank in the state GOP platform, but it was never the state party's defining issue.

When our 1956 convention ended, many in the press could see that the Lily White label was no longer our emerging GOP identity. "They don't even like to be called the Lily White [party] anymore," *The Clarion-Ledger* announced, "and with justification because they are now officially the Mississippi Republican Party. ... After the Thursday afternoon session you would hardly recognize it. ... It was pretty clear that Governor Sheldon no longer dominated the party."[5]

Only one Republican entity remained to be challenged,

Perry Howard's Black-and-Tan group. Howard began to mockingly call us "The Grand Old Party of Mississippi." It was now time to take him on in August at the upcoming San Francisco Republican National Convention.

• • •

In May, Howard had gathered his forces at Jackson's Hill Auditorium on Farish and Griffith streets to elect delegates for his own mock-state convention, which he eventually held June 15.[6] Methodist pastor J.W. Hair, Howard's convention chairman, boasted his group would be seated in San Francisco over ours. "I believe just as firmly that we will be seated as I believe I'm going to Heaven, and I've been preaching 50 years to get to Heaven," said Hair. "If we are not seated, the Republican Party will lose the Negro vote of the nation, and we have leaders in the party to see to that." A virtual king among his doting court, Howard named his entire delegation. He predicted they all would be seated at the national convention over the "interlopers and hijackers." If his group was not seated, "there are four-million Negro votes in this nation" that could "swing the presidential election" to the Democrats, he promised.[7]

Howard and I were soon called to Washington, D.C. to speak before a GOP national credentials committee to make our cases for which of our two groups should be recognized as Mississippi's Republican representatives at the upcoming GOP national convention. I went first. I told the committee that I had already talked with Republican leaders from all 48 states who backed us as the state's legitimate Republican Party organization.

I have no real sense of what Howard said. I had immediately left after my presentation, joining Spencer and Mrs. J. Balfour Miller, our national committeewoman, at the White House for a two-hour meeting with presidential aides. My good friend and Republican leader, Charles McWhorter, accompanied us.[8]

Our meetings at the White House went well. Spencer reminded these aides about Howard's numerous patronage and vote-selling scandals. Our group would not align with Howard's group "under any conditions," Spencer stated. "If you recognize Perry Howard," Spencer told Eisenhower's aides, "just count us out."[9] We had worked too hard in legitimate ways to form a real GOP state party.

The Clarion-Ledger speculated that for "the first time in history" the national GOP might recognize someone other than Howard and his group. The paper rightly predicted the battle would peak in credentials meetings during the week before the 1956 Republican National Convention.[10]

Prior to the convention, Howard kept denouncing our delegation. He said E.O. Spencer was "like a man who joins the church one Sunday and wants to be bishop the next Sunday."[11]

Our group said the issue boiled down to two facts: 1) The courts had recognized our right to be called "Mississippi Republican Party"; and, 2) virtually all national GOP leaders were privately ready for Howard to disappear. "Everyone we talked to up [in Washington]," I told *The Clarion-Ledger*, "wants to get rid of Howard."[12]

Howard stayed in Washington, almost cocky, one news account said. "Seated in the modest but pleasant offices of his law firm—not far from the plush, national headquarters of the GOP—Howard professes so much faith in the Republican Party that he reminds one of a small boy whistling as he passes a graveyard."[13]

Our group could not take anything for granted. So we drafted a 19-page brief detailing startling activities of the Howard group. It also included a document in which the Republican National Committee had promised Spencer in 1952 to "endeavor to have the Mississippi Republican Party recognized as the official Republican Party in Mississippi."[14]

With this document in hand, it was time for the big August 1956 showdown in San Francisco.

• • •

The Democrats held their national convention in Chicago a week prior to ours, even as our national pre-convention deliberations were beginning. The Democrats nominated Adlai Stevenson for president and Carey Estes Kefauver, senator from Tennessee, as his running mate.

The Democratic National Convention was a tense, embarrassing time for the Mississippi delegation, to put it lightly. Mississippi's governor, J.P. Coleman, spent a great deal of time with the press refuting NAACP allegations, including that blacks trying to vote in Mississippi had to answer the following question to qualify to vote: How many bubbles are in a bar of soap? "I deny that ever took place," the beleaguered governor said.[15]

Coleman pled with Democrats from around the nation to "spend more time fighting the Republicans and less time fighting among ourselves."[16]

But Coleman could not even hold his state party apparatus together at this point. "Mississippians for States' Rights," a splinter group left over from the 1948 Dixiecrats Party, gathered 500 supporters at Jackson's Heidelberg Hotel and bolted Coleman's main state Democratic Party; they named eight "unpledged" electors to the state ballot for president, though they had no candidate. The move was a lame protest aimed purely at advocating segregation as a way of life. "We are standing for principle rather than a candidate," proclaimed W.B. Fontaine, the convention chairman.[17]

Amid such state Democrat infighting, our state's Republican factions were about to hash out our own differences before a national audience.

• • •

San Francisco is a fabulous city. Our new GOP group stayed in a small hotel near the more prominent St. Francis Hotel. National convention organizers assigned hotels for all the different state delegations. Ours was a great location.

My wife, Mary, and I had just married in 1956. We

were newlyweds during the August San Francisco convention and enjoyed the experience. Our number of Mississippi delegates had risen between 1952 and 1956 from five to 15, due to the national party's formula of awarding states more delegates for each congressional district that had delivered more than 10,000 votes in the previous presidential election.[18]

Our group and Howard's both brought our sets of 15 delegates (and a corresponding 15 alternates) to San Francisco to force a nationally televised showdown at the famed Cow Palace arena. Media coverage of Mississippi at the 1956 Republican National Convention was greater than usual. Leonard Hall, a one-time U.S. congressman from New York, chaired the Republican National Committee. He knew Howard's group was fraudulent, but he feared Howard's perceived national political leverage with African Americans.

The tension was immense during our week of pre-convention meetings. On pre-convention Tuesday, Aug. 14, Hall proffered a "compromise" plan to seat eight of Howard's delegates and seven of ours. Howard also temporarily would remain our state's GOP national committeeman, but I would be recognized as state GOP chairman at the current 1956 convention and thus I would have patronage power for the next four years, not Howard.

The national committee also invited me to give Richard Nixon's seconding speech for vice president. I declined the offer because I did not want at all to appear to be bought off. In retrospect, I should have given the speech, if only to gain more momentum for our newly formed state party.

Howard accepted Leonard Hall's compromise plan, but all of us in the new Mississippi GOP were furious. None of us had been notified prior to the preconvention meetings that such a compromise had been in the works. Spencer told *The Clarion-Ledger* that we were all packing our bags and coming home; the paper said Spencer "frankly admitted that there was little chance" of a reversal of mind.[19]

45

But too much was at stake. *Clarion-Ledger* reporter Gene Wirth correctly speculated that, after this convention, our group would "be officially recognized by the national party."[20] At the end of the convention, we would have full control of our state party. So while the compromise proposal didn't suit the idealist in me who wanted an absolute break from the weak leadership of the Black and Tans, it was nonetheless the best we could get and promised a brighter future.

Soon came a moment that thrust me into the national spotlight. About midway into the pre-convention week, Hall announced that this "compromise" Mississippi delegation had been formed.

"I understand that the Mississippi situation has been settled," Hall announced from his microphone.

When he said that, it was too much.

I jumped up and said, "Mr. Chairman, the Mississippi situation may be effectively settled, but you know and others know it's a fraud."

Flashbulbs popped. The media erupted.

I just couldn't handle him saying that. When he said that everything had been "settled, " I just said, "No it hasn't." It had not been settled with any fairness or any integrity. I hit him with that—right on the floor of the national committee meeting.

As state chairman, I wasn't going to let Hall make people think we were happy. We had been deceived and betrayed. I was probably the unhappiest person there because I was an idealist.

The Mississippi Democrats mocked this surprise political turn. Democrat State Party Chairman Bidwell Adam wrote Spencer saying he should come over to their side.

> Now that Perry Howard has been recognized as the Republican party head of the State of Mississippi and this party has demonstrated that your effort, labor and work are not appreciated, may I suggest that you come back home, hang your coat and hat on a Democratic rack and join with the political forces of Democracy in administer-

ing a thorough repudiation of the Howard forces. I call upon you to help us show just how few votes Perry Howard can deliver in Mississippi. ... I believe this is your golden opportunity to pay off the crowd of Republicans who thought more of Howard than they did of you.[21]

E.O. was at his wit's end. He issued another statement on Thursday, Aug. 16, saying that we all were coming home and were "not going to participate" in the upcoming week's convention. "Most of the delegates are coming home. The few delegates remaining will do so as spectators."[22]

But by Sunday, some of us were feeling somewhat better.

To assuage heated minds, the two factions would sit in separate sections at the Cow Palace convention hall and be listed separately on the roll call. We both would respond to the vote as if we were two different states.

Our fundamental message in the new Mississippi Republican Party delegation was not what national press understood it to be: they, of course, claimed we as whites would not sit with blacks, period. On the contrary, our move was rooted in highlighting that the eight Black-and-Tan delegates were not valid and we would not recognize them as members of the Mississippi Republican Party. Furthermore, our own slate of delegates included the first African American ever to serve as a legitimately chosen delegate from either the Mississippi Democratic or Republican parties: Dr. Laurence C. Jones, founder of the Piney Woods Country Life School outside of Florence, Mississippi.

• • •

This was my first taste of a national convention.

The main event of the convention was a no-brainer: Eisenhower was nominated and Richard M. Nixon was named his running mate again. I told the media I was not sure Nixon was "the strongest man ... as far as Mississippi is concerned," but he was acceptable.[23]

There was a feeble effort by a few Southern GOP leaders to protest Eisenhower's integration plan, but it went nowhere.

Compromise wording promised that any federal integration plan would be run by local officials.

Roving national network reporters combed our state delegations' two factions to conduct interviews. I wasn't overawed by it. We were doing the right thing in our new party and had a good group of people doing it—period.

As the convention played out, E.O. Spencer did, in fact, return early to Jackson. The rest of us eventually returned from the 1956 convention to great statewide media coverage and interest. I think people were quite proud of what we had managed to accomplish. We had not shrunk before our national leadership, as state Democrat leaders had.

The Jackson Daily News on Aug. 23, 1956, reported that our San Francisco delegation returned proclaiming the "Black and Tans Doomed." Note that the following article *still insisted* on calling our group the "Lily Whites":

> The youthful chairman of Mississippi's Lily White Republicans returned from San Francisco Thursday claiming his group has broken the 32-year-old control of the Black and Tan Republicans in Mississippi.
>
> Wirt Yerger Jr., Jackson insurance executive, stepped from an airplane at Municipal Airport and said his group won a "ninety to a hundred percent victory" during the factional infighting at the Republican National Convention.
>
> Yerger said the naming of Perry Howard, Washington Negro attorney and long-time Black and Tan head, as national committeeman and Negro Edna Redmond of Jackson as national committeewoman would have no effect on his faction winning control by 1960.
>
> "Perry Howard is on his way out. We will definitely be able to unseat Howard at the 1960 convention," Yerger declared.
>
> "We won everything but the figurehead posts of national committeeman and committeewoman."

... By having control of the Republican state executive committee, the Lily White faction will be able to oust the Black and Tans, Yerger said.

"All Howard won at San Francisco was a four year delay," he added.

... Yerger expressed disgust at the seating of the Mississippi delegation in San Francisco. The national party seated eight of the Black and Tan faction and seven of the Lily Whites.

"The seating was entirely unsatisfactory but three or four of our group sat with the Black and Tans," Yerger said.

... Yerger said he ignored Howard and the Black and Tan group in San Francisco.

Col. T. E. Rhodes of French Camp, a white Black and Tan delegate, called him and invited the Lily Whites to a meeting, Yerger said.

"I told him no. Rhodes asked me if we thought we were better than they were. I told him yes, that we were better politically," Yerger said.

Yerger said his group "will always consider E.O. Spencer as our national committeeman and work with him." He predicted Spencer would win official recognition but "it may not be until 1960."

Yerger said he returned from San Francisco "more convinced than ever that the Republican party is the best for Mississippi."

...Yerger also predicted "that chances are mighty" good for Eisenhower carrying Mississippi this November.[24]

• • •

All of these political developments were occurring amid immense societal fermentation. Integration and the corresponding issue of race were inescapable, hot-button issues.

A Gallup poll in 1956 showed that seven out of ten citizens nationally believed the government should gradually, over a long period of years, integrate schools per the 1954

Brown v. Board of Education ruling.[25] A few attempts had been made during 1956 and they met with little success, including:

- Ten blacks tried to integrate Clinton, Tennessee's all-white school, provoking some violence and catcalls. Rumors were some troublemakers might dynamite homes of white families whose children integrated.[26]

- An attempt to integrate in Mansfield, Texas, was abandoned.[27]

- A Clay, Kentucky school was integrated by two children escorted by National Guard troops; two teachers resigned; all but 11 white students stayed home.

The NAACP was increasing its presence in Southern states and was raising large amounts of money to use in its efforts, such as allegedly paying a black youth $11,000 in 1956 to integrate a Texas college.[28] The Montgomery bus boycott ran throughout 1956. Mississippi bus officials said they would continue to ignore the U.S. Supreme Court edict to mix seating on their buses.[29]

Jackson, Mississippi's paper warned in its editorial section that "the peaceful, law-abiding, self-respecting, hard-working colored people of the South must not be blamed" for such recent unrest, adding the blame fell "squarely on the shoulders of the dim-witted old men who form the personnel of the Supreme Court."[30]

The editorial warned: "Back and behind all this agitation is the spirit of Communism."[31]

Most Southern states also now had Citizens' Councils, formed privately and claiming to monitor race issues and promote "public relations" efforts to counter racist accusations. In Mississippi, the legislature in May also had created the State Sovereignty Commission; its stated goal was to be a publicity machine and a "counter-secret service against racial agitators."[32]

• • •

On Sept. 3, 1956, Eisenhower sent me a telegram inviting me to a meeting with Nixon, him and other state party chairmen at his Gettysburg, Pennsylvania, farm. "We hope that you and others who are working for our common cause can join us. In the meantime, I know that you will be doing everything you can to see that every eligible voter ... can vote."[33]

I was now going out and selling our party to our state's people, and I would do so for another decade. "Not until Mississippi adopts a two-party system will we take our rightful place in national affairs," I began proclaiming.[34]

When the presidential election night came in November of 1956, we held a banquet at the Walthall Hotel and honored Charles McWhorter, who had helped me get started with the GOP. Ike and Nixon won in 42 states over Stevenson and Kefauver, registering 35.6 million votes to 26 million respectively.

Though I backed Eisenhower, he never proved to be the true conservative I was hoping for. In the meantime, as one Washington correspondent said, our new GOP in Mississippi was riding "high in the saddle."[35] It was time to start building a solid state party infrastructure.

WIRT A. YERGER, JR. (center) was chosen as the winner of the 1956 Jackson Junior Chamber of Commerce distinguished Service Award. He was presented with a plaque by Jeff Underhill, Jr. (right), Junior Chamber of Commerce president, at a banquet held at the Edwards Hotel last night. Hugh Clegg (left), Director of Development and Assistant to the Chancellor, of the University of Mississippi, was the principal speaker.—Photo by Kelly.

TRICKED: RNC Chairman Leonard Hall, pictured here in 1951, double-crossed Mississippi's new GOP during the 1956 GOP national convention in San Francisco. Photo source: www.gpo.gov.il

BUSY YEAR: Mary and Wirt Yerger married in 1956, then departed from Jackson, Mississippi's airport that same year for San Francisco, where they attended their first Republican National Convention. There, Wirt took a strong stand against long-time Mississippi Republican Party Chairman Perry Wilbon Howard, managing to win future patronage rights away from Howard. It was a key victory for the new Mississippi Republican Party, of which Wirt now became the undisputed state party chairman.

EISENHOWER INVITES YERGER

TO MEETING AT GETTYSBURG

PRESIDENT EISENHOWER WIRED MISSISSIPPI'S REPUBLICAN STATE CHAIRMAN TODAY-

WASHINGTON D. C. SEPTEMBER 7, 1956

"WIRT A YERGER, CHAIRMAN REPUBLICAN STATE EXECUTIVE COMMITTEE
ON SEPTEMBER 12th AT 4:00 PM, MRS EISENHOWER AND I ARE HAVING AN OUTDOOR
MEETING AT OUR GETTYSBURG FARM WITH THE VICE PRESIDENT AND MRS NIXON TO TALK
OVER THE CAMPAIGN, AND ESPECIALLY THE PROGRESS BEING MADE THROUGHOUT THE
COUNTRY TO OBTAIN MAXIMUM VOTER REGISTRATION. WE HOPE THAT YOU AND OTHERS
WHO ARE WORKING FOR OUR COMMON CAUSE CAN JOIN US. IN THE MEANTIME, I KNOW
THAT YOU WILL BE DOING EVERYTHING YOU CAN TO SEE THAT EVERY ELIGIBLE VOTER
SUPPORTING OUR CAUSE REGISTERS SO THAT HE OR SHE CAN VOTE. I SHOULD APPRECIATE
KNOWING IF YOU WILL BE ABLE TO BE WITH US. TRANSPORTATION FROM WASHINGTON TO
GETTYSBURG AND RETURN WILL BE ARRANGED.

I LOOK FORWARD TO SEEING YOU, AND TO YOUR REPORT ON
REGISTRATION PROGRESS AND OTHER DEVELOPMENTS IN YOUR STATE.

WITH WARM REGARDS

DWIGHT D. EISENHOWER

in receipt of invitation and

Also planning on attending are Mr and Mrs. E.O. Spencer (Mr. Spencer in his
official capacity of State Chairman of the Mississippi Citizens for
Eisenhower)
Mrs. R.E. Shands, New Albany, Co-Chairman of Mississippi Citizens for Eisenhower,
and Mrs. J. Balfour Miller, Natchez

July 5, 1956

Dr. Laurence C. Jones
Piney Woods Country Life School
Florence, Mississippi

Dear Dr. Jones;

We have a vacancy in our delegation to the
Republican National Convention beginning
August 20th. in San Francisco and we would
like very much to have you serve as one
of our delegates and attend the Convention.

We appreciate your interest and the splendid
service you have rendered as a member of our
Citizens for Eisenhower Committee on Negro
Welfare and we hope you will serve as a
Delegate to the Convention and represent the
interest of our good Negro citizens in Mississippi.

We await your advice in this matter with great
interest and look forward to the pleasure of
having you serve with our delegation.

Sincerely yours,

E. O. Spencer
National Committeeman

EOS/s

A KEY SELECTION: The Mississippi GOP delegation to the 1956 Republican
National Convention was proud to include an outstanding African-American
Mississippian, Dr. Laurence C. Jones, founder of the Piney Woods Country
Life School outside Florence, Mississippi.

Wirt Yerger, Jr., [is] ... a nice, soft-spoken young man and comes from one of the finest families in Mississippi. But what he doesn't know about that rough-and-tumble American game called politics would fill any good-sized library in the nation. His political pin-feathers have not even shown signs of sprouting and he is as wide-eyed and credulous as Alice in Wonderland. ... Wirt Yerger, Jr., has gone far from the faith of his fathers. Probably Wirt Yerger, Jr., is beyond all semblance of the power of reason or appeal to bring him back to the fold. It seems to be a case of "Ephraim is joined to his idols. Leave him alone."

—The Clarion-Ledger, 1957

If you crave a close-to-hand example of how great has been the change in the attitude of the people toward Republicans, consider young Mr. Wirt A. Yerger, Jr., ...

Quite a few people thought that when young Mr. Yerger—he's only 26—came out boldly as a Republican and worked hard and long last year to push the candidacy of President Eisenhower, that he was "sticking his neck out" and that he'd get his head chopped off.

So what happens? Instead of reprisals, he harvests honors. And the Republican Party, as such, is fast developing into a sure-enough, gen-u-wine going organization in the Magnolia State. ... Young Mr. Yerger's militant efforts in behalf of ... more interest in good government evidently [have] struck a responsive chord. ... And this writer can report, after talking with Mr. Yerger, that Republicans are NOT (original emphasis) fiends in human form. ... He showed no evidences whatsoever of being a "bloated plutocrat."

—Carl Walters, 1957
Mississippi columnist

4

1957

OUT-ORGANIZING THE DUSTY DEMOCRATS

In January of 1957, Eisenhower began his second presidential term. I stood in the Washington sunlight with 20,000 others watching Eisenhower take his second oath of office.

In his inaugural speech, Eisenhower said that we lived in financially prosperous times, but also times without "ease or rest." He added that "new forces and new nations stir and strive across the earth. ... The divisive force is international Communism and the power it controls."

Eisenhower worried America might face a massive nuclear attack by Russia. Reports were saying that "a surprise attack" could involve "about 500 warplanes carrying as much as five billion tons of nuclear explosive force."[1]

Our GOP delegation enjoyed attending the Inaugural. We stayed at a beautiful hotel. Fred LaRue, Jackson hotel owner and son of one of the state's major oilmen, "Big Ike" LaRue, attended a GOP national finance committee meeting. My plane arrived late into Washington, so I missed that meeting. But my wife, Mary, and I were special guests of the national Young Republicans at a state chairmen's gala thrown by Vice President Nixon and his wife.

At Constitution Hall, Mississippi's own soprano, Leontyne Price of Laurel, sang; our local paper called it "an outstanding triumph."[2]

When we Mississippi Republicans returned home from the Inaugural, everyone was predicting the GOP might pick up as many as six congressional seats in Southern states in the 1960 elections. Our Mississippi contingents, therefore, wanted to start acting right away to make the most of our chances.

Charles McWhorter came to Jackson shortly after Eisenhower's inauguration. It was Charles' fourth state visit in a year's time. He lambasted Governor J.P. Coleman, the state's leading Democrat, for having dismissed our tiny party during the recent 1956 elections. Coleman had told state citizens to ignore us. Though Coleman was less strident on the race issue than most state Democrats, in 1956 it was he who had, with the state legislature, created the state-funded State Sovereignty Commission, a would-be watchdog group monitoring Communists and civil rights activists; it was he who sat on that commission as chairman. His successor as governor, Ross Barnett, would set the commission to work from 1960 to 1964 secretly funding the Citizens' Council.

McWhorter reminded both Coleman and the Democrat-run *Clarion-Ledger* that our GOP "state party ran second only to the Democrats. And returns showed that the Mississippi Republican Party is a great organization."[3] He said that I had "done a wonderful job" organizing the November 1956 vote. With more time to organize, "a great independent movement in the South" would harvest more GOP votes in Mississippi in 1960, he predicted.

But the President's personal political leanings were not going to help us new Republican conservatives inside Mississippi. The South's affections for Eisenhower were due to his war record and his perceived ability to counter creeping Communism, not due to his big-government inclinations. In this, we Mississippians mirrored average Americans everywhere. Sixty percent of Americans in 1956 had said Ike's war record sold them on him as president; by early 1957, that had dropped to 42 percent.[4]

Eisenhower espoused what he called "Modern Republicanism," a big-budget brand of taxing and spending adored by Northern pinstripe Republicans; more and more, his positions advocated big government and federally-run programs. Eisenhower was now advocating more taxes to fund more government-controlled programs. He now also put forth his own federal civil rights bill to Congress.

Mississippi U.S. Congressman John Bell Williams joked that Eisenhower's Modern Republicanism was simply Roosevelt's old New Deal "in flimsy disguise." Another Southern Democrat congressman predicted that the President's big-government policies would drive conservative Republicans such as me "away from their leadership."[5] Eisenhower's $70 billion budget for 1957 was, in fact, a record.

Once, in 1957, Eisenhower noted his love for Robert E. Lee, George Washington, Benjamin Franklin, and Abraham Lincoln; portraits of all four hung at his personal retreat in Gettysburg, Pennsylvania. But one Mississippi Gulf Coast journalist now joked that Ike must be confused. "Franklin was an exponent of thrift, Washington did not believe in entangling foreign alliances. Lincoln believed in complete segregation of the races, and Lee fought for states' rights."[6]

So why did we new Mississippi Republicans nonetheless pin our hopes on the national GOP versus the Democrats? For one, no Democrat could rival Eisenhower's strong defense and free-enterprise efforts. The GOP also offered us in Mississippi a clean slate for starting a real conservatism that was not merely race-based and not tied to the terrible baggage both of the national and state Democratic parties; and, of course, being a Republican offered us the chance to introduce a viable second party into Mississippi.

In addition, a rising, younger group of national Republicans—men and women including the great thinker and writer,

William F. Buckley, Arizona U.S. Sen. Barry Goldwater, and Texas U.S. Sen. John Tower—were starting to exercise influence to move our entire national GOP toward a more well-rounded, conservative position on most issues. It was with this very new movement that I cast my lot.

Our state goals were basically twofold: 1) get a second party—the GOP—into Mississippi; 2) help fashion the national GOP into the national party of true conservatives. Achieving these goals would not happen merely by flipping a switch.

• • •

In early 1957, Republican political advisor Lee Potter, an Eisenhower staffer, came to Mississippi to help me recruit citizens to our state GOP. "The opportunities for the Republicans in the South are great," Potter told a Jackson gathering.[7]

We new GOP leaders in Mississippi—many of us young businessmen—were willing to put our money where our mouth was for a two-party system. Unlike the status-quo, big-government Northern Republicans such as the Rockefellers and Romneys, we didn't have lavish personal and corporate wealth at our disposal; and unlike the Southern, old-line Democrats, we didn't have the good-old-boy system of funding politics via backroom meetings and illegal use of local tax dollars all over the state. Instead, we would field a real, rank-and-file party membership from the bottom up; it would give all party members a real say and a chance to express themselves and even to run for office.

So we began doing something our old-line Democrat counterparts never had done: we publicly raised funds at the county level; people stepped up and began giving sacrificially. I asked them to make it regular, like their church tithe. Unlike the state Democrats, we started raising funds county by county, party member by party member. Where people put their money, they often put their hearts. This new program helped us secure many strong commitments.

We started an automatic bank draft system, the United Republican Fund of Mississippi, becoming the first state GOP party in the nation to do so. Money was withdrawn directly from people's bank accounts each month. C.E. "Buddy" Klumb, a Crystal Springs lumberman, capably ran the program.

Our goal was to raise enough money to fund a full-time GOP state headquarters in Jackson. The Democrats did not have one of those, either. We believed a central office would further our long-term goals of forging a county-by-county and precinct-by-precinct organization.

Klumb publicly predicted the URF could solve our fundraising problems once and for all. He was largely correct. In 1957 alone, Copiah County raised 135 percent of its quota; Leflore County raised 66 percent of its goal in under three weeks. Seven other counties—Sunflower, Lowndes, Warren, Hinds, Lauderdale, Pike, and Jackson—ran strong URF programs from the start.

Our top state Republican donors now were out-giving the Democrats' largest public givers. Our four major contributors were Dumas Milner of Jackson ($1,000); Alexander F. Chisholm of Laurel ($1,000); L.O. Crosby of Picayune ($1,000); and Richard A. Campbell of Natchez ($1,000). By comparison, the Democrats' top donors were Ralph Cox of Alligator and T.G. Wilson of Tupelo, both giving $500. We also were getting some help from outside the state via gifts from Citizens for Eisenhower: James E. Kemp of Dallas ($1,000) and B.G. Byers of Tyler, Texas ($500).[8]

We were becoming harder to overlook.

The Jackson Junior Chamber of Commerce had even awarded me its 1956 Distinguished Service Award. It seemed to validate all of our efforts to promote free enterprise in our state. A relatively new state-wide paper, *The State Times*, editorialized that "the Jaycees did not err in picking 26-year-old Wirt Yerger for the coveted prize." I had, said the paper, conducted "a house-cleaning in the MRP ranks. It is his intent to make the state faction as politically pure as possible, a commendable task for any party leader. If Mr. Yerger has done no more than rid Mississippi of the spectacle of 'Black and Tan' rump sessions, ramrodding leadership and other unsavory practices, he has earned a niche in state history."[9]

We new state Republicans had just started.

We were a new breed of business-minded Southerners, coming of age amid post-World War II industrialization. Mississippi was no longer a one-faceted agricultural state. We in the business sector wanted and needed to compete outside our state. We needed a party to represent our free-enterprise position. Neither Ike's team of Northern Republicans nor national Democrats saw this. They still saw all Mississippians as Roosevelt-type New Dealers. The Southern image of a "pot-bellied run-down sheriff" did not fit us businessmen, one national writer correctly observed.[10] "The South today is no longer sectional except in the minds of some of the people outside the South," one U.S. senator from Florida noted.[11] Our region was in "ferment," he added.

• • •

In early 1957, Montgomery, Alabama, experienced five shootings after a federal court ordered integrated bussing in late December 1956.[12]

I cannot speak for all, but I can say that I despised such violent acts. Indeed, several years later in 1964 when three civil rights workers were killed and buried in an earthen dam near Philadelphia, Mississippi, I was summoned to grand jury duty. I gladly answered the call and hoped against hope that the defense would pick me; I believed I could help ensure the jury would deliver the strongest guilty verdicts possible to all those deserving them. I was not picked. Years later, one of the defense attorneys admitted to me that they knew I would have taken a principled stand against the violence and would have worked to convict those proven guilty. Seven of 18 men tried in 1964 on charges of violating the three victims' civil rights were found guilty and served time; it took until June 20, 2005, however, until Edgar Ray Killen was found guilty of manslaughter and imprisoned for 60 years.

There were two lines of thought developing in 1957 about how the Southern Republican movement might grow amid this difficult climate:

1. A few pundits predicted we in the Southern GOP would make a new, all-out push for civil rights, citing our state Democrats' ineptitude and outright racial animosity. Black voters would then naturally move into the Southern GOP as a backlash against Southern Democrats. One political reporter actually wrote: "No Southern Republican leader will at this time make public comment, but most of them privately are urging an all-out fight to pass the so-called right-to-vote legislation. If Negro citizens are really permitted the ballot, and are safe-guarded in it, Dixie GOP leaders see a very real chance to make a great leap forward in establishing a two-party system. They believe they could within the foreseeable future elect more congressmen and some state officials."[13]

2. Another line of thought was that we in the Southern GOP must not focus overtly on the race issue, except by continuing to call for calm, reasoned efforts amid the challenge; this was uniformly our approach. The GOP would not harp on race; scream it to voters or in the media; constantly publish about it as Southern Democrats were doing. The reality was that Eisenhower, our national leader, was at the time *advancing* integration bills. We were not going to oppose our national leaders and therefore become schismatic. This was what our state Democrats had long been doing with their national leaders.

Eisenhower's big-government social policies did not enhance my popularity as a Republican in the Magnolia State, but I never apologized for him, though I favored small-government solutions.

Being for small-government solutions does not equal racism. I have never felt that any race was superior. I felt in 1957, and I still feel, that all are due the same opportunities, treatment and respect. My hopes and allegiances in 1957 were fixed on promoting a color-blind conservatism.

I wrote a letter to President Eisenhower and Republican National Chairman William Miller representing my constituency's concerns over expansion of federal-government powers and increased spending on pet social projects, which sometimes seemed designed to court certain groups' votes more than to follow principle. I told Eisenhower that slower, steadier heart and legal changes would best solve the long-term race issue. "We urge you to reconsider," I wrote to Eisenhower regarding his 1957 civil rights bill.[14] But I was not going to press any harder.

I told Miller that such expressions of my concern were not meant to indicate that we should not accept African-American voters into the GOP, but rather they were meant to emphasize that to set a pragmatic, political course that counted on a great number of new black voters to form our future base was unwisely risky. Liberal Northern Democrats already had the union/labor and black vote largely sewn up outside the South, both practically and philosophically, and we would not find much water in that well. It was a political fact. "I am not writing off completely any vote, but I do think it is best to go hunting where the ducks are," I told Miller. Goldwater made this same metaphorical statement, and I believed he was correct. Today a growing number of African-American conservatives are in the GOP because of their solid convictions. That is the way it should be with us all.

By mid-1957, one pundit foresaw a new national standoff forming among Democrats: "For the Democrats, the years ahead pose a real political dilemma."[15] How would they resolve the Southern Democrats' stances with the Northern Democrats rapidly emerging position on race? National Democrat leadership increasingly ignored their Southern party leadership. The Southern party leadership, in return, continued to defy and decry their national leaders—and, as in 1948, some soon would publicly break again from the national Democratic Party into a temporary protest faction.

Republican Richard Nixon was biding his time for a future presidential run, quietly favoring Ike's social policies, but also currying Southerners' favor. I once told Nixon that a secondary thing that bothered me about the new rash of civil rights laws was that these laws were not applied equally in Northern and Western states compared to in the South. Racial violence, hatred, and *de facto* segregation were occurring everywhere, but many Northern and Western Republicans (and Democrats) did not want to hurt their chance to keep their own white voter bases in their poltical districts. Therefore, they pointed all their efforts southward.

For instance, in January of 1957, an Oakland, California mob of 1,200 roughed up two white policemen, with more than 30 people arrested.[16] A "free-for-all" in Milwaukee left several detectives with abrasions.[17] Some African Americans were as upset with their conditions in these places as in the South— and many said they were more upset.

Mississippi's Citizens' Council promised that integration efforts would be dead within five years "as long as the people will fight for it."[18] Of course, this amounted to an aggressive dare to federal officials to defeat them.

Some of our state's black leaders actually opposed new civil rights laws. These black leaders opposed what they cited as the "revolution" called for by the NAACP, which they regarded as too radical and agitating; instead, they favored a more gradual evolution toward better relations accompanied by continued demonstrations of African American excellence that none could refute or disdain.

Without federal force, "a steady evolution for the better towards the Negro citizens" was already underway, wrote

Percy Greene, the black editor and owner of *The Jackson Advocate*. He added that "good, sound, logical reasons" existed for moving slowly, rather than using forced, outside action toward integration.[19]

Commenting on the strife happening in 1957 in Montgomery's 382-day bus boycott, Greene contrasted Jackson's bussing situation:

> Here in Jackson ... there has been a steady evolution for the better towards Negro citizens on the local buses.
>
> Any Negro, or any other person, who will use a little time in observing can see that Negro passengers on the Jackson buses, serving the predominantly Negro neighborhoods, take seats anywhere they please, and generally fill the buses from front to back, sometime with hardly room for the driver to operate. ...
>
> For all practical purposes, despite outside critics, segregation on the buses serving predominantly Negro neighborhoods of the city is now only a question of emotions and imagination, and on the buses serving predominantly white neighborhoods, the first come first served basis works conversely to that on the buses serving predominantly Negro neighborhoods. ...
>
> Both past and present history points to a far better future for Negroes of Jackson via the evolutionary process than by indulging in revolutionary activities and movements.[20]

Greene is remembered as someone who "time and time again put his life on the line fighting for black people. The battle for the vote, court battles, his friendship with President Truman all helped Southern blacks," said James Rundle, who once worked with Greene.

When accused in the 1950s of being a sellout, Greene replied: "Any Negro is an 'Uncle Tom' who ... seeks to maintain a friendly and respectful attitude toward the responsible white people of the community."[22] Greene lamented that liberal activists had also made a "prime target" out of Dr. Laurence

C. Jones, "founder and head of the now world famous Piney Woods Country Life School in Piney Woods, Mississippi."[23] Northern liberal blacks including W.E.B. DuBois demeaned such conservative-oriented African Americans, chief of whom was Booker T. Washington, founder of the Tuskegee Institute in Alabama.

Greene predicted in 1957 that "the masses of Negroes of the South ... are being led over a precipice by the siren calls of the new Negro leadership to be repeatedly submerged in an ever maddening whirlpool of hatred, fear, frustration and bewilderment."[24]

When in 1957 four African-American churches in Montgomery were dynamited, everyone's world shook. A horrid act had been waged against bussing desegregation. There was no decent principle in such bombings. Montgomery's mayor issued a curfew for all children. He worried about potential anarchy.

About this time the National Communist Party met and vowed to continue assisting activist liberal leadership with their desegregation plans in the South. These types of published statements by the U.S. Communist Party always added to hysteria among some Southerners about the degree of Communist involvement in the civil rights movement. One pundit said the civil rights and Communist movements were co-joined and "hell-bent" on their objectives in the South.[25] An Associated Press report out of Washington, D.C. in 1957 said the recent Communist convention had discussed plans to "infiltrate Negro and other mass organizations in the United States" to penetrate the "main stream of American life."[26] Even the *Chicago Tribune* warned of Communist plans "to aggravate racial tensions [in Chicago]."[27]

Many reasonable Southerners struggled to understand the real facts. At that time, it was not always easy to know. In the meantime, we in the state GOP stayed the course toward building a responsible second party.

• • •

In 1957, I chose B.B. McClendon, Jr., a former Hinds County district attorney who had moved into private practice, to take my place running Mississippi's Young Republican organization. Both E.O. Spencer and I told the newspapers that we felt "very fortunate" to have someone of B.B.'s quality. Our goal was to have a Young Republican chapter in every Mississippi county.[28]

Again, we were way ahead of state Democrats, who had little organizational opportunities for their youth or at the county level. Our first Young Republican chapter was in Jackson. We elected James K. Child, chairman; Thomas K. Crockett, Jr., vice chairman; Mrs. B.B. McClendon, secretary; and Mrs. George P. Hewes, III, treasurer.

Mrs. James A. White of Durant was president of the Mississippi Republican Women's Club. She started holding proactive gatherings of ladies around the state, preaching the importance of a two-party system, "one which is representative of the true Republican peoples of Mississippi," she said, "if we are to be heard on the national level."[29]

The national GOP and I were now fully cooperating to build our state infrastructure. Such organizational systems today are taken for granted in politics. But at the time, *Democrats in our state had never even had or needed such a framework.*

On another front, Mississippians, like most Americans, were feeling pretty good about their pocket books in 1957. Forty-two percent in one Gallup Poll said "business would be better" in 1957 under Republican leadership versus 12 percent who said it would be "worse"; 36 percent said their family would be better off, versus 12 percent saying "worse off."[30]

I could sell this prospect of economic prosperity to our citizens.

In addition, a national Young Republicans study showed that college students were shifting toward our GOP, and they were most often William F. Buckley conservatives. For the first time in history, a majority of college students in the State of South Carolina—52 percent—voted Republican in 1956. "There is no doubt that the Republicans have made considerable headway among Southern youth in recent years, including Mississippi and other states traditionally loyal to the Democratic Party," one editorial said. "This means that Democrats must ... concentrate on 'youth appeal.'"[31]

B.B. and I traveled to a Lexington, Kentucky, strategy meeting with top-level Republicans. Eisenhower spoke to us by long-distance phone. He urged us to run candidates statewide in future elections. National GOP Chairman Meade Alcorn and Charles McWhorter spent a lot of time in Lexington with B.B. and me. Charles pledged he "would do everything possible" to help us in our state.[32]

We returned to Jackson and, in mid-May, announced plans to run candidates in the next statewide races. Sen. John C. Stennis predicted that we were a flash in the pan.[33] Stennis couldn't see the future for the past.

Something else would soon dynamite Stennis' beliefs. An earth-shaking personality was asserting himself nationally. Barry Goldwater was a lively, idealistic young conservative who hoped to take GOP control for conservatives from Eisenhower's Modern Republicans. Goldwater was a member of the "Regular Republicans," those holding a more philosophical set of true conservative beliefs.

• • •

By mid-June, our state GOP leadership was attending the Young Republicans National Convention. B.B. McClendon, Tom Crockett, and Jack Geary joined me as our state's first true delegation to a Young Republican national convention, which we all greatly enjoyed. During a two-hour gala for the Eisenhowers, the President told us of his "never-failing concern for every last human being in America, no matter what his religion or color of his skin." We all applauded. "That, as I see it, is Republicanism," he said.[34]

Then, in September of 1957, our nation turned its eyes to Central High School in Little Rock, Arkansas. A federal judge planned to force Arkansas Gov. Orval Faubus to integrate the school immediately. Faubus *already* had integrated Arkansas' bussing system, in compliance with the Brown v. Board of Education ruling of 1954; newspaper reports said Faubus was inquiring at that very time about how best to integrate his state's schools. But the activist federal judge would not wait. He issued a federal order. Faubus, a Democrat, resisted. Then Eisenhower entered the fray; he sent Faubus a telegram warning him to back down. A few days later the two men met in Newport, Rhode Island. The President labeled the meeting disappointing. On Sept. 24, 1957, Eisenhower federalized Arkansas' National Guard, setting these Arkansans against the majority of their fellow citizens to enforce integration, saying this was a stand against "anarchy." Faubus threatened to challenge Eisenhower in federal court.

After Little Rock, Mississippi Governor J.P. Coleman insisted he would close any public school where integration was attempted. An editorial cartoon in *The Clarion-Ledger* showed a chalk board shaped like the State of Mississippi. On the board was written, "A Clean State," with a caption below boasting, "In a Race Class of Its Own."[35] Another headline boasted that "Jackson Remains a Fortress"; pundits predicted Eisenhower's action "may spell [a] third party."[36]

Our GOP state leadership had planned an organizational meeting in Jackson for Oct. 2, but Eisenhower's moves in Little Rock changed things. Instead, we now gathered to monitor reaction in Mississippi to our Republican president's moves. As my friends Jere Nash and Andy Taggart—the former a liberal and the latter a conservative—noted in their very fine 2006 political history, *Mississippi Politics: The Struggle for Power, 1976-2000,* "The most profound crisis in the growth of the Republican Party in Mississippi had been triggered by a Republican president."[37]

Actually, it ultimately was a more profound crisis for the state's old-line Democrats than for us; but it did challenge our plans to stimulate growth in our party. Ike's move was the final straw for E.O. Spencer. He had almost bolted our new party when Eisenhower's national committee had tricked us into a compromise deal with Perry Howard's Black and Tans at the San Francisco 1956 convention. Spencer could not believe that Ike would pit federal troops against Americans in the South. He announced after our Oct. 2 meeting that "Citizens for Eisenhower" in Mississippi had been "completely destroyed" by the act, claiming it had ruined "everything accomplished in Mississippi during the past five years."[38]

Observes Joseph Crespino, "President Eisenhower's use of federal troops to enforce school desegregation in Little Rock confirmed segregationist fears that the Republicans were and always would be the party of Lincoln."[39] GOP members from every Southern state now began defecting our ranks in droves.[40] I understood Spencer's emotions. In a press statement, I insisted our state owed him a great debt. Privately, I also knew that he was a man bound by his own times. Our party stood for much more than anything involving the integration issue.

And though I disliked Eisenhower's use of federal force—it produced an extremely painful wound—I knew that the future must be kept in mind. So on the same day that Spencer announced his decision, I told Mississippians that I planned to stay in the GOP and continue working "within the framework of the national party ... for the free enterprise system and constitutional government." I added, "It is more than ever certain that Mississippi and the Southland have their hopes in the two-party system."[41]

Few understood how I could remain in our Republican leadership. "What white man in Mississippi would want to associate himself with the present administration?" asked one former associate, Mayo Reed, whose tirade at me was published in *The Clarion-Ledger*.[42]

I was not altogether popular. But my principles were solid and long-term, and the idealist in me knew they would last.

Meanwhile, another youthful idealist, John F. Kennedy, had now started informally to campaign in Mississippi, speaking to a gathering of Democrats in Jackson. He was beginning what would become his presidential campaign.

As state GOP chairman, I challenged Kennedy through the media to make clear his own position on the integration issue when he met with the state's old-line Democrats, who somehow were so enthralled with him that they hypocritically would not question him on the matter. National and local media attacked me for asking Kennedy the most important question any Mississippian had at that time.

Time magazine printed an article about my challenge to Kennedy, making it sound as if Kennedy's response was heroic. The article follows:

DEMOCRATS

Through the Roadblock

Long before federal troops flew into Little Rock, Massachusetts' Democratic Senator John Kennedy, an undeclared but unabashed candidate for his party's presidential nomination in 1960, accepted an invitation to speak to Mississippi Young Democrats at Jackson, in the deepest of the Deep South. But ever since Arkansas' Governor Orval Faubus kicked over the Democratic civil rights applecart, Kennedy's Southern friends have been begging him to back out. Their argument: anything Kennedy would say that was faintly conciliatory to the South would be used against him in the North, yet if he spoke the Northern view he would necessarily offend his Southern supporters. Jack Kennedy disagreed: he felt that he had to live up to his speaking commitment and, further, that he had to speak out on civil rights. Last week he did both with auspicious political results.

"I Accept the Challenge." Landing in Jackson, Kennedy read the local papers—and in them, a challenge from Mississippi Republican State Chairman Wirt Yerger Jr. for him to state his views on integration and segregation. While he kept an overflow reception crowd waiting in the Roof Room of the Heidelberg Hotel, Jack

Kennedy hid out in his room, lolling in a warm bath while he thought through a revised version of his speech.

That night Kennedy arose before a sellout audience, boyishly tugged at his ear, tweaked his nose, ran a finger around the inside of his shirt collar, and announced bleakly: "I am particularly happy to be here tonight." The crowd sat silent, waiting, Kennedy continued: "It will be possible for us to disagree as Democrats within our party organization." The silence grew heavier. Kennedy plunged ahead, reading the text of Republican Yerger's tricky challenge. Said he: "I accept the challenge. You who have been gracious enough to invite me here realize that we do not see eye to eye on all national issues. I have no hesitancy in telling the Republican chairman the same thing I said in my own city of Boston, that I accept the Supreme Court decision as the supreme law of the land. I know that we do not all agree on that issue, but I think most of us do agree on the necessity to uphold law and order in every part of the land."

"I'm All For Him." Kennedy paused, and for a brief, desperate moment there was more silence. Then Kennedy quickly added: "And now I challenge the Republican chairman to tell us where he stands on Eisenhower and Nixon!" The crowd came to its feet, alive, roaring and stomping its approval: Jack Kennedy had won it by his own display of courage and by turning all good Democrats against the odious Republicans. He was still a long, hard way from the Democratic nomination, but he had broken through a major roadblock.

Said one local congressman admiringly: "I never thought I'd see anybody in Central Mississippi speak up for integration and get a standing ovation." Said a slightly tipsy young Democrat, as he pumped the hand of Roman Catholic Jack Kennedy: "You know what? All these Baptists and Methodists are going to vote for you, my Catholic friend. And I'm proud to say I'm one of them too." Said Mississippi's influential Governor James P. Coleman: "I think he is our best presidential prospect for 1960, and I am all for him."[43]

History, of course, reveals that Kennedy also later used troops in Mississippi at Ole Miss. Those same "giddy" old-line Southern Democrats then became the greatest Kennedy-bashers ever. My desire for Kennedy to let Mississippians know where he stood versus spouting rhetorical flourishes proved reasonable. But at this point in time, I was mocked. *The Clarion-Ledger* soon added its two-cents about my challenging Kennedy. The scathing *Clarion-Ledger* article of Oct. 20 follows:

Our New Political Leonidas

Wirt Yerger, Jr., successor to E.O. Spencer as GOP political patronage boss, wanted to be noticed by Senator John F. Kennedy, guest at the rally of the Young Democratic forces held here Thursday.

Wirt got noticed all right, and is perhaps now wishing he hadn't.

Let it be said by the way of fuller identification or introduction of Wirt Yerger, Jr., that he's a nice, soft-spoken young man and comes from one of the finest families in Mississippi. But what he doesn't know about that rough-and-tumble American game called politics would fill any good-sized library in the nation.

His political pin-feathers have not even shown signs of sprouting and he is as wide-eyed and credulous as Alice in Wonderland, in this instance the wonderland being that weird political organization created last year calling itself "Citizens for Eisenhower,"—political malcontents who felt that they couldn't possibly support Stevenson— admittedly a hard thing to do—and felt that Eisenhower, if elected, would be the lesser of two evils.

Mr. E.O. Spencer, leader of "Citizens for Eisenhower," was completely disillusioned about Eisenhower, when the President sent troops to Little Rock to enforce integration at the bayonet's point. Spencer quit in disgust and frankly said so. But not our political fledgling, Wirt

Yerger, Jr. ... Like many another political novice, he rushed right in where others feared to tread.

He was a Leonidas hurling himself into the breach when he assumed command of the remnants of the "Citizens for Eisenhower" movement, and he certainly got some hot shot in the seat of his breeches when Senator Kennedy asked him frankly to make public his views of Eisenhower and Nixon.

It will be recalled that Yerger asked, prior to Kennedy's arrival in Jackson, an explanation of why Kennedy has not raised his voice against the vicious segregation decision of the Supreme Court.

That question Kennedy could well have hurled right back at Yerger, asking what he thinks of the Black Monday decision on integration.

Kennedy's simple reply was that he respects the Supreme Court decision because it is the "law of the land." From the purely legal viewpoint, Senator Kennedy is correct. It will take something more than dissent, derision, or disgust to change that decision. Moreover, please bear in mind Senator Kennedy didn't say he agreed with that decision. Like many other good Democrats in the north, he wished it had never been rendered.

But, regardless of Kennedy's agreement or dissent concerning the decision, that did not justify a fine chap like Wirt Yerger, Jr., son of an old and highly respected family, sticking with Eisenhower regardless of what happened in Tennessee and Arkansas in the way of forcing Negro pupils into white schools.

Wert [sic] Yerger Jr., by the very act of [remaining within the Republican party structure] ... gives full consent and approval to use of Federal troops poking bayonets in the stomachs of citizens while rudely ordering them about, even if integration is "the law of the land."

By taking over as titular head of the party in Mississippi

he gives full approval in the actions of Eisenhower, all of them plotted and planned by that political lick-spittle, Herbert Brownell, Jr., who takes his orders from the NAACP.

Nothing serious in enforcement in Mississippi has been attempted but [it] will happen and will very soon, make no mistake about it. What is Mr. Yerger going to do when the same problem is dumped on your own doorstep? What is our new political rooster, who has not yet learned to crow, going to do when Federal troops invade Mississippi?

Wirt Yerger, Jr., has gone far from the faith of his fathers. Probably Wirt Yerger, Jr., is beyond all semblance of the power of reason or appeal to bring him back to the fold.

It seems to be a case of "Ephraim is joined to his idols. Leave him alone."[44]

In writing the above editorial, *The Clarion-Ledger* attempted to cast me as a political expedient, seeking to advance myself by grabbing attention and aligning myself with those whose politics and actions I opposed. The mirror, of course, would soon be turned on them.

MONEY MATTERS: While our state Democrat opposition kept running its good-old-boy system of funding campaigns and trading power, the new state GOP initiated a fund-raising system copied by many other GOP state parties.

THE WHITE HOUSE

WASHINGTON

July 18, 1957

Dear Mr. Yerger:

Now that the Republican Regional Conferences have been
concluded, may I assure you of my deep appreciation of
your contribution to their success. I know that with the
aggressive participation of every Republican leader we
can assure the election of a Republican Senate and House,
as well as Republican State and local officials in 1958.

The plan that the Regional Conferences enthusiastically
approved, providing similar conferences in each state in
the fall of 1957 will, assuredly, meet with the same success. Your vigorous promotion of this important part
of the program for victory in 1958 will be of immeasur-
able aid.

With warm regard,

Sincerely,

Dwight D. Eisenhower

The Honorable Wirt A. Yerger, Jr.
Mississippi Republican Party
Box 1139
Jackson, Mississippi

YOUNG REPUBLICAN NATIONAL FEDERATION
1625 Eye St, N.W. Washington 6,D.C.
National 8-6800

CHARLES K. MCWHORTER   May 28, 1957   JOYCE I. BOVIK
CHAIRMAN   CO-CHAIRMAN

Mr. E. O. Spencer
National Committeeman
214 Walthall Hotel
Jackson, Miss

Dear Mr. Spencer:

Thank you for your letter of May 24th. So long as S.W. Miller
is un-willing to request the Secretary of State of Mississippi to withdraw
any official status for the Mississippi G. O.P. (Black and Tan) Party, I
think it would be useless and dangerous to give him any consideration or
recognition in connection with personnel matters. I do think it is important,
however, that we should work out in the immediate future, the procedures
for bringing this personnel operation under the auspices of the Mississippi
Republican Party.

I am delighted that you and Wirt are going ahead and organizing
a Young Republican Federation throughout the State of Mississippi and that
there will be a full delegation on hand for our Convention this June.

I will certainly do all I can here in Washington to cooperate
with you and Wirt in every way concerning any problems you have with the
Republican National Committee. One suggestion that I would like to pass
on is for you to consider changing the letterhead of your Party stationery so that you and Mrs. Miller are designated as something other than
National Committeeman and National Committeewoman. Perhaps " National
Representative" would be a better discription. I say that only because
Perry Howard has apparently made persistent phone calls to Meade Alcorn,
stressing that the present title on your letterhead violates the action of
the Republican National Convention taken in San Francisco last August. I
would be glad to discuss this with you over the telephone if you want
any further information or comments.

I hope all is well with you and your family and my warmest
personal regards,

                                        Sincerely,

                                        s/

                                        Charles K. McWhorter

CK/bw

                                        c

Mississippi Republican Party

Peace • Progress • Prosperity

PHONE 108

E. O. SPENCER
NATIONAL COMMITTEEMAN
214 WALTHALL HOTEL
JACKSON, MISSISSIPPI

MRS. J. BALFOUR MILLER
NATIONAL COMMITTEEWOMAN
HOPE FARM
NATCHEZ, MISSISSIPPI

WIRT A. YERGER, JR., CHAIRMAN
STATE EXECUTIVE COMMITTEE
108 LAMAR LIFE BUILDING
JACKSON, MISSISSIPPI

FRED LaRUE, CHAIRMAN
STATE FINANCE COMMITTEE
107 WEST PEARL STREET
JACKSON, MISSISSIPPI

G. DEWEY COLLINS, SECRETARY
STATE EXECUTIVE COMMITTEE
TYLERTOWN, MISSISSIPPI

R. B. THOMAS, TREASURER
STATE EXECUTIVE COMMITTEE
WIGGINS, MISSISSIPPI

October 1, 1957

Mr. Wirt A. Yerger, Jr., Chairman
State Executive Committee
Mississippi Republican Party
108 Lamar Life Building
Jackson, Mississippi

Dear Mr. Yerger:

I hereby resign as a member of the Mississippi Republican Party and as National Committeeman effective immediately.

Sincerely yours,

E. O. Spencer

EOS:mj

January 9, 1957

State Executive Committee
Mississippi Republican Party

Dear Committeeman:

This morning, your Chairman received three telegrams requesting a meeting of the Executive Committee on January 14th at 4:00 P. M.

As I understand it, the majority of the committee does not desire to come to Jackson for meetings, unless it is of utmost importance and urgency, and them not very often. Neither these telegrams, nor Anson Sheldon, who claims to be the spokesman, have given sufficient reason for calling a meeting as early as January 14th.

I have arranged to be in Washington for the Inauguration and hope to receive important information to relay to you. After the Inauguration, if we have the pertinent information from the Republican National Committee, a meeting of the Executive Committee will be probably in order.

One thing I will say now is that if we of the Mississippi Republican Party cannot act with a spirit of cooperation, dignity, and integrity, we will not have a voice in one single appointment during this Republican Administration.

As a member of your Executive Committee and your Chairman, I will fight for the interests of the Mississippi Republican Party always, as long as I am convinced the majority are not "post office politicians".

Let's all work together for a much stronger, more widely organized Republican Party in Mississippi.

Sincerely,

Wirt A. Yerger, Jr.
Chairman

WAYJr:ese

Mr. President, is there any way that we can be sure that when we send a letter to you personally that you will see that letter?

> —Wirt A. Yerger, Jr., to President Dwight D. Eisenhower in a private, 1958 meeting of the 48 GOP state chairmen

---

You must be either an integrationist or a segregationist. You can't carry water on both shoulders.

> —Ross Barnett in 1958 campaigning as a Democrat for governor of Mississippi

---

We have come a long way in a short time, but we must keep moving forward. In order to do this we must have a state headquarters. ... No, I haven't gone crazy ... Now is the time to forge ahead.

> —Wirt A. Yerger, Jr., to the Miss. Republican executive committee, Aug. 1958

5

1958

Confronting Eisenhower and Kennedy

When President Eisenhower sent federal troops into Little
Rock in 1957, it obviously smashed our GOP momentum in
Mississippi. So we state Republicans kept a low profile in
1958, concentrating on building state party infrastructure as
this "racial controversy blew across the region."[1] We were "re-
covering from Little Rock and preparing for the 1960 national
convention."[2]

The only U.S. group in which GOP voter strength increased in 1958 was African Americans, from 22 to 30 percent.[3] College-educated people voting Republican dropped
from 64 percent in 1954 to 53 percent in 1958. Farmers voting GOP dropped from 56 percent to 46 percent. Professionals
and business people dropped from 61 percent to 51 percent.
Whites voting for Republicans dropped from 48 to 42 percent.

Reports said that a "defeatism" had crept into the GOP,
with only about three in ten Republicans nationally expecting
any GOP wins in the 1958 November congressional elections.[4]

As for Mississippi's Democrats, now more than ever they
fanned flames of segregation. But at the same time, their na-

tional party was becoming increasingly liberal. In 1958, while Southern Democrat voters weren't really watching, 22 Democrat U.S. senators voted the entire liberal agenda line of the Americans for Democratic Action group, versus only four Republicans. The Democratic Party was moving further to the Left.

Meanwhile, Democrat attorney Ross Barnett was tilling the soil for a 1959 bid for the governor's office. He was populist and racist. He told one Kiwanis Club gathering in 1958:

> If integration is practiced long enough in any state or nation, it will destroy that [state or nation]. Look at Egypt, once the greatest of nations and now a doddering nation. The good Lord is the original segregationist, for he made the races of many colors and placed oceans between them to make certain they stayed that way. We should dedicate ourselves to maintaining the integrity of both the white and the Negro races in this country. Eisenhower should know that any people who integrate will soon go down hill. We must protect the future of our children and, if we don't care about the purity of their blood, either white or black, then we are in a dangerous plight. You must be either an integrationist or a segregationist. You can't carry water on both shoulders.[5]

Barnett would be elected governor and would further saddle his state party with a perverted brand of conservatism.

• • •

In 1958, my brother Swan and I approached a former military buddy of his, Clarke Reed, who lived in Greenville. Reed had been the manager of the officer's club at Berkeley Air Force Base in Mobile, Alabama. Swan had been his assistant manager, while also performing other military duties.

I called Clarke and asked him to help build a new Republican Party in our state. He told me that he didn't have time to get involved in politics. He said he was too busy at work and being president of the Greenville Country Club. I sat on the other end of the phone line thinking, "Here I am trying to save the nation and he's concerned about being the president of the country club." Clarke would eventually follow me as GOP state party chairman in 1966.

John F. Kennedy kept courting old-line state Democrats, announcing that he planned to speak again on April 14 to our Mississippi Economic Council. He had spoken to the same group in April of 1957, but had refused at that time to field questions from our state media. State Democrats let him get away with this. They did not want Kennedy to answer uncomfortable questions.

I publicly berated state Democrats for hiding Kennedy from our voters. I noted that our Republican leadership always made themselves available to all media questions. "Last October Senator John Kennedy of Massachusetts journeyed to Mississippi in order to speak to the Young Democrats of Mississippi," I said. "Immediately following his speech he went into seclusion and refused to be interviewed by press members of Jackson. After Kennedy had left our state, the Young Democrats boasted of their success in keeping the press members from interviewing Kennedy while he was in Mississippi."[6]

Just days after Kennedy's April 1957 visit to Jackson, I. Lee Potter, Special Assistant to the Republican National Chairman, spoke on the Mississippi Gulf Coast and talked freely with the local press. I noted the difference in our parties' treatment of the media: "Mississippi... Republicans feel that the people of Mississippi are entitled to the true facts about Kennedy, the so-called friend of Mississippi."[7]

Of course, state Democrats ignored us. Once again, the lack of any real two-party system and the media's friendly relationship with state Democrats meant state citizens were poorly informed. But then Kennedy suddenly decided to back out of his second scheduled Mississippi appearance, snubbing our state. At that point, even Charles M. Hills, a statewide columnist, admitted we Republicans had a point about Kennedy's soft-glove treatment.

Wrote Hills: "The Massachusetts potential candidate for

president, who has been most skittish of the Mississippi press ... is vulnerable now, sure enough."[8]

Everywhere, state Democrats either attempted to ignore us or obscure our presence. For instance, in Hinds County there were just three state representatives to the state legislature, when by population there should have been 12. Democrats wanted the low number, since having 12 would increase the chance that a non-Democrat might win a seat. Also, Republicans had our best numbers in business-oriented Jackson, while the Democrat power base was in rural areas.

In April of 1958, Democrats once again killed a reapportionment plan for the state legislature. "What are you doing?" I asked Democrats in a public statement.[9] "What have you, our representatives, done to help us gain our rightful representation? We do not like taxation without representation, and having the minority control the majority."[10]

• • •

I traveled to Washington, D.C. during the third week of June 1958 for Republican strategy meetings. They called it a "campaign school." The goal was to help state chairmen develop in-state candidates and voter strength. I told the state press that it was a chance to "exchange ideas with other state GOP chairmen" and to "work for a strong second party—the Republican Party—in the South."[11]

That same week, a major scandal broke with Eisenhower's White House Chief of Staff Sherman Adams, former governor of New Hampshire. He was implicated in taking big gifts—amounting to bribes—from a Boston industrialist in exchange for preferred treatment. "The 48 Republican state chairmen couldn't have picked a worse time to come to Washington," one political writer noted.[12]

This put our state chairmen's meetings in the spotlight. At the end of one closed-door strategy session, Meade Alcorn, chairman of the Republican National Committee, warned all of the chairmen that the media lurked in big numbers just outside our meeting room. "Gentlemen, as you know, there has been some unfortunate publicity about one of the members of our party. Before you leave the room, I want to warn you that the corridors are jammed with newspapermen who will want your comments on the situation; be prepared."[13]

We found a remedy. We all removed our name-tags. As we walked into the hall, the press could not know who we were and where we were from.

Sherman Adams always limited access to Eisenhower, and we state party chairmen were disgusted with him. He kept Eisenhower from receiving our input on policy matters. But during our state chairmen meetings, we chairmen did meet personally with Ike at the Statler Hotel. He gave us a nice pep talk and then opened the meeting for questions. Nobody seemed able to open their mouths.

I have always felt a leader should be willing to ask hard questions.

I stood up.

"Mr. President," I said, "is there any way that we can be sure that when we send a letter to you personally that you will see that letter?"

He said, "I can guarantee you."

A sudden thunder of applause swept the room.

Everyone was happy. I had simply asked the obvious question.

I believe the world would be different if more people would step up and say what they think versus sitting around scared.

Ike got my message. Meanwhile, Adams stood there, fuming. Over the next month, Adams survived calls to step down. The President always stood by him, saying, "I can't believe that anybody on my staff would ever be guilty of an indiscretion."[14]

• • •

On the last day in July 1958, the United States Senate approved Alaska as the 49th state. Eisenhower started calling for

Hawaii's acceptance, as well. This was happy news in an otherwise depressing year.

In Cleveland, Ohio, another "49th" was occurring. The NAACP was holding its 49th national conference, drawing about 1,000 delegates from 40 states. Just a week earlier, Eisenhower had met with Martin Luther King, Jr., and three other civil rights leaders at the White House.[15] The NAACP had just financed a suit by three Mississippi blacks that was the first federal court legal challenge to our state's voter registration laws.[16] While an ability to read was the basic standard for voting at the time, very often county clerks in Mississippi used demeaning tactics to keep African Americans from registering: our state constitution said those registering had to explain part of the United States Constitution and some county clerks asked blacks questions no one could answer.

Just days after this Jefferson Davis County suit, a Northern newspaper wrote a series of articles claiming Communists were infiltrating every strata of the civil rights movement. Our own *Clarion-Ledger* reported that *The Standard-Times* of New Bedford, Massachusetts "links the pink-shirted crowd to Little Rock in the planning of strife, agitation ... and their roles in the barrage."[17] Again, this was the sort of information that weary Mississippians were trying to process amid very stressful local conditions. Meanwhile, a Gallup poll in August of 1958 said that six out of ten Southerners believed "violence will break out if integration is enforced immediately in Southern communities."[18] This did not mean most Southerners wanted violence; this simply meant they knew it would come.

• • •

We in the state GOP apparatus chose to focus our attention on defeating the entrenched state Democrat machine.

In August of 1958, we went on the attack once more, accumulating a "score card" of state laws we claimed killed free enterprise by letting certain manufacturers organize cooperatives to gain unfair tax advantages. We cited "the temporary shutdown and lay-off of 80 workers at Spencer Chemical Co. fertilizer plant at Vicksburg" that very July.

"The hard, cold reason for this shut-down," we said through the press, "is the subsidized quasi-co-op fertilizer plant that pays a much lower tax rate and can therefore sell fertilizer to farmers at a much lower price."

The co-op was Mississippi Chemical Corp. in Yazoo City. Had MCC operated under the same laws as Spencer Chemical, MCC would have had to pay $1.7 million more in taxes; but by dodging these taxes, MCC not only hurt Spencer's business, but also left our state coffers $1.7 million poorer. "Such money was used to compete unfairly with a private enterprise firm," we emphasized.[19]

Furthermore, the owner of Spencer Chemical Co. also owned a major tire manufacturing company and a major tractor manufacturing company. We argued that because of our state's existing tax laws, there would be only a "remote possibility of eight of these firms locating a plant in Mississippi in the future."

People today want to know why more industry did not come to Mississippi in the second half of the 20th century. It was due to a short-sighted Democrat-controlled legislature in the 1950s and 1960s. We are still paying for this today.

Republicans were doing our best to educate the general electorate on the benefits of a strong free-enterprise system that could keep taxes low and encourage business. We knew that we were the party to take Mississippi in this direction.

The business potential was there. For instance, that very month of August 1958 as we challenged the state Democrats' lack of business vision, *U.S. News & World Report* said that Jackson showed the greatest increase in banking activity among 80 major cities studied nationwide. Jackson's income was up 6.9 percent versus 1 percent nationally. The magazine said Jackson was one of the nation's "cities where business is best."[20]

The dramatic rise of Jackson as a business hub would eventually favor our state Republican Party.

• • •

The State of Mississippi was energized in September of 1958 when our own Mary Ann Mobley was named Miss America. She burst into tears at the Atlantic City announcement, and our state burst into rejoicing with her. We needed some good news. More than that, she represented our state with so much class.[21]

Our state Republican leadership certainly lacked Mary Ann's charisma, but our silent work in 1958 would bring positive press to our state. One political scientist has noted: "The leadership of the GOP was becoming more effective. The addition of younger men to the party, like Wirt Yerger, Jr., seemed to invigorate it and add to its stature and respectability."[22]

We decided in 1958 not to run any candidates in that year's U.S. congressional elections. Any potential candidate would have had to get 1,000 signatures on a petition to run for U.S. Senate or 200 to run for U.S. House of Representatives. Qualified candidates were still biding their time.

But we were getting ready for that day.

I kept prodding our state GOP leadership that it was time to establish a central office. "We have come a long way in a short time," I wrote in an August 1958 memo to the state executive committee, "but we must keep moving forward."

I added:

> In order to do this we must have a state headquarters with a secretary and the necessary equipment. This office could handle all of the administrative details. ... From personal experience I can say to you that this office is a necessity. My estimate of the minimum cost of running this type of office ... is approximately $80,000 per year. Our organization should also have a full time executive secretary to supervise administration and liaison matters and travel the state expanding the county organizations to the greatest extent possible. This is the only way we will ever grow as rapidly as we should, and I believe that if we could find the right man he could do wonders in building the organization and raising the money from

year to year. The man we need should be young, a bona fide Republican, a native Mississippian, a college graduate, energetic, willing to travel in his own car, and by all means a man with real ability. ... No, I haven't gone crazy, I'm simply trying to analyze our needs and the overall solution to our goal of a real two-party system for Mississippi. ... Now is the time to forge ahead.[23]

We eventually did announce plans for a permanent Mississippi Republican headquarters in Jackson with a full-time executive director.

"The present efforts of the party in Mississippi are toward the establishment of a 'from the precinct level' organization," I told state media. We had raised more than $25,000 "by personal contacts and letters" and we promised that 80 cents out of every dollar we received would be kept in the state organization versus the national. I told the media we expected to be active in the 1959 election campaign for state and county seats.[24]

"A contribution to the Mississippi Republican Party," I said, "will help make the great American ideal of a sound Mississippi. ... The free enterprise system, which more than anything else has made America a prosperous and great nation, is in jeopardy. ... In order to function effectively, we must have the active and financial support of intelligent, farsighted Mississippians."[25]

At the State Fair in October of 1958, we distributed pamphlets saying, "Government is Everybody's Business."[26] We wanted to do things above board. We wanted to bring as many new people into the political process as possible.

While we were building this solid state political system, state Democrats, literally, tried that autumn of 1958 to copy us. They tried to start their own "Dollars for Democrats" public program to counter our effective fund raising. But they had been doing business too long under the table—exchanging money that sometimes amounted to bribes for votes. Now, when they needed to access local Democrat leaders' names to start an above-the-board program, they could find no real re-cords of them. "State headquarters doesn't have any record of who the members of the county committees really are or what, if anything, they are doing for the party," admitted Sam Wil-hite, regional officer for Democratic National Party, lambast-ing our state's Democrats.[27]

For now, their old-boy system of picking and funding lo-cal candidates still worked. About the time of Wilhite's pub-lic remarks, Mississippi's Secretary of State Heber Ladner announced the names of political candidates for November's statewide elections. It illustrated the task we Republicans still faced. Of the more than 200 candidates running for local, county, and state offices, *all were Democrats.*

EXCLUSIVE POLL OF HOW G.O.P. CHIEFS VIEW ADAMS

HIGH COTTON: Beginning at age 26, Wirt was quickly thrust into Republican leadership not only in Mississippi but also nationally. This photo, which ran in *Life* magazine, June 30, 1958, shows Yerger (#1 at the top left of the staircase) among 38 state GOP chairmen gathered to debate the merits of Dwight Eisenhower's policies and of the President's reliance on his controversial chief of staff, Sherman Adams. *Life* polled forty-two state GOP chairmen asking: "Should Adams resign?" Wirt was among 13 who said "Yes." Twelve said "No," and 17 were "undecided."

REPUBLICANS MEET

Wirt Yerger, Jr., of Jackson, chairman of the State Republican Executive Committee in Mississippi, is greeted by President Eisenhower in Washington where Yerger went for a meeting of Republican leaders from throughout the nation.

BOLD: Wirt was never intimidated in the presence of United States presidents. During one meeting with Eisenhower and the nation's other GOP state chairmen, Wirt stood up and asked the president a question that was on every man's mind: "Is there any way that we can be sure that when we send a letter to you personally that you will see that letter?" Ike's affirmative response drew thunderous applause among the many frustrated GOP state chairmen.

Mississippi Republican Party
P.O. Box 1139
Jackson, Mississippi

PRIVATE & CONFIDENTIAL (PLEASE)   August, 1958

TO: Members of the State Executive Committee

FROM: Wirt A. Yerger, Jr. - Chairman

Periodically, from now until 1960, I will send each of you a report on our
activities. You will notice that I have divided this report into several
categories.

FUND RAISING: As many of you realize this is perhaps our biggest weakness.
Thus far, over the past eleven months we have managed to raise just under
$4,500.00. Of this we have sent $1,000.00 to the Republican National Committee. As you know, our Republican National Committee quota for this year
is $8,547.00. In March each county was assigned a quota, and I am proud to
say that a number of counties have met and exceeded their quota. However,
as you can easily see from the small amount raised a number of counties have
sent in little or nothing.

To the best of my knowledge, there is no easy solution to our difficulty, however, I am positive that we can be successful in our efforts if;

    (1) County Organizations are strengthened,
    (2) All forms of activity at the state, county and city level are
         expanded,
    (3) An overall state finance committee is established with its member-
         ship composed of men and women with exceptional ability to raise
         money,
    (4) People in every income group are asked to contribute,
    (5) Fund raising campaigns are conducted annually,

FEDERAL APPOINTMENT & LIAISON MATTERS: What we need most in this field is
a full time paid administrator and more operating capital to pay for the added
expenses which would be incurred. Under the existing conditions, however, recommendations on postal appointments and at least some others are proceeding
smoothly. Everything is being handled strictly on a county committee basis,
as it should be. In the few counties where we have no committee we make no
recommendations:

VISIT OF NATIONAL CHAIRMAN: Meade Alcorn is definitely planing a visit to
Mississippi. He and I. Lee Potter, Special Assistant to the Chairman, will
probably come to Mississippi sometime after the 1st of January, 1959. Naturally,
complete arrangments will not be finalized until a date is certain, but we must
be thinking about how we can benefit the most from his history making visit.

The present idea is to have him address a $7.50 per plate banquet and try to
get a large statewide audience. We will also schedule an Executive Committee
meeting while he is here. This will be the most important Republican event in
Mississippi in sometime, and we must therefore, put forth every effort to make
it successful.

STATE CHAIRMEN'S CAMPAIGN SCHOOL: As most of you know I attended the campaign
school for four days in June at the Statler Hotel in Washington. It was literall
a school of politics and I learned a great deal about organization and campaignir
which I hope will be of tremendous benefit to the Mississippi Republican Party ir
the near future. I also made friends with most of the other forty-three state
chairmen who were in attendance. If their support is ever needed, I believe we
can count on it.

It was indeed a pleasure to learn that nearly all of the chairmen were disgusted
with the Administration's handling of a number of things, including Earl Warren and
Little Rock. I learned once again that the Republican Party is much more conservative and for "state's rights" than President Eisenhower seems to be.

We all had breakfast with the President one morning, and we also went to the home
of the Vice President for a visit with Dick and Pat Nixon, who, in my opinion, ar
both wonderful people.

(CONTINUED)

FORESIGHT: This 1958 two-page document written by Wirt proposed highly
ambitious ideas that would eventually help bring the Mississippi GOP into
prominence, a status few could foresee. "No," Wirt wrote, "I haven't gone
crazy."

Mississippi Republican Party
P.O. Box 1139
Jackson, Mississippi

-2-

YOUNG REPUBLICANS: B. B. McClendon, Jr., State Chairman of the Mississippi Young Republicans, is busy enlarging the organization on a statewide basis.

He would greatly appreciate your help in finding the young people between 21 and 35 who are willing to work actively as young Republicans.

WHERE THE MONEY IS GOING: Since we have no person on a salary and with the exception of the $1,000.00 mentioned above which was sent to Washington, the little money we have is being spent on printing, telephone, limited travel, and the **MISSISSIPPI REPUBLICAN NEWSLETTER.** Also, we are paying ROSS & YERGER, INC. $100.00 per month for the use of the Company's Office, equipment, secretary, telephone, supplies, and postage meter. The actual cost of all of what we call on Ross & Yerger, Inc. for is much higher, but if you think this is in any way unreasonable please let me know right away. Frankly, my firm is not at all happy with the situation and would like to see the Mississippi Republican Party matters handled at another location.

RECOMMENDATIONS OF THE CHAIRMAN: We have come a long way in a short time, but we must keep moving foward. In order to do this we must have a state headquarters with a secretary and the necessary equipment. This office could handle all of the administrative details including the mailing lists for the **NEWSLETTER** and any other publications. From personal experience I can say to you that this office is a necessity. My estimate of the minimum cost of running this type of office together with the work it should do is approximately $8,000.00 per year.

Our organization should also have a full time executive secretary to supervise administration and liaison matters and travel the state expanding the county organizations to the greatest extent possible. This is the only way we will ever grow as rapidly as we should, and I believe that if we could find the right man he could do wonders in building the organization and raising money from year to year. The man we need should be young, a bona fide republican, a native Mississippian, a college graduate, energetic, willing to travel in his own car, and by all means a man with real ability. We might be able to hire such a person for roughly $6,000.00 per year. His travelling expenses would probably run an additional $2,000.00 per year.

No, I haven't gone crazy, I'm simply trying to analyze our needs and the overall solution to our goal of a real two-party system for Mississippi. I haven't mentioned it specifically, but it goes without saying that we must run good candidates for local offices on local issues. This is also a MUST in the immediate future.

Now is the time for us to forge ahead. What do you think about it? I am looking forward to hearing from you in detail SOON.

STATEMENT OF PRINCIPLES: We are drafting a statement of principles to be published in quantity so that other people will know what the majority of our organization stands for. I hope to submit it to you in the immediate future.

BOOTH AT STATE FAIR-OCTOBER: The Mississippi Republican Party may have a booth at our annual Mississippi State Fair. The booth would be actively operated by volunteer members of the Jackson Republican Club and literature such as the statement of principles mentioned above will be distributed. Contributions will also be accepted.

REMINDER: The information contained herein is confidential and private, and I am counting on your cooperation in this respect. This includes the mention of the proposed activity at the State Fair.

A step toward a two-party system in Mississippi at the local level ... might mean a liberal or radical minority could slip in with a balance of power and dictate the choices for offices in the county.

—The Clarion-Ledger, 1959

The Southern way of life [will be] endangered if a Republican is allowed to get into the legislature.

—Charles M. Hills, Columnist,
The Clarion-Ledger, 1959

6

1959

SETTING UP HEADQUARTERS

Nineteen-fifty-nine was a year of firsts for our state Republican apparatus.

In April, U.S. Sen. Barry Goldwater (R-Ariz.) spoke in Jackson to our new GOP leadership base.

In June, 75 of 82 Mississippi counties sent a Republican representative to a GOP seminar in Jackson to be trained in county-level work. Each was assigned a quota of money to raise.

In September, we opened a full-time GOP state headquarters with a full-time field representative.

In October, we ran the very first GOP candidate in decades for an office in Mississippi. He did not win, but the victory was in running him.

And in December, Edward S. Shattuck, California GOP state chairman and also chairman of the 13-state Western States Conference of the Republican Party, met with our state's GOP leadership.[1]

My correspondence in 1959 with key national leaders also increased, as did my personal influence in national affairs.

• • •

Even as Hawaii became the 50th state, Mississippians and Americans were distracted more and more in 1959 by fears from outside and within.

Fidel Castro deposed Cuban President Fulgencio Batista on January 2. A Communist regime was suddenly as close to U.S. soil as Jackson was to Memphis. Cuban refugees flocked to our Gulf Coast region.

Two days later, the Soviets launched a 1½ ton rocket, which they said would become the first artificial planet, "a satellite of the sun."[2] Soviets said they planned a manned space flight soon.

Ross Barnett announced his candidacy for governor of Mississippi. "My purpose will be to build and not tear down," he said.[3] History proved otherwise. Meanwhile, the national chairman of the Democratic National Party, Paul Butler, said his party did not need the South. Bidwell Adam, Mississippi Democratic Party chairman, demanded Butler apologize to "the white men and women of the South for this shocking insult," adding, "You have spoken to our people as though they were hedgehoppers and political pygmies subject to the whiplash and the authority in the hands of a Hitler."[4]

Butler ignored him.

"What then, Mississippi Democrats?" our state GOP asked. "You say you'll continue with the Democrat Party. ... Northern Democrats don't need the Southern vote. ... You say you'll break from the Democrat Party and form a third party. What effect will this have on national policy and legislation? NONE."[5]

We invited the Democrats to join the GOP. We noted, "The Republican Party is for free enterprise, is for conservative government, is for local control, is for individual initiative. Why not stop voting the Democrat ticket? Just because great, great grandfather and great, great grandmother did? Times change."[6]

Democrats' old ways of doing business had lulled voters to sleep. For example, in Hinds County, only 32,000 of 52,000 registered voters had paid their poll tax, which was required to vote. It was a clear sign of apathy and did not "furnish any feathers for the cap of the 'one-party system'," I noted.[7]

Democrats held on to their voters using fear tactics. Bidwell Adam claimed the NAACP's goal was to "make the South a bed upon which to start a colored colony that will ultimately transform the nation into a land of chocolate-colored people."[8]

Meanwhile, top state Democrats saw no need to develop a real statewide office as we were doing. Gov. J.P. Coleman said that having one might be "entertaining ... but it does not accomplish anything."[9]

And so as our opposition sat idly by, we opened our full-time party headquarters in Room 414 of the Lamar Life Building, the same building where my Ross & Yerger Insurance offices were located. I told the press, "This is the first time that a permanent state headquarters has been established and a full-time staff representative named—by either party in the state."[10] It was "another step toward the fulfillment of a strong Republican working organization in the state," I said.[11]

Our state staff was so effective.

- Louis Kincaid was our first full-time field representative.

- Vivian Collins Matthews, formerly the secretary for E. O. Spencer during the Citizens for Eisenhower years, became our executive secretary. She was a godsend.

- Dean Miller, a geologist, became the first editor of *The Mississippi Republican News*.

- Joe Marion was our first state party finance chairman; a host of influential businessmen and industrialists served on his finance committee.

- And timber dealer G. Harold King, 39, a Republican from Canton, was appointed to the Federal Reserve

Board, the youngest-ever reserve board member. *The Clarion-Ledger* said that I was "taking bows for the appointment."[12]

I was in and out of the party headquarters daily, trying to balance my insurance business and family with the never-ending political demands. I also oversaw another political plum. Because the U.S. president was a Republican, I ran our state's next census. This was a massive boost for our state party. I oversaw a 40-person staff in each congressional district and 200 to 300 enumerators going door to door tabulating data.[13] This helped greatly in building political contacts.

We also started bringing county GOP leaders to Jackson. In 1959, we held a 3½ hour training session for leaders of 75 counties on doing the census, then another on the importance of a two-party system in our state.[14] I. Lee Potter led a third session.[15]

Meanwhile, national GOP interest in us grew. At a meeting of the Southern Association of Republican State Chairmen, I spent three hours with Vice-President Richard Nixon.[16] A Gallup poll said Nixon led Nelson Rockefeller 56-to-23 percent for the 1960 Republican presidential nomination.[17]

• • •

Our grass-roots organization was valuable, but nothing ever boosted GOP interest within Mississippi like Barry Goldwater. At my invitation, he first came to Mississippi on April 16, 1959, for a breakfast gathering of state Republicans and the Mississippi Economic Council. I invited Sen. Eastland to introduce his U.S. Senate colleague. Eastland told the crowd that Barry was "so popular in Mississippi ... he could be elected to any office he sought in the state."[18] Everyone applauded.

Goldwater's popularity in Mississippi shot up with each phrase he uttered during that speech. In his electrifying style, Goldwater told us to keep our course, and he recalled how hard it had been when he first was building Republican support in Arizona.

Soon, the magazine *Human Events* claimed Barry was a popular favorite to make a presidential run in 1960. The magazine listed six reasons why:

> (1) [Goldwater] won a smashing victory last fall as a Republican [in Arizona], ... a state with an overwhelming Democratic registration; (2) he's right on the ball on this labor question; (3) he's from the West and carries no taint of New York or Tom Dewey; (4) the pros are impressed by his obvious popularity among average citizens and his capability in arousing enthusiasm among followers; (5) he has a warm, human, infectious personality—attracting people of all sorts; (6) nomination of candidates from small-population states are unprecedented—but these are times of realignment of parties, political flux and crumbling of party traditions.[19]

Meanwhile, a 40-man study committee of the National Republican Party asked: "What [does] the GOP need to meet the demands of the American voter?" A new study answered: "Conservatism ... is the true and only progressive political philosophy for America."[20]

State Democrats began to fear us and started cracking their political whip at the local level. For instance, Joe Marion and I met with Jackson County leaders who wanted to know more about us. Jackson County Democrats heard of this and punished these local men. Jackson County Democrat Chairman Robert H. Oswald "promptly read [the men] out of the Democratic Party."[21] Tom Ethridge, a staunch old-line Democrat journalist, actually came to our defense, saying it was "no worse for a few Gulf Coast citizens to associate with a few state Republicans" than it was "for influential Democratic leadership in Mississippi to throw a big banquet honoring" John F. Kennedy.[22]

Today, some people stereotype Mississippi Republicans as intolerant, but these Democrats ran away with that award.

• • •

The 1959 governor's race still consisted only of Democrat candidates. Lt. Gov. Carroll Gartin, Charlie Sullivan, and Ross Barnett were in the race heading for the Aug. 24 Democratic Party election primary, which amounted to the general election since no second party had a candidate.

As of mid-June, Sullivan and Gartin both led Barnett. But then Barnett went all-out on the subject of race, making it his campaign's one-note theme. About this time, *The Clarion-Ledger* editorialized on its *front page*: "Ross Barnett Is Our Choice." The unprecedented front-page endorsement stated, in part:

> Mississippians have three weeks more in which to consider, compare, and evaluate the men who aspire to be the next chief executive for our state. ... *The Clarion-Ledger* today announces its support of the candidacy of Ross Barnett and his platform. Mr. Barnett is a most outstanding attorney, a successful businessman and a humble Christian who serves his fellow man in many ways. ... He will bring to that office the dignity, intelligence and positive leadership so necessary for the next four years. ... We commend this man to Mississippi voters.[23]

Barnett won the August Democratic Primary and was unchallenged in November's general primary. Meanwhile November's election saw a Republican first: our state GOP qualified a local candidate to run. William V. Westbrook, a Jackson manufacturer, ran for state senator as a Republican in Hinds County. "Westbrook's candidacy introduces a new era in Mississippi politics," our state office proclaimed.[24]

Hinds County Democrats, however, tried hard to prevent it. Westbrook had to collect 50 names on a petition to get on the ballot—a daunting task for a Republican back then. Few people wanted publicly to sign a Republican candidate's petition that, in essence, was going to lead to a challenge of the local Democrat power brokers. Attorney General Joe Patterson announced that no one who had voted in the

August Democratic gubernatorial primary could "either sign Westbrook's petition or vote for him in the Nov. 3 general election since they were obligated to support the Democrat nominee."[25]

My brother, Swan, plus B.B. McClendon, Tom Crockett, and James Child, provided legal representation for Westbrook, who rounded up far more than 50 names on his petition, just in case any state Democrats challenged signatures. Westbrook turned in his petition, but then on Sept. 23, 1959, the Hinds County Board of Election Commissioners (composed of three Democrats) rejected it. Gov. J. P. Coleman publicly warned voters that letting Westbrook run would "produce a Mississippi system of primary elections" that would be "an empty mockery."[26]

This was a perfect example of "old-fashioned machine politics," I retorted.[27] A day later, the Hinds County election commission reversed its decision and approved Westbrook's petition.

Westbrook campaigned September through November on a platform of strong local government, equal representation in the state legislature for Hinds County, and more industrial development.[28] But the local Democrat machine preyed on voters' fears, saying that voting for Westbrook would be "a step toward a two-party system in Mississippi at the local level, which might mean a liberal or radical minority could slip in with a balance of power and dictate the choice for offices in the county."[29]

The Clarion-Ledger warned: "The Southern way of life [will be] endangered if a Republican is allowed to get into the legislature."[30]

When the November election day arrived, I made sure we had poll watchers. Local voters had never experienced poll watchers, since only Democrats had been running for office. They did not know how to respond to them, and our state paper made them out to be fiends. "Some [election day] workers at the polls complained of Republican observers at the counting," *The Clarion-Ledger* glibly wrote, "insisting that the young [Republican] people made themselves objectionable by their close observations of the counting, making nervous the clerks not accustomed to such steady surveillance. At some polls, the Republican observers were asked to leave and did so. At other places they remained throughout. Presence of observers at the polls is legal but is not the usual practice here."[31]

Westbrook lost to the incumbent Democrat, 9,024 to 1,519. But we had not backed down. This was an important first foray into seeking a two-party system. Voter turnout was ten-times greater than the previous general election.[32] Our poll watchers also noticed that about two thirds of the voters that November day seemed to be senior citizens. That told us that by attracting younger voters, we could bury the one-party system.

MISSISSIPPI REPUBLICAN NEWS

VOL. 2—No. 12   JACKSON, MISSISSIPPI   DECEMBER, 1959

JOE MARION
Finance Chairman

WIRT YERGER, JR.
State Chairman

LOUIS KINCAID
Field Representative

GREAT TEAM: *Mississippi Republican News* was an early newsletter begun by the state's fledgling GOP that helped galvanize like-minded people statewide by bringing them into the GOP fold and espousing true conservative ideas. Wirt is shown here with two of his early right-hand men, Joe Marion and Louis Kincaid.

THE OPPOSITION: Democrat State Chairman Bidwell Adam and Governor Ross Barnett were vocal segregationists.

We have this challenge—the challenge to prove to other Mississippians that a two-party system is the state's only hope for political survival.

> —Wirt A. Yerger, Jr., 1960
> speaking to the media

Let me tell you this, Mr. Yerger, Jim Eastland will be fighting tomorrow against Civil Rights bills you Republicans introduced yesterday!

> —Bidwell Adam, Mississippi
> Democratic Party Chairman,
> speaking at the 1960
> Neshoba County Fair

I get the shakes in the middle of the night when I think of some of the leading Democratic candidates that might be president.

> —Arizona Sen. Barry Goldwater,
> 1960, speaking to the Mississippi
> Republican Party State
> Convention

7

1960

NIXON AND GOLDWATER STORM MISSISSIPPI

John F. Kennedy. Richard M. Nixon. Ross Barnett.

All three became household names in 1960, and increasingly so did the phrase—"Mississippi Republican Party." On Jan. 7 Gov. J.P. Coleman gave his farewell address, boasting that "the rules of racial separation" had stayed intact on his clock.[1] On Jan. 19, Barnett took his oath of office. In his inaugural speech, he warned that his state Democrats "should think hard" before backing the national party's presidential nominee that year.[2]

Our state's Republicans had no such worries. We were welcomed by our national leadership and we felt largely in line with them. Goldwater was at the forefront of a strong true conservative movement, though Richard Nixon was to be our 1960 presidential nominee.

In January of 1960, Nixon lectured a Washington D.C.-based Republican Leadership Training School. Mississippians B.B. McClendon, Joe Moore, Tom Crockett, and Louis Kincaid attended.[3] We were ready to back Nixon's candidacy, and Gallup said that Nixon led all Democrats in the South.[4]

After his inauguration, Barnett sloughed off caring for our state's real business, and instead he dashed to South Carolina to speak at a $20-per-plate gathering of that state's Citizens' Council, telling them that moderation on integration was unacceptable, and that Southern states must unite to "preserve the greatness of America."[5]

Barnett said he would revive the Mississippi Sovereignty Commission, which had waned under Coleman.[6] He said he wanted to protect the "segregated life of Mississippi."[7] Just days later, he spoke to the Louisiana Citizens' Council, saying, "We are all under attack by the same enemies, so why shouldn't we get together to plan the ways in which we can win this fight?"[8]

• • •

Barnett was bent on starting his own national segregationist movement, while we Mississippi Republicans were on an entirely different wavelength; we were building a real state party infrastructure on real principles and solid political strategies. I traveled March 18 and 19 to New Orleans to the Southern Association of Republican State Chairmen meeting. Republican National Committee Chairman Thurston B. Morton, I. Lee Potter, and Barry Goldwater were there and our spirit of cooperation was in stark contrast to state Democrats with their national leadership. "A friendly attitude" filled our party, I told the media.[9]

At SARSC, we mulled with national leadership over our plans to hold legitimate precinct and county meetings in Mississippi preparing for our June 11 state convention. This would include 75 of Mississippi's 82 counties, an unprecedented accomplishment.

"We have this challenge," I told the national media, "the challenge to prove to other Mississippians that a two-party system is the state's only hope for political survival."[10]

Also at SARSC, Goldwater accepted my invitation to give the keynote speech at our upcoming 1960 GOP state convention. I predicted it would be a "fighting conservative speech."[11]

Though Barry was not formally seeking pledges of presidential electoral delegates, he was getting them anyway. On

March 27, South Carolina Republicans threw all 13 of their national delegate votes to Barry amid a thunderous ovation by 400 South Carolina state delegates and constituents. Barry predicted that "thousands of conservative Southerners will vote the GOP ticket this year."[12]

I was meeting frequently with county-level GOP leaders, joined by my fine state field representative, Louis Kincaid. We watched as Forrest County Republicans elected Clarence W. Woods, Jr. to be their chairman and C.E. Tolar their vice chairman. We soon visited Lowndes, Lauderdale, Jackson, Hancock, Harrison, and Leflore counties. Warren County residents formed their Republican Party organization.[13]

Three Republican men were about to announce plans to run either for the United States Congress or United States Senate.[14]

- Joe A. Moore, 36, of Pascagoula announced for the United States Senate;

- W. A. "Bill" Clark, also 36, of Greenwood announced for the Third District Congressional race against incumbent Frank Smith; and,

- Edward W. Scott of Starkville announced his First District Congressional race against incumbent Thomas Abernethy.[15]

In May, we held vital GOP precinct meetings. "No individual has the right to complain about either political party," I warned our people, "unless he takes an active part in the precinct meetings of the political party which comes closest to representing his or her views. Only at the precinct level can anyone's voice be heard."[16]

On Saturday, March 14, throughout our state historic GOP county precinct elections occurred. There had never been such grass-roots, democratic representation of all Mississippians. Each precinct elected at least one delegate and one alternate to their county convention. Precinct delegates in turn chose their county's delegate to our June 11 state convention. Most precinct meetings were attended by eight to ten people.[17] A new army of Mississippians would choose 12 delegates to our national GOP convention. "I believe this will be one of the most important conventions ever held in the state," I told Republicans statewide.[18]

Then came our state convention on June 11, 1960. It was truly historic. It was held at the State Capitol, where no Republican at that time held a seat as a state legislator. There had only been 35 people at our 1956 GOP state convention. In 1960, we were 250-strong. Every seat of the Mississippi House of Representatives chamber was filled—*with Republicans*. It must have made Democrats watching on TV sick. Thousands of Mississippians watched via WJTV television station. WJDX radio broadcast all the proceedings. Tall signs designated counties. It seemed like a national convention. I stood to give the official call to order. As I looked out at that morning gathering I was amazed at how far we had come.

I introduced I. Lee Potter, who left us in stitches with his jokes about Democrats.[19] Potter then introduced the main attraction, Barry Goldwater. For a full half-minute, the applause from 250 supporters was deafening. "The Republican Party stands for what the Democrats stood for before the socialists took them over," Goldwater bellowed.

Thunderous applause.

"The Democratic Party is not what it used to be. How a Jeffersonian Democrat can stomach the things the Democratic Party is doing today is more than I can understand."[20]

More applause.

"[National Democrats have] tried to make 'Dixie' a dirty word, but I think it the most beautiful word in the language."[21]

Still louder applause!

Here was a Republican United States senator, standing in the center of the lion's den—the podium of Mississippi's legislative hall—berating Democrats! On TV, of all things!

"I get the shakes in the middle of the night when I think

of some of the leading Democratic candidates that might be president," Goldwater continued. "I know. I have seen them in action. The vast majority of Democrats in Congress vote against states' rights, sound money policies, the free-enterprise system and strict interpretation of the Constitution."[22] Then Barry endorsed Nixon as someone who "has recognized states' rights" more than any "of the Democratic candidates ever have."[23]

Now is the time in this book to look more closely at this phrase "states' rights," which has always meant different things to different people—Paul Johnson's old-line Democrat definition was not the same as Michigan Governor George Romney's or Richard Nixon's or Barry Goldwater's, but all used the term, as did I. In the 1960s some liberal politicians and liberal media were going all-out to isolate the more racist rendering of the phrase "states' rights" and to turn it for their own political ends. They knew that Barry Goldwater's movement endorsed a more reasoned, race-neutral states' rights philosophy of smaller, decentralized government, increased free enterprise, and a strict adherence to the U.S. Constitution, all of which are legitimate, excellent political stances being reasserted today in conservative circles fearful of Barack Obama's government expansion. William F. Buckley had written much about this states' rights idea, but those who abhorred such beliefs began calling Goldwater a states' rights segregationist and linking him to the Southern white Democrats' usage of the phrase. This is very important to understand: someone can be a states' rights proponent, as was Thomas Jefferson (who advocated freeing all slaves), without being a segregationist. And Barry Goldwater was just that.

To this day, some far-Left leaders misconstrue the best meaning of the phrase, furthering stereotypes of those they dislike. They claim it is "code" for supporting segregation; how shallow to reduce so simplistically an entire, viable political philosophy. This is akin to insisting today that all Democrats who use the word "progressive" are actually socialists. For instance, in 2007 two top bloggers battled in a nationally noted debate over the true meaning of the phrase "states' rights." A liberal writer insisted Ronald Reagan made a racist slur by saying he believed in "states' rights" during his Aug. 3, 1980 speech to 20,000 at Mississippi's Neshoba County Fair, where some argue that he launched his presidential race.

Reagan actually had made his beliefs very clear in that speech for anyone who truly cared to know and to honor his words in context: "I believe in people doing as much as they can for themselves at the community level and at the private level. And I believe that we've distorted the balance of our government today by giving powers that were never intended in the Constitution to that federal establishment."[24]

The liberal argued that Reagan was utilizing a "symbolic gesture of approval for good old-fashioned racism" when he mentioned "states' rights." A top conservative writer retorted that Reagan was, indeed, for the historical, race-neutral concept of "states' rights," not some "distortion that's ... spread like a weed" and that "was concocted for partisan reasons: to flatter the prejudices of one side, to demonize the other and to simplify a complicated reality into a political nursery tale."[25]

Barry's own words in his 1960 book *The Conscience of a Conservative* make clear what true "states' rights" thinking is: a viable political system that opposes big-government nannies. He wrote:

> It so happens that I am in agreement with the *objectives* (original emphasis) of the Supreme Court, as stated in the Brown decision. I believe it *is* (original emphasis) both wise and just for Negro children to attend the same school as whites, and that to deny them this opportunity carries with it strong implications of inferiority. I am not prepared, however, to impose that judgment of mine on the people of Mississippi or South Carolina, or tell them what methods should be adopted and what pace should be kept in striving toward that goal. That

is their business, not mine. I believe that the problem of race relations, like all social and cultural problems, is best handled by the people directly concerned. Social and cultural change, however desirable, should not be effected by the engines of national power. Let us, through persuasion and education, seek to improve institutions we deem defective.[26]

Barry did well that June day as he keynoted our Mississippi Republican Convention.

"In fact," he told our delegates, "the GOP transition in Mississippi in recent years has been amazing. ... As every schoolboy knows, the Republican name has been a stigma to Mississippi since the Civil War. The new party is out to create a new image. With it they are bringing a touch of freshness to the political scene. ... These boys are real dedicated. They may get there yet."[27] Our delegates were ready to march. A United Press International reporter covering our convention was blown away. UPI reporter John Herbers wrote: "The Mississippi Republican Party ... apparently has succeeded in laying the foundation for a successful second party."[28]

We passed a 12-plank state platform along with the nine-plank national platform. This act alone was in massive contrast to our state Democrat counterparts, who did not spell out real platforms for our state's voters. Our state platform affirmed the following, in order:

1) A two-party system—We believe that the people of our state deserve the right of choice in political philosophy.

2) Segregation—We feel as most thinking Mississippians feel that segregation of the races is absolutely necessary. This is a state issue and one that can best be handled by Mississippians.

3) Reapportionment—We believe that every citizen is entitled to an equal voice in our government and only through a true reapportionment of the Mississippi

House of Representatives based on current population distribution, can this be accomplished.

4) Local Option Prohibition—We heartily endorse the principle of both the "Local Option Bill" and the "Bone Dry Bill" and deplore the hypocritical and shameful status of "prohibition" in our state today.

5) Tax Equality—We believe that revision of Mississippi's tax structure is necessary. All businesses and organizations engaged in competitive business should be taxed on an equal basis.

6) Voting Requirements—We believe that the two-year residence requirement should be reduced.

7) Right To Work Law—We believe in the right-to-work and endorse the placing of the Mississippi Right-to-Work Law in the State Constitution.

8) Bureaucracy in State Government—We advocate the streamlining of state government to promote efficiency and economy.

9) Industrial Development—We endorse every effort now being made to balance the agricultural economy of Mississippi with sound basic industry.

10) Individual Liberty—We hold foremost those concepts of maximum opportunity and liberty for the individual.

11) The Legislature—We condemn the shameful inaction and wasteful spending of the 1960 Mississippi legislature.

12) Economy in State Government—We believe in a balanced state budget and deplore the wiping out of surplus in the state treasury.[26]

This was our democratically affirmed state Republican platform, forged by locally elected delegates from throughout Mississippi.

The Laurel Leader-Call editorialized: "Twenty years ago Mississippians would have laughed at the idea of a Republican talking about Jeffersonian principles. Not so, today, for things have changed a bit. ... Goldwater's [state convention speech] points up the coming trend in American politics: Conservative versus Liberal. It means that party labels do not mean what they once did and this will become more evident as time goes on."[30]

• • •

Our 1956 state GOP platform, upon my insistence, had not included a plank affirming segregation. This 1960 platform, voted on by 250 delegates, did. This was the will of our delegates. Still, I am happy that the Mississippi GOP's position on segregation was markedly milder than the Democrats'. Joe Moore, our 1960 candidate for the U.S. Senate, spoke on the campaign trail about this and was fairly representative of our Republican position. "We must reach for [the African-American voter's] heart and mind. We cannot lend ourselves to actions which would pollute with hate and fear the entire climate of race relations. The time has come for Republicans to make clear that tolerance and goodwill cannot be legislated. The sure road to the achievement of equality so fervently and rightly desired by all minorities is paved with good will, tolerance and understanding, not with laws or executive decrees."[31]

This position strongly resembled Goldwater's own stand. Barry had actually publicly supported the NAACP's organizing in Arizona. He also had lent his support to desegregating that state's National Guard. He did those things voluntarily, based on his states' rights principles rooted in advocating the right for local governments to make, change, or allow laws to evolve in the manner deemed best for their own citizens.

Barry did not support, however, federal heavy handedness. He did not back the unwieldy Civil Rights Acts of 1957 or 1960, or, later on, the Civil Rights Act of 1964. Barry's truly conservative mind could not accept using federal force to solve any matter he felt was fundamentally of the mind and heart and was best worked out on a state-by-state basis, given each state's varying challenges.

One could not "legislate morality," he famously insisted.

Most important for now, our state party had put forth, without ranting and with calm sincerity, a real platform taking stands on all of our state's key issues. After our convention, I challenged Bidwell Adam to make his state party's platform broader than merely one issue: segregation. "Mississippi Democrat leadership is obligated to take stands on such vital issues as reapportionment, prohibition, tax equality, right to work, economy in state government, individual liberties, and bureaucracy in state government."[32]

I said, "We Mississippi Republicans are on record. Now it is up to the state's Democrat leadership to do the same. Anything short of a positive stand on these issues will be shirking of responsibility."[33]

• • •

Our Jackson headquarters was deluged with supportive calls from disgruntled Democrats. "Mississippi Republicans are unified in their direction," we boasted in a newsletter, "not stumbling along blindly behind leaders who offer vague reasoning, untried and unproven ways."[34]

Newspapers said Mississippi actually could go Republican in the November election. As our strength became more evident in 1960, so did the state Democrats' weaknesses. The two parties' national conventions vividly illustrated that point.

State Democrats had two factions attend their July 1960 national convention in Los Angeles. Bidwell Adam, James O. Eastland, John C. Stennis, and J.P. Coleman—the "loyalists"—stayed with the national party, pledging 23 Mississippi delegate votes to Kennedy. Ross Barnett and his crew put forth an independent set of 23 delegates whom they claimed truly represented the state's wishes. They would not support any presidential candidate who did not back their hard-line views on segregation. Barnett's supporters actually nominated him for president, drawing boos in Los Angeles' Memorial Sports Arena.[35]

The convention nominated Kennedy, who picked Lyndon B. Johnson of Texas as his running mate. Barnett ridiculed the Democratic National Convention's 1960 platform as something that "could well have been written in Moscow."[36] Soon after, Barnett gathered his followers at his Blair House Hotel suite to discuss launching a second Dixiecrat "revolt."[37] South Carolina Sen. Strom Thurmond and former Mississippi governor, Fielding Wright, attended. They had been the presidential and vice-presidential ticket when the Dixiecrat Party had emerged in the 1948 election, winning the majority of Democrat votes in Mississippi, Louisiana, Alabama, and South Carolina.[38]

The next week, July 15-28, our Republican National Convention was held in Chicago. For me, it was a time of real joy. There was no infighting. Mississippi Republicans released a press statement predicting Barnett's splinter effort would "amount to a vote for Jack Kennedy for president, or else to throwing away one vote."[39] In our pre-convention committees, many people were now noting my leadership as the youngest Republican Party state chairman in the nation. I told the media that our 12 delegates were backing Barry Goldwater to be Nixon's vice presidential running mate, but we did not support nominating Barry to run for president since that might drive a wedge in the party.[40]

Then one of the worst political tricks ever was played. For months, Nelson Rockefeller—a world-class spoiled sport if there ever was one—had continued making liberal demands concerning the 1960 GOP national party platform, though his own candidacy for the nomination was dying. But now Nixon met secretly with Rockefeller for "eight hours through the night" at Rockefeller's New York City apartment—*at the same time that our platform committee was laboring in Chicago!*[41]

In their secret meeting, Nixon conceded key platform points to Rockefeller. When this finally came to light, everyone was enraged. Nixon lost credibility. The fiasco became known as the "Rockefeller Fifth Avenue apartment deal."

What was so fundamentally troubling about this deal was that new Republicans in the South detested the liberal-leaning Republicanism of the North. We felt Nixon had understood this. It had been fully communicated to him many times, and he had indicated his understanding. We were joined with others nationally in a passionate fight for a new conservatism in our party, one that Rockefeller rabidly opposed for years to come. Nixon had now summarily dismissed us, and that hit hard. At that point, many conservatives wanted Goldwater to put his hat in the ring for the nomination, and he could have garnered a large vote. He already had 21 delegate votes pledged, and if our state and a few others had been added, it would have formed "a solid protest," media noted.[42]

I was receiving telegrams and phone calls from home urging that we throw our weight behind Goldwater.[43] I never trusted Nixon after that. He would do anything to make a deal. Principles went out the window. That is why when it came to Nixon's second effort to be elected in 1968, I wouldn't touch him.

During the 1960 convention, Goldwater gave his dramatic, historic speech in which he withdrew his name from presidential consideration while also urging conservatives to work long-term to take the GOP's reins. We cheered wildly. When the time came to announce our vote for Nixon, I took the convention floor microphone and said that Mississippi, "the home of the last two Miss Americas," cast our 12 votes for Nixon.[44] This was a time to make wise, long-term decisions. We would find our vindication in 1964 when Barry Goldwater would gain the national GOP candidacy for president.

Nixon now carried our banner. "I'll make a prediction," Nixon told convention delegates. "Millions of Democrats will join us—not because they deserted their own party but because their party deserted them at Los Angeles."[45] He was correct;

he was never short on political savvy. Nixon saw the potential power of the South.

I returned from the national convention to congratulations from state citizens.[46] *The Clarion-Ledger* predicted that 1960 could be "the liveliest [presidential race] in our history," adding, "The weather in Mississippi will begin to get a mite cooler soon. Not so our politics—they've just begun to boil."[47]

• • •

Mississippi's famed Neshoba County Fair ensued on Aug. 10. I stood on a stage with U.S. Rep. John Bell Williams, Mississippi Democratic Party State Chairman Bidwell Adam, and Charles Sullivan, who had recently been nominated for United States president by yet-another splinter party, the Constitutional Party formed in Texas. We each spoke.

I reminded the crowd that our GOP state delegation had been treated with respect at our national convention, quite a difference from our state Democrats' experience. "We won some victories in the Republican platform, in contrast to the all-out failure by the Mississippi Democrats at Los Angeles."[48] Bidwell Adam then took the microphone and mocked me. He said that I was "flourishing a bride's bouquet flung to [me] by Perry Howard, after the Negro of 50 years with the Mississippi Republicans has got too old to act."[49] I had already departed the stage and was at a house a block from the stage as Adam's harangue continued. I could hear him screaming, *"Yerger! Where's Yerger?"* His voice bellowed over the loudspeaker. I had to smile.

For 20 minutes he lashed at me: "You scraped the barrel to find an opponent for Sen. Jim Eastland," he said. "You have boasted that you will run opponents against Democrats from constable to governor, and look what you've come up with, a man who ran second in three of his counties' 30 boxes and last in the other 27 in a race for county attorney. I refer to Joe Moore of Pascagoula."[50]

Adam blamed me for his Gulf Coast's beaches starting to

be integrated. "Republicans have given us prospects of a pol-ka-dot beach at Biloxi. They haven't yet explained away Little Rock. ... And let me tell you this, Mr. Yerger, Jim Eastland will be fighting tomorrow against civil rights bills you Republicans introduced yesterday!"[51]

Adam would write me sometimes, daring me to match him word for word in public discourse. His bellicose attacks were great publicity for us. Our state GOP's excellent showing at our national convention, coupled with the wild antics of state Democrats such as Barnett, had people looking our way. We poked at Barnett's quixotic splinter faction of delegates. "We Republicans have the elephant and the Democrats [have] their donkey," we stated, adding,

> No symbol has as yet been made official for the [Barnett] "independent" ticket. It is in keeping with their philosophy that we suggest the ostrich as an appropriate symbol for their campaign. It is common belief that an ostrich buries its head in the sand when it is in danger of having to face facts. ... It [also] is an extremely fast runner (this will be of great help in getting back into the herd of donkeys after the election). ... It is also important that an ostrich egg weighs over three pounds—a good-sized egg for this part of the country. This will be a characteristic well in keeping with the size of eggs to be laid by this "independent" group in the coming months before November.[52]

Dean M. Miller was often responsible for these rhetorical jewels in the *Mississippi Republican News*.

• • •

While the state Democrats were coming apart at the seams, in late August all of the South's Republican leadership came to Jackson for a strategy session at the King Edward Hotel. We were joined by top national leaders, including National Party Chairman Sen. Thurston Morton; Nixon's man, Robert

Finch; I. Lee Potter; and Ab Herman, campaign chairman for the Republican National Committee. Potter said Jackson was "an area of the South where progress was being made."[53]

At this meeting, Nixon confirmed he would speak in Jackson on Sept. 7, keeping a promise made at the Republican National Convention to campaign in every state. "If the vote were held tomorrow in Mississippi," I predicted, "we would win, the loyalists Democrats would be second, and 'independent' Democrats would bring up the rear."[54]

By mid-September, *The Clarion-Ledger* was at it again. In an editorial, they endorsed the hyper-racist ghost-group—Ross Barnett's unpledged set—while admitting it would have no say in the national election's outcome.[55]

But *The State Times*, a new newspaper now competing with *The Clarion-Ledger*, offered a different voice. Editor J. Oliver Emmerich, unquestionably the most respected newspaperman in the state, wrote that Barnett's independent electors could accomplish nothing: it must be Democrat or Republican. The National Democratic Convention's platform was "more dangerous to America at home than the threat of Communism from afar."[56]

"We have made our choice," Emmerich editorialized. "We will support Richard Nixon for president." He added: "The time has come for Mississippi to cease applying an 1875 image to the 1960 reality of the Democratic Party."[57]

This was more proof that our Republicanism was a legitimate option.

Columnists including *The Clarion-Ledger's* James Ward still did not know how to handle our real, organized second political party. In one column, Ward seemed to wish for the olden days when reporters in Mississippi did not have to cover real political competition:

> Wirt Yerger, Jr., chairman of the Republican Party in Mississippi, has issued another statement.
> Wirt is letting his mimeograph machine run overtime these days.

Now, Wirt is an intelligent fellow. He is handsome. He is likeable and to tell the truth, he looks right spiffy when he appears on national TV networks.

But Wirt says Mississippi Democrats "do not have the courage to face the issues." Wirt also says that Mississippi Democrats "are trying to have their cake and eat it too."

... Want to hear some more of what Wirt says?

He says, "We say these men [Democrats] are insulting the intelligence of Mississippi voters." Wirt doesn't like the idea of having independent electors. Wirt also sounds like he dislikes Democrats in general.

This is no effort to run Wirt's campaign for votes, but he isn't likely to win many friends to Nixon's cause by telling people how stupid they are.

It might be interesting to note that Louisiana faced up to some of Wirt's alleged "realities" four years ago.

Let's see now. What is going on in the land of reality?

Thanks to some Southern Democrats—which Wirt dislikes so much—there hasn't been a single law passed in Congress requiring schools to integrate. However, over in Louisiana some Republican-appointed Federal marshals are trying to serve some papers on Gov. Jimmie Davis, a Democrat who is trying to keep the schools of New Orleans and elsewhere operating in the time-tested Southern traditions of segregation and home rule.

Louisiana voted Republican four years ago. Louisiana displayed some of Wirt's gallant courage and "facing issues." Louisiana got some cakes. They also got some cookies. They've been eating cakes, cookies and they are being forced to eat some ice cream, too.

It's chocolate ice cream, Wirt.

Chocolate ice cream served straight out of a Republican-controlled freezer in Washington.

We say somebody is trying to insult the intelligence of Mississippi voters. Guess who?[58]

As Nixon's appearance in Jackson drew near, we assembled an impressive September fundraiser at the King Edward

Hotel, which *The State Times* said "smashed predictions by Republican State Chairman Wirt Yerger Jr. of Jackson, who has said that 'more than 250' would be present."[59]

In fact, 505 guests showed, raising $60,999 at a $100-per-plate function to hear Texas' Republican U.S. Congressman Bruce Alger decry Southern Democrats. I told the crowd that "it would be nice to have some Mississippi congressmen" with conservative records like his.[60]

Guests were treated to a closed-circuit broadcast from President Eisenhower, Vice President Nixon, and New York Governor Nelson Rockefeller, the latter of which "got almost no applause from his Mississippi audience."[61]

Then came Sept. 23, a beautiful, historic day. An estimated 10,000 people crowded along Jackson's Capitol Street in front of the Mississippi's Governor's Mansion. For the first time in about 100 years, the U.S. presidential candidate of a major national party came to Mississippi to speak during his campaign. Nixon did not shirk Mississippi.

The crowd applauded wildly as Nixon and his wife, Pat, appeared. Thirteen times Nixon's speech was interrupted with applause. It was a beautiful sound. Just a few months earlier, the National Young Republicans had named me to their Young Republican Hall of Fame. That was truly an honor, but it could not compare with this thrilling moment.

Nixon lobbed political bombs, evoking all the right responses. He said the Democratic Party was the party of liberals such as historian Arthur Schlesinger and Connecticut Kennedy advisor Chester Bowles, and it was not the party of Thomas Jefferson or Andrew Jackson, *or* Jackson, Mississippi. He waved his right hand skyward promising he would "start with the people and work up to Washington," not the other way around. He hit Communism and mocked Nikita Khrushchev.

Kennedy and Nixon were running so tightly that the race seemed impossible to predict. Nixon lost any slight edge, however, he may have had when, just three days after speaking in Jackson, in the first of four scheduled televised debates, he appeared tired and dull while Kennedy came off polished, youthful, and confident. It was a real blow to Nixon's campaign.

• • •

Sen. James Eastland had been in the U.S. Senate since 1943. As long as he brought home the bacon, he seemed immovable. Only ten days after the 1954 Brown v. Board of Education ruling, and sounding very much like Ross Barnett, Eastland had declared from the Senate floor,

> The Southern institution of racial segregation or racial separation was the correct, self-evident truth which arose from the chaos and confusion of the Reconstruction period. Separation promotes racial harmony. It permits each race to follow its own pursuits, and its own civilization. Segregation is not discrimination ... Mr. President, it is the law of nature, it is the law of God, that every race has both the right and the duty to perpetuate itself. All free men have the right to associate exclusively with members of their own race, free from governmental interference, if they so desire.[62]

Now, in 1960, state Republican Joe Moore challenged Eastland for office. Moore was the first in our new Republican ranks to try to unseat the political giant. We wanted to hold Eastland accountable because during the Democrats' 1960 national convention, he endorsed the Kennedy-Johnson ticket, while trying to tell Mississippians he was not for the Kennedy-Johnson platform.

Moore publicly decried the senator's sidestep. "Eastland attempted to divorce himself of the Democratic platform when he endorsed Kennedy and Johnson. ... How can Mississippians now have respect and admiration for Senator Eastland when he advocates that they elect men who endorse a platform that makes no reference to the responsibilities of our citizens to preserve, protect and defend the Constitution?"[63]

But Moore faced the final wall of defense that guaranteed

Mississippi Democrats their national elected offices: seniority. If Mississippians were to vote out Eastland or Stennis, our Southern state would lose immense political strength accumulated by those men over years of elected service.

On Oct. 14, *The Clarion-Ledger*, which already had endorsed Barnett's unpledged electors, ran a front-page editorial proselytizing for Barnett's splinter faction again. Entitled, "Let Our Voice Be Heard," the editorial once again told readers to cast a protest vote:

> We continue to believe that the Magnolia State, even if it stands alone, should withhold its electoral vote from the two major parties, which are so strongly committed to programs in direct conflict with the way Mississippians want to live their lives. ... Mississippi well could be starting a minority group that would grow and gain a balance of power. It is not unlikely such a force could become a majority group in time.[64]

As the November election approached, our state headquarters knew we would lose this particular battle; but we could see that the war was winnable. Nixon lost to Kennedy on Nov. 4. A new era of big-government spending and liberal activism quickly began. The national vote was the tightest in the century, with 34.2 million votes for Kennedy and 34.1 million for Nixon.[65] Barnett's unpledged electors won our state's vote; Kennedy Loyalists ran second; our Nixon GOP campaign ran third.[66]

Newspapers published a photo of former Mississippi governor, Hugh White, who had supported the Kennedy ticket, smiling while talking on the phone. A second photo showed State Sen. John McLaurin of Barnett's unpledged electors campaign, laughing. Then there was a photo of me. I looked tired. My photo caption read: "State GOP Chairman Wirt Yerger saw his vigorous campaign for the Nixon ticket in Mississippi go down the drain to defeat as the Republicans ran last on the ballot."[67]

But I would have the last laugh.

HISTORY: On Sept. 23, 1960, Wirt hosted Richard Nixon, who was running for president against Democrat John F. Kennedy. It was the first time in more than 100 years that a major presidential nominee was willing to speak in Mississippi. For Wirt, it was another sign that the new state GOP was headed in the right direction. In this photo, Pat Nixon sits next to Wirt as they listen to Richard Nixon (not pictured) speak before a massive gathering on Jackson's Capitol Street.

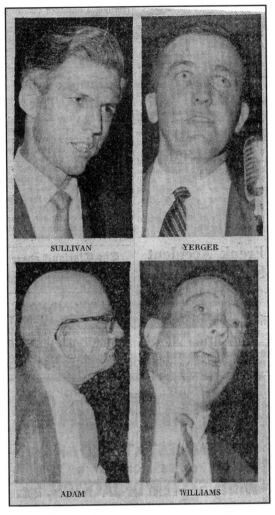

NESHOBA COUNTY FAIR: Since the Mississippi Republican Party had no major elected officials, it fell to Wirt to present the party's case in every major political forum. During the 1960 Neshoba County Fair, Wirt raised the ire of his arch-foe, Bidwell Adam, while they were joined by two other candidates: Charlie Sullivan (then nominated for U.S. president by a splinter party, the national Constitutional Party), and U.S. Congressman John Bell Williams.

Southern GOP Leaders

Leaders of the National Republican Party — both Southerners themselves — met with Mississippians at the March meeting of Southern Association of Republican State Chairmen, New Orleans.

Pictured, left to right, are Bill Westbrook, past president of Jackson Republicans; Wirt A. Yerger, Jr., state Republican chairman; Senator Thruston B. Morton of Kentucky, chairman of the National Republican Party; Hon. I. Lee Potter of Virginia, assistant to the chairman, assigned to "Operations Dixie"; and Lewis Kincaid, field representative, Mississippi Republican Party.

SOME PULL: Under Wirt's direction, national GOP leadership routinely traveled to Mississippi, eager to help Wirt construct a new Republican Party in the state.

GOP LEADERS IN JACKSON for a regional strategy conference this weekend appeared before a television audience Sunday afternoon and announced an appearance in Jackson by Vice-President Richard Nixon Sept. 7. Answering questions on the televised press conference are (from left) Robert Finch, Los Angeles, Nixon's national campaign director; Sen. Thruston Morton, (R-Ky.), National Republican Chairman; Wirt Yerger Jr., Mississippi GOP chairman; and I. Lee Potter, Virginia chairman and head of "Operation Dixie."—Photo by Perry Nations.

July 5, 1960

Honorable Barry Goldwater
U.S. Senator
U.S. Senate Office Building
Washington, D. C.

Dear Senator Goldwater:

No doubt you are familiar with past efforts to accomplish an electoral college reform. Our state convention passed a Resolution calling for chancing the electoral college system on the basis of Congressional Districts. Since then I have written Republican state chairmen over the country on this matter and nearly all I have heard from are strongly in favor of this reform. Through our two members assigned to the 1960 Repbulican National Committee Platform Committee we plan to push for the adoption of this in the 1960 Republican Platform.

We think that if we were successful- it would be a great step in being able to adopt the principle. We believe that the present electoral college system is one of the main things that hinders majority rule in this country at this time, through its influence on presidential elections.

We want to know if you will endorse what we are doing? What is your impression of our chances? Will you help?

Looking forward to hearing from you, I am

Sincerely,

Wirt A. Yerger, Jr
Chairman

WAY Jr/vm

CONSTANT CONTACT: Wirt stayed in frequent contact with the top national Republican leaders, who turned often to him for political advice both on how to make inroads into the Mississippi electorate and among the national electorate.

July 5, 1960

Honorable Richard M. Nixon
Vice President of the
    United States
U.S. Senate Office Building
Washington, D. C.

Dear Vice President Nixon:

Congratulations on the way you have been handling yourself recently. Chances for a victory in November appear to
be good although I am sure it will be a real battle.

No doubt you are familiar with past efforts to accomplish
an electoral college reform. I am sure you personally favor
this, because I know that you are for what is equal and fair
to all concerned, and most certainly this would simply be
that. Our state convention passed a Resolution calling for
changing the electoral college system on the basis of Congressional Districts. Since then I have written Republican
state chairmen over the country on this matter and nearly
all I have heard from are strongly in favor of this reform.
Through our two members assinged to the 1960 Republican National
Committee Platform Committee we plan to push for the adoption
of this in the 1960 Republican Platform.

In addition to being just and fair we believe that
both on the short-run and long-run it will be good for the
Republican Party. We trust you will support us, and we will
appreciate an expression from you as to your feelings in the
matter.

Sincerely,

Wirt A. Yerger, Jr
Chairman

WAY Jr/vm

I don't want to be charged with being derelict in my duties. I don't want it said that I was too late in recognizing the Republican threat. ... Mr. Yerger has been reading the stars. I have news for him. The barometer of his vanity shows unfair weather ahead. The voters of Mississippi will bury these Republican boys in a tomb of ice and outlines of their political failures will be painted upon the canvas of bitter disappointment.

—Bidwell Adam, 1961
Miss. Democratic Party Chairman

8

1961

"Two-Party Air Blitz" Yields Our First Win

In his famous 1961 inaugural address, John F. Kennedy said, "Ask not what your country can do for you, ask what you can do for your country." It is undoubtedly one of the finest lines a president ever spoke.

It was our state Republican Party, however, not the Mississippi Democrats, implementing this philosophy in 1961. We were challenging a good-old-boy system that discouraged competition and hard work, and that subverted principle in favor of pragmatism.

Kennedy's Jan. 20 speech had Mississippians hoping "perhaps ... Kennedy will follow a more conservative path, after all."[1] But then, just days later, his first State of the Union address was full of "gloom and doom predictions."[2] It lacked his normal sense of optimism.

The idealistic Kennedy told Congress that he was "staggered" by what he had discovered in his first ten days in office, "the harsh enormity of the trials" he was inheriting.[3]

Kennedy's inaugural words made "good reading," I told our state GOP, but, in reality, "instead [of Kennedy] asking the people to 'do for your country,'" he was quickly rattling off "program after federal program. All tax supported."[4]

"President Kennedy's motives are not in question. His methods and views are, however, questioned very seriously," I said.[5]

He cleverly enlarged the House Rules Committee to help him push more welfare programs through Congress. He stuffed his cabinet with liberals. He said he wanted to increase legislation to increase the growth of Social Security spending, federal subsidies for education, housing and "depressed areas," and to hike the minimum wage from $1 to $1.25 per hour.

By March, our state GOP proclaimed, "There is no question about which direction Kennedy means to go. He believes, quite honestly, in a centralized form of government. The platform on which he stands—and the action he has taken—are more convincing than words."[6]

• • •

The Mississippi Republican Party was no longer the party of Perry Howard and the Black and Tans. *The Clarion-Ledger/Jackson Daily News* actually called our Republican election efforts in the previous year of 1960 "the most intensive GOP campaign ever."[7] It added: "For the first time in more than 100 years ... the Republicans staged their greatest ... political races."[8] Jackson's Junior Chamber of Commerce gave me their Distinguished Service Award a second time, intended to highlight our successful GOP efforts.[9]

Our staff issued twice-weekly news releases to 220 media outlets; we published a four-page newsletter every other month to 25,000; and we had now launched an impressive speaker's bureau of people capable of representing us at service clubs, women's groups, and other organizations around the state.[10]

We had $6,500 in the bank and we set a fund-raising goal for the year of $250,000.[11]

Buddy Klumb, 33, our state finance chairman, successfully led the United Republican Fund program, which was copied in future years by many other states.[12] By year's end, URF's bank draft system would be underwriting most of the office's fixed costs. The office ran in the black all the way through October, and a war chest was growing for upcoming campaigns.[13]

Our GOP leadership wasn't, however, always greeted with cheer on fund-raising visits. Some people's Republican commitment did not extend to their pocket books. Others, perhaps, still feared being listed among our donors. Our first executive director, Bob Enlow, often met with local businessmen about URF only to find their secretaries more motivated to give.[14]

Once Enlow asked a big executive for $100. The man wadded up a $100 bill and threw it at him. Recalled Enlow: "I should have thrown it back."[15]

As for Governor Ross Barnett, he proved horrible in basic accounting. Barnett was now spending $1.10 for every dollar collected.[16]

In late April, I announced plans to run a candidate for governor in 1963, saying Democrats would have to take "full responsibility for Gov. Ross Barnett." I was asked to clarify my comments: "I think it speaks for itself," I said, adding Barnett made our state "look absolutely silly."[17]

The governor's mansion was our eventual goal for 1963. In 1961, we now hoped to run GOP local candidates and break a nine-decade-long drought of no Republican municipal officials in Mississippi.

Just to qualify a Republican to run for office was like walking through quicksand. First, a temporary municipal executive committee had to be formed and a "mass meeting of the electors of the party residing in the city" called, plus our political intentions had to be published once a week for four weeks; all potential candidates had to be gathered and a permanent committee elected to choose our official candidates for local offices; this committee informed the county executive committee of its official candidates and the executive committee then elected three election commissioners. Official candidates then had to register with their city clerk thirty days before the first primary date.[18]

In Meridian, we announced four GOP candidates: Henry E. (Gene) Damon for mayor; Beth Sellers, W.C. Cruise, and Thomas J. Peter for the city council. All were active Lauderdale County Republicans.[19]

In Ocean Springs, candidates were Dr. Richard T. Furr for mayor and Charles L. Ferguson for alderman. And in Pascagoula, our mayoral candidate, John D. Gautier, was the son of a former National Democratic Committeeman Hermes Gautier.[20]

Gautier was in the heart of Bidwell Adam country and challenged Adam to spell out how his party actually funded elections.[21] "We all know that the Democrat primaries are financed out of county or municipal funds derived from general taxes and that each Democrat candidate finances his own campaign out of his own pocket."[22]

The Democrats were truly arrogant. Barnett crassly admitted his desire to suppress the state GOP. "Why should we ask for competition?" he asked media; our response was, for "better candidates and better government."[23]

Our state office urged citizens statewide not to fear retaliation for voting for a Republican. "The American tradition of secret ballot—and Mississippi law—both give unquestionable right to Mississippians to vote for whom they choose in the ... general election."[24]

In 1961, 254 of the state's 266 municipalities held political races.[25] We managed to oppose the Democrats in 56 of them.[26] We forced a general primary in three towns, but lost them all.[27] But progress had been made.

• • •

Goldwater's star was rapidly rising in 1961. He was handsome like John F. Kennedy, but also had the wisdom of years.

His words hit home with many Mississippians. "The

conservative viewpoint has been scornfully attacked by modern radicals in the past half century," he said in one national speech. "The conservatives have not fought back."[28]

He was no stereotypical conservative—backwater, politically repressive—nor was he an elitist like Rockefeller. Contrary to many media and historic accounts, Barry's conservatism did not fear change, as long as that change was guided by right principles.

When Barry spoke for himself, versus the media putting words in his mouth, as they were prone to do, it was a powerful thing. Note his reasoned eloquence on what constitutes a real, classical conservative:

> The conservative recognizes that benevolent, well-intentioned overpowering authority can, and inevitably will, become tyranny. The conservative knows that man is a child of God—that freedom comes to man from God—and is not bestowed upon him by any political organization. Governments are necessary because without them we would have anarchy. But the conservative recognizes that if freedom and liberty are to be maintained and to be properly exercised by responsible citizens, we must consistently oppose the creation of power centers in government, business, education, or labor unions.
>
> The opponents of this basic faith who abuse the word by describing themselves as 'liberal' consistently support greater concentration of power in the national government and, consequently, a diminishing of freedom and opportunity for the individual. Many of the suggestions supported by the opponents of conservatism appear to have lofty objectives.
>
> Yet upon closer examination, we discover that these lofty objectives can only be attained by using the power of the super-state to compel the individual citizen to become a part of the over-all program. The Constitution of the United States was created by men who depended upon divine guidance. It is truly a remarkable document and it reflects

the experience of men who had suffered from the operation of unlimited central authority in the Old World.

Most of the language in the Constitution is devoted to limiting the power of the central government. The founding fathers recognized the need of a central government to perform certain duties which the individuals could not possibly perform as individuals. Fortunately, for us and for freedom, they were also determined to so limit the power of the central government of this republic as to prevent the creation of the tyrannical authority of the Old World governments.

Those who oppose the conservative position say, "Yes, all this was true, but the world has changed." The world has changed, but there has been little change in man. Basically, the problems of peace and justice and an ordered society which confronted the founding fathers are the same today as they were then.

In the last 40 years, we have moved with frightening speed from a philosophy of government which we inherited from the wisdom of the founding fathers to adoption of the machinery of the super-state.[29]

Goldwater did not call for human oppression, but for a reasoned, careful human progression. He called both for true civil rights and appropriate states' rights for all Americans. By contrast, many felt we were headed with Kennedy toward a super-state, and at a super-sonic speed.

Kennedy introduced the first compulsory government health-care bill—far before Hillary Clinton's or Barack Obama's time; thankfully, it did not pass. Our *Mississippi Republican Newsletter* predicted it would eventually "bankrupt social security."[30]

State Democrats were wilting with each new, rapid-fire Kennedy initiative. I told the media: "Mississippians were told repeatedly last year by ... Coleman, Smith, Stennis, Eastland, and Adam that—with Kennedy in the White House—

Mississippi's voice would be heard because they could talk to and reason with Kennedy. ... Now, Mississippians are being treated to a strange silence on the part of the 'Kennedy Club of Mississippi.' "[31]

Bidwell Adam was squirming.

For the first time he admitted a GOP "threat" and he called a special state Democrat summit in mid-May where he pleaded for Democrats to take action against us "before it's too late." He said: "I don't want to be charged with being derelict in my duties. I don't want it said that I was too late in recognizing the Republican threat."[32]

Adam said the party should consider opening a state political office, and he formed a six-man committee to explore the possibility. He said our GOP was trying to "take over Mississippi"; I replied, "He's absolutely correct."[33]

The Clarion-Ledger called me Adam's "pet peeve."[34]

"Mr. Yerger has been reading the stars," Adam said in bellicose fashion. "I have news for him. The barometer of his vanity shows unfair weather ahead. The voters of Mississippi will bury these Republican boys in a tomb of ice and outlines of their political failures will be painted upon the canvas of bitter disappointment. ... [Yerger's] Republican remarks are like endless echoes in the chasm of uncertainty. I am afraid that his plume of glory will soon wither in the sunshine of truth."[35]

My response?

"The difference in us and the Democrats is that we will always welcome healthy competition in a two-party state," I said. "... We certainly appreciate all the recognition our efforts are receiving from Mr. Adam and his cohorts."[36]

Goldwater conservatism was on the rise in Mississippi and across the nation. At one major Republican meeting, he received a 40-second standing ovation; Eisenhower spoke and got a 15-second standing ovation.[37]

Our Republican conservatism was consuming both the national and Southern GOP sectors. "A new generation in the South is seeking an alternative to the Democratic Party dominated by radicals and liberals," reported national newspaper columnist Raymond Moley.[38]

Clarke Reed of Greenville was finally ready to join this new GOP generation by July, after Enlow asked him once more to run our GOP Washington County URF program. "I have decided that I will take you up on your offer," Clarke wrote Enlow.[39]

• • •

Federal spending, Communist threats, and racial tension ...

All were rising in the first year of the Kennedy administration. Here is a brief update on where each issue stood relative to our state and our political battles.

FIRST:

Fiscally, in Kennedy's first six months, his federal spending machine ran at a $47 million-per-day clip.[40] Eisenhower had left an $80 million surplus; Kennedy's federal government was headed into deficit.

Republican National Chairman William Miller called it "wild sums of additional spending, and the centralization of more bureaucratic empires in Washington." He said a true conservative Republicanism was the cure. "When I use the word 'conservative' I stress the first part of the word—'conserve.' ... Unlike the spenders-in-residence in the White House, we don't favor change for the mere excitement of change. We do not believe that power flows from Washington outward. Power rests in the people and Washington has nothing and gives away nothing that it does not first take away from the people. We believe that the best government is the local level of government that is capable of handling a specific problem."[41]

SECOND:

Internationally, Communist tensions kept rising in 1961.

Communist forces vied for power in Laos. Fidel Castro cut ties with the U.S. embassy. The Soviet Premier told the world patronizingly that he would give the new U.S. president a little time to "get organized before putting on the pressure again."[42]

Only nine days after his inauguration, Kennedy publicly, childishly, asked the Soviets to think about cooperating in space exploration. Khrushchev responded by sending a 7-ton Sputnik into orbit two weeks later. By mid-March, Khrushchev told the Soviet people that they were winning the Cold War, adding, "We shall be happy when people of all countries stand under a banner of Marxism-Leninism and the Communist banner flies over the whole planet."[43]

In early September, the Soviets exploded an above-ground nuclear bomb in central Asia; three days later, they set off a nuclear bomb in the air; then, yet another explosion a day later. Finally, Kennedy decided he should renew U.S. nuclear testing.[44] But he promised with idealistic flair that the nuclear "fallout" would be carefully controlled.

Kennedy and Khrushchev also kept swapping barbs about Berlin. The Soviet leader on Aug. 7 warned that the West was "carrying out measures ... threatening to start a war" over Berlin.[45] By Aug. 13, the Soviets had, overnight, erected their "Berlin Wall," prompting shouts of "swine!" and "dogs!" from angry West Berliners who suddenly were separated from family members trapped in East Berlin.[46]

National civil defense officials told all Americans to build fall-out shelters in case of a nuclear blast or "face slow death without one."[47] Kennedy promised to do all possible "to prevent the world from being blown up," perhaps not the best choice of words.[48]

By late October, fallout from an exploded Soviet hydrogen bomb was hovering over the United States in the form of a 100- to 150-mile-wide cloud.[49]

And U.S. and Soviet tanks were facing off at point-blank range on the West Berlin-East Berlin border in what was being called a "cat-and-mouse game" as 50,000 American troops were rushed to Europe.[50] On Nov. 1, the Soviets exploded two more atomic bombs.[51] On Nov. 4, the Soviets exploded another atomic bomb.[52]

By Dec. 1, Robert Kennedy's Justice Department had indicted the U.S. Communist Party for refusing to register in our country as a "subversive tool of the Soviet Union." Robert Kennedy, himself, declared that Communists were working in America and currently going underground.[53]

THIRD:

On the race front in 1961, John F. Kennedy and Ross Barnett were now clashing vividly on integration: Kennedy stressed the notion of civil rights with less regard to states' rights; Barnett stressed states' rights with little regard to civil rights. Their battle would climax in 1962.

The Clarion-Ledger fomented strife in 1961 when it called for a year-long 100th anniversary celebration of the state's 1861 secession from the Union. It promised a year-long, weekly column, "This Week In 1861," about the state's first year in the Civil War. The paper's message: white citizens should stand with their ancestors.

Meanwhile, on March 6, 1961, a then-anonymous black man told United Press International he planned to enroll in the University of Mississippi "for the good of my people, my country, my state, my family, and myself."[54]

In rapid-fire fashion, Robert Kennedy was filing a blur of civil suits against Southern states and cities, including one against a New Orleans school district and another against Jackson and McComb, Mississippi's transportation systems.

In previous years, former Governor J.P. Coleman had managed the rapidly evolving race issue more quietly, but now Ross Barnett, a dedicated Citizens' Council member, was loudly defiant and already was assuring that group $5,000 a month in state funding.

The Citizens' Council even claimed tax deductible contributions, despite IRS disputations.[55] The Sovereignty Commission also had "stepped up its activity under Barnett."[56]

Mississippi's NAACP mailed letters to Mississippi black churches asking for funding to counter such resistance. They planned: 1) to sue the University of Mississippi to admit blacks; 2) to support NAACP Mississippi field director Medgar Evers in a contempt of court case; and, 3) to support African-American Clyde Kennard's suit to enter the University of Southern Mississippi," and more.[57]

On May 24, 27 civil rights-activist Freedom Riders were arrested after crossing in busses the Mississippi state line from their previous protesting stint in Alabama. Robert Kennedy, two days later in a world-wide broadcast, predicted a black could be elected United States president in 40 years. (He was not far off on this prediction.) He promised the riders in Mississippi full federal protection.[58]

Mississippi novelist William Faulkner for a second time warned Americans that the Kennedys were moving too fast. "It will take education—more education than both white and black people have had so far—to avoid more racial trouble of the kind that erupted in Alabama." He believed that no one outside the South really understood the racial interaction in the South. Americans "really know too little about one another to be tolerant of each other."[59]

On May 31, 27-year-old Kosciusko native James Howard Meredith, a nine-year Air Force veteran, announced that he was, in fact, the man who had anonymously applied back in March to enter the University of Mississippi; he now re-applied to enter. The NAACP's national lawyers filed a suit for Meredith's entrance; it was summarily refused by U.S. Judge Sidney C. Mize.[60]

Soon, a convocation of activists came to Jackson, including Martin Luther King, Jr., and Ralph Abernathy plus other leaders from Southern Christian Leadership Conference, the Christian Leadership Council, and the Student Non-Violent Coordinating Committee. They met on June 27 and promised more Freedom Riders in Jackson. *The Clarion-Ledger* called Martin Luther King, Jr., a "troublemaker" and "dangerous leader" who was "king-sized only in producing troubles for other people."[61]

The NAACP sued Greyhound [bus] Lines and the Illinois Central Railroad over segregated seating in Jackson waiting stations. Mayor Allen Thompson called for the South to unite to oppose pressure groups. "Mississippi, the last stronghold of complete racial segregation, is under full-scale attack," *The Clarion-Ledger* bemoaned, and Robert Kennedy was "responsible."[62] Almost simultaneously, President Kennedy issued an executive order beginning nationwide affirmative action. My friend Buddy Klumb called it "ridiculous" and "anti-business."[63]

Gallup polls soon estimated that 53 percent of all Americans worried that race relations were about to get worse due to the Freedom Riders; two out of three Southerners said the same.[64] Gallup said 61 percent of Americans felt integration was best brought about "gradually."[65]

Then, on Dec. 13, James Meredith was turned away from entering the University of Mississippi, setting the stage in the coming year of 1962 for perhaps the biggest single civil rights fight ever in Mississippi, and one that would change its political landscape forever.[66]

So much was happening so fast that many Mississippians lived daily both confused and on edge. The Communist scare and the racial tension mixed into one thick soup; then there were the federal spending issues.

To some of us, the Kennedys seemed recklessly fast in their handling of Communism, racial issues, and government spending.

And this was just their administration's first year.

• • •

Amid so many difficulties, Mississippi Republicans experienced an encouraging end to 1961.

First, Klumb, Enlow, "Mack" McAllister, Jr., of Meridian, and I took our "GOP Two-Party AIRBLITZ" across the state

Nov. 1-3. More than 350 Mississippi Republican leaders and key workers attended "BLITZ" gatherings in Indianola, Greenwood, Columbus, Meridian, Jackson, Vicksburg, Natchez, McComb, Hattiesburg, Laurel, and the Gulf Coast.[67] Media hailed the tour as "exceedingly successful from all counts—enthusiasm, participation and URF pledges signed." Scores of new URF pledge cards were signed.[68]

Second, on Nov. 17, the 13 GOP state chairmen elected me to lead their Southern Association of Republican State Chairmen. I was now 31 and would follow Florida GOP chairman G. Harold Alexander into the office. He told my fellow chairmen that Mississippi had one "of the best records in the Southern states for its advancement of the Republican Party. It has a very stepped-up program."[69]

News of my election by the Southern GOP chairmen was splashed on the front page of *The Clarion-Ledger*, which had for so long avoided covering us. Meanwhile, news of the death of 84-year-old Perry Wilbon Howard in 1961 was barely reported in Mississippi or anywhere else. Our new Republicanism in Mississippi was now so different from the doormat and laughing stock it once had been.

As Christmas 1961 approached, our state party was riding the crest of a major wave. On Dec. 7, GOP National Chairman Bill Miller spoke at our $100-per-ticket First Annual URF Appreciation Dinner in Jackson. More than 500 attended. More than 50,000 Mississippians watched the event by television. Miller's speech was interrupted 31 times by applause.[70]

In a December special election, Joe O. Sams of Columbus, a Republican, had defeated his Democrat opponent to become Lowndes County prosecutor.[71] Sams told the King Edward Hotel crowd "that being a Republican in Mississippi is not political suicide."[72]

More and more distinguished Mississippi businessmen were now joining our ranks, including William Vaughey (Jackson), William Gresham, Jr. (Indianola), and Warren A. Hood (Jackson), who said the state GOP was taking "a positive stand" for "individual freedom and the free enterprise system ... that have made our country great."[73]

I was now ready to travel to our Republican National Committee's meetings in Oklahoma City, grateful for all we had accomplished in 1961. There, Goldwater would wow our 50 state chairmen and 50 state committeemen.

Something special was in the works.

Over 350 Mississippi Republican leaders and key workers attended the "GOP Two-Party AIRBLITZ" meetings November 1-3. The "Blitz" was made by State Chairman Wirt Yerger, Jr., State Finance Chairman Charles Klumb, and State Executive Director Robert Enlow. They visited Indianola, Greenwood, Columbus, Meridian, Jackson, Vicksburg, Natchez, McComb, the Coast, Hattiesburg, and Laurel. Pictured at Meridian, left to right, are: L. L. "Mac" McAllister, Jr., of Meridian, Yerger, Klumb and Enlow. Yerger stated that the tour was "exceedingly successful from all counts — enthusiasm, participation, and URF pledges signed."

COPY OF ORIGINAL IN

AIR BLITZ: Wirt and other key state GOP leaders took to the air in 1961, the first year that the state party seriously ran candidates for office. Wirt spoke to large and small crowds in towns statewide.

State GOP Chairman Yerger was named head of Southern Association of Republican State Chairmen.

A Spirited Fighter

Yerger Named To Top Southern Post At Atlanta Meet

NATIONAL LEADER: In 1961 Wirt was elected to lead all 13 Southern GOP state chairmen, solidifying his place of national influence for years to come, a development that proved very helpful to the Mississippi GOP.

149

GOP VICTORY — William E. Miller, National Republican chairman, second from left, is shown raising the hand of Republican Joe Sams Jr. of Columbus in victory, after Sams Tuesday won a race for Lowndes County attorney by a two to one margin. Mrs. Sams, left, looks on while Wirt A. Yerger Jr., chairman of the State Executive Committee, beams his approval. Chairman Miller was in Jackson to attend the first annual appreciation dinner of the United Republican Fund of Mississippi. (Staff Photo by Bart Parker)

BREAKTHROUGH: Wirt's persistent efforts helped spur Mississippi's GOP's early victories, such as Joe Sams, Jr.'s win in Lowndes County.

Can a Republican be elected President as a conserva-
tive? Our answer is "Yes."

—Statement from a Minnesota
gathering of national GOP leaders,
including Wirt Yerger.

9

1962

"Southern Strategy" at a Minnesota Lodge, Goldwater Gala in Mississippi

A conservative Republican had not held the White House, arguably, since Calvin Coolidge in 1923. As the newly chosen chairman of the Southern Association of Republican State Chairmen, I now wrote my fellow state chairmen:

> The time has come for true conservatives to decide whether they wish to be active conservatives or to continue in the ranks of the conversationalists and surrender our freedom. Conservatives have, unless they sit on their hands, the best opportunity in history to impose their views on national policy. ... Senator Barry Goldwater can be nominated and he can be elected, but we must demonstrate very clearly between now and 1962 and 1964 that if nominated, he will without a doubt carry Mississippi and the South.[1]

Could a conservative *really* win our party's presidential nomination in 1964?

In mid-April of 1962, in a Minnesota forest, our strategic gathering of about 15 national GOP conservatives answered "Yes." At a Wonewok, Minnesota lodge, we all agreed that Kennedy's approach to leadership was pessimistic and floundering. We agreed that the right man with the right sense of patriotic optimism could not only win the 1964 Republican presidential nomination, but also defeat Kennedy.

As mentioned at the start of Chapter 2, this meeting was led by New York City conservative Clifton White.[2] We talked all weekend about the conditions among varying voter demographics. We talked about various key issues. Ultimately, we all knew that there was a man out there who would ignite the right combination of people and issues to achieve victory: Barry Goldwater.

Goldwater's writing and oratory clearly proved he was that man. "President Kennedy and the spokesman for the New Frontier have ... suggested this nation has lost its purpose, that we are torn with disunity and internal strife," Goldwater wrote in one of his columns entitled, "How Do You Stand Sir?" His newspaper column continued:

> It is not at all remarkable that the New Frontier chorus should be chanting this dirge of defeat. ... The brave, bold rhetoric of the New Frontier and its magnificent phrases stand naked and shivering. ... Deficit spending and government aides to this and have not cured the patient.

> The new look in foreign policy, the bold new look, results first in the loss of Laos, and this has been followed by the tragic act of indecision which doomed the uprising in Cuba, the President's first attempt at personal diplomacy with Khrushchev. ... The Berlin crisis is over.

> Khrushchev presented the work with a *fait accompli* when he was allowed to build his solid wall. Anything which now may be negotiated will be meaningless. Russia resumed its nuclear teaching, and revealed what some had believed all along—that Russia had never in fact stopped nuclear experimentation and never intended to do so.[3]

Goldwater now turned his thoughts to his readers, issuing a challenge:

> ... If it is true that our nation has lost its national purpose and is no longer sure of its national goals, then you and I share a part of the blame. ... We who are Republicans must face the past without bitterness and without any attempt to point our fingers. ... There is little profit to be made from name calling or from attempting to cast the blame on the present administration or on those presently in control of the Democratic Party. ... We are, I suggest, required to offer to the people of this nation, Republican and Democrat alike, a program which will successfully correct the errors of the past and provide a value basis for new hope."[4]

What a contrast to Kennedy!

The second day in Minnesota we gathered by regions, then jointly again. The afternoon was spent in detailed discussions concerning election techniques. We talked about galvanizing the Young Republicans, Young Americans for Freedom (William F. Buckley helped form YAF in 1960), and women's groups. Sunday morning offered a final session, and then planes began departing from Wonewok.[5]

When finished, we all agreed Barry could lead us to victory. The following paper, "Can a Conservative Republican Win?", was masterminded by Clif for our meeting. It is repeated in part:

> Can a Republican be elected President as a conservative? Our answer is "Yes"—an answer backed both by the facts of the case, and by our past record of the Republican Party. Four times in recent years the GOP has attempted to win the Presidency by appealing to "moderates" and "liberals" in the urban centers of the East—1940, 1944, 1948, and 1960. Each time the GOP failed. The two Eisenhower campaigns cannot be placed in this category because, as is widely admitted, Eisenhower won by virtue of [being] a trans-partisan war hero, and not on the basis of any ideological convictions or issues.

If the strategy of appealing to the "moderates" and "liberals" has failed, is the Republican Party doomed to perpetual minority status as a nationwide entity? We must answer "No," because there is (original emphasis) a strategy which can win the Presidency for the Republicans, a strategy of fusing together an Electoral College majority from the basically conservative areas of the nation: the Midwest, the Mountain States, and the South. ... Could a conservative Republican win the South? The answer, again, is "Yes"—but on the assumption that the GOP would promise to call off the national vendetta against the South, and take the constitutional stand on states' rights. Although the area has not yet fully developed a two-party system, it will vote for a suitable Republican national ticket. Eisenhower took most of the South, and even Nixon—without any special appeal—won Virginia, Florida, Tennessee and Kentucky, and made serious inroads everywhere. Goldwater is immensely popular in the South. ... The victory of Republican Senator John Tower in Texas supports this thesis, since Tower won only by running with a "Goldwater conservative" label.

Nor should we simply write off all of the urban areas. Census Bureau figures show that in the decade between 1950 and 1960 the "central city" population of the United States increased only 1 percent. The greatest jump in this decade was in the suburbs—which grew 44 percent. These suburban areas are middle-class, basically conservative, Republican areas. Yet the Republican Party has not exploited its full potential in these areas by campaigning on a platform of fiscal responsibility. ...

A third factor is "troops." Liberals in the Democratic Party have been able to make their political gains primarily through the use of union campaign workers. In the campaigns, and especially on Election Day, thousands of union shop stewards and officers are, in actuality, working for the Democratic Party rather than for the companies that employ them. ... The Republican Party must find some body of workers—beyond what it already has—if it is to offset these professional union organizers. In fact, such a body of workers is (original emphasis) available—but again, only if the Republican Party is willing to stand on principle and run a conservative candidate. We refer to those conservatives, and primarily young people, who are willing to work for a conservative candidate.[6]

A course was set during our time in Minnesota. Now all that was left was to follow it.

I departed Minnesota confident in our cause.

But by early June, my old friend Bill Miller, chairman of the Republican National Committee, was showing signs of letting the RNC be controlled by the GOP's moderate Rockefeller wing. Miller looked the other way as Rockefeller, along with Eisenhower and Nixon, formed a self-serving group, the National Republican Citizens' (NRC) committee. GOP conservatives had not been consulted.

"Bill," I quickly wrote Miller, "... what happened to the Bill Miller who was in Jackson last December, and whom I know to be a wonderful, fighting state chairman? ... Eisenhower talked you into giving your blessing to this citizens' group idea."[7]

Miller and Goldwater fell out with each other over the NRC being formed.[8] We conservatives saw the group's formation as Rockefeller's power grab to galvanize forces for his upcoming presidential campaign.

So I approached Barry with the idea of starting another organization—a national, state GOP chairmen's group—one that would let the state chairmen speak for themselves. I told Barry that the Republican National Committee at this point was "nothing but a rubber stamp operation, which is not the least bit reflective of the view of the Republican precinct, county, and state leadership throughout the country."[9]

We GOP conservatives must now act for ourselves, I said. And our power base was waiting to be organized. The state chairmen of our party were, on balance, Goldwater people.

But we had no unified voice. I told Barry that as chairman of the Southern Association of Republican State Chairmen I wanted to assemble all the GOP's state chairmen to discuss forming our own organization.

"Barry, from the events of recent weeks, it is most obvious that the battle is on in full force," I said, "but let me assure you that in my sincere opinion, under your leadership, we will win decisively after a bitter struggle. However, let's not kid ourselves into thinking that we can defeat a well-organized, well-financed force without one of our own."[10]

About this time, *Time* magazine featured me as a part of "The New Breed" of GOP leadership, along with the GOP state chairmen of Alabama, South Carolina, and North Carolina. "There have been admirals in the Kentucky navy with more power and prestige than many Republican state chairmen in the South since the Civil War," *Time* stated. "As leaders of a small and suspect minority, many GOP chairmen shrugged off any chance of winning state elections, dozed on dusty courthouse steps, and dreamed of the election of the next Republican President and the patronage that would flow down from Washington."[11]

The *Time* article said that "things are changing in the old Confederate states," led by "a new breed of politician—furrow-browed, button-down, college-trained young amateurs who, one by one, took over control of the state parties from apathetic and aging professionals. The new wave is now in command of Alabama, Mississippi, and South and North Carolina."[12]

Time called us "the four rebel state chairmen."

We were: "South Carolina's Robert F. Chapman, 36, a towheaded Spartanburg lawyer"; "North Carolina's William E. Cobb, 39, a slender, crew-cut lumber broker in Morganton"; and "Alabama's John Grenier, 31, ... a vigorous Birmingham lawyer." Here is what *Time* said about me:

> Mississippi's Wirt Yerger Jr., 32, who works in his father's
> Jackson insurance agency, is chairman in a state where

home-born Republicans were lately regarded as freaks. Yerger's chief rival for Mississippi Republican supremacy was the late Perry Howard, a Negro, who was national committeeman for 36 years, lived most of that time in Washington, and racked up a record of almost absolute ineffectiveness. Yerger has organized local leaders in nearly half of the state's 82 counties, has small sympathy for those party members who are along just for the ride. Says he: "I don't care who it is, bank president or anybody, if he's just going to give us conversation, we don't want him. We want people who are going to get out and fight." Several hundred of Mississippi's fighting Republicans have agreed to let the party draw drafts on their personal checking accounts for $5 to $100 a month.[13]

Added *Time*, "The efforts of the new breed have already paid off in small ways. In the last two years, Republicans have elected a mayor in Mobile, put the first two party members in the South Carolina legislature since Reconstruction, and sent Texas' John Tower to the U.S. Senate. Southern Republicans talk of doubling their number of Congressmen from seven to 14 this November, a hope that may prove forlorn. Clearly, the new breed has a long way to go. But at least and at last it has made a beginning."[14]

The growth of our state's party had, obviously, been a team effort. Bob Enlow had done a fine job as our first executive director. He planned to resign soon to reenter a career in journalism. So now we hired a young man straight out of Ole Miss—one of the best hires I ever made. Bill Wilkins, over the next decade, would not only become our state GOP executive director, but also would prove to be a master of political strategy.

With such men at work, I was further freed to strategize and implement ideas both locally and nationally. One of the finest efforts to this end was a massive training seminar in Jackson in 1962 for all of our state, municipal, and county workers.

Paul DesRochers, organizational director for the Texas Republican Party, spoke, as did Jim Leonard, the Texas party's executive director, plus several other Texas leaders. They helped us see how Republicanism was growing in their state. James Bertron, who had been John Tower's campaign director in 1960, guaranteed our people that if we would organize at the precinct level, we would take 87 percent of the vote in the next general election.[15]

Texas Sen. John Tower closed our workshop with a strong speech. At that time I told Tower of my concerns about moderate power plays at the national level. "John," I said, "I know you must realize that the Rockefeller group is highly organized, lavishly financed, and well staffed. We are entirely too naïve if we think we can stand up in the face of the Rockefeller steamroller."

Tower agreed, saying, "We are currently working on means to stop it."[16]

I had told Clifton White of my same concerns. "Clif," I once wrote, "... We are kidding ourselves at this point if we think we can do the job with a token, loose-knit group, when we are combating a staff which is fifty times as well financed and staffed as we have."[17]

Both White and Tower liked my idea for organizing the state GOP chairmen. I even told Bill Miller and he affirmed it.[18] Most importantly, Goldwater okayed the idea. "Barry, please remember this," I told him in a letter. "It takes plenty of manpower and money to successfully promote the Goldwater image throughout the country. Naturally, since he has had it in abundant amounts and you haven't up to now, it is not surprising to see polls showing Nelson Rockefeller as the frontrunner. The people in America deserve a better choice than that between Kennedy and Rockefeller, and while I'll admit to being prejudiced on the subject, I firmly believe that they will have another choice."[19]

I flew to New York City during the second week of August. Clif told me he was ready to alert all of his people.[20] I. Lee Potter, special assistant to RNC chairman Bill Miller, also told me he was "glad to know that you are making progress in your plans for a national state chairmen's meeting."[21]

But Miller was playing both sides of the political fence.

Our conference of state GOP chairmen had been set for Dec. 13 and 14 in Dallas. I had kept Miller in the loop all the way.[22] More than 35 state party chairmen planned to be there. But as the date approached, I began getting letters expressing regret, and/or expressions of confusion, from state chairmen after Bill Miller suddenly preempted our gathering by calling a special RNC meeting the week prior to our scheduled Dallas event. But despite Miller's move, our voice had been heard. The National Committee of Republican State Chairmen eventually formed in early 1963. Miller and the RNC also organized a panel of the four regional state GOP chairmen to troubleshoot the RNC. Our findings included some major reorganization of staff and function and a less-powerful RNC executive committee.[23]

• • •

Our state GOP challenges were trivial compared to our state Democrat counterparts. They were rocked in 1962 by a series of political and ethical disasters.

First, Mississippians learned in early 1962 that a Parchman Prison convict, Kimble Berry, appeared to have been released intentionally by some state Democrats in order to retrieve an estimated $519,000 in securities he had stolen.[24] These Democrats were close to Governor Barnett. Parole Board Chairman Martin Fraley, Parchman Prison Supt. Fred Jones, Lt. Gov. Paul Johnson, and Barnett all were implicated; some were forced in February to testify before a joint state legislative committee.

Second, because of the Berry incident, scrutiny of state prison operations intensified. An investigative report showed 600 inmates had received suspended sentences, or "leaves," during Barnett's tenure; the governor called the report "misleading."[25] "A veil of mystery hung over the entire" matter, said a state senate's special investigatory committee.[26] Parchman Supt. Fred Jones was fired on April 24 by Barnett.

Jones complained he had been made to put his "head on Ross Barnett's chopping block" in the matter. Jones said inmates got paroles by paying off prison employees who were "good friends of the governor."[27] Barnett then vetoed four penitentiary reform bills. Critics called it "one of the more serious mistakes he's ever made," adding, "he has completely forgotten the will of the people."[28]

I suggested that Bidwell Adam and Barnett should hold "a peace powwow in the Governor's wigwam ... to get their tribal braves on the right legislative trail."[29]

Third, Barnett remodeled the Governor's Mansion at "ridiculously high costs," I stated to the media. About $300,000 was spent fixing up the mansion; $20,000 of real-gold bathroom fixtures were installed. "Gold toilets" became a joke around the state. Even worse, Barnett awarded the remodeling job to Democrat friends at exorbitant rates.[30]

Fourth, revelations became public of widespread kickbacks among Democrat county supervisors statewide. The state legislature created a six-man commission to investigate.[31] Supervisors were getting kickbacks from heavy machinery dealers to buy their products. One supervisor owned a $35,000 home and drove a new Cadillac on a supposed $350-a-month salary. "Five years ago this same supervisor couldn't even charge a suit of clothes at a local store," I noted.[32] Just as bad, news broke that only 12 of the state's 82 county sheriffs—all Democrats—had paid their state income tax.[33]

Mississippians could now see how corrupt a one-party political system could be. It was a mounting corruption like this that, along with our excellent new GOP, caused many state citizens to look our way. This fact is totally missed by many historians who tend to point only to Goldwater's effect in raising voters' desire for a second party. The fact is that our base was growing long before the 1964 Goldwater run. I predicted that "the voters will have added reason to change parties in 1963 and vote for Republicans who will follow through with thorough investigations and, where necessary, prosecution."[34]

State Democrats' unavoidable association with John F. Kennedy added to their misery. Kennedy proliferated federal edicts at a dizzying rate through 1962. It was as if he could not create enough new federal programs. Here are some of Kennedy's activist efforts only from the first half of 1962:

- He wanted a cabinet position for urban affairs, as well as a big-government plan for America's farming industry that, said *The Clarion-Ledger*, was "political dynamite brewing."[35] Kennedy's "ABCD" farming program—"abundance, balance, conservation, and development"—sought to restrict farmer's production of food supplies. The proposal would "clobber farmers," said the head of the American Farm Bureau Federation. Kennedy said it would bring "balance."[36] Farmers rose up in opposition. A meeting of 101 Mississippi Delta farmers voted 100-1 against the Kennedy farm plan.[37] It was "another of a growing list of dictatorial moves that would drain away still more individual freedom," I said. Mississippi Farm Bureau president Boswell Stevens noted, "We found no one who supported [Kennedy's farm plan]. ... People realized it would create a dictatorship."[38]

- Kennedy sent a new welfare-for-needy-families plan to the U.S. Congress. Many Republicans and Democrats called it socialism.[39]

- He pushed big steel companies to cut back production, opposing free enterprise.

- Eisenhower now criticized Kennedy as "floundering— thrashing aimlessly and a bit desperately, amid dire economic times," revealing "an inadequate understanding of our American system."[40] Eisenhower told American businessmen, "Wake up ... take a look at what's happening to you ... and you better get in politics quick." He said that "only some resurgence of Republican control over government" would save the country from terrible times.[41]

- A Gallup poll said voters thought Kennedy was veering to the Left.[42]

- Kennedy called for U.S. and Soviet nuclear disarmament; his own secretary of state, Dean Rusk, had to disavow the president's actions with the Soviets.[43]

- A day after the Supreme Court outlawed requiring prayer in public schools, Kennedy gave the move his blessing.[44]

Meanwhile, the Berlin Wall was stronger than ever. Kennedy said he would keep talking with the Soviets because it was better to "jaw-jaw than war-war"; West Germany Chancellor Konrad Adenauer said the talks were going nowhere.[45]

Castro was entrenched in Cuba. Chinese Communist forces attacked the strongholds of the royal Laotian army.[46] On May 14, Kennedy ordered more land, sea, and air forces into Laos and South Vietnam.[47] On May 17, our marines hit Thailand's shore, as Kennedy pledged to back up South Vietnam and Thailand against Red forces that had already swept into northwestern Laos.[48] Kennedy thus secured his legacy for starting an undeclared Vietnam War.

The year was only half done. And this does not include the hundreds of federal lawsuits against organized crime and for civil rights filed by Robert Kennedy in the same period of time.

Many Americans felt overwhelmed by the Kennedys' torrid pace.

• • •

In the fall of 1962 our state's citizens hit absolute overload. James Meredith was about to enter the University of Mississippi. But it was the interplay of Ross Barnett and Robert Kennedy that undid so many. *It was a classic case of state and national Democrat hypocrisy.*

Meredith, a smart man, spent much of the year in court trying to gain entry to Ole Miss.[49] By September of 1962, the NAACP had made little progress. Kennedy would not "get enough votes in Mississippi to wad a shotgun," Ross Barnett joked while visiting the World's Fair in Seattle in September.[50]

Four days later, on Sept. 10, U.S. Supreme Court Justice Hugo Black said that Ole Miss must let Meredith enroll. Barnett's reply was plain: "No."[51]

Medgar Evers wrote Barnett asking that he "use the designated as well as Christian influence of your office to effectuate a smooth transition at the University."[52] Instead, Barnett announced that he would use a special "interposition" statute passed by the state legislature to prevent Meredith's entry. The statute said, rightly or wrongly, that "Mississippi is a sovereign state and has never delegated to the federal government its right to educate and nurture its youth and its power and right of control over its schools, colleges, educational and other public institutions and facilities."[53]

The interposition idea was advanced by an editor in Richmond, Virginia. It was rooted in several past cases where "states interposed their will over the dictates of the federal government when they contended that state statutes should hold sway over U.S. mandates." It claimed to have its root in the 10th Amendment of the U.S. Constitution concerning state powers not expressly given to the federal government.[54]

On Sept. 13, Barnett officially interposed himself as governor between Ole Miss and federal authorities. Ole Miss would not be integrated, he said. The next day, *The Clarion-Ledger* editorialized concerning Barnett's speech that "regardless of misinterpretations of the constitution in recent years," Barnett's stand was right. This was "an assault on States' Rights," the paper said. "We must neither falter nor fail in this supreme test."[55] Henceforth, average Mississippians would know almost exclusively only what *The Clarion-Ledger* and Ross Barnett wanted them to know.

No Mississippian of any public significance except U.S. 3rd District Rep. Frank Smith opposed Barnett; Smith had just lost an election and his congressional seat to Jamie Whitten and would soon be leaving the U.S. Congress.[56] The state house of representatives backed Barnett 130 to 2; the state senate backed him unanimously.[57] Former governors and lieutenant governors wired support. The Mississippi Association of Supervisors gave its "full" support.[58]

Meanwhile, out of the public eye, Robert Kennedy conducted secret phone conversations with Barnett.

Through the rest of the Meredith showdown, the two talked. Sometimes John F. Kennedy phoned Barnett as well.[59] In a midnight meeting on Sept. 19, the state legislature passed a measure empowering Barnett to arrest Meredith if he tried to enroll, on a criminal charge of false voter registration years prior in Hinds County.

Meanwhile, Meredith was arriving on the college campus to enroll the next day. "I have no argument, no fight or struggle with segregation," Meredith said. "I don't know what other people want, but I seek only to find a common ground for settlement of our mutual problems. Let's make a friendly relationship between races in Mississippi possible. Then give me my rights and nothing more."[60]

On Thursday, Sept. 20, Barnett—now appointed as the college's official registrar and accompanied by Lt. Gov. Paul Johnson—walked out of the Continuation Center at four in the afternoon to a crowd of about 250. "James Meredith has been denied admission," he proclaimed to a cheering crowd.[61] Protected by scores of highway patrol offices, Meredith had arrived on campus to hisses, curses, and choruses of "n----r, n----r, n----r". That night, Barnett's sister died of a stroke.[62]

My old foe, Bidwell Adam, chairman of the state Democratic Party, was finally undone by the Kennedys. Adam now did the unthinkable: he asked me—his sworn political enemy—to join him in publicly opposing the Kennedys. Adam's letter follows:

> After the slaughter of the last vestige of human decency
> by the Republican organization in the days that followed
> the Civil War under the leadership of carpetbaggers and
> scalawags and Thaddeus Stevens, I could never become

reconciled to sitting in the [party] that Perry Howard vacated and gave to you a free simple title. You have overreached yourself in your wild imagination. I suggest that you wash the banner you now so proudly wave and give it a good fumigation. It still has the odor of a tragic era.

Your memory of Herbert Brownell, Republican Attorney General, and Eisenhower's Little Rock soldiers with fixed bayonets is extremely short. Let you and me send a joint telegram to the northern leadership of both major political parties, telling them to go jump in the Potomac River. Have you got the guts to sign your name to such a wire?

Come on, little man, get off of your ivory tower and let's make things sizzle. This game of politics is for men and not little boys. You can't wear spats and kid gloves. I will come to Jackson for a conference whenever you want to set up a good lunch.[63]

I replied to Adam that I would not join him in his demagoguery. I wrote Adam the following:

The trouble with sending a joint telegram to the leaders of both major political parties, telling them to jump in the Potomac River, is that on the whole, Mississippi Republicans are quite proud of their national leadership at the present time. Our Party leadership is basically conservative, and when compared to the New Frontier, which is representative of the national Democratic Party, our Party looks even more conservative.

Honestly, you have my deepest sympathy, and I am quite surprised that you have not told your national chairman and the Kennedys to jump in the Potomac River a long time ago. Let's recognize the facts for what they are today.

Your letters are a great morale booster, and it is always a pleasure to hear from you.[64]

The NAACP asked President Kennedy to arrest Barnett for contempt.[65] On the next Monday, the state college board yielded to the 5th U.S. Circuit Court of Appeals and agreed to let Meredith attend Ole Miss. On Tuesday, Sept. 25, Meredith again tried to enroll; again Barnett faced him down.[66]

Bidwell Adam could not take it any more. He announced from his Gulf Coast home that he was finished with the Democratic Party. "They'll have to get somebody else to carry their banner down here."[67]

The next day, Thursday, Lt. Gov. Paul Johnson filled in for Barnett and blocked Meredith again on the Oxford campus. By Friday, 600 U.S. Marshals amassed in Memphis. "Mr. Meredith will be registered," Robert Kennedy said.[68]

Reports were that the state was rushing in up to 500 of its own officers as a counter force.[69] The major general from Arkansas who had commanded that state's National Guard's forcible entry of African-American children into Little Rock schools (and later had regretted it), Maj. Gen. Edwin A. Walker, now told media he was traveling to Oxford to lead a massive resistance, "10,000 strong from every state in the Union" to block Meredith.[70] "We can't win a shooting war with the U.S. Army," one state legislator warned.[71]

On Friday, Sept. 28, the 5th Circuit Court of Appeals in New Orleans convicted Barnett of contempt.[72] The same day, Mississippi's senators and five of its six congressmen sent a telegram to President Kennedy asking that he not use troops in Oxford. "We respectfully submit, Mr. President, the successful registration could not be worth the price."[73]

On Saturday, President Kennedy conscripted the Mississippi National Guard even as national media on the Ole Miss campus ogled co-eds walking by, "not one unattractive, ... at least half actually pretty and an astonishing number beautiful."[74] The same day, Barnett watched the Ole Miss football team beat Kentucky, hosting the president of Hertz Corp., the chairman of the board of Holiday Inns of America, and a Mississippi car dealership mogul.[75]

At the game's half-time, Barnett stood before a massive Confederate flag and bellowed, "I love Mississippi. I love her people. I love our customs. I respect our heritage," as the football fans cheered.

But by Sunday night, Barnett again was scheming on the phone with President Kennedy, who was about to make a nationally televised speech about the Ole Miss quagmire. Barnett, without anyone's knowledge, *had already cut a deal with the President to let Meredith enter Ole Miss.* Publicly, however, Barnett led Mississippians to believe otherwise. Just before Kennedy's TV speech, Barnett issued a public plea for calm. He decried the federal force and the co-opting of "10,000 good Mississippians" from the National Guard "to oppose me and my own people. I know that we are physically overpowered."

Meanwhile, a helicopter was delivering Meredith onto the campus. All day long, hundreds of people—students, outside agitators, local teens—had flocked onto the campus, an unwieldy crowd. As President Kennedy took the podium to speak on national TV, about 2,500 students and others, including Maj. Gen. Walker and local Oxford youths, jeered federal marshals as they guarded the dorm where Meredith was staying.

About the time that President Kennedy was speaking to a national TV audience, pledging to carry out Meredith's enrollment and defending the need for troops, tear gas was fired amid a rioting crowd. And gunshots. A foreign newsman was killed, as was a 23-year-old Oxford-area resident. A U.S. marshal was shot in the throat. Another man died of a heart attack.

Students drove a bulldozer to the Lyceum steps. Maj. Gen. Walker then led "a charge of about 1,000 of the students against the marshals," throwing bottles and bricks at the marshals.[76] "In the darkness and confusion which existed Sunday night, it was difficult to say exactly what happened," stated *The Clarion-Ledger*.[77]

And then it was over.

Two days later, about 135 leading Mississippi businessmen, most either Republicans or soon to be, met with the media at Jackson's King Edward Hotel, urging no more violence.[78] I wrote a friend, saying, "I believe Barnett belongs in

169

jail."[79] Ole Miss was integrated, as most knew to be inevitable. Too great a price had been paid: killings and horrid violence. Another terrible new wound had opened.

Such trauma made significant political change in Mississippi inevitable now. It would be impossible to think otherwise. All over the state, people saw the national Democrats, as led by John F. Kennedy, as unacceptable now in the extreme. It was no longer possible for many Mississippi citizens to entertain the notion of a bipolar relationship between state and national Democrats.

"Dear Barry," I wrote to Goldwater on Oct. 2, 1962. "From reports I have been getting ... tremendous voter preference change [has occurred] ... in the recent days in Mississippi as a result of happenings here."[80]

• • •

In the ensuing weeks, federal troops occupied the campus, searching dorms without warrants, arresting students at will, and confiscating whatever they desired. Young ladies were subjected to embarrassing personal searches. Whatever "side" one was on, the entire matter was humiliating. "People still are in a state of shock and ... incapable of too much decisive action in any direction," one local GOP leader told me.[81]

Out of sight, Bill Simmons, head of the Citizens' Council, offered a postmortem to his members throughout the state. "With the express approval of Khrushchev, Castro, the Communist Party of the United States, certain professors at Ole Miss, and certain clergymen of Oxford, Kennedy has placed and is maintaining at Ole Miss a negro whose application for admission was revoked. ...

> Mississippi citizens have been subjected to insulting, unlawful, unreasonable, and illegal searches of their person and property and Mississippi citizens have been brutally treated. All of this is reminiscent of the treatment of the American Colonists by the troops of George III, which our forefathers sought to prevent in the future by what

is known as the Bill of Rights to the Constitution of the United States.

... In considering these abuses and the brutal treatment of students and the atrocities committed on Mississippi citizens, one is well aware that the Attorney General of the United States has openly said that the Constitution is obselete (sic) and [that] the end justifies the means. Their actions in this regard demonstrate this belief. In view of this situation there are two questions that arise: (1) How did this come to be? (2) What can be done about it?[82]

Simmons detailed his thoughts on how, over many decades, powers had been taken from the national legislative branch and assumed by the executive and judicial branches under Democrat administrations starting with Franklin D. Roosevelt. He added:

Our contribution to this destruction of constitutional government has been a blind devotion to ... the Democratic label.

... Although the situation is dark, nevertheless it has many bright sides. ... [It] has caused thinking men everywhere to realize that if we are ever to turn back it must be now.

... I submit for your consideration the following action:

1. Support the Goldwater Rally in Jackson, Mississippi on Nov. 29, 1962. Goldwater is the only national figure who has had the courage to say that states have the right to control their own schools and that the action in Oxford was unconstitutional.

2. Get our Alabama friends to either get a commitment from Senator Hill that he will vote with the Republicans to organize the Senate or either throw their support behind Mr. Martin.

3. Form a coalition with the Mississippi Republicans to get

support on a national level. This would include, if necessary, the election of candidates on a Republican ticket.

4. ... Put pressure on ... [elected] Representatives and Senators to vote with the Republicans to organize the 88th Congress.[83]

Almost immediately after the Meredith incident, hundreds began showing active interest in our party. Significantly, we were there and organized and ready to put them to work. A flood of top state leaders suddenly came on board the organization committee for "one of the greatest demonstrations of conservative strength ever exhibited in Mississippi," stated our Goldwater banquet chairman, Fred LaRue.[84]

Forty top state leaders affiliated with the Goldwater banquet committee in mid-November; 42 more announced days later; 30 just days later; and then another 48. These were men who had held out on the GOP—men like WLBT's Fred Beard and Vicksburg State Sen. Ellis Bodron; and other men who normally eschewed politics. It was an unprecedented list. Even billionaire Texan H.L. Hunt contacted me, and I invited him to the Goldwater rally. "We have here in Mississippi the greatest potential, in my opinion, of any state in the country for being a solid conservative state," I told Hunt.[85]

After years in the desert—and years of being mocked by national and state Democrats—people were now seeing the stark reality of how embarrassing and corrupt Barnett's state Democrats were and, at least for many, how intolerable the increased use of federal force could become. "Listen," one older Kosciusko man told me, "if Barry Goldwater or some other conservative is the Republican nominee, he will carry Miss. over one hundred thousand votes. I've been here a long time living among them. I know how they feel. The present Democrat Party has no leadership now."[86]

• • •

By November, President Kennedy issued an executive order

mandating integration of all federal housing. He again by-passed Congress. I told the media, "In Khrushchev, Castro, and Kennedy style, President Kennedy has ignored Congress and the Constitution completely and put out another of his executive orders. This dictatorial action on the part of the President must be stopped if individual freedom and constitutional government is to be preserved. Why didn't he ask Congress to pass a law to accomplish in housing what he decreed? The answer is he didn't feel it would pass."[87]

There was a clear, logical way to respond to Kennedy, I said. "Hundreds of Mississippians dedicated to this goal will gather in the Heidelberg Hotel Thursday evening, Nov. 29, to meet, hear, and support Senator Barry Goldwater."[88]

The snowball now rolling for our Goldwater banquet was unstoppable. Tickets sold out and we printed more, finding extra space for guests. We bought statewide television time for Goldwater's address, but then Barry balked at being televised, likely due to the recent Oxford incident. I did my best to allay his worries.

"Everything is in readiness for your visit next week," I wrote Barry on Nov. 21, "and I think you will be highly pleased with the reception you receive. While your reception will be enthusiastic in every way, please don't misunderstand anything at all because we are not in any sense trying to launch the Barry Goldwater for president boom from Jackson, Mississippi.

"Regarding the situation in connection with the Oxford incident, please be assured that absolute calm prevails, and while people are very bitter at the Kennedys, there is a very relative quiet. Please put your mind to rest about the situation being any different here now than from any of your previous visits."

"Naturally," I told him, "Charlie Klumb and myself are quite disappointed since we do strongly feel you would have no problem, and can certainly stick to what you have already said and written without having to say any more. In connection with the television itself, the television time has been bought, and the main reason we were interested in this is that it does multiply our audience, and gets across to the people who cannot afford to attend the fund-raising dinner."

I asked him to hit "hard at the third party or unpledged group who continue to muddy the water" in Mississippi, "and urge that they join the only conservative party in the Nation, the Republican Party. In addition, you would make some strong mention of the need for adequate funds and the importance of fund raising; I think that would be most appropriate.

"... Barry, if you still want to close off the thousands of people that cannot pay to come to the dinner by not letting us televise it, then please let us know, and we will try to get out of our contract, but as I said, we can see no harm that would come to televising it over one local station which is all that was planned."[89]

Barry remained unconvinced, so we cancelled the TV time.

As the day drew near, Bob Enlow, who despite resigning as our state executive director was still working with us on this event, scurried with final plans. One day he received a phone call. Enlow recalls:

> In the midst of selling tickets for the Goldwater dinner, I received a call from Medgar Evers ...
>
> "Mr. Enlow," he said politely, after introducing himself, "I'd like to buy some tickets for the Goldwater dinner."
>
> When I realized who was on the phone, I paused to be sure of my response, then said: "Certainly, Mr. Evers, how many tickets would you like?" He said he'd stop by the office later in the week but never did.[90]

The day came for the Goldwater banquet.

I met Barry in Dallas and we flew into Jackson together. Meanwhile, Fred LaRue had run a full-page ad in *The Clarion-Ledger*, featuring a big photo of Barry. In big, bold letters, the ad read in part: HAD ENOUGH? Join other conservative Mississippians to meet, hear and support ... Senator Barry Goldwater. ... This is your chance to take positive action ... don't miss it!"

And they did not.

Fifteen hundred people showed up that night at the Olympic Room of Jackson's Heidelberg Hotel, each paying $100 per plate—unfathomable by any political organizer in any state in the Union at that time.[91]

"The South is awakening to the fact that the only practical protection for them in this country is in the Republican Party," Goldwater told the electric crowd. "You are not alone."

He added: "The radical Left is scared stiff because they now see the South leaving the house of the 'Double Deal'."

The issue of integration was not the real issue for us, Barry insisted. Barry made clear what he and I always had felt: we had to stand on core principles that transcended any one issue. "The Southerner of both parties is turning to the Republican party for reasons far more serious." Among them, he said, was the danger Kennedy's New Frontier programs presented to free enterprise.

Barry urged us all to unite, "not divide America," and he also offered a realistic, prophetic thought: "I will warn you conservatives. You will be called reactionary. But what are we reacting against? Do we resist the centralization of power in Washington? You're darn right we do."

He added: "Is a reactionary one who resists replacement of the free enterprise system with socialism? If so, then we must plead guilty. Is it reactionary to resist a weak-kneed foreign policy? To resist a growing disregard for the Constitution?"

"I think the day is long past that we should stop this unholy appeal to persons because of their race, creed or color, just for votes," Barry added.[92]

That night I felt much as I had when Nixon had visited Jackson earlier. All of the work, all of the harassment endured—every bit was worth it. The gratitude I felt was enormous. The hope I felt in Goldwater's leadership was beyond words. I had opened the evening with this quip: "Welcome to the world's largest phone booth!" a reference to the now-old Democrat joke about the size of our 1956 GOP state convention meeting.

The place erupted with laughter. Our Republican ranks were now solidified. Hundreds of letters flowed into our GOP state office after the event.

In early December, I wrote a letter of thanks to Barry. "Support is still flowing in, in the form of personal comments, cards and letters, and not the least of all ... money," I said, "as a result of your overwhelming speech. We had expected great things, but ... this is the largest gathering ever fed in a hotel in Mississippi's history. ... Let's continue to keep in touch, and I want to assure you not only for the principles on which you stand, but also for your warmth and sincerity from the heart."[93]

In 1962, I had witnessed three unprecedented events: 1) the beginning of the end of the old Mississippi Democratic Party; 2) the integration of my alma mater under federal gunfire; and, 3) the jet-propulsion of support for Barry Goldwater and a true conservatism.

Little did I know that we were soon to identify an excellent gubernatorial candidate for 1963, Rubel Phillips.

STRONG TIES: Wirt became friends with Ariz. Sen. Barry Goldwater, who traveled to Mississippi to speak upon Wirt's invitation. As chairman of the Southern Association of Republican State Chairmen, Wirt helped orchestrate Goldwater's presidential run.

AS BARRY ARRIVED at the Jackson airport, the greeters were headed by Charles Klum, left, Senator Goldwater, Wirt Yerger, Jr., and Fred LaRue, who were major figures at the Goldwater dinner Thursday which drew a record crowd.—Photo by Claude Sutherland.

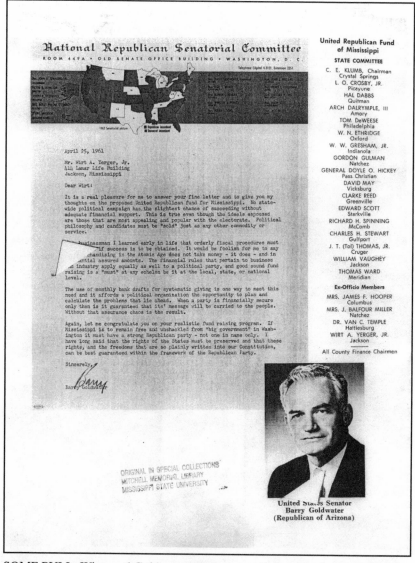

SOME PULL: Wirt used Goldwater's influence to help rally the troops in Mississippi, as this letter solicited by Wirt from Goldwater shows. This letter was distributed among Mississippians.

F. CLIFTON WHITE & ASSOCIATES, INC.

File Conservatives For President

ROOM 3505
122 EAST 42 STREET
NEW YORK 17, N. Y.
MURRAY HILL 2-4767

April 7, 1962

RECEIVED
APR 10 1962

Mr. Wirt A. Yerger, Jr.
Mississippi Republican Party
414 Lamar Life Building
Jackson, Mississippi

Dear Wirt:

Plans are now pretty firm for our meeting the week end of April 13.
I will be arriving at the Hotel Lowry in St. Paul around 8 p.m. on
the 12th. I assume that you, Charlie Klumb and Fred LaRue will be
arriving together. If you are coming in on Thursday evening also,
please call me collect in New York as soon as possible and reservations will be made in your names at the Lowry for that night. Or
if you wish information with reference to your privateplane flight
to Minneapolis-St. Paul and then on to the Lodge, let us know also.

Friday morning we will officially convene at 10:30 a.m. in Room 1210
at the St. Paul Athletic Club. Our meeting will run through lunch and
at 2:30 p.m. we will depart for the Lodge. The rest of the group will
be getting into the Lodge around 6:30 p.m. when we will have some
refreshments and dinner. That evening, I will give a report to the
group and then we will have some time for socializing.

The next morning following breakfast there will be a work session by
regions, which will include putting names on the state forms that I
have sent to the regional men. At 10:30 a.m. until lunch, we will have
a general discussion and reports from the regions. Following lunch,
we will spend the afternoon in detailed discussion concerning techniques, work with groups that should be associated with us, reports on
the Young Republicans, Young Americans For Freedom, women's groups,
as well as a discussion of our work with the National Committee.

Saturday evening there will be a brief discussion of techniques that
are being used in some states that might be useful to all of us. Sunday
morning will be a general summary session. Planes will leave Wonewok
Sunday morning on a schedule to meet the convenience of the members of
the group. As we will be operating in an informal atmosphere and I hope
to get a great deal of work accomplished, casual clothes will be in order.

Looking forward to seeing you.

ORIGINAL IN SPECIAL COLLECTIONS,
MITCHELL MEMORIAL LIBRARY
MISSISSIPPI STATE UNIVERSITY

Sincerely,

Clif

F. Clifton White

SMALL BEGINNINGS: In April of 1961, a small group of idealistic conservatives with national pull gathered quietly in the Minnesota woods to plot
ideas that eventually became part of "The Southern Strategy," used by Goldwater and ultimately Nixon and Reagan to coalesce true conservatives into
the GOP. Clifton White of New York City organized the meeting, which White
discussed in the letter above.

MINNESOTA MIND-MELD: True-conservative Republican national leaders ironed out the following paper to elect a like-minded man as president of the United States. Their man would be Ariz. Sen. Barry Goldwater.

CAN A CONSERVATIVE REPUBLICAN WIN?

I. Can a Republican be elected President as a conservative? Our answer is "Yes"--an answer backed both by the facts of the case, and by the past record of the Republican Party.

Four times in recent years the GOP has attempted to win the Presidency by appealing to the "moderates" and "liberals" in the urban centers of the East--in 1940, 1944, 1948 and 1960. Each time the GOP failed. The two Eisenhower campaigns cannot be placed in this category because, as is widely admitted, Eisenhower won by virtue of being a transpartisan war hero, and not on the basis of any ideological convictions or issues.

If the strategy of appealing for the "moderates" and "liberals" has failed, is the Republican Party doomed to perpetual minority status as a nationwide entity? We must answer "No", because there is a strategy which can win the Presidency for the Republicans, a strategy of fusing together an Electoral College majority from the basically conservative areas of the nation: the Midwest, the Mountain States, and the South. Such a fusion would consist of:

The Midwest and Mountain States: Arizona, Colorado, Idaho, Illinois, Indiana, Iowa, Kansas, Montana, Nebraska, Nevada, North Dakota, Ohio, Oklahoma, South Dakota, Utah, Wisconsin and Wyoming. Total electoral votes: 135.

The South: Alabama, Arkansas, Florida, Georgia, Louisiana, Mississippi, North Carolina, South Carolina, Tennessee, Texas and Virginia. Total electoral votes: 128.

Beginning with this base, the Republicans would have to carry only New Hampshire and Vermont, both Republican and conservative strongholds, in order to achieve an Electoral College majority.

Of the Midwest and Mountain states listed, all except two went Republican in 1960, and these two--Nevada and Illinois--could be retrieved by a conservative candidate. Illinois politics in 1960 was affected by displeasure with Republican Governor William Stratton, whose unpopularity hurt the party's showing downstate. But this downstate area is one of the most conservative areas in the nation, and would rally to a conservative candidate. As for Nevada, Goldwater is as popular and well-known there as are the two Nevada senators.

Could a conservative Republican win the South? The answer, again, is "Yes"--but on the assumption that the GOP would promise to call off the national vendetta against the South, and take the constitutional stand on states' rights. Although the area has not yet fully developed a two-party system, it will vote for a suitable Republican national ticket. Eisenhower took most of the South, and even Nixon--without any special appeal--won Virginia, Florida, Tennessee and Kentucky, and

-. 2 -

made serious inroads everywhere. Goldwater is immensely popular in the South, and we have the word of Senator Strom Thurmond (the only Senator in modern times to win through a write-in campaign) that South Carolina, as "deep south" a state as one can imagine, would vote for Goldwater. The victory of Republican Senator John Tower in Texas supports this thesis, since Tower won only by running with a "Goldwater conservative" label.

II. Nor should we simply write off all the urban areas. Census Bureau figures show that in the decade between 1950 and 1960 the "central city" population of the United States increased only 1 per cent. The greatest jump in this decade was in the suburbs--which grew 44 per cent. These suburban areas are middle-class, basically conservative, Republican areas. Yet the Republican Party has not exploited its full potential in these areas by campaigning on a platform of fiscal responsibility. The appeal to the city minorities lost votes in the suburbs, and gained none in the cities. The Negro, Puerto Rican and Mexican wards of New York City, Chicago and Los Angeles still went for Kennedy in 1960 by majorities of 10-1 to 15-1, while the suburbs gave a relatively lukewarm 60 per cent majority to Nixon. Republican strategy should be aimed at increasing its majorities in the suburbs, rather than the hopeless one of attempting to get the in-city minority vote.

III. A third factor is "troops". Liberals in the Democratic Party have been able to make their political gains primarily through the use of union campaign workers. In the campaigns, and especially on Election Day, thousands of union shop stewards and officers are, in actuality, working for the Democratic Party rather than for the companies that employ them. States such as California and Pennsylvania have been won to the Democratic column primarily through the work of professional union political organizers. (We do not mean to imply that the union _vote_ is lost to conservative Republicans. The union hierarchy does _not_ represent the views of all the union membership, as Senator Taft proved by winning the union vote in Ohio despite--or because of--fierce opposition from the union bosses.)

The Republican Party must find some body of workers--beyond what it already has--if it is to offset these professional union organizers. In fact, such a body of workers _is_ available--but again, only if the Republican Party is willing to stand on principle and run a conservative candidate. We refer to those conservatives, and primarily the young people, who are willing to work for a conservative candidate but refuse to actively support a "me-too" candidate.

Polls taken by the Indianapolis _News_, for example, show that majority of delegates of the 1960 Republican convention are conservative, and would support Senator Goldwater much more enthusiastically than someone more liberal. Similarly, it is generally recognized now that a conservative revival of major significance exists among young people. The Young Republicans in recent years have taken a

- 3 -

much more conservative position than the national party. It was primarily young workers that were responsible for the surprise victory of John Tower in Texas.

Even in such seemingly hopeless areas as metropolitan New York City, young people are joining conservative organizations faster than these organizations can accept them. In a little over a year, for example, the Greater New York Council of Young Americans for Freedom, the conservative youth group, has taken in more than 4000 active members. This is more than the combined membership of the New York Young (Men's) Republican Club and the Young Women's Republican Club, two old and established clubs that enjoy full Party support. These YAF workers, and others like them, have the time and energy necessary to offset the campaign efforts of the professional union organizers, but they will not work for anyone but a conservative candidate.

10 The Clarion-Ledger   Friday, June 29, 1962

REPUBLICAN RALLY in Jackson Thursday night featured the presence of Jim Bertron, Houston, Texas, second from left, Harris County Republican Chairman. He was greeted here by many Jackson and Mississippi Republican leaders, including, left to right, Conner Smith, chairman of the precinct committee for Jackson, Mr. Bertron, Charles Klumb, Crystal Springs, state finance chairman, Billy Simmons, president of the Jackson Republican group, and Wirt Yerger, Jr., state chairman.

RALLYING TROOPS: Wirt was constantly moving from national gatherings such as the Minnesota meeting to small, county-based gatherings in Mississippi where he sought to build the state GOP from the bottom up.

NOT AFRAID TO ASK: Wirt issued Goldwater an invitation to speak to an Indianola, Mississippi, gathering. Goldwater declined, citing his commitment to spend some time with his wife.

CC: Seymour B. Johnson

November 5, 1962

Honorable Barry M. Goldwater
Old Senate Office Building
Washington, D. C.

Dear Barry:

Attached is a letter which I have the opportunity to forward to you inviting you to be the main speaker for the Delta Council Annual Meeting in May, 1963. As you can easily see from the list of speakers they have had, this is no ordinary organization.

The Delta Council is one of the most effective organizations of its type in Mississippi and even in the South. Their meetings draw large audiences, and they have excellent press coverage.

By way of introduction, Seymour Johnson, Chairman of the Sunflower County Republicans, has perhaps the outstanding county organization for our Party in the State, and I think it is altogether fitting that the invitation for you to appear on the program has been extended by him.

Barry, we recognize fully your crowded schedule, but this is definitely one invitation I would urge you to accept, if at all possible. It would do the cause a tremendous amount of good, and I can assure you that you would thoroughly enjoy the visit to the Mississippi Delta. The meeting is held in Cleveland, Mississippi and I can guarantee you that they will take care of your every wish, and I am sure would even be willing to arrange private air transportation from, and/or to, Washington, or any other convenient spot. Many thanks,

Sincerely,

Wirt A. Yerger, Jr.,
Chairman

fb

.S. If this stationery looks familiar, it's no coincidence!

November 1, 1962

Honorable Barry A. Goldwater
National Republican S natorial Committee
Room 449A - Old Senate Office Building
Washington, D. C.

NOVEMBER 29th VISIT

Dear Barry:

This is just a note to keep you posted as to progress on our
United Republican Fund meeting on November 29th.

As I have told you several times before, this dinner is to be
the high-light of our activity for the year. In connection with the
publicity on this, we are planning to have our Governor designate
November 29th as Goldwater Day in Mississippi. This, we feel, will
be a big help to publicity; and unless we hear from you to the contrary, we shall assume that this is all right with you.

As soon as you know what flight you will be arriving on, or
when you would like for us to arrange to pick you up in a nearby city,
we would appreciate your advising us accordingly.

Barry, your conservatism is very appealing to folks here in
Mississippi and I can assure you that November 29th is going to be a
day you will long remember.

With every good wish, I am

Sincerely,

fb

Wirt A. Yerger, Jr.,
Chairman

November 21, 1962

C O P Y

PERSONAL

Honorable Barry M. Goldwater
United States Senator
Washington, D. C.

Dear Barry:

Everything is in readiness for your visit next week, and I think that you will be highly pleased with the reception you receive. While your reception will be enthusiastic in every way, please don't misunderstand anything at all because we are not in any sense trying to launch the Barry Goldwater for president boom from Jackson, Mississippi.

Regarding the situation in connection with the Oxford incident, please be assured that absolute calm prevails, and while people are very bitter at the Kennedys, there is a very relative quiet. Please put your mind at rest about the situation being any different here now than from any of your previous visits.

Mrs. Coerver conveyed to me the message in connection with the press conference and television, and naturally, Charlie Klumb and myself are quite disappointed since we do strongly feel you would have no problem, and can certainly stick to what you have already said and written without having to say any more. In connection with the television itself, the television time has been bought, and the main reason we were interested in this is that it does multiply the audience, and gets across to the people who cannot afford to attend the fund-raising dinner.

Regarding your speech itself, everybody's brother has suggestions, and I hope that you will hit hard at the third party or unpledged group who continue to muddy the water, and urge that they join the only conservative party in the Nation, the Republican Party. In addition, if you would make some strong mention of the need for adequate funds and the importance of fund raising, I think that would be most appropriate.

According to Mrs. Coerver, we are to pick you up in Dallas at 12:54 P.M. on Thursday, the 29th, then fly our private plane to Jackson. Accordingly, she said that you wish to leave after the dinner and fly to St. Louis for a flight out of there early the next morning back to Phoenix.

Barry, if you still want to close off the thousands of people that cannot pay to come to the dinner by not letting us televise it, then please let us know, and we will try to get out of our contract, but as I said, we can see no harm that would come to televising it over one local station which is all that was planned.

Thanks again and again for all your help, and I can assure you you will be very glad you made this visit.

With every good wish, I am

Sincerely,

Wirt A. Yerger, Jr.
Chairman

WAYjr/jc

C O P Y

OLE MISS FALLOUT: Wirt wrote Goldwater after the integration of Ole Miss by James Meredith assuring him that it was politically safe to keep a commitment to speak to a massive GOP gala planned in Jackson. Goldwater kept his commitment. The event gave the state GOP a pivotal push. But Wirt could not convince Goldwater to let the state GOP televise Goldwater's speech.

August 29, 1962

Honorable Robert Wilson
House Office Building
Washington, D. C.

"Conference of Fifty State Chairmen"

Dear Bob:

For some time, a number of people have suggested that the fifty state Republican Chairmen to get together at least annually to exchange ideas and become closer acquainted. Our Southern Association of Republican State Chairmen is taking the initiative in calling for and hosting the first meeting, which will be in Dallas, Texas, December 14. The present plans are to have a social affair in the evening of the 13th, and then have the meeting run all day on the 14th, and conclude that evening with the dinner.

Bill Miller is highly enthusiastic about the meeting, and he suggested that I first write Senator Goldwater to get a date on his calendar and let you and he know when it is so that you could plan to attend. Since we are about settled on the above dates, we certainly hope that you can plan to be with us, as we will want you to have a part on the program. Please advise as soon as you can that you have marked your calender accordingly, and I will keep you posted as plans progress.

The Precinct Education Program, which was developed by your Congressional Committee, is excellent, and we are planning on instituting it throughout the state.

Sincerely,

Wirt A. Yerger, Jr.
State Chairman

FRUSTRATED: By 1962, Wirt felt national leaders seemed to be dismissing the views and input of many GOP state chairmen. He called for a new organization of the fifty state GOP chairmen, a group that would allow them to plan and speak as one. The move also would create more influence for Goldwater's backers among the state chairmen. The resulting national group was begun.

July 23, 1962

Honorable Dwight D. Eisenhower
Gettysburg, Pennsylvania

Your activities during recent weeks have been most discouraging
to quite a few young men in the Republican Party, including myself. First, let me say that I strongly supported you both in
1952 and 1956, and with JFK in the White House I, along with
many others, miss you as our President.

The fact that you were politically naive has been obvious for
quite sometime, and this was borne out by the fact that we lost
every Congressional election while you were President and the
Presidential election after you were through. This record does
not seem to indicate one who is an authority on how to strengthen
the Republican Party.

One of the most shocking things during the past few weeks was
your endorsement of the publication entitled "Advance". If you
have been reading this publication and truly endorse it, then I
am surprised that you still consider yourself a member of the Republican Party, because, in my opinion, the people who edit this
publication to a man belong in the Democrat Party.

One thing which I suggested to you several times to no avail when
you were in office was that you come out into the country, not
just to the big cities, and get more acquainted with your consti-
uents. Perhaps if you had seen fit to do this, and not remained
in a lofty tower for the better part of eight years, the Republican
Party would today be the majority party.

President Eisenhower, my remarks are necessarily blunt, but I assure
you that I still have the greatest respect for you, and I don't
blame on the troubles of the Republican Party on you, but I do
think that you will have to take responsibility for a great many,

and if the statements attributed to you and the actions attributed to you during the past few weeks are indicative of your
feelings now, then perhaps you need to re-examine your position.

Respectfully,

Wirt A. Yerger, Jr., Chairman
Mississippi Republican Party

CRITIQUE: Former U.S. President Dwight Eisenhower was never immune
from critique by Wirt, who wrote Ike several tough letters. Once, Wirt accused
Ike of having a "blind spot."

August 29, 1962

Honorable Dwight D. Eisenhower
Gettysburg, Pennsylvania

Dear General Eisenhower:

This is simply a note to compliment you on the splendid
article that you wrote for the SATURDAY EVENING POST.
Your points were extremely well taken and well developed,
and this is the type of thing that is encouraging to the
Republican Party and to the country.

The only thing that I noticed in the article which I would
take exception to is your chiding President Kennedy on Civil
Rights, but since you always did have a blind spot on this
subject, I wasn't too surprised.

There are still a great number of people in our country
that have the utmost rexpect for you and your opinions,
and I certainly think that it is wise for you to express
yourself as you did in this article.

Respectfully,

Wirt A. Yerger, Jr.
State Chairman

WAY,jr/mas

DDE

GETTYSBURG
PENNSYLVANIA

September 4, 1962

Dear Mr. Yerger:

Thank you very much for your complimentary
note concerning my article in the Saturday
Evening Post.

I got a chuckle out of your comment about
my "blind spot." My only remark is that
I have believed in and respected the Constitution; I have always and shall always support
it.

With very best wishes,

Sincerely,

Dwight Eisenhower

Mr. Wirt A. Yerger, Jr.
State Chairman, Mississippi Republican Party
414 Lamar Life Building
Jackson, Mississippi

Republican candidate Rubel Phillips is a "moderate"
by his own admission.

—Mississippi Democratic Party,
1963

The National Republican Party, including Sen. Barry
Goldwater, is making overtures to Negro voters in all
corners of the nation. This makes it somewhat ridicu-
lous for the fledgling GOP group in Mississippi to at-
tempt to woo Mississippi voters.

—*The Clarion-Ledger* in 1963

It is amazing to note the panic of the State Democratic
Executive Committee over the rapid growth of the Mis-
sissippi Republican Party.

—Wirt Yerger in 1963

The German people were persuaded in 1933 to pledge
their loyalty to the Nazi Party. The Russian people to-
day are pledged to the Communist Party, and now it is
suggested that Mississippians sign a pledge to vote for
a party label, irrespective of the candidate, the issues,
or the platform.

—Rubel Phillips, Mississippi's first
modern GOP gubernatorial
candidate, regarding state
Democrats' call for a loyalty oath

10

1963

OUTLAWING OUR GOP?

"Vote for white conservative unity," one state Democrat ad pleaded in 1963. "Elect all your Mississippi Democratic Party Nominees."

Democrats after the 1962 Ole Miss crisis now preyed on Mississippians' fears merely to keep their vote.

"BURY GOP SCALAWAGS," one 1963 Democrat ad read, derisively comparing state Republicans to post-Civil War federal Reconstructionists.

Democrats were beginning to feel desperate and seemed to care only for keeping power, certainly not for principled politics. A few years later this would be further demonstrated; when faced with having lost much of their voting base to our GOP, their most pragmatic politicians suddenly, miraculously, would change their political convictions, aligning with ultra-liberal forces. This will be detailed in Chapter 12 on 1965.

In 1963 they feared Rubel Phillips, our first GOP gubernatorial candidate. They dug up a 1956 letter in which Rubel, as then-state public service commissioner, said he supported "taking the moderate course in respect to all social legislation" and backed "progressive government."[1]

This proved Rubel was a dangerous man, Democrats claimed: we Republicans were *too moderate*.

In 1963 probably less than five percent of all white Mississippians were full-blown integrationists. In this context, people like Rubel were, in fact, moderate on this hot-button issue, preferring to emphasize a larger positive vision. Democrat state leaders, on the other hand, increasingly spewed almost exclusively their racist rhetoric. Rubel, four years later in 1967, would be the first white state political leader to give the state's first truly farsighted speech on race relations.

Our new conservatism had intellectual and social appeal to rising numbers of college-educated Mississippians, whose numbers were growing. One major magazine in 1963 actually ranked Jackson fourth—behind Cambridge, Massachusetts; Madison, Wisconsin; and Pasadena and Berkeley, California—for most college-educated citizens for its size.[2]

The difference in racial views was naturally shifting by generation. For instance, Mississippi's George Godwin, Jr.'s views were seemingly much different than his father's. Back in the 1960s Godwin, Jr. "was secretly ghostwriting some of Phillips' more 'progressive' material."[3] Bill Wilkins, my former state GOP executive director, only recently told me this. The Godwins operated the state's top ad firm, and George Godwin, Sr., was—as Wilkins states, "very deeply entwined with the old Mississippi Democrat power structure."[4]

• • •

A January 1963 Gallup presidential poll showed Nelson Rockefeller was favored by 46 percent of Republicans and Barry Goldwater by 26 percent.[5] Even the admirable national news commentator Paul Harvey predicted Rockefeller over Goldwater in the 1964 elections the coming year.[6]

James Meredith had just finished his first semester at Ole Miss and was back in Jackson. He told the media he might not return to Ole Miss. But on Jan. 30, Meredith announced he would return in the spring; the Kennedys prodded him to do so.[7]

Rubel, about this time, publicly stated that if he had been governor he would have admitted Meredith.[8] Our first Republican gubernatorial candidate detailed many progressive issues he wished to champion as governor. Among them:

- staffing our state government agencies with professional workers not subject to the whims of a governor's appointment process, thus ensuring quality, trained people;

- bringing more industries to the state;

- revamping worker's compensation to help business growth.[9]

But trying to run a positive, issues-oriented campaign in 1963 was tough because Democrats so viciously played the race card, both in and out of the state.

Gov. Ross Barnett in early 1963 took his show on the road to Harvard, preaching his hyper-segregation stance. State Democrats adored the speech, which drew a Harvard crowd larger than had speeches by Harry S. Truman or Billy Graham.[10]

The Clarion-Ledger warned that "the National Republican Party, including Sen. Barry Goldwater, is making overtures to Negro voters in all corners of the nation. This makes it somewhat ridiculous for the fledgling GOP group in Mississippi to attempt to woo Mississippi voters."[11]

Our internal polling showed that we had some work to do to win over Mississippi voters. In February of 1963 we commissioned Dallas, Texas-based Louis and Bowles Research Consultants, who surveyed 509 Mississippians.[12] This survey showed that:

- "The anti-Kennedy feeling [was] so strong" that it was "inconceivable" "that voters of Mississippi would support the President for reelection."

- Governor Barnett and Lt. Gov. Johnson were "highly regarded," and Eastland and Stennis, even more so due to their supposed stand against the Kennedys.

- The way to state Republican growth was by slow disengagement of voters' current affiliations: "It would be a mistake to assume that voters because they detest the Kennedys are conditioned to line up behind Republican leaders."[13]

Survey data showed that our Republican leaders statewide were little known compared to Democrat state leaders: I was the best-known Republican, with a total awareness rating of 60 percent. Rubel's total awareness rating was 59 percent. By contrast, Barnett's was 100 percent, Paul Johnson's was 98 percent, and William Colmer's was 74 percent.[14]

When Louis and Bowles *conversationally* asked what issues a person thought were most important (versus asking the person to rank the issues numerically from a printed list), respondents prioritized issues in a fashion that may surprise some people today. The list follows:

1. Education: more schools, improve schools —22%
2. Liquor Control: legalize whiskey, solve local option —12%
3. Economy: taxes too high, eliminate waste, etc. —12%
4. Economic Development: more industry, jobs; raise pay —9%
5. Welfare Control: investigate welfare fraud, etc. —9%
6. States' Rights: keep federal government out —7%
7. Segregation: "keep Negroes from mixing with whites" —7%
8. Highways and roads: more and better ones—6%[15]

But when respondents were told to mark on paper "for" or "against" on key words and phrases, their responses broke down as follows:

For	Against	
93%	1%	States' rights
88%	3%	Segregation
87%	2%	Individual freedom
76%	2%	Free enterprise
61%	9%	Less government
58%	10%	Conservative principles
12%	48%	Liberal principles
9%	63%	More government
2%	82%	Socialism
2%	88%	Integration
2%	88%	Federal control[16]

Such clear data meant that I faced a challenge as state GOP chairman to balance our message.

Future Republicans—especially top businessmen such as Jack Reed, then-president of the Mississippi Economic Council—were already calling for citizens to "face up to the fact" that integration was coming and that we all must move forward; meanwhile the Citizens' Council hammered us new Republicans as too moderate, which was a damaging label in our state at that time.[17]

The national GOP gave me nine pages of campaign ideas, including a suggestion to tout a long list of civil rights measures passed under Eisenhower.

Politically and philosophically, however, proliferation of "civil rights" legislation has always troubled me at points.

Politically, we wanted to be a balanced party and not overstate hot-button issues. Already, pundits speculated that the "job [would] be harder" to build a solid GOP in Mississippi than in other states because our state GOP seemed to need to "establish first, that it can offer the South what it wants ... a platform with guarantees against forced integration and encroachment on states' rights."[18]

Philosophically, big federal bills (and all civil rights bills are stuffed with pork) always offer the carrot of increased federal funding in exchange for increased federal control at the state level. Federal funds put you in bed with more and more federal laws and mean a loss of local rule. As for the Kennedys' civil rights laws, they: 1) seemed to coerce states into positions that the states' own voters roundly rejected; 2) seemed blatantly to ignore *de facto* segregation throughout the North, which even Bobby Kennedy admitted was "more subtle, more sinister than in the South"; and, 3) seemed often redundant and unnecessary, if the laws currently on the books were eventually enforced.

Robert and John F. Kennedy actually believed and stated that their spate of new civil rights laws in the early 1960s, almost exclusively, would largely overcome structural racism and accomplish equal treatment of blacks *in just ten more years*, when the reality was and is that even a parent can not overcome a child's stubborn bad behavior in such a brief period. Human nature is not so easily changed. They had admirable qualities, but the Kennedys were young, naive, and brazen. Said Robert in one 1963 interview: "We have to go through that kind of thing [racial strife and racists' opposition] for the next maybe ten years before we are going to have *full equality* (emphasis mine)."[19]

By contrast, the more mature Barry Goldwater and Rubel Phillips kept saying that "full equality" required chiefly heart change, not just the quick stroke of a political pen and the corresponding federal coercion. And, perhaps, had Rubel been elected governor in 1963 and had Barry been elected president in 1964, they could have brought Mississippians along more deliberately and peacefully toward change by moving citizens' hearts to comply with pre-existing laws. But since neither were elected, we will never know. I think that Rubel and Barry believed as I do, that people usually resist high-pitched coercion. Laws may reveal the evil in a heart, and even restrain that evil somewhat, but laws alone will never change a heart, much less cure its resident evil in ten years. As for me, I longed for the day when, as I told one constituent, "the majority of Americans would ... be appealed to as Americans, not as members of a particular class based on income or race."[20]

That was our Republican message. And it was so different from our state Democrat opposition, who demonstrated no desire to look at improving or altering race relations.

For instance, when Ross Barnett in March of 1963 opposed Mississippi State University's basketball team playing integrated or black teams in an upcoming NCAA tournament, Rubel disagreed.[21] Rubel's stand was not as popular with our citizen voters, but it was correct.

One man's response to Rubel was typical: "If your statement is based upon a sincere dictate of your decision, then I grant you the right to so think. You may hold that the question of integration is inevitable, it may be, but I can tell you I am one who will never acquiesce freely.... I had looked forward to casting my first vote for a Republican governor, but since you have shown that you will compromise the mores of our people, all I can say is thank you for so advising before [the] election. Now I can use the dictates of my own conscience and not vote for you."[22]

• • •

Along with Rubel's campaign, I was working on several national fronts in my position as chairman of the Southern Association of Republican State Chairmen.

In March of 1963 in Washington, D.C., our new Republican State Chairmen's Advisory Committee finally convened, culminating all of my 1962 efforts to start a GOP state chairmen's organization. Arkansas State Chairman William L. Spicer congratulated me, saying that the group would "serve as a sounding board for our party and at the same time" let the state chairmen "feel the pulse from all parts of America."[23]

But then, almost instantly, a power-play surfaced among our state chairmen. Texas U.S. Sen. John Tower—already aspiring to run for president, no doubt—tried to gain control of our next meeting of the Southern Association of Republican State Chairmen, of which I was the chairman. Tower tried to change the meeting's time and dates and to have someone other than me elected to moderate.

I quickly wrote the other state chairmen: "Why do we need a Conference Chairman since we are simply having a one-day meeting, and all we need for the meeting that was originally envisioned is a moderator, and this was undoubtedly my responsibility?"[24]

I added: "One luxury Southern Republicans can ill afford is bickering or feuding among ourselves with personal ambitions involved."[25]

While this played out, our state headquarters was running at a breakneck pace. At the start of 1963, we already had $25,000 pledged for Goldwater's 1964 run. Rubel was campaigning hard, and State Sen. Stanford Morse had announced his Republican candidacy for Lt. Governor, switching from the Democratic Party.[26]

There was a sense of great momentum for us. I. Lee Potter at the GOP national office felt we had "an excellent chance to win the governorship in Mississippi this year."[27]

And, then, a major breakthrough occurred.

Finally, in a February 1963 special election, L.L. (Mack) McAllister—chairman of our Mississippi Young Republicans—defeated his Democrat opponent 3,066 to 2,298 to win a seat in our state legislature representing the Meridian area.[28] *He became our first elected Republican state legislator in modern history.*

Mack would eventually win a full term in the ensuing regular election in November.[29] "This ... is the key which frees the people of Mississippi from the imprisoning walls of one-party politics," I told the media.[30]

Panic-stricken, Ross Barnett literally asked the state legislature to create a law ensuring that Mississippi would remain a one-party state; his successor as governor, Paul Johnson, would make an even bolder attempt at this in 1964![31]

I hammered Barnett, saying this was an "attempt to completely deprive the people of this state of their freedom of choice at the ballot box. Some Mississippi politicians apparently see the power they once wielded about to slip from their selfish grasp and are growing desperate."[32]

Barnett's actions simply reflected the underlying realities in our state. Democrats publicly bragged they could and would overrule Mississippians' popular vote if it went for Rubel, since they controlled all of the state's county electors. When we challenged them on this, even *The Clarion-Ledger* said our protests "may be well-founded."[33]

Mississippi governors were bound to one term in the 1960s, so Lt. Gov. Paul Johnson in mid-April declared his candidacy to succeed Barnett as governor. Immediately, Johnson made his position clear regarding a second party: he would oppose allowing a second party, he said, adding that any second party "would put a minority bloc of Negro voters in the position of holding the balance of power, and they could influence elections from supervisor to governor."[34]

One man told me at the time that "Paul is obviously out for power and plunder," adding, "Any person with responsible intelligence should be able to see this. We are not interested in any ... dictator nor ... a police state."[35] Of course, my feeling continued to be: as a democracy, let all citizens vote and compete. The best ideas would win.

Rubel and Stanford Morse were speaking and meeting with citizens all over the state. Rubel hit every county, and most more than once. Some funny things can occur in politics; you can get some pretty petty complaints. One Indianola banker told me Rubel had a "fishy handshake," adding, "personally, I recommend that he shake hands firmly."[36] Such was the minutia of politics. "It is a little thing," I replied to the banker, "but it is the type of thing that can make a whale of a difference."[37]

The fact was that Rubel made a great speech and impression. Our candidates were consistently sharp.

• • •

By the spring of 1963, Bidwell Adam had cooled off from the previous year's Meredith incident and he remained state Democrat chairman.

Now, like Barnett, he tried his own political trick. He declared that any Mississippian voting in the coming gubernatorial Democrat primary in August (which was virtually everyone who voted) must swear a loyalty oath that they would also vote for the Democrat nominee in November's general election.

I quickly countered that Bidwell's edict "smacks of dictatorship tactics and it is against the American ideal of freedom of choice," adding, "It is strange that this is the group that fought against the National Democratic Party's loyalty oath in 1956 and 1960. ... It is amazing to note the panic of the State Democratic Executive Committee over the rapid growth of the Mississippi Republican Party."[38]

At a Tupelo Lion's Club gathering, Rubel criticized Bidwell's loyalty oath as "a rank insult to the intelligence and integrity of the people who have the legal right and moral duty to vote their convictions on a secret ballot. The German people were persuaded in 1933 to pledge their loyalty to the Nazi Party. The Russian people today are pledged to the Communist Party, and now it is suggested that Mississippians sign a pledge to vote for a party label, irrespective of the candidate, the issues, or the platform."[39]

Newsweek magazine on May 13 wrote an article about our state GOP efforts, citing our rise and the Democrats' sad tactics. It stated:

> The most important political event of 1963 is likely to be the statewide election in Mississippi. Its results may well cast light upon what may happen in 1964 in the nation. A new governor and a legislature are to be elected, and a new and vigorous Republican Party is in the field to capture both the governorship and a considerable number of legislative seats. No one could have dreamed until now that Mississippi, deep in the Deep South and treasuring rich Confederate memories, might be the first real Southern state to elect a Republican governor.
>
> Until very recently, the leaders of the Republican Party in most of the Southern states were political hacks,

little respected in their communities. ... The Republican leaders I have met in this extended tour of the South are young, respected citizens more interested in creating a strong Republican Party than in anything they may get personally.

Leading the Republican Party in Mississippi are Wirt Yerger Jr., 34-year-old state chairman and an insurance executive; national committeeman Fred LaRue, a successful businessman who is 34; and Rubel Phillips, candidate for governor. He is 38. Charles Klumb, state finance chairman, is 35.

The state Republican committee has had a full-time staff at headquarters in Jackson for four years. Its published material is lively and attractive. Phillips and Yerger have been campaigning over the state and meeting enthusiastic crowds. Their appeal is for a genuine two-party system, with Republicanism dedicated to principles of conservatism—limited Federal government, sound money, economy, private enterprise, and local self-determination.

Since all candidates of both parties are against school integration, this is not an issue in the campaign. And since most of the more vocal segregationist are firmly Democratic, the Republicans permit that problem to stay in the Democratic Party.[40]

• • •

As if Mississippians did not live amid enough turmoil, the added frenetic pace of racial change that our citizens faced remained impossible to process or absorb. Most Mississippians simply had to work and raise families and meet countless other obligations, while this epic, complex, drama swirled around them.

In Birmingham, Alabama, in May a jailed Martin Luther King, Jr., led protests, facing barking police dogs and the debilitating spray of fire hoses.[41] By late May, 3,000 federal troops quartered near Birmingham, and Governor George Wallace protested to the Supreme Court.[42]

Soon, the first two blacks entered the University of Alabama; Gov. George Wallace made a belligerent show, then backed down before 100 federal troops with M-1 rifles.[43]

Black protestors in Jackson issued demands, claiming to represent the city's 50,000 blacks. Demands included black police officers and a biracial panel to discuss desegregating eating facilities and drug stores, as well as public schools. They met with Mayor Allen Thompson, who told them, "I ... want to hear your ideas ... to improve the climate of understanding and goodwill which will best ensure ... making Jackson a better community." The black leaders told the mayor, "We know the Negro community as you probably do not," adding 75 percent of the city's blacks would back any action they called for.[44]

The next day, after 500 blacks rallied at a local church, whites and blacks conducted a sit-in at the local Woolworth's; a Walgreen's closed "for public safety." NAACP officials, including Medgar Evers, said many pickets were planned; skirmishes were reported.[45] A day later, May 30, 19 people were jailed.[46] Mayor Thompson repeated requests for peaceful talks.

The NAACP asked the Kennedys for federal troops in Jackson as protection; the mayor said it was outside "agitators" who were creating the problems.[47]

On June 12, a twisted ex-marine living in Greenwood, Mississippi snuck through a honeysuckle thicket, raised his bolt-action .30-caliber rifle, and murdered Medgar Evers.

Immediately, police, city leaders, and the *Jackson Daily News* pooled more than $22,350 in reward money for his capture.[48] Martin Luther King, Jr., NAACP national secretary Roy Wilkins, Chicago comedian-turned-activist Dick Gregory, and scores more top black leaders joined thousands at Evers' June 15 funeral in Jackson.[49]

A week later, Byron De La Beckwith, a lifelong loser of a man and a California native, was arrested in Greenwood for Evers' murder.[50] Eleven days later, De La Beckwith was indicted.[51]

On July 14, 41 percent of Americans said integration efforts now were moving "too fast," compared with 14 percent saying "not fast enough" and 31 percent saying "about right," according to a Gallup poll. "President Kennedy's civil rights stand has caused many Negroes and white Southerners to revise their thinking about the Administration's integration time-table," Gallup reported. Among blacks polled concerning the issue, the number saying integration was going "not fast enough" was dropping, from 46 to 34 percent.[52]

On July 23, the last 250 federal troops finally began leaving Ole Miss.[53] A day later, Martin Luther King, Jr., admitted that a New York man working as a staff employee for Southern Christian Leadership Conference was a Communist; a special U.S. Senate investigative committee called him a Communist "zealot."[54]

John Kennedy told media on Aug. 1 that continually applying his civil rights pressure probably hurt him politically, but he felt he "must meet his responsibility."[55] On Sunday, Aug. 18, James Meredith walked the aisle and received his college degree at Ole Miss.[56] Ten days later King gave his famous "I Have a Dream" speech before an estimated 200,000 marchers in Washington, D.C.[57] Three weeks later, four black girls were killed when a bomb exploded in a Birmingham church.[58]

• • •

It had been a tempestuous summer for all Mississippians. We in the state GOP had tried to stay focused on our central message.

Former governor J.P. Coleman and Delta politician Charles Sullivan had eventually announced as candidates challenging Paul Johnson for the nomination as the Democrat gubernatorial candidate. Starting in June, the three began attacking one another, with their language becoming more extreme as their August Democrat primary approached.

None were happy that, eventually, their winner would have to face our Republican candidate, Rubel Phillips, in November. "Democrats in Mississippi ... have a new problem this year," said one Democrat political commentator. "… A new kind of Mississippi politics is at hand."[59]

Rubel kept the three Democrat candidates somewhat honest.

For instance, before the Mississippi Education Association, Sullivan and Coleman had little of substance to say. Rubel, however, was specific and appealing. He told the crowd that he was "the only ex-school teacher running for governor"; his mother taught for 33 years; his four brothers, his wife, and his in-laws were teachers; he promised to find more money for teacher salaries; he opposed using the National Teacher Examination to decide pay raises, favoring "incentive increases"; he wanted more technical and vocational training; he called for a state lay-board of education.[60]

Paul Johnson?

He merely promised the teachers' association that he would "do all that is within my power to aid education." No specifics.[61]

Observers saw a difference in our Republican candidate. One writer noted:

> Republican Phillips, a mild-mannered individual with a "sockem and rockem" platform that would revamp a large segment of government operations, may be able to saddle up alongside his Democratic counterparts until the first primary is over. … Phillips could come in for some mighty roasting from Democrats, even though only one of the three now campaigning could run in the finals. … Phillips, as a Republican, won't be running in the Democratic Primary, but he will be around and perhaps to be reckoned with.[62]

In stark contrast to the tepid positions taken by his Democrat rivals, Rubel told voters that our state had "more agencies per capita … than the federal government. We have more state employees per capita than the federal government," adding, "too often a new governor finds he's got more friends than he has jobs." He advocated a simple system to reduce state employees by attrition. "I hope nobody who votes for me is expecting a state job, because there won't be any."[63]

Whenever Paul Johnson spoke, it was front-page news. Rubel's news was mostly buried in the back of papers. On July 5, a full month before the Democrat primary, a front-page *Clarion-Ledger* editorial endorsed Johnson for governor, applauding his stand at Ole Miss as exemplary. "A vote for Johnson is a vote for continued battling against the forces seeking to oppress us."[64]

On primary day, Aug. 6, Johnson was thrown into a run-off with J.P. Coleman, whom Johnson began mercilessly to attack as being too moderate. Coleman fought back, running an ad that detailed revelations that Paul Johnson and Ross Barnett had cut a deal over the phone with John F. Kennedy to let Meredith enter Ole Miss.[65] "Everybody knows my opponent talked five different times to Bobby Kennedy," Coleman told crowds. He challenged Johnson to "tell the people what he told the Kennedys."[66]

But Johnson just kept blasting Coleman as a Kennedy supporter. On Aug. 27, Paul Johnson beat Coleman, and our Republican forces now had our November opponent.

• • •

Throughout the whole state Democrat primary, I also was leading Goldwater's efforts in Mississippi *and* the South.

In the spring of 1963, Goldwater had opened the door to a possible 1964 presidential run. Our "Draft Goldwater Movement," which had been conceived by our Minnesota group, already had raised $3.2 million nationally; Barry was generally cooperating with us, though he kept insisting that he was not our man.[67]

CBS ran a three-part special, "CBS Reports ... Barry Goldwater—The View from the Right." It portrayed Barry as a businessman, a politician, and an "itinerant philosopher."[68] A day later, a March 9 Gallup poll said Goldwater had risen to a 44 percent favorable status with voters, while Rockefeller was at 45 percent, a big shift.[69]

By April, Barry announced that he no longer opposed our persistent draft campaign.[70] Barry's favorability numbers kept rising in May.

My predictable foil, Bidwell Adam, wrote to me that Barry was my "golden idol." Adam continued: "It has been said that you can dish the political mustard," Bidwell told me. "I am wondering whether you can take it."[71] I told Bidwell to read Barry's book, *The Conscience of a Conservative*. "Incidentally," I jabbed, "We appreciate your statements more than you know."[72]

On top of involvement with Rubel's and Barry's campaigns, I was engaged in a number of GOP national events.

- Our Republican State Chairmen's Advisory Committee met on June 20 in Denver.[73] Enthusiasm for Barry ran very high.

- The Young Republicans national convention in San Francisco was wowed by Goldwater. "Modern liberalism is only a form of rigor mortis," Barry said, "The old, respectable, and sometimes noble liberalism of 50 years ago is gone for good. The young people of this nation are looking to the Republican Party."[74] In a presidential preference poll among delegates, Barry defeated Rockefeller 320 to 40.[75] One commentator said, "If those who were here [at the convention] are really the future hope of the GOP, it's going to be quite a party."[76]

Liberal Republicans had "controlled every modern party convention," but they were now "frantic."[77]

By mid-July, Rockefeller was firing away, saying a Goldwater nomination would "not only defeat the Republican Party in 1964, but would destroy it altogether"; he said that sincere conservatives in the party were a "lunatic fringe."[78]

But Barry saw that we youthful Republicans were different from the old-line, Northeastern deal cutters. Paul Harvey said we thought "in terms of political philosophy instead of opportunism."[79]

By late August, Barry polled at 30 percent to Rockefeller's 22 percent.[80] Another August poll showed Goldwater defeating Kennedy among Southern voters by a 54-to-33 percent margin.[81]

This was good for our GOP candidates in Mississippi. It gave us some much-needed help as we now faced Paul Johnson in September and October leading up to the November general election.

• • •

Besides Rubel for governor and Morse for lieutenant governor, we Mississippi Republicans had 22 candidates running for the state legislature.[82] And as part of our election strategy, we developed our "magic number" program to let every GOP county chairman know how many votes he needed to pick up for us to secure victory.[83]

Charles Klumb was doing great work with our fundraising. In early August, key Republican leaders helped Klumb develop a list of people in each county able to give $1,000 to the campaign. Rubel planned to visit each man. "Time is rapidly running out," Klumb said, "and we are a long way from our objective."[84]

We were as ready as we could be. My old friend, John Grenier, Alabama state GOP chairman, bid us well. "Wirt," he said, "Go get 'em and give us Johnson's head on a platter!"[85]

Our county precinct leaders were our best hope against Paul Johnson. One rural woman described well the challenge we faced. "When you get out to the backwoods, with the dirt roads and pickup trucks, ... these are the people who really hold the balance of power in Mississippi, and they vote Democratic because their daddies voted Democratic and <u>they</u> did because their <u>daddies</u> did (original emphases)."[86]

Johnson quickly rallied his forces against us. The Mississippi Association of Supervisors completely backed him, saying we were "trying to sell a fairy tale to the people of Mississippi" and would "destroy our traditional, time-tested and honored heritage and principles."[87] The Mississippi Municipal Association endorsed Johnson and every other Democrat candidate in Mississippi, saying we Republicans were trying "to make a place for themselves in Mississippi politics" and would "destroy the unity of our white conservative majority." Johnson told the MMA that a two-party system "would mean more social equality" for blacks and increased minority voting.[88]

Meanwhile, Johnson avoided appearing on stage with Rubel.

As the campaign wrapped up, we tried to hit every county. Rubel later regretted that. He told me he "thought we should have concentrated those outings on about 10 key rallies, rather than trying to hit almost all the counties. That might have left more time for 'handshaking tours'."[89] In reflection, Bill Wilkins said we never took "off the gloves" against the Democrats.[90] All year long, I had urged Rubel to stress the importance of a two-party system. Rubel told me after the race that he should have listened to me on that. "You advocated for this yourself," he told me, "and at the time I did not agree with you. We found ourselves on the defensive regarding the need for a two-party system and this would not have happened if we had made it one of our principal issues."[91]

As the campaign wound down, I sent Rubel tactical ideas. The following Sept. 19 memo is exemplary:

"CAMPAIGN TACTICS"

1. ... I would suggest a statement emphasizing that a sizable percentage of local officials who have all been elected as Democrats are wholeheartedly supporting us because they feel that what we advocate is best for their state, and I have no fear of a two-party system because they are doing a splendid job and will be reelected as long as they continue to do a good job.

2. ... Point out the absolute untruths that are contained in [Johnson's] smear literature.

3. Continue to emphasize over and over and over again that the Kennedys are pulling for the election of Paul Johnson and [Democratic Lt. Gov. nominee] Gartin because of the great slap in the face they would receive nationally if Mississippi did not elect the Kennedy-crat candidates. Incidentally, I would suggest that we start calling those who place the Democratic Party ahead of their principles, and consequently their state and their country, "Kennedy-crats."

4. Let us continue to attack the one-party system as having elected Kennedy, and let us point out the fact that due to the one-party system, our state is 50th among all 50 states in the Union in per-capita income and 12th among all 12 Southern states. We could stress here Senator Barry Goldwater's statement that in Arizona, both Democrats and Republicans agree that the greatest single factor in the rapid growth in recent years in the State of Arizona has been the development of the two-party system, and Arizona is the fastest growing state in the United States.

Also, in attacking the one-party system, we need to emphasize that these advocates of the one-party system are tampering with a precious American freedom—that of freedom of choice, and consequently, the issue is whether we have a monopolistic and dictatorial one-party system, such as in Cuba and Russia, or whether we have competition, which is good not only for business but also for politics.

5. ... Emphasize that the last [Democrat] fund raising dinner ... was in 1958, and the speaker was none other than Senator John F. Kennedy. They gave him a royal reception.

6. Ross Barnett should be properly blasted for waiting 3½ years to close up gambling on the [Gulf] Coast and never even making an effort to enforce prohibition, which is still allowed in our state.

7. If John F. Kennedy is to be defeated in 1964, he will be defeated by united conservatives working together, not by conservatives who are divided.

8. The University of Southern Mississippi, in comparison with all Mississippi state universities, has come up on the short end of the stick in appropriations, and since this is now the largest state university, I suggest that we might emphasize the fact that they should be entitled to a much larger percentage of what is allocated.[92]

But for all our efforts and every piece of ground we took, the Democrat machine most often took it back. On the night of Oct. 8, Paul Johnson played the ace card in his hand. He staged rallies in every Mississippi county on the same night. His cronies attacked Republicans for presenting a "serious assault on our traditional political system."[93]

I sent out local Republicans to monitor each county and write a report to me. I told them "the press is so prone to distort the facts," so they should take good notes.[94]

What follows are firsthand accounts from that night; they were turned into me from our people in the field. They paint a sad picture of what the old Democrats were like.

- "I attended the so-called Victory Rally at the Pearl River County Court House in Poplarville last night. There were between 50 and 60 persons present. ... I got the impression that the Johnson people were disappointed in the attendance. ... There seemed to be very little interest by the general public. ... Boyce Holleman, district attorney from Wiggins, Miss. and Roy Strickland, county representative from Stone County, were the principle (sic) speakers. ... Holleman spoke primarily about the Republican Party in Mississippi 100 years ago. ... Holleman, also of course, brought up the discredited contention that a two-party system would split the white conservative vote and leave the balance of power in the hands of the negro (sic) minority. Apparently, their entire campaign will be waged on this theme."[95]

- A Mrs. Mitchell, an office manager in Cleveland, was dispatched by Lowry Tims, president of Lowry Tims Company in Cleveland. She wrote: "J.C. Feduccia ... [made] a few remarks relative to the one-party system—the Democratic Party Mississippi. He stated that all Mississippians are one as far as preserving 'our way of life' is concerned. He touched on the regret that there might be too much apathy on the part of some of the Democrats of Mississippi. He then introduced Judge Ed Green. Judge Green elaborated on the benefits from the one-party system, and brought out the things that occurred in our state during the reign of the Republicans just after the Civil War—how Negroes served in a higher post of our state government, etc. Judge Green [said] the 1960 Republican platform ... boasts of the progress the Republicans had made in civil rights—more progress in the last four years than in the 80 years before that—and that the Republican Party would continue to do everything possible to [make sure] all people have the same privileges. ... The Mississippi Republican Party <u>has not divorced the national Republican Party</u> (original emphasis). But, Democratic Party of Mississippi has divorced the national Democratic Party, and is aloof and alone. We will not have to vote for the Democratic nominee of the national Democratic Party. There have been questions about the nomination of the Republican candidate. I do not know whether he was nominated or not, but I do know the political boss of that party, Wirt Yerger, approved him. The Republican Party of Mississippi reminds me of the little boy with a small fish in one hand and knife in the other, telling little fish, "Be still, be still, I am not going to hurt you, just cut you in two."[96]

- From Marshall County: "The same issues were discussed—splitting the White Majority, and the Republican Party being the Negro's party."[97]

- From Washington County Court House Rally on Oct. 8, 1963. "... Phillips has been railroaded into this race by the Republican boss Wirt Yerger of Jackson. Several years ago there was some talk about Phillips running in the Democratic primary this year. He apparently went around the state looking for some support of his ambitions and failing to get it made a deal with Yerger. ... About this fellow, Yerger. During the last national convention, he went out to San Francisco as a "Lily-White' delegate, but had to accept the convention's decree that half of the Mississippi delegation had to be black. So we had the disgraceful picture on television of Wirt Yerger making up part of the black-and-white delegation from our state. ... A 2-party system is the worst thing that could happen to us in Mississippi. ... take for instance New York State. There the regular Democrats and Republicans are pretty evenly balanced numerically. The balance of power is held by the Negro-Liberal party. ... Because of the large Negro population here in Mississippi, this would surely become the case here, and the way would go all of our cherished institutions, such as segregated skills, public accommodations and transportation, states' rights and all the rest. For these reasons, we must bury Republicanism once and for all, and so deeply, that our way of life will be preserved for the next hundred years."[98]

Under such attacks, Rubel started highlighting Johnson's part in the hypocritical show at Ole Miss with Meredith. "Tell the people about [your] secret deal," Rubel challenged Johnson during a speech in Booneville.[99] Sadly, most state newspapers showed little or no interest getting to the truth of this matter.

But then a *Newsweek* article published excerpts from phone conversations between Ross Barnett and the President. "*Newsweek* hasn't told you the half of it," Rubel claimed to Mississippians.[100] Said Rubel: "At the very moment your Lieutenant Governor was having a rooster fight with U.S.

Marshals at Ole Miss ... he had already made a deal with Bobby Kennedy."[101]

Johnson was upset. "Bobby has been leaking information!" he said. And Johnson, with the help of some press, managed to somewhat turn the issue around to his political advantage, saying it proved "Kennedy would rather see a Republican elected governor of Mississippi than Paul Johnson."[102] Johnson kept attacking. His cronies went to war for him, as well, citing another *Newsweek* article saying that Nixon was sure "the Republican Party does not have a segregation wing. Sen. Goldwater is not a segregationist."[103]

The Democrats' racist rants poured forth daily now and the state's top papers published them. Rubel finally challenged *The Clarion-Ledger*: "You have never seen anything unfavorable printed in that Jackson newspaper against the [Barnett-Johnson] administration. You haven't and you won't."[104]

But the campaign was nearly finished. The damage was done.

Johnson, feeling confident, began promising that Democrats would never have to worry again about facing a Republican in a general primary. Said Johnson: "I know it is distasteful to have this campaign strung out to extreme lengths and I promise you, when the legislature meets in January, the laws will be changed so that it will never happen again."[105]

In America. ...

In 1963. ...

We were about to elect this man to our state's highest office.

Johnson continued his irreverence. He said that "Squirt Yerger" had chosen Rubel Phillips to run for governor to avoid a Republican primary.[106]

Two days before the election, I appealed to the people of Mississippi.

> "The question is not whether or not we have a two-party system because we've got one now. ... [The] Johnson

machine is trying to sell the people of Mississippi the greatest propaganda snow-job ever perpetrated on a free people."[107]

I continued: "Because of the two-party system, the people of Mississippi know what they didn't know in August and that is that our state can ill afford to trust as governor a man who has secretly betrayed the people of his own state."[108]

On Nov. 5, 1963, Mississippi voters turned out in large numbers as Johnson won what Bidwell Adam called an "electrocution."[109]

Johnson took right at 60 percent of the vote.

The Clarion-Ledger editorialized that voters were saying "there was no excuse for a second party in Mississippi. ... It would be a dangerous and devastating plan in our state."[110] The state had bought Johnson's bill of goods. But we Republicans had taken about 40 percent of the popular vote. We were a serious force now. And over in Meridian, Mack McAllister won a full term in the state legislature in the general election—another first for us.

In a statement to the people of Mississippi, I reminded everyone that only four years prior, in the 1959 general election, not a single Republican was on the ballot.[111] Therefore, the 1963 election was "a giant step forward for conservatives" towards a "competitive two-party system ... that has been talked about for years but is now a reality in Mississippi'."[112]

Today, we all owe a great debt to Rubel. Only six percent of Mississippians in 1963 said that they actually were Republicans, yet Rubel received about 40 percent of the vote. If he had not switched to the Republican Party, I believe he could have been, and likely would have been, elected governor as a Democrat.

• • •

All during Rubel's campaign, I also had been launching our state's "Draft Goldwater" drive. We were seeking 50,000 signatures on petitions to urge Barry to run for the 1964 Republican presidential nomination. I told the media our goal was "to mobilize the tremendous grass-roots support that is being evidenced in Senator Goldwater's behalf."[113] "He is the only man who can beat John F. Kennedy in 1964," I claimed.[114]

In the fall, Barry had begun a 10-state tour, speaking and building conservative constituency.[115] "We must offer the chance for sound policies here and at home and for freedom around the world," he told an Oklahoma crowd. "... We want real Republican voices and choices. ... Those who would put chains on that choice do not serve Republican principles."[116]

Barry's message was so powerful. It was drawing all kinds of people to his side. A radio man in Jackson, Lew Heilbroner, general manager of WJQS, could not support Barry publicly, but he wanted to: "There is no doubt in my mind that this great American is the only salvation this country has for its future, and if he is not nominated and elected, we have a dark future ahead of us."[117]

As Goldwater traveled the country, he clarified for any who would listen (and, of course, most liberals, especially Northern Democrats and Republicans, simply were never going to try) the reality of what we Republicans in the South were doing. He told the Oklahoma audience:

> I say to you that the South today, with its growing restiveness over radical Democrat economic policies, offers the Republican party one of its most important political advantages in many decades. Those who believe that Republicans in the South are somehow mysteriously tied to racism ignore the obvious facts.
>
> They ignore the fact that Republican influence in the South is growing in direct proportion to the South's moderation on the race issue. They ignore the fact that Republican strength in the South is located in the cities and urban areas where a new view is emerging, while Democratic strength is more and more being confined to the rural communities where the race issue has undergone little change.

> ... I disagree with people who insist that we must forget all about the Negro vote, and that we might as well concede the labor vote. ... I [am not] willing to accept the premise that segregation is the great delineation between the parties. Far more important than the race issue to most Southerners has been federal encroachment on local government, the curtailment of individual liberties, growing federal control of just about everything.[118]

Goldwater had described what those of us who had founded the modern Mississippi Republican Party believed. This was who we were.

By early October, Barry had increased his lead in the polls over Rockefeller, jumping from 38-percent to 42-percent voter strength, compared to Rockefeller's 29- to 26-percent drop.[119] Even liberal, Pulitzer Prize-winning Greenville newspaperman Hodding Carter was saying Barry would probably take nine out of 11 Southern states if he ran.[120] A surprise to some, Barry (48%) polled close to Kennedy (52%) for the female vote.[121]

• • •

John F. Kennedy had planned a three-day visit to try to patch up some perceived splits in the Democratic Party in Texas, no doubt caused in part by Barry's rising popularity.

Apples were 10 for 39 cents; Thanksgiving turkeys, 29 cents-per-pound. In football, Oklahoma was picked to beat Nebraska, 24-20; and Harvard to top Yale 10-0. Hopalong Cassady had just re-signed with the Detroit Lions; John Wayne's *McLintock!* was being called "magnificent." And national broadcaster Paul Harvey predicted that "for the first time in thirty years," Americans "could have an opportunity to choose [in 1964] between two divergent views on national and international affairs. A confrontation between Kennedy and Goldwater could separate the issues and inspire the electorate."[122]

And then the Nov. 22 bulletin scorched every Americans' TV ...

John F. Kennedy had been assassinated by a sniper's bullet in Dallas.

Many of us gathered that terrible day in a downtown barber shop that had a TV. I soon went straight out and bought a TV for Ross & Yerger Agency and told Bill Wilkins to buy a TV for our GOP office; I felt we needed to be able to get news as quickly as we could.

Lyndon Johnson was immediately sworn in as President of the United States aboard Air Force One.

Suddenly, old rivals were stricken with grief.

"I am profoundly shocked and grieved," Ross Barnett said. "... It was indeed a wicked and cowardly act. ... President Kennedy was a man of great ability, a man of courage, and one who had the courage of his convictions."[123]

The Clarion-Ledger ran a political cartoon of a distraught Uncle Sam on his knees, hands clasped in prayer. Its caption read, "Seeking Guidance."[124]

• • •

We all were shaken.

Barry personally liked Kennedy very much. And now, more than ever, Barry was unsure whether to run in 1964.

As time passed, we had to pick back up our campaign plans. Now, however, we faced uncertain opposition. Some thought Robert Kennedy would run. Everyone felt Lyndon Johnson would run for a full four-year term in 1964. "I have talked with a number of Southern leaders who feel that Lyndon Johnson, with a Southern accent, could make a speech for which Bobby would be matched, and still get the votes of many Southern Democrats," said Rep. Robert E. Bradford (R-Va.) in a letter to me. "... The Senator [Goldwater] himself is undergoing an agonizing reappraisal in view of the events of the past few weeks."[125]

The pundits said that Lyndon Johnson would be much harder for us to beat, with his Texas-Southern roots.

"Any suggestion that the South will be in the bag for the

ultra-liberal Lyndon Johnson in 1964 presidential election is an insult to the integrity of Southern voters," I announced through the media. "The average Southerner is a conservative and places principle and the good of his country first. Johnson, an ardent left-winger, has consistently denied that he is a Southerner, but even if he were, this would not mean he could count on the South's support."

I continued: "... We have complete confidence in the integrity of the Republican Party leadership and feel in 1964 the national convention will express the honest convictions of the majority of the party and the choice of nominees and platform. This is the purpose of the convention."[126]

So much rested on next year's Republican National Convention.

So much now rested on Barry Goldwater's shoulders.

GOLD RUSH: Wirt rallied Mississippi's GOP, holding planning sessions (top) that led to the massive Goldwater Dinner (below), which put Mississippi squarely in Goldwater's camp for good.

February, 1964   CONSERVATIVE CHALLENGE

GOLDWATER DINNER SCENE — Part of the crowd is shown at the "Go Goldwater" dinner held in the Olympic Room of the Heidelberg Hotel Jan. 29. Gov. Henry Bellmon of Oklahoma stood under a huge picture of Sen. Goldwater to deliver a speech which was frequently interrupted by applause. Seated at the table with him were State Chairman Wirt Yerger, Jr.; 1963 GOP gubernatorial candidate Rubel Phillips, who served as dinner chairman; National Committeeman Fred LaRue; Dr. James Moye of Laurel, who served as master of ceremonies and other top fuctionaries of the party.

REPUBLICAN STATE CHAIRMEN'S CONFERENCE
Denver, Colo., June 20, 1963

REPUBLICAN SURGE, NOT BURIAL: Top, Wirt's influence grew among GOP state chairmen. Bottom, Miss. Gov. Paul Johnson's campaign literature called for citizens to "bury Republicanism in Mississippi from now until the year 2,000, at least!"

"Two Party" Pay-off...

Los Angeles, California-(Associated Press Report)

Amelia M. Tucker, the first Negro woman elected to the Kentucky State Legislature, said here Friday (Sept. 13) "the Negro will not be politically liberated in the South unless the Republican party is strengthened to give the area a two-party system."

THE BEST DEFENSE FOR OUR WAY OF LIFE IS UNITY OF THE WHITE CONSERVATIVE MAJORITY UNDER MISSISSIPPI DEMOCRATIC LEADERSHIP

Yes, you can see the pay-off of the "two party system" in such states as Kentucky, Michigan, Pennsylvania, California, New York, etc. . . . where two parties bid for the votes of an organized minority. The organized minority, holding the "balance of power", wields influence out of all proportion to its numbers. And conservative citizens —still a majority in America—see their cities scarred by crime, their development stymied by socialist schemes and high taxes, their governments infiltrated by alien ideologies.

This is the kind of two-party system these so-called "Republicans" seek to establish in Mississippi.

Your defense against Mississippi's handful of Republicans and the possibility of a growing Negro vote is the continued unity of our white conservative majority.

As long as one party controls all of the governmental machinery within Mississippi, and as long as that party is dominated by loyal, white, conservative Mississippians, you and your loved ones and your way of life are as safe as they can be in this troubled world.

The Mississippi Democratic Party, "segregated" from both national parties and solely an instrument of the citizens of this State, now is safely in the hands of the conservative, responsible majority of Mississippi voters.

The unity of this majority is reflected by the solid support accorded the Mississippi Democratic nominees by the municipal, beat, county, district and state officials which YOU have elected.

Back up the public officials you have elected. Eliminate once and for all the two-party threat. Help get out the biggest vote in Mississippi history November 5 . . . and bury the Republicans under such an avalanche of ballots it will take them another 100 years to dig out!

VOTE NOVEMBER 5 FOR WHITE CONSERVATIVE UNITY

ELECT ALL OF YOUR MISSISSIPPI DEMOCRATIC NOMINEES .

under the leadership of

PAUL B. JOHNSON for Governor
CARROL GARTIN for Lt. Governor

(approved by Gene Triggs, Campaign Manager)

TWO PARTIES vs. "OUR WAY OF LIFE:" Old-line Miss. Democrats constantly said state Republicans endangered white Mississippians' "way of life," a veiled reference to Democrats' hyper-segregationist platform.

HAD ENOUGH?

Go Republican!

MISSISSIPPI REPUBLICANS
STAND FOR:

★ STATES' RIGHTS
★ FREE ENTERPRISE
★ ECONOMIC PROGRESS
★ RESPONSIBLE GOVERNMENT

MISSISSIPPI REPUBLICANS
ARE WORKING FOR:

★ REMOVAL OF KENNEDYS
★ RESTORED CONSTITUTIONAL
   GOVERNMENT
★ POSITIVE ACTION TOWARD CUBA
★ GOLDWATER FOR PRESIDENT

HOW DO YOU STAND?

It's time for Mississippians to stand up and be counted! Get the facts on how you can help restore Constitutional government to our state and nation. Complete and mail the coupon below today!

WIRT A. YERGER, JR., Chairman
MISSISSIPPI REPUBLICAN PARTY
414 LAMAR LIFE BUILDING   PHONE
JACKSON, MISSISSIPPI   FL 4-5719

Without obligation, send me information about the Republican Party in Mississippi.

NAME

ADDRESS

TOWN

● CLIP AND MAIL ●

FIGHTING BACK: Faced with Miss. Gov. Paul Johnson's attempt to outlaw the state GOP, Wirt and his Republican's fought back.

LAST MINUTE CALL FOR HELP

JACKSON, MISSISSIPPI

DEAR FELLOW MISSISSIPPIAN:

PAUL JOHNSON'S LEGISLATION DESIGNED TO ABOLISH THE MISSISSIPPI REPUBLICAN PARTY GOES FAR BEYOND THAT AIM BY **ACTUALLY ELIMINATING THE GENERAL ELECTION** THROUGH MAKING IT NEARLY IMPOSSIBLE FOR ANYONE OTHER THAN A DEMOCRAT TO EVEN GET HIS NAME ON THE BALLOT. WE KNOW THAT YOU ARE A MISSISSIPPIAN WHO HAS SUPPORTED THE CAUSE OF INDIVIDUAL FREEDOM AND STATES RIGHTS IN THE PAST. THIS IS WHY THIS EMERGENCY APPEAL IS ADDRESSED TO YOU. IF THE PEOPLE OF MISSISSIPPI ARE PROPERLY INFORMED ABOUT THIS VICIOUS LEGISLATION AND FULLY AWARE OF ITS **POLICE STATE CONSEQUENCES** IT WILL EITHER BE DEFEATED BY THE PUBLIC PRESSURE GENERATED OR THE INDIGNATION OF FREEDOM LOVING MISSISSIPPIANS WILL INFLUENCE THEM TO RISE UP AS NEVER BEFORE TO ASSURE THE DEFEAT OF THOSE WHO WOULD SNATCH AWAY OUR PERSONAL FREEDOM AND THE ECONOMIC FUTURE OF MISSISSIPPI. **TO GET THE MESSAGE OF TRUTH BEFORE ALL MISSISSIPPIANS IN THE SHORT TIME REMAINING, ADEQUATE FUNDS MUST BE SECURED TO PROVIDE TV, RADIO & NEWSPAPER MESSAGES.** MAKE NO MISTAKE ABOUT IT — THIS IS AN EMERGENCY GREATER THAN ANY MISSISSIPPIANS HAVE FACED IN THIS CENTURY. THE BATTLE WILL BE FURIOUS BUT WE CAN WIN IF WE GET THE HELP NEEDED FROM YOU AND OTHERS WHO PERCEIVE THE DANGER STARING US IN THE FACE. **VICTORY MAY WELL DEPEND ON YOUR GENEROSITY.** PLEASE MAIL YOUR CHECK PAYABLE TO THE NON-PARTISAN MISSISSIPPI FREEDOM OF CHOICE COMMITTEE, RICHARD SHAW, CHAIRMAN, IN THE ENCLOSED ENVELOPE NOW BEFORE YOU FORGET. **THANK YOU.**

WIRT A. YERGER, JR.

THE COLD TRUTH: The following brochure, which is continued on the next two pages, sets forth state Democrats' racist, anti-Republican, power-hungry stand.

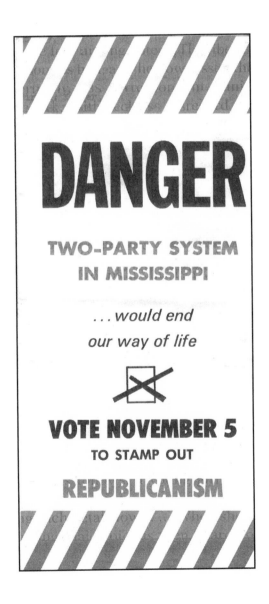

Mississippi Republicans Endanger Mississippi With Two Party System

The "overnight" Republicans in Mississippi are playing with political dynamite by advocating a two party system in our State.

These inexperienced, so-called Republicans proudly boast that "they are not bound by any deep-seated taboos and prejudices handed down blindly from past generations" but they never discuss the real dangers of a two party political system in a state like Mississippi with a "block-voting" minority group that represents over 45 per cent of our population.

These self-styled "young men and women and older people with young ideas" either do not know or they deliberately ignore the facts of life as they exist in Mississippi today.

A DIVISION OF CONSERVATIVE MISSISSIPPIANS INTO TWO POLITICAL CAMPS, as now being attempted by these self-styled Republicans, WOULD GIVE THE BALANCE OF POWER IN MISSISSIPPI TO OUR MINORITY GROUP. This would be the end of our way of life in Mississippi and the peace, tranquility, law and order we now enjoy in all of our communities would soon come to an awesome end.

To have Mississippi Democratic nominees and Republican nominees running for every public office . . . municipal, county and state . . . every four years . . . would constitute an unnecessary nuisance and would bring to Mississippi the same political evils and dangers that now beset such states as Illinois, New York, Michigan, Pennsylvania and California.

Mississippi Has All The Benefits Without The Very Real Dangers

As Mississippi Democrats we are enjoying all of the so-called "benefits" of a two party system, through our State Democratic primary elections, without exposing the people of Mississippi to the disastrous events and conditions that would surely follow the division of conservative Mississippians into two political camps thus giving the balance of power into the hands of a minority.

Our Mississippi Democratic Party is entirely independent and is free of the influence or domination of any national political party, and it offers an adequate framework for candidates of widely varying views to offer their services to the people. Mississippi has no need for a two party system that would divide our people and stretch our political campaigning over many additional months with resulting expense, confusion and disunity.

Today, Mississippi is enjoying the greatest economic and industrial growth and prosperity in its history. We have more people gainfully employed than ever before. More new industries with their new job opportunities are coming into our State than at any previous time in the State's history. Industrialists, seeking new plant sites, like the political climate in Mississippi. They compliment Mississippi for refusing to go "down the socialistic drain" with either of the two national political parties. They know that Mississippi has attained a degree of mutual cooperation between government, the people and industry without equal elsewhere in the world.

Have You Had Enough "Politics" For One Year?

The first and second Mississippi Democratic primary elections were completed in August, but the campaigning really began in January. In the tried and true tradition of the Mississippi Democratic Party these primaries gave candidates with wide degrees of views and opinions full opportunity to submit their services to the people of this State. Over 475,000 Mississippi men and women participated in these primaries, selecting their Mississippi Democratic nominees for all county and state offices.

Certainly, we have already had enough of politics for one year! But now come these Republicans with over 25 candidates for governor, lieutenant governor, for the State Senate and the House of Representatives and for Boards of Supervisors, forcing an additional period of political activity upon you.

If you've already had enough of politics for 1963, then help stamp out Republicanism on November 5.

Let's bury these Republican "upstarts" so deep under good, solid Mississippi Democratic votes that it will be the year 2000 before you hear of Republican candidates for Mississippi offices again!

Republican Party Always Rejects Their Conservative Leaders

Mississippi's latter-day "Republicans" are trying to sell a fairy tale to the people of this State. They are telling you that their National Republican Party is "conservative". The truth is that neither national party is "conservative". Both the National Republican Party and the National Democratic Party are the dedicated enemies of the people of Mississippi. The national leadership of both — consistently, across the years — has pursued courses of action which have moved our beloved country ever leftward . . . which have threatened our citizens with ever more centralized power at Washington.

The National Republican Party has followed the National Democratic Party like a shadow. Both have moved toward socialism as they catered to organized "have-not" minorities in the heavy populated urban centers, ignoring the great, silent, unorganized majority of decent, responsible citizens in this country.

Our "new" Republicans in Mississippi make much of their connections with the National Republican Party which has won the presidency only twice since 1932 (and both times with Eisenhower). They have failed to even nominate a presidential candidate who spoke with the voice of a militant conservative. The Republicans have rejected their most conservative men in the past in favor of men whom they thought could compete with the Kennedy type for the support of "the block-voting masses". And they have lost, again and again. And their party has declined steadily in national influence. Why? Because the National Republican Party has not had the moral courage to stand before America as the party of the "right" . . . the defender of free enterprise against socialism, the defender of Constitutional government against the welfare state, the defender of individual liberty and state sovereignty against the Washington power concentration. The Republican Party is no more "conservative" than are the Kennedys.

Neither national party as constituted today offers any hope to free men and women who value their independence and their honor. Both parties — if their platforms and their past actions are any guide — threaten our Mississippi traditions, institutions and segregated way of life.

The Mississippi Democratic Party — which long ago separated itself from the National Democratic Party, and which has fought consistently everything both national parties stand for — offers to the citizens of Mississippi, and to the troubled white conservative majority throughout America, their only chance to raise a conservative voice in the land.

Our "free elector" plan will fill the vacuum on the political right in America. The white conservative majority which has seen its choice limited to Republican liberal vs. Democrat liberal (varying only in degree), now will be offered an alternative on the right.

The Mississippi Democratic Party is not subservient to any national party. It has its own statement of principles adopted in convention in Jackson, and these are in direct conflict with the position of both national parties. We are free to oppose any policy which threatens our people. We do not have to "go along" with the big city bosses and sectional leaders who dominate both major parties. Our free electors may vote for any American leader who will espouse the principles in which we believe.

We do not have to belong to and participate in an integrated national party, which tolerates in its ranks radical leftists like Governor Nelson Rockefeller and Senator Jacob Javits of New York and "Black Monday" Earl Warren, in order to cast Mississippi's electoral votes for a true conservative. We do not have to make an "accommodation" with liberals, and we do not have to compromise our principles, in order to make our electoral votes count for freedom.

By the greatest vote in our State's history, Mississippians have repudiated the influence of the National Democratic Party in Mississippi. We don't want any National Republican Party influence here either! So let's finish the job.

Let's defeat the National Republican Party's candidates on November 5 by a vote so overwhelming that it will bury forever these "overnight" Republicans who would like to divide our State and hand it over to a minority group.

MISSISSIPPI REPUBLICAN PARTY

514 LAMAR LIFE BUILDING • P. O. BOX 1178 • JACKSON, MISSISSIPPI • 354-5719

June 17, 1965

- U R G E N T -

Dear Key Leaders:

Attached you will find an analysis of voter registration law changes
proposed by Governor Johnson.

The Governor's proposals go far beyond the Federal Voting Rights
Act. Literacy requirements would be completely abolished under
these bills. If the bills are passed there will be little hope of
ever again making literacy a prerequisite to voting in Mississippi.

The LBJ Voting Rights bill will suspend our voter registration laws
regardless of their content until such time as we can prove that
we are no longer discriminating against negroes in voter registration. Even if the laws proposed by the Governor were enacted
and were not suspended by the federal bill, voting requirements
would be no lower under the Governor's proposed bill than they
would be under the federal proposal.

We must think toward the future. When we are able to prove that
we have ceased discrimination and are able to come out from under
the federal voting law, the laws that are on our statute books,
even though they may have been suspended during the time the federal
voting bill was applied to our state, will again be applicable and
enforceable.

If we remove literacy requirements from our Constitution now as the
Governor has proposed, we will be unable to garner the necessary
votes to reinsert these provisions in our constitution after the
federal bill becomes inapplicable as the state legislature which
must propose an amendment by a two-thirds (2/3) vote and the state
electorate which must ratify an amendment by a majority vote will
have radically changed in character because of the impending mass
registration of negro voters.

Our only hope for having an intelligent electorate in the future
is through the insertion of a non-discriminatory literacy provision
in our Constitution now, rather than repealing literacy provisions
as the Governor has proposed.

If we are to preserve the quality and upgrade our electorate, our
Constitution should be amended to require that all voters have a
sixth grade education or its equivalent as evidenced by an impart-
ially administered objective literacy test. The test could be prepared by a professional testing firm.

You are urged to contact your legislators over the weekend and
discuss this very serious matter with them. If the current
Special Session of the Legislature follows the course chartered by
our Governor, the quality of our electorate will be drastically reduced for all time to come and the welfare state will be upon us.

Please contact your legislator and talk this matter over with him.

Sincerely,

Wirt A. Yerger, Jr.,
Chairman

LITERACY: Wirt fought for state voting standards that would have required
basic proof of literacy as the only criteria besides citizenship.

DOMESTIC SERVICE			INTERNATIONAL SERVICE
Check the class of service desired; otherwise this message will be sent as a fast telegram		**WESTERN UNION**	Check the class of service desired; otherwise the message will be sent at the full rate
TELEGRAM	X	**TELEGRAM**	FULL RATE
DAY LETTER		1206 (4-55)	LETTER TELEGRAM
NIGHT LETTER		W. P. MARSHALL, PRESIDENT	SHORE-SHIP

NO. WDS.-CL. OF SVC.	PD. OR COLL.	CASH NO.	CHARGE TO THE ACCOUNT OF	TIME FILED
			Miss. Republican Party	3:00 P.M.

Send the following message, subject to the terms on back hereof, which are hereby agreed to

February 22, 1963

Hon. Ross R. Barnett
Governor's Mansion
Jackson, Mississippi

As the Governor of our great state of Mississippi and representative of all
Mississippi citizens you are cordially invited to officiate at the formal
opening of the new State Headquarters for the Mississippi Republican Party.
The official ceremonies will be held at 10 O'clock tomorrow morning at
514 Lamar Life Building, directly across Capitol Street from the Governor's
Mansion. The event will be covered by newspapers, television and radio,
and we believe you will want to recognize publically the advent of
political maturity in Mississippi by cutting the ribbon which will usher
in a true two-party system in our state. Your acceptance of this honor
will be in keeping with your recent defense of Mississippi's great
traditions at Harvard.

Yours for the preservation of American
freedoms,

Wirt A. Yerger, Jr., GOP State Chairman

COULDN'T RESIST: From time to time, Wirt rattled off a telegram or note
to his competition, needling them, as he did to Ross Barnett in the telegram
above.

227

*There's a growing group of Mississippians who believe
... that Barry Goldwater ... will be the next President of
the United States.*

> —*Jackson Daily News* columnist
> William Peart, 1964

———————

If Goldwater wins the nomination it will take a miracle, and how this country needs one!

> —*The Tulsa Daily World*, 1964

———————

*Mississippi is put to shame before the entire nation
by efforts to legislate the Republican Party out of existence.*

> —Wirt Yerger on Mississippi
> Democrats' attempt to outlaw
> a second party in 1964

11

1964

JOUSTING WITH JOHNSONS FOR GOLDWATER AND MISSISSIPPI

In 1964 I battled two "Johnsons"—U.S. President Lyndon Johnson on the national scene and Mississippi Governor Paul Johnson on the state scene. Locally, Governor Johnson literally tried to outlaw a two-party system and, by extension, our state GOP. Nationally, I was now helping lead a charge for Goldwater to defeat Lyndon B. Johnson for president of the United States.

It was an overwhelmingly significant year in the life of our state Republican Party.

Paul Johnson truly proposed 22 laws to kill the state Republican Party. He said he wanted to prevent Democrat nominees from "being harassed" in the future. I countered that he "would then [create] the same one-party system that has been found so satisfactory by a Mr. Khrushchev and Fidel Castro."[1]

With Lyndon Johnson's liberalism escalating in 1964, an articulate conservatism continued to grow to answer Johnson; it was led by men including Russell Kirk and William F. Buckley.[2]

A confidential poll of the Republican National Committee in 1964 showed that white Mississippians were shifting affinities. It asked: "Do you consider yourself more of a Republican or Democrat today?" A staggering 62.6 percent answered Republican versus 29.9 percent Democrat; 7.5 percent did not reply. More than 74 percent said the GOP "most nearly supported their views of how the country should be run."[3]

What had changed? In the wake of Kennedy's death, Lyndon Johnson was pressing a continually brazen liberalism, and even Michigan's moderate Republican Governor George Romney said he was "concerned about the declining responsibility of local and state governments and local individuals."[4]

The same 1964 GOP poll also said Mississippians now more associated the phrase "states' rights" with the Republican Party (76.6 %) than with the Democratic Party (16.1 %); 7.3 percent did not respond.

I told our Mississippi Republican Party Convention in July of 1964 that our belief in true states' rights was a belief in the ability of local government to effect good policies if given a chance versus fomenting animosity among our citizens. When I said we could not "honestly believe that laws alone will solve this problem. We must make existing laws work. Years of real progress are at stake. The tension we see between races is a matter of the heart. And that is where it must be solved. That is the only place it ever truly can be solved! Those who condone by their silence or openly encourage violence on either side, ... bitterly delay real solutions."[5]

I added: "There is violence of a different sort that is done when politicians set any segment of the nation against any other: employees against employers, consumers against producers, the less fortunate against the more fortunate. The answer to progress in this land is enlargement of opportunity for all. ... We can and must grow and prosper together—not in compartments of political favor."[6]

But a concerted effort was now proving successful to pervert our message and, ultimately, distort Barry's views. "[Goldwater's] positions," said Maryland's 1964 GOP chairman in a disheartening letter to me, were "badly distorted."[7] The work of these liberal propagandists lingers like poison to this day. As a result, many have been hesitant to use the term "states' rights" to describe their political beliefs for fear they will be called a racist.

The presidential race of 1964 would disillusion many and absolutely fatigue Goldwater, but in Mississippi it would verify and increase our party's growing power on several fronts.

It was a crazy, difficult, strategic year.

• • •

On Jan. 1, 1964, F. Clifton White, executive director of the national Draft Goldwater movement, told the Associated Press that we were thrilled about Barry's expected announcement for president in three days. "We're ready to do whatever he wants us to do. ... I'm sure [Goldwater] will accept the call to public duty."[8]

Our Draft Goldwater movement had made great strides. Stephen Shadegg, Goldwater's campaign manager in his first two senatorial campaigns, later had this to say about us: "These men were not novices playing in a new arena. They neither were innocent nor naïve. They were not seeking power or glory or prestige for themselves." On the contrary, said Shadegg, each of us in the Draft Goldwater movement "believed their country was in danger."[9]

We had pushed hard to convince Barry to run. Nelson Rockefeller already had political operatives in place everywhere by late 1963.

Conservative political philosopher Russell Kirk estimated Rockefeller "had more wealth at his disposal, directly or indirectly, than any other American."[10]

In California alone, Rockefeller had "hired sixty professional campaign workers, at a hundred dollars a day each," to build up his strength for the primary. My friend Bill Spicer, Arkansas GOP chairman, did some math: starting in February of 1964 and running through June 30 of 1964, this equaled

$900,000, a sum inconceivable at the time. That was just for one state, and only to achieve the Republican presidential *nomination!*[11]

Rockefeller "had recruited a staff of researchers, speech writers, and political experts—all assembled in his handsome headquarters at 22 W. 55th Street in New York City. His advance men were in the field making overtures to such knowledgeable Republican organizers as Larry Lindemer, one-time state chairman in Michigan; and Mort Frayn, the state chairman of Washington."[12]

In 1964 Rockefeller loomed as a menacing giant ready for battle.

The rumors already were that "the boys in the back room" would "have anybody but Barry Goldwater."[13] Those boys were Rockefeller, Romney, and Pennsylvania Governor William Scranton—all of whom ran for president that year. "If Goldwater wins the nomination it will take a miracle," *The Tulsa Daily World* stated realistically in January, adding, "and how this country needs one!"[14]

And while Barry was the man to beat these moderate, establishment Republicans, he was already making some strategically bad appointments to his campaign staff. He chose an old friend and former New Deal Democrat, Denison Kitchel—an Arizona transplant and native New Yorker—ostensibly to run his upcoming 1964 Senate reelection campaign.[15] Kitchel was an immediate disaster, but Barry could not ever see it. Denison did not know very many politicians, nor did he have the instincts of one. People felt him to be "cold, distant, and unapproachable."[16] Even worse, Kitchel did not work well with our Draft Goldwater movement. "The arrival of Kitchel in Washington, D.C. signaled the beginning of the end of the Draft Goldwater Committee," says Jay Hartz, formerly of the Ashbrook Center for Public Affairs.[17]

Kitchel was Barry's first bad campaign move.

Then Barry brought in Dean Burch.

Eventually during the July GOP national convention,

Barry would help maneuver Burch into the greater position of chairman of the Republican National Committee.[18]

A good many of the rest of Goldwater's staff were assembled in poor fashion. Just why, I don't know, but Barry made no place for J. Clifton White on his staff, while making Richard Kleindienst (later a part of Richard Nixon's Watergate scandal) his second in command.[19]

No one from the Draft Goldwater committee was put on Goldwater's core staff. On Jan. 4, as Barry announced his candidacy for president, he said he did not plan to concede the South to Lyndon Johnson, "a Southerner ... at least he calls himself one."[20]

• • •

Six GOP state chairmen, including me, had been serving on the Draft Goldwater movement. In January, we traveled to Washington, D.C. for Republican National Committee meetings. Arkansas GOP chairman Bill Spicer called us "rebel-mustangs." We were: John Grenier, Tom Brown, Jim Dorsey, Drake Edens, Pete O'Donnell, and myself, and we stormed the party meetings with pro-Barry talk.[21]

Hotel mogul William Marriott entertained us and introduced us to Michigan Governor George Romney; but we were not moved by him. Pennsylvania's Scranton did not faze us. "Barry Goldwater is the overwhelming choice of Republican Party leadership from the precinct level up," I told a top Pennsylvania Republican, "and these people are not about to let Madison Avenue and the left-wing press frustrate their desires."[22]

I returned to Mississippi from Washington and told the men's "Y" club in Jackson that "if conservatives can convince the Republican Party throughout the nation the South will go for Senator Barry Goldwater, there will be no stopping him."[23]

But in Mississippi, state Democrats were now launching a full, frontal attack of drastic proportions against our state GOP. By March of 1964, Mississippi's Governor Paul Johnson began his absolutely anti-Democratic ploy to legislate away the possibility of a two-party system in Mississippi. On March 11, he and a stacked team of state legislators called for a package of 22 bills to revise the state's election laws. This, despite the fact that we Republicans submitted to the exact laws as Democrats did at that time.

In 1964 we had only one Republican in the state legislature, Mack McAllister, so no real hope existed for me and our state party leadership to lobby the state legislature to oppose Johnson's efforts. Fred LaRue was our state's Republican National Committeeman at the time. He asked in one of our GOP meetings: "Who is going to lead this battle to defeat Johnson's bill in the legislature?"

I said, "I am."

A few of us GOP state leaders eventually appeared before the elections committee of the state legislature to plead our case. "Our party is small and growing," I reminded the legislators, noting that as recently as 1959 we had run no Republicans for any office in the state. In 1963 we ran 33 candidates among the 2,500 statewide offices. None of our candidates were facing primary races simply because we were so few, and thus we had no numbers for such contests within our own party. "If two or more Republicans had filed for the same office, they would have had to run in a primary election, just as opposed Democrats do."[24]

I added: "We Republicans are mostly Mississippians, born, reared, and educated in Mississippi. We raise children, worship God, support our communities, pay taxes, and have honest convictions just as each of you. We seek no special privileges but only justice and fairness under the law, just as all Mississippians regardless of their political philosophy. We deeply resent ... any attempts ... to take away precious freedoms which many Mississippians have given their lives to protect."[25]

Johnson's proposed laws sought to require Republican candidates to run in party primaries even if they ran unopposed; this was designed to force our state GOP to spend our precious time and money so none remained for the general-election races against the Democrats. The proposed laws also wanted to force all state citizens who voted in the Democratic primary (virtually everyone at the time) to also vote Democrat in the general election, no exceptions; thus, no one could switch and vote for a Republican in the general election. Johnson's bills also sought to set a line so that only the parties achieving ten percent of votes statewide in primaries could field a candidate in the general election, another almost impossible standard for our state GOP at the time.

Johnson offered citizens his justification for seeking these laws: "We abhor the selection of candidates for the general election ballot by a few, self-proclaimed party leaders." *The Clarion-Ledger's* Charles M. Hills called Johnson's plan fair. There would be no "maudlin" sympathy for us, Hills insisted.[26] Even the Mississippi Economic Council initially refused to take a stand against Johnson's dictatorial plan.[27]

I challenged the governor to a televised debate about his proposals; he declined. Our state GOP announced plans to sue. "These 22 laws ... affect every citizen of this state," I said. "[Johnson] is asking for a police state. ... The fear of the Republican buildup in the state, and the fear of competition, prompted these laws. ... It would seem as if his program was lifted directly from 'Mein Kempf'."[28]

I added: "If these laws are passed, young people, who are now leaving the state in droves, would have no reason to remain and you can bet that industry does not wish to locate in a police state."[29]

Bidwell Adam called me "the tin-god of the GOP in Mississippi" and the "champion belly-acher of Mississippi," who did not want my "political playhouse" taken away.[30]

By March 18, the Elections Committee of the Mississippi Senate had affirmed Johnson's proposal.[31] On March 26 the State Senate passed 18 of the 22 bills. But a few legislators were finally starting to show reservations. State Sen. Bill Caraway from Leland predicted, "It is going to leave Democrats with no place to go if their own party is taken over by liberals."[32]

Suddenly the Senate tabled the bills and sent them back to the House. Tempers flared as State Sen. Bill Alexander of Cleveland proclaimed, "We're crushing people [the Republicans] here. Are we afraid of these so-called Republicans?"[33]

I began alerting the national news media, which uncharacteristically took our side. "Mississippi is put to shame before the entire nation by efforts to legislate the Republican Party out of existence," I said.[34] United States Senate Minority leader Everett Dirkson, (R-Ill.) said the plan was "repugnant to the American way of life" and "parallels the Communist conception of a single party state."[35]

By April the legislature and Paul Johnson were trying to soften the laws.[36] On May 12, in a remarkable turn, the State House formally voted to kill the bills.[37] On May 30 at our Mississippi Republican Convention, we celebrated the defeats of what I called "the forces of evil." I noted how "a wave of righteous indignation swept across this state as seldom seen."[38]

• • •

Barry's national presidential campaign kept gaining steam. He came in second in New Hampshire's primary to Henry Cabot Lodge, Jr. Rockefeller ran a distant third. Then Barry took South Carolina; Georgia threw him their 34 delegates; North Carolina's 26 delegates endorsed him. By the end of March, George Gallup's poll showed that a massive 48 percent of Americans surveyed backed Barry.[39] Goldwater just kept winning GOP primaries, taking Illinois in mid-April and Texas on May 2 with 48,991 votes.[40] He swamped all Republican comers in Maryland's GOP primary.

Barry began to campaign hard in California as we Mississippians met on May 28 for an historic Republican state convention. We were Goldwater all the way. Only eight years earlier, a mere 35 people had attended our state convention; now we had more than 500 from more than 70 counties. We now enjoyed another first: Prentiss Walker, a farmer from Mize, Mississippi, was running for U.S. Congress in the

Fourth District against incumbent Democrat, William Arthur Winstead. I wish we had been able to find candidates to run in all of our congressional districts. We named 13 delegates and 13 alternates to the upcoming July Republican National Convention. We spelled out our state Republican platform, highlighting our concern over a recent Supreme Court decision against school prayer.[41]

About this time Goldwater also announced that he supported federal involvement in school integration. It was a surprise; some felt his Arizona Mafia had pressured him to compromise his small-government principles. Barry told a press conference on the eve of the California primary, "I am glad I can recognize when I am wrong."[42] Barry swept California's primary. Rockefeller finished second but won the primary in his home state of New York, taking 76 delegate votes and thrusting him into second place as San Francisco's national convention loomed.[43] Still, Barry was projected to take the nomination on a first ballot.[44]

And that is when the ugliness escalated.

On June 8 Rockefeller arrived at the annual National Governor's Conference. He, Romney, and Scranton were now planning to unleash a very public "Stop-Goldwater Movement," with Romney saying "he would spare no effort to keep the GOP nomination from Barry Goldwater."[45] "A stand must be made," Scranton told a gathering in Maryland, "but the hour is late. The Republican Party is in danger."[46] Eisenhower actually met with Scranton and gave the appearance of an endorsement, but later publicly he retreated from that. I quickly wrote Ike, taking him to task. He replied to me: "While I do not want to give even the appearance of suggesting the importance of my own support, ... I do want to make it clear that after the nomination, I want to be in a position to support that name, whatever his identity."[47]

Eisenhower ended up offering very little help to Barry once he received the GOP nomination, though I entreated Ike to stand up to Romney and Scranton's hostile opposition. "I

237

hope that your disappointment in this group of pure phonies will be displayed by an all out effort on your part to insure Barry Goldwater's election," I wrote to Eisenhower, but apparently to no avail.[48]

Scranton called Barry's grass-roots supporters a "minority" that was "naïve, irresponsible, reactionary, and heartless."[49] Sadly, he would stoop even lower in the coming weeks. The national media continued scathing Goldwater, trying to paint him as a covert segregationist. I did my best to defend him: "Never in the history of this country has such a hatchet job been done on any political candidate by the molders of public opinion," I claimed. "Goldwater has never been a segregationist and we have never claimed that he was. His statements have been taken out of context and distorted to make him appear ridiculous."[50]

Soon Henry Cabot Lodge, Jr. threw his 43 delegates behind Scranton.[51] Two days later, Rockefeller threw his 125 estimated delegates to Scranton, whose delegate total now ran about 245.[52] Rockefeller's own candidacy had been harpooned by a private marital scandal. More than 270 delegates still remained uncommitted around the nation. "The hour is late, but ... the moderate cause can still be won," Rockefeller said.[53]

As all of this political maneuvering played out, a crucial drama unfolded in the United States Senate, one with election implications. The U.S. Senate's vote on the Civil Rights Bill of 1964 was about to be cast, and Scranton kept pressing Barry to shift his stance in favor of it. Scranton had the gall to say Goldwater lacked courage to support the bill. The Arizona Mafia was no help to Barry, who by June 17 was still deliberating on how he would vote. He said he still felt the bill's clauses on equal employment were unconstitutional in principle.[54] Again, Scranton called for Barry to "repudiate his opposition" to the bill.[55] But on June 19, 1964, Barry stood by his principles and voted against the bill. "I am unalterably opposed to discrimination or segregation on the basis of race, color, or creed," he said at that time. "I cannot in good conscience to the oath that I took" vote for it, he added. "Let me suffer [in the polls]. ... Just let me be judged in this by the real concern I have voted here and not by words that others may speak or by what others may say about what I think."[56]

It was a brave stand, but the media again used it against Barry.

Yet another horrible event soon wrenched every decent American and escalated the emotional pitch of the presidential election.

On June 23, 1964, three civil rights workers—James Chaney, 21, Andrew Goodman, 20, and Michael Schwerner, 24— were among about 1,000 Northern students registering black voters in a Freedom Summer event in Mississippi. The three disappeared and their charred station wagon was soon found empty in the Bogue Chitto swamp. President Johnson sent top FBI agents to Neshoba County to investigate.[57] National press descended. Our worst element in Mississippi again had struck. The three men's dead bodies were eventually found buried in an earthen dam. This despicable violence undoubtedly had a secondary effect of further skewing Barry's run for president.

By the end of 1964, I had been summoned to jury duty on the case of these murders. Everything in me longed to give these young men's families justice. Earlier that very year, on April 17, Byron De La Beckwith's second jury trial had ended in a mistrial. That was a gross injustice to Medgar Evers and his family, one that was finally rectified in 1994.

As I mentioned in a previous chapter, getting justice for these three civil rights workers would have required jurors who did not fear threats of reprisal by ugly, backwoods thugs. I wanted badly to provide tough leadership to the jury to make sure the right call was made. But no defense attorney was going to let someone like me sit on the jury; I was quickly dismissed.

Amid all this, I boarded a plane to San Francisco to attend our Republican National Convention.

• • •

"There's a growing group of Mississippians who believe ... that Barry Goldwater ... will be the next President of the United States," wrote *Jackson Daily News* columnist William Peart as our national convention began.[58]

Nowhere was this fact more evident than at our Republican National Convention in San Francisco. Our pre-convention meetings were controlled by our Goldwater forces. Scranton was making a feeble play for about 80 Goldwater delegates he felt could be won to his side, but the Associated Press predicted Barry would carry the nomination on the first ballot.[59]

For me, the pre-convention week was so satisfying. I told the media, "For the first time in many years, the South seems about to play a decisive role in naming a man whom we believe will be the next president of the United States." Then I received another surprise: CBS's Walter Cronkite invited me to lunch. *The Clarion-Ledger* reported this on their front page July 8, as if the paper was both shocked and delighted to discover that I had challenged the anchor about his coverage of our state. "I gave him a good sales talk on Mississippi," I told our voters back home.[60]

During our meal I told Cronkite that the national media was being unfair in its coverage both of the South and of Barry. "Well, we're working on that," Cronkite uncomfortably told me.

On Friday, July 10, Goldwater arrived to the convention amid a rousing welcome. As he arrived, Charlie Klumb and I were with the platform committee making sure Scranton's forces did not impose their will.[61]

The GOP presidential platform gave us most everything we wanted for Barry. Among other things, it called for:

- keeping prayer in public schools;

- recognizing a true Cuban government in exile;

- serious reductions in federal spending;

- greater firmness in opposing nuclear threats from other countries;

- more decisive action in Vietnam;

- maintaining superior, not merely equal, military strength to that of the Soviets.

This ground-breaking, conservative platform was a precursor to those adopted during the fine Reagan years of the 1980s. "After decades of complacency on the part of many Republicans, as well as Democrats, about the constant aggrandizement of Federal power, the new platform calls for a halt," reported an enthusiastic *Wall Street Journal* guest editorial. The *Journal* editorial added: "It represents considerably more than some kind of negative attack on the Federal government. Its positive aspect is that by restraining heavy-handed officialdom it opens up new prospects for individual respect and local responsibility. Our whole history is testimony that this approach is the guarantor of political freedom and a spur to economic progress."[62]

I met privately with Barry on Sunday, July 12, and I felt very good about his spirits. "He looks like the next president of the United States," I told media. Goldwater reportedly had secured the backing of 727 delegate votes, an insurmountable lead; he only needed 655.[63]

Speaking as the chairman of the Southern Association of Republican State Chairmen, I told the media that I believed Barry would take the South. Mike Goldwater, Barry's fine son, agreed, noting that, "Yerger is probably the strongest voice in the Republican Party in the South."[64]

During that pre-convention week, rumblings emerged that Barry might pick Scranton as a vice-presidential running mate. I immediately sent a telegram to Barry urging him not to choose Scranton. The very next day, I received a telegram from him saying, "I can guarantee you Scranton will not be my choice." I was fortunate to have such access and I tried to use it wisely.

The power in our party was shifting from Eastern elites to middle-class Americans. "Here in San Francisco," wrote one reporter, "not only are the one-time Eastern kingmakers a disorganized and dispirited group, even the Eastern delegate has less power than at anytime in history. ... The kingmaker from the Northeastern part of the United States does not figure to come back—ever."[65]

I told the media, "The kingmakers are dying hard."[66]

All sorts of conspiratorial claims began to be launched about Goldwater. The Northeastern elites, helped by the media, said Barry had "penetrated" "all factions of the party" "with representatives of the radical right"—citing as their example Brent Bozell of *The National Review,* which was an absurd notion. They called Bozell and others "right-wing Neanderthals."[67] Today Bozell holds the respected status of a time-tested, political fixture, hardly a radical.

Finally, Nelson Rockefeller took to the convention podium for his allotted speaking time. A chorus of boos ensued. His speech was all sour grapes aimed at our right wing, which he at times spuriously alleged was linked with the KKK and the John Birch Society. Absolute falsehoods and smears were now his standard fare.

Even during Rockefeller's speech, we Mississippians had a fantastic time; we blew and shook noisemakers, wore dumb hats, and waved Goldwater signs. Our people were not about to wave a Confederate flag or hoop any sort of perceived "Rebel yell"—both of which were standard practices among our Southern Democrat opposition.[68] The national media still sought anything to stereotype our Mississippi GOP. Frank McGee was an NBC television reporter. Like others in the media, he had an agenda. I was standing on the convention floor when McGee interviewed me. He opened with some preliminary conversation. Then, with the lights glaring, he asked, "Mr. Yerger, are blacks welcome in the Mississippi Republican Party?"

Several members of our delegation standing around me almost fainted. I looked at McGee and stated the truth: "If they are conservatives, they're welcome."

All I did was give an honest answer. I never worried about

media spin because I always told the truth. There was no genius to it. Someone once said that if you tell the truth you never have to remember what you said. Many politicians find themselves locked in this constant quagmire of spinning past statements.

The real moment of truth in San Francisco came the evening of July 15. At 9:36 p.m. at the Cow Palace, bedlam broke out. South Carolina announced for Goldwater, and he exceeded the 655 delegates needed for the nomination. It was a "smashing" victory, Associated Press writer Douglas Cornell stated. Scranton, Romney, and all their gang finally conceded and moved that all 50 states recast their votes to give Barry a unanimous tally, and it was done. "A showdown ... between conservatism and liberalism" was over, Cornell said. "An era is over," wrote another reporter, Arthur Edson.[69]

The next night, thunderous applause swelled as Barry ascended the podium to accept the nomination. "Thursday July 16, 1964 was a sweltering night in San Francisco's Cow Palace," notes scholar Jay Hartz, who offers a wonderful recounting of what happened next: "Barry Goldwater took his place on a wooden platform to address the assembled delegates at the Republican National Convention and a national television audience. The red, white, and blue balloons settled around him as Goldwater began his acceptance speech—a speech that was to ... [culminate] a grassroots drive to obtain the Republican nomination for a conservative, and to begin a Goldwater-controlled presidential campaign. Goldwater accepted the Republican nomination with a 'deep sense of humility' and called for a united and determined campaign. He spoke of the 'columnists that had closed their minds' and were preparing to make him the 'whipping boy of the campaign.' Then Goldwater called for all Republicans to 'think victory, talk victory, act victory—and we will win victory in November.' Unexpectedly, the rhetoric of Goldwater's address changed. He issued a warning to all those who did not share his understanding of the purpose of government, or the nature of the American republic: 'Any who joins us in all sincerity, welcome. Those who do not care for our cause we do not expect to enter our ranks in any case. And let our Republicanism, so focused and so dedicated, not be made fuzzy and futile by unthinking and stupid labels. I would remind you that extremism in the defense of liberty is no vice. And let me remind you also that moderation in the pursuit of justice is no virtue.' With this utterance, the assembled delegates jumped to their feet and cheered wildly. ... Goldwater ended his speech with these marching orders: 'This party, its good people, and its unquestionable devotion to freedom will not fulfill the purposes of this campaign which we launch here and now until our cause has won the day, inspired the world, and shown the way to a tomorrow worthy of our yesteryears.' With this, the floor and galleries of the Cow Palace again erupted. Goldwater stepped away from the podium, slipping his ever-present black glasses into his lapel pocket, and smiled."[70]

It would take 16 more years until Americans elected Barry's principled conservatism into the Oval Office in the form of Ronald Reagan, a Goldwater disciple. But the seeds were now planted, and we at the time believed we were going to win the White House.

At the close of the convention, I was standing in a chair by the aisle on the convention floor to get a better view. Romney was walking up the aisle. The Michigan governor looked my way. I looked over at him and said, "Governor, I hope you can get behind the ticket. Help Barry." Romney gave me the most vicious scowl I ever recall having seen. He was just outraged that I would dare say anything like that. His ego was so big. I'll never forget it. It was pure anger, hatred, and resentment—all those things rolled into one. Bill Wilkins, who was our state GOP executive director at that time, had a similar experience at the convention. "I recall a similar exchange I had that night with Nelson Rockefeller, who stuck his tongue out at me," Wilkins says. "I later came to learn that he was notorious for somewhat more crude gestures so I guess I got off light!"[71]

Upon returning home after the national convention, I told one group of Mississippians, "We had the liberals absolutely squirming in their seats."[72]

• • •

What now ensued was sad. The national media, along with Romney, Scranton and Rockefeller, fomented inaccuracies and stereotypes all throughout the general election.

Immediately after Barry gave his acceptance speech, media latched onto one phrase in it and rode it during the entire general campaign. That phrase was: *"Extremism in defense of liberty is no vice. ... Moderation in the pursuit of justice is no virtue."*

The lines actually are said to have been penned for Barry by Harry V. Jaffa, now a distinguished fellow of the Claremont Institute. Many think they were based on a quote from Cicero, but Jaffa says they were an adaptation of a statement by the great American Thomas Paine, who had said: "A thing moderately good is not so good as it ought to be. Moderation in temper is always a virtue; but moderation in principle is always a vice."[73]

The Arizona Mafia's ensuing limp response to the media's stir over this quote was another sign that Goldwater's closest advisors were going to ruin him. They began putting Barry out to apologize for this statement, rather than to build upon it. He even wrote to Richard Nixon soon after the speech, explaining feebly that what he really meant by "extremism" was "whole-hearted devotion."[74] Barry had now officially begun kowtowing to his enemies. If John F. Kennedy had uttered that same quote on "extremism," it would have been treated by the media as pearls of wisdom for the history books. If he had condemned "moderation in the pursuit of justice," children would be memorizing the line today.

GOP moderates like Romney and Scranton were supposed to be "Republicans," but they were more devoted to themselves than to their party. The media loved them. They had held control of the party for so long, and none of them could stand that another wing of the party was now in leadership.

Rockefeller was the consummate spoiled brat. Instead of rushing to defend his presidential candidate, Rockefeller stabbed him in the back. He told the media, "To extol extremism—whether 'in defense of liberty' or 'in pursuit of justice'—is dangerous, irresponsible, and frightening," adding that Barry's statement "raises the gravest of questions in the hearts and souls of Republicans in every corner of our party. I shall continue to fight extremism within the Republican Party."[75]

Paul Harvey offered Barry better advice: "Senator Goldwater, in his acceptance speech in San Francisco, said, 'Extremism in the defense of liberty is no vice.' The enemy attacked. The Goldwater forces retreated. 'He didn't mean "extremism," he meant "patriotism",' they apologized. What the Republicans should have done was to make a lapel-button campaign slogan of that splendid statement and stand on it! There is no great military leader in history who was not extremely courageous. There is no statesman worth remembering who was not extremely dedicated to the politics he advocated."[76]

A guest editorial in *The Wall Street Journal* defended Goldwater by looking at his platform: "Indeed, the specifics in the platform proceed from a philosophical recognition that the root issue today, at home and abroad, is the age-old one of whether man is to be the servant or the master of the State. ... [Goldwater's] platform hardly ranks as extremism. It is in fact a moderate alternative to the extreme proponents of unlimited Federal power."[77]

The hypocrisy of Rockefeller and other old-line liberals was unbridled. Instead of celebrating new party growth, they pouted at not having all the marbles. "If they can't whip Goldwater," Harvey said, "... they will try to make him over into their image."[78]

One liberal commentator set out to paint those of us now gaining power in the Draft Goldwater movement as "new political money" and "a white Protestant country club set which doesn't understand the problems of the big city, the struggles of immigrants and minority groups ... nor does it care much."[79] And what of Rockefeller's, Romney's, and Scranton's elitist backgrounds? *What hypocrisy.*

Just three days after the convention, Lyndon Johnson announced a White House-sponsored plan to attack "extremist" groups in America. It was interesting timing and absolutely a ploy to encourage fear among voters. The liberal Republicans had given Johnson his fuel, and he now tossed the match on it.

From Germany, CBS correspondent Daniel Schorr did his own dirty work. With reckless disregard to anything resembling the truth, he reported that Barry was going to have a post-convention meeting in Berchtesgaden with German "right-wing elements," an allusion to Nazis and a total lie. *Time* magazine even called Schorr's work "a smear."[80]

The New York Review of Books "depicted Goldwater in a wild caricature, saluting in a manner unmistakably reminiscent of a Nazi salute."[81] A member of *The New York Times* editorial board said that Goldwater's use of new organizational structures called "cell groups" in his 1952 and 1956 senatorial campaigns sounded fishy.[82]

It seemed the national smear campaign could not get any worse, but it was about to do just that. On the evening of Sept. 7, during an NBC Monday Movie entitled *David and Bathsheba*, a now-infamous and totally villainous commercial ran. Today the commercial is simply called "Daisy," and it has its own Wikipedia page, which correctly says, "[the commercial] was a factor in Lyndon B. Johnson's defeat of Barry Goldwater ... and [it was] an important turning point in political and advertising history."[83]

The ad goes as follows: a young girl is "standing in a meadow with chirping birds, picking the petals of a daisy while counting each petal slowly. ... When she reaches '9', an ominous-sounding male voice is then heard counting down a missile launch, and as the girl's eyes turn toward something she sees in the sky, the camera zooms in until her pupil fills the screen, blacking it out. When the countdown reaches zero, the blackness is replaced by the flash and mushroom cloud from a nuclear explosion."[84]

Lyndon Johnson's voice is now heard in the ad, even as the fearful explosion takes full form. Johnson says, "These are the stakes! To make a world in which all of God's children can live, or to go into the dark. We must either love each other, or we must die."

Then another voice is heard, that of a professional announcer. He says, "Vote for President Johnson on Nov. 3. The stakes are too high for you to stay home."

The image corrupted the rest of the presidential race.

Barry's home paper, *The Arizona Republic,* chided the smear and asked why decent liberals were not decrying the ad's message. Said the paper, "When members of the right impugned the motives of leftists, the fire-breathing liberal guardians of American morals rose to meet the challenge posed by those who engaged in 'smear tactics' and 'guilt by association,' and they were joined by many American conservatives. But today, when a great part of the left is engaged in smearing an outstanding conservative, the liberal fire-breathers not only say nothing against the smears but, in fact, join in them with all the fervor of one embarking on a jihad—as indeed they are convinced they are."[85]

Johnson's campaign officially denounced the ad, but for the rest of the campaign, all that Johnson had to do was mention the word "trigger happy," or even hint at the notion, and the public swayed to his side.

• • •

Voters' emotions kept escalating during the 1964 campaign, fanned into flames by fear of nuclear disaster, along with the issues of racism and Communism.

At our late-May Mississippi Republican Party Convention we did not skirt these matters. In our platform, we had affirmed 1) free enterprise, 2) a fight-to-win policy in Vietnam, and 3) eradication of unnecessary state government agencies. We also had taken a strong stand against Communism. Citing myriad reports from FBI Chief J. Edgar Hoover, we had called for "all divisions of the U. S. government and specifically [the] U.S. State Department [to] be purged of Communist sympathizers and left-wing socialists who have advocated 'no win' wars all over the globe, relinquishment of Armed Forces to the U.N. Security Council, ... replacing these with God fearing individuals." In a more tempered fashion than the Mississippi Democratic Party, we had said segregation seemed to be the best solution at that time for the State of Mississippi.[86]

Meanwhile, racial strife now was tearing through the North as well as the South. For a third day in a row in late July, almost 1,000 African-Americans rioted in Harlem in Nelson Rockefeller's state, throwing bottles and light bulbs at police, who shot at them. More than 30 had been injured when strife erupted after a 15-year-old black youth was shot and killed by a white policeman. European papers labeled it the "cancer called Harlem."

Though this violence was spreading everywhere, Mississippi would forever remain the media's symbol of racial strife due to the horrible murders of Emmett Till; of Chaney, Goodman, Schwerner; and of Medgar Evers. And the efforts of Northern activist college students to goad Mississippi's worst elements also proved effective. By design, these young activists sought to incite violence, drawing sympathetic national media attention. *The Harvard [University] Crimson* newspaper reported as much: "This summer will witness a massive, daring, probably bloody assault on the racial barriers of Mississippi," the paper had said, predicting that the students' actions would: "precipitate a crisis of violence which they [the activist-students] consider prerequisite for further progress."[87]

The Dallas Morning News said our state faced "the unjustified, uncalled-for invasion [of Mississippi] ... by a bunch of Northern students schooled in advance in causing trouble under the guise of bringing 'freedom' to Mississippi Negroes." The press would be given more fodder to pummel Mississippi and the South "every time an incident arises as a result of this invasion."[88]

Even national political columnist Drew Pearson, a liberal who had been very tough on Goldwater and Mississippi, appealed to the student activists to let up on Mississippi. "I would earnestly disagree with you that now is a time to risk lives and incite passions by sending an army of white students to Mississippi. ... It is only fair to give the South an opportunity to live with and adjust to this new code [of recent civil rights laws]. I say this also because there have been changes in the South and because it is necessary to give the more enlightened leadership of the South an opportunity to lead. They should not be handicapped by outsiders whose presence incites bitterness and resentment."[89]

On July 22, Martin Luther King, Jr., returned to Jackson. He spoke to a mass gathering at the Lynch Street Masonic building during a four-day state tour in conjunction with the 1,000 student activists' work during the Mississippi Summer Project. He condemned Barry Goldwater and praised Lyndon Johnson at every stop. He also asked Johnson to send federal marshals to Mississippi to help the 1,000 Freedom Summer activists.[90]

Even as he spoke, racial riots were pouring forth in the streets of Harlem. Lyndon Johnson was at a loss regarding what to do about the Harlem riots. He told the nation, "I did not become president to preside over mounting violence."[91] He asked Barry to agree to avoid any mention of the issue of civil rights in their televised debates. One might ask, "Why?", since he was the one who was pressing for more and more of such legislation? Why would he now seek to avoid debate on this, his centerpiece issue? Had the violence not been anticipated? Was he now unsure of what to do about declining popularity for his measures in the polls? Barry, ever the gentleman, agreed, though he shouldn't have.

Meanwhile, Martin Luther King, Jr., went to Philadelphia, Mississippi, encouraging blacks to vote. Two days later,

King was off to Harlem, where police faced more violence.[92] Bidwell Adam bid King a sarcastic goodbye. "I suggest [Martin Luther King, Jr.] go back where he came from and attend the people who need him for advice, say in Brooklyn and Harlem."[93] On Saturday, July 26, King left Mississippi, promising to return.[94]

That weekend the race riots in Harlem escalated to a "small war," reports said, running "dusk-to-dawn." Looting was beyond control. A Communist was once more implicated in the riots: "William Epton, 22, an admired Communist who runs the Harlem defense council," was arrested.[95] Rockefeller said the rioting would be "met by the full force of the law," adding, "there are disturbing indications that there may be organized efforts to incite or abet such disturbances."[96] Really? Of course, when Southern leaders had noted this same problem, men like Rockefeller and Lyndon Johnson scoffed at them.

"Pistols and make-shift arms were triggered," one national writer said. "Molotov cocktails thrown, clubs wielded. Gangs, mostly of tough strong boys, raced the streets, fighting police hand-to-hand. Store after store was looted. The air crackled with police pistols firing."[97]

Suddenly, the national press, Rockefeller, and President Johnson's tone concerning race matters seemed to tilt. A Richmond, Virginia, newspaper spotted the irony: "The race riots of Harlem and Brooklyn offer a sore temptation to Southerners whose nerves have been rubbed raw for the past 10 years by the piousity of their brothers in the North. The violence in New York is so much worse than the violence of Birmingham, St. Augustine and Oxford, Miss. that no fair comparisons can be made. One might propose, following the North's example, that the South send hundreds of college girls, rabbis, ministers, trouble-making lawyers, and do-gooding ladies to educate the benighted North in better race relations."[98]

This in no way is meant to impugn the brave work of true civil rights leaders, versus racial inciters.

· · ·

About this time in late July, the Mississippi Democratic Party was ready to hold its state convention. This moment proved to be pivotal. A new group of blacks and whites now announced plans to unseat the old-line Mississippi Democratic Party at the party's upcoming national convention Aug. 24 in Atlantic City. The new group called themselves the Mississippi Freedom Democratic Party. Old-line Democrats detested this group more than they did our state GOP. And when the MFDP tried to register with the state, Secretary of State and old-line Democrat, Heber Ladner, rejected their application one day before the party's state convention began.[99]

Nonetheless, when the state Democratic convention opened, two slates were presented—one by the traditional old-line Democrats and the other by the new MFDP, which was enjoying some support from the Democratic National Committee. Eventually, delegates decided to recess until September, a move by the old-liners to buy time to make a new, anti-MFDP plan. Bidwell Adam publicly admitted that many white Democrats now wanted to back Goldwater.[100] Eventually, the old-line Democrats tried to maneuver things so that the State of Mississippi might prevent the MFDP from using the word "Democratic." But this did not stick. Attorney General Joe Patterson said the group was "a conspiracy" and a "sham"; the MFDP countersued.[101]

At this point, the two state Democrat groups traveled to Atlantic City to take part in the party's national convention. The State Executive Committee of the Mississippi Democratic Party decided not to share seats with the MFDP group. Paul Johnson said he would not meet with Lyndon Johnson to discuss the problem.[102] Martin Luther King, Jr., led a rally for the MFDP at Atlantic City.[103]

Old-line Mississippi Democratic Party delegates boycotted the national convention's opening night.[104] The next day they voted 53-3 to boycott the rest of the convention, and most returned to Mississippi. Paul Johnson said that "a rift" with the "National Party had been caused that will not heal."[105]

Old-line state Democrats were furious with this new state Democrat group. "Mississippi has been libeled before the nation by a motley crew of agitators calling themselves the 'Freedom Democrats'," bemoaned Mississippi Associate Supreme Court Justice Tom Brady. "These misguided specimens were joined in their vicious triage against the good people of Mississippi by the Big Three of the Negro Revolution—Roy Wilkins of the NAACP, James Farmer of CORE, and the apostle of violent non-violence, Martin Luther King. The obnoxious conduct on the part of the rabid Negro and white high-salaried executives of [the civil rights groups] ... were heard and seen by the civilized world in all their stark vulgarity."[106]

The spectacle of shamed, confused Mississippi leaders at the Democrat's national convention led me to tell Bill Wilkins to round up TV clips of the national proceedings for our possible future use. "Wirt had an immediate sense of the present and future value of this incident in so far as Republican party building and instructed me to do whatever it took to buy as complete a set as possible of news video tapes," Wilkins recalls. "For a price they eventually found their way out a studio door and as I recall we wound up with about six hours of 'dynamite' footage, which proved quite useful in future campaigns."[107]

The height of irony came when Bidwell Adam, after Lyndon Johnson's eventual nomination, suddenly began telling Mississippians that they could vote either Democrat or Republican in the upcoming 1964 presidential election. "There can be no penalty put upon the voter because he crosses a party line," he hypocritically stated, just months after trying to outlaw the Mississippi GOP.[108] My attitude was that any citizen's vote was a good vote if it was for Barry, and so I invited disaffected Democrats to vote with us.[109]

State Democrat leaders hoped to avert an out-right exodus of state voters to the Mississippi Republican Party, while still encouraging voters to back Goldwater as a protest to their national party. They pledged their 44 electors to Goldwater, but tried to say they were "separate-but-united" from our Republican Party.[110] Paul Johnson even wanted a special legislative session to set up more new laws to do this.[111] The very man who had tried to kill our GOP now told others to vote for a Republican, but he still wanted to stay a Democrat! And Johnson's mouthpiece, *The Clarion-Ledger*, editorialized in one headline that "Democrats-for-Goldwater Makes Sense in Forthcoming Election."[112]

It was now clear for all to see: both *The Clarion-Ledger* and the state Democrat leaders cared only about themselves.

In September, the Mississippi Democratic Party reassembled to settle the issue of its presidential electors. They faced a quandary: To tell their loyal supporters to vote for Barry "could mean the state Republican Party will no longer be a teenager," stewed *The Clarion-Ledger*. Former Governor Hugh White, who planned to vote for Barry, admitted: "It will take a devil of a lot to get the people back to the Democrats if they vote for Goldwater in November."[113]

I replied: "The overwhelming majority of Mississippians do not want to play games with the ballot. They want to unite behind Barry Goldwater."[114] The reality was that a fresh Gallup poll showed that 66 percent of Southerners now believed the South would be better off with a two-party system.[115]

The state Democrats were in trouble.

On Thursday, Sept. 10, the re-convened state Democratic convention put on a pitiful display. Party bosses pledged their set of electors to the National Democratic Party, but at the same time they also insisted this was not an actual endorsement of Lyndon Johnson's candidacy. This was nonsensical. President Johnson's seven confirmed state Democrat electors would appear on the November ballot and go for Johnson, they said, but the party would not be identified with Lyndon Johnson; rather, argued Paul Johnson, "I think the Pledge of Allegiance will be in the mind of every Mississippian when he enters the voting booth on Nov. 3. The conservative American candidate will carry the State of Mississippi by a tremendous majority," an obvious allusion to Barry, insisting that "the Lyndon Johnson-Hubert Humphrey ticket is ... the most dangerous political combination in the history of this nation."[116]

Even *The Clarion-Ledger* saw the bigger writing on the wall. "If [Goldwater] does win—and conservatives retain control of the Republican Party—it's at least likely that Mississippi Democrats will assume the Republican label."[117]

The hyper-racist, dictatorial Democrats—as Mississippians had long known them—faced extinction.

• • •

Both national parties now had their presidential candidates, and it was time for the campaigns to hit full force.

Barry's Arizona Mafia quickly led him down the wrong path. We long-time Goldwater backers immediately sensed an increasing shift in his speeches. In his opening speech of the general campaign, Barry mentioned the word "peace" so many times that he sounded like a San Francisco beatnik—18 times in all. "We are preoccupied with peace," he said. "The Republican Party is the peace party." "We seek peace for everyone." In lacing Goldwater's speeches too heavily with feel-good words, Kitchel and Kleindienst destroyed Barry's oratorical power. It was an appeasement to liberal media attacks, with no sense of the candidate's voter base.

Barry did try to talk about the issues. He promised to abolish the draft altogether. He outlined a plan to cut the federal income tax by five percent for five years in a row.

Goldwater's presidential campaign had always been a grass-roots affair. Halfway through the general election campaign, our grass-roots campaign workers had contacted more than 5.3 million households by personal visits and 1.8 million by telephone, compared to 2.3 million and 1.5 million on the Democrat side.[118]

Still, mid-September polls showed Lyndon Johnson with a 65-29 percent lead over Goldwater; 27 percent of normal Republican voters were said to be "defecting."[119] The characterizations against Barry by those within his own party, as well as by Johnson and his vice-presidential running mate, Hubert Humphrey, were working.

Worse than that, the Arizona Mafia continued to tie Barry's hands behind his back, forcing him to pull rhetorical punches. I urgently wrote Republican National Chairman Dean Burch, "It is high time we took off the gloves and started fighting. ... It is high time for some strong words. We've got all the issues, and all that is lacking is our determination to lash out with them in a forceful manner."[120]

Johnson enjoyed vastly more TV time than Goldwater by using his presidential prerogative. He kept telling the nation that it ran the risk of being taken over by "reckless and rejected extremes" and that "the heart of our American way of life is under attack."[121]

Barry's image had been remade by his enemies. But he still filled football stadiums of people in the South who cheered upon his every phrase. Strom Thurmond, the U.S. senator from South Carolina, announced in mid-September he was switching to the Republican Party; this helped Barry in the South, but Thurmond's baggage also hurt Barry elsewhere.[122] Editors of Mississippi's top newspapers all were for Goldwater.[123]

Even Bidwell Adam spoke for Barry during a joint appearance with me before the Mississippi Women's Cabinet of Public Affairs. I poked at Bidwell. "It's ironic," I quipped to the ladies' group. "Adam and I support the same candidate. But it's progress." Just a few months ago, Bidwell had gloated, "At the proper time I will be glad to preach the funeral oration over the political carcass of Wirt Yerger."[124]

I told the women's group that we all should vote for Goldwater, but we also needed to maintain long after this election the healthy competition of a two-party system. "Let [Republicans and Democrats] compete for this precious influence," I said.[125]

My volunteer and my paid staff and I were out there conducting "Goldwater Victory" rallies throughout Mississippi. Former Governor Hugh White, a Democrat, chaired our Jackson rally; noted writer Clayton Rand chaired our Gulfport event; Victor Mavar, our Harrison County chairman, and Manly Molpus, chairman of the Mississippi Young Republican Federation, figured prominently, as did State Senator Ellis Bodron, who chaired our Mississippi Citizens for Goldwater-Miller Committee. Top businessman Warren Hood was our Hinds County chairman.

And then, suddenly, top local state politicians began announcing they were switching membership from the Democratic to Republican party in Mississippi. Eight men in all. The most well-known one was a young Jones County up-and-comer named Charles Pickering. I wrote to congratulate Charles on his move and welcome him; he replied that he wanted to help "build a bigger and better Republican Party in Mississippi to help in the fight to return our nation to a philosophy of conservative, constitutional government."[126]

I couldn't help but note that our two United States senators, James Eastland and John Stennis, were remaining silent during the presidential campaign. I told the media they appeared to be "working strongly behind the scenes" for Johnson, not Goldwater.[127] "It is time the people asked what Senator Eastland's real convictions are. ... It is high time that the blanket of deceit was ripped off."[128]

• • •

As the 1964 presidential campaign wound down, Barry and I both were out there saying the U.S. State Department was soft on Communism. "It is high time the American people insisted upon a president who has the highest moral principles, a belief in individual freedom, and conviction of firmness with the Communists and faith in God," I told a local political gathering.[129]

In October, suddenly the Communist scare abroad flared again.

Nikita Khrushchev was edged out of office in the Soviet Union, replaced by Leonid I. Brezhnev. Then the Chinese exploded their first atom bomb on Oct. 16. Voters said the "Red Scare" was now a bigger election issue than the issue of race,

46 percent to 26 percent.[130] The North Vietnamese were surging into Laos as Johnson considered adding 16,000 more troops a year into a fight that the media called "a U.S.-backed guerilla war that is plainly worse than it was a year ago."[131] Even Rockefeller said Americans were not getting "the full story."[132] A NATO council admitted that Communist-controlled Cuba was a greater threat than previously thought.[133]

In mid-October, the Communist Party, U.S.A., in its magazine *The Worker*, called for Lyndon Johnson to be elected with an "unmistakable mandate." The Communist news organ for America said it was vital to stop Goldwater "from turning our streets into bloody racist battlegrounds," adding Goldwater wanted to take America back "to the dark ages of Hitler Germany." *The Worker* further predicted "a great coalition" including "the Negro people, almost to a man, the labor movement," and others who would now form "the great society."[134]

• • •

In those final days, some of us in the Mississippi Republican Party decided to try something on our own to boost Goldwater's chances. Mississippi's GOP had experienced tremendous fund-raising success in 1964. We had exceeded our quota assigned by the national party. We had almost $200,000 left in our fund—money that needed to be spent.

We felt that the most powerful resource Goldwater had remaining in his campaign arsenal was somehow to re-broadcast the great speech that had been made during the campaign by Ronald Reagan for Barry. I called one of Barry's media agents and asked what was going to be run on TV the night before the election. He said, "Brunch with Barry." The Arizona Mafia had taped this silly show called "Brunch with Barry," which already had run once, and it was scheduled to run again the weekend before the election. The whole goal of "Brunch with Barry" was supposedly to show Barry's softer side, seeking the female vote. I could not fathom anything so off base.

I said, "Well, what about re-airing the Reagan speech?"

Barry's media man liked the idea, but he said the air time for "Brunch with Barry" was already purchased, therefore Reagan's speech would have to run on another station. "Well I don't want to put a penny up for 'Brunch with Barry,' " I said. "We'll definitely put up the money to run Reagan's speech again."

So the Sunday before the presidential election, Reagan's speech was rerun nationally on ABC. It cost the Mississippi Republican Party approximately $145,000. Years later, I was with Ronald Reagan and told him that his speech had been aired with money from Mississippi. He thanked me with his gracious smile. Mississippi had much to do with his success. It was not until later that I learned that the "The Speech" that Reagan delivered actually had originally been written for Goldwater.

Barry, years later, told me in a personal letter:

> The speech that Ron Reagan made, that got him started, was a speech that I was supposed to have made in Milwaukee, but when I received it, and read it, I said this is not for me. It doesn't sound like me, I don't have the fluency to do it, so I said send it to Ron Reagan and let him use it, and that's what we did.[135]

When Barry had read the speech, he somehow hadn't felt capable of pulling it off and had mailed it to Reagan to use. "The Speech" launched Reagan's national star in the conservative political movement and helped put him on the eventual road to the White House. In this sense, the funding of that speech by the Mississippi Republican Party helped launch the national political career of Reagan. In the same letter, Barry defended to me his selection of Kitchel, but also indicated his regret that long-time supporters such as myself were cut out of the loop. He wrote: "I have known Denny Kitchel all of my life. I knew him first when he came to Arizona as a young lawyer, particularly bent to the left, and I watched through the years as he became a great Constitutionalist, and a very devoted conservative. He would be the first one to agree that he did not know a whole lot about running a campaign."[136]

More telling, Barry told me of the fatigue and fatalistic feelings he had experienced even before receiving the nomination. He had eventually come to feel the 1964 race was not possible to win.

> Wirt, ... I don't offer this as an excuse, from the time the Convention was over, and the nomination was ours, to the time we started working, was not more than a few weeks, trying to put together a fine, productive team in that length of time was impossible. I must tell you though, that no Republican, I don't care what his name was, could ever have won the election in 1964. The country was not ready for three presidents in two and a half years. I will admit that I probably could have done better, but I have to confess something to you, that you probably already know, I never had a real "fire in my belly" to conduct that campaign. I just did the best I could.[137]

As the race wound down, Stets Coleman, a prominent businessman from Virginia, secured the Mississippi GOP two seats on the Goldwater campaign plane, the "Yia Bi Kin" (Navaho for "House In The Sky") for the Wednesday, Thursday, and Friday of Oct. 22-24, just before the election. State Finance Chairman Charlie "Buddy" Klumb and I boarded the Boeing 727 with Barry and flew from Washington to New York to attend former President Herbert Hoover's funeral. On Wednesday, Oct. 22, we re-boarded the plane and flew to Los Angeles. We were the only people with him besides his immediate staff. We then took a train with Barry to San Diego, making stops along the way.

Barry was his warm, friendly self. He looked remarkably relaxed and confident. We gave him a check for $100,000 raised from our "Goldwater Victory" rallies, and he was impressed and appreciative. On the plane, I was talking on the phone with Mary, my wife, who was back in Jackson; then Barry took the phone and he and Mary conversed; he also spoke with my three children and accepted Mary's invitation to visit us after the campaign was over.[138]

Since September, when the general election started, Denny Kitchel had been avoiding my letters and phone calls. I'm sure that he was shocked and chagrined to see that I was on the plane with Barry and him.

Kitchel and I at one point found ourselves standing at the plane's front. He was clearly shocked that I was even on the plane at all. He said, "Wirt, I understand you are not real pleased about the campaign."

"Denny," I said, "that's the understatement of the century."

He said, "What you've got to understand, Wirt, is that we're trying to show Barry in a non-emotional form."

I looked at him and responded, "Congratulations, Denny, you've succeeded 1,000 percent. You are doing that to him while the Democrats are running ads showing little girls being blown apart by atomic bombs and social security cards being torn up. And you say that you want to show Barry non-emotionally?"

How could anybody have been that off base? Kitchel and the Arizona Mafia intentionally played down Barry's greatest strength—his passion and his rhetorical ability.

There was little more to offer on my part. I did write Dean Burch with one last suggestion: all of us who loved and supported Barry Goldwater could, on election day, turn our car lights on as a symbolic expression of our hope of "turning on the lights in the White House and the lights of freedom by voting for Barry Goldwater."[139]

One last time, I hit the speaking circuit, which already had taken me on hundreds of stops through our state. I told the Natchez Kiwanis Club, "History may well record that Tuesday's election battle was simply one of the first battles in the all-out war by Americans to regain their freedom."[140] As the weekend before the Tuesday election arrived, I issued a passionate two-page statement:

> Goldwater does not believe our Constitution is outmoded. He realizes that it was conceived by men who feared

big government and he believes there is as much justification for fearing big government today as there was in 1776. He is of the opinion that the government should do nothing for anybody that he can do better himself. This does not mean that he would withhold government aid from those who find themselves in unfortunate circumstances over which they have no control. It does mean that he would first do everything possible to place these people in a position to help themselves. Barry Goldwater is a man in love with his country. ... He knows that there will always be those who threaten us and our national security and he would keep the peace through a thorough program of preparedness. ... He believes that only through utmost individual freedom and states' rights can we achieve the goals we are capable of achieving. The present administration ... would take away the initiative of the average American and make him a ward of the government. Through poor leadership it has allowed a climate of fear to develop—fear for the future in our dealings with Communist nations and fear for personal safety in the streets due to increasing crime and immorality. Barry Goldwater is a man of confidence and he can restore America's confidence. ... For these reasons, we urge Mississippi voters to go to the polls Tuesday, Nov. 3, and elect Barry Goldwater President of the United States.[141]

Dean Burch and others predicted a massive, unexpected surge for Goldwater. Barry's election was not, however, meant to be.

On Nov. 3, Mississippi delivered 87.3 percent of its votes to Barry Goldwater. He carried only Mississippi, South Carolina, Louisiana, Georgia, Alabama, and Arizona. Nationally, Barry was trounced by Johnson, who took 61.1 percent of the popular vote and 486 electoral votes to Barry's 38.5 percent of the popular vote and 52 electoral votes.

• • •

Considering the spoiled-sport actions of Romney, Rockefeller, and Scranton, as well as the biases of the media, in hindsight it is amazing that even 38.5 percent of Americans voted for Barry.

On Nov. 4, I put the national media on notice: "We conservatives through this land have just begun to fight," I said. "We would like to serve this notice on Chet Huntley, David Brinkley, and Walter Cronkite, who, together with the owners of these networks and the people who work under them are the most powerful men in America. The brainwashing that has been engaged in recent years and particularly in the recent months by these gentlemen and the bulk of the national press corps has been utterly fantastic and in our opinion represents a national scandal. These men were the principle culprits in making it appear that Lyndon Johnson was a saint and Barry Goldwater was the devil himself. ... Barry Goldwater would rather be right than president, and conservatives across this nation feel the same way, and theirs is the cause that will some day triumph."[142]

I issued an invitation for principled men and women to come join the new Republicans in Mississippi. "There can be no doubt but that the Republican Party will remain the conservative party of this nation for the rest of our lifetime," I predicted.

Today, I have seen this come to pass. After Ronald Reagan's 1980 presidential election, national political commentator George Will wrote, "It took 16 years to count the votes [of the 1964 election], and Goldwater won."

Across the United States in 2010, the radio airwaves are filled with the tough, clear banter of scores of accomplished, articulate conservative talk-show hosts. Our televisions tune to the 24-hour Fox News station that has a willingness to tell the conservative side of the political story and to hold the old, "major" stations honest. My own state sends mostly Republicans to the United States Senate and House. At the time of this writing, our governor and lieutenant governor are Republicans. They are men who try hard to govern by conservative principles.

In 1998, Barry died. I wrote a letter to the editor of *The Clarion-Ledger.* I poured my heart out in honor of this great man, who visited in my home, who had led a movement that helped change our country, and whose memory I cherish. I wrote:

> Long-time U.S. Senator Barry Goldwater of Arizona died last week. He has been eulogized, but what has not been reported is the tremendous role he played in the development of a two-party system in the South, and particularly a two-party system in the State of Mississippi. Barry Goldwater, owner of Goldwater's Department Stores in Phoenix, Arizona, was elected to the U.S. Senate in 1954 in one of the most bitter contests ever with organized labor doing everything possible to defeat him. The people of Arizona in the face of this opposition elected him then and many times later to the U.S. Senate where he was a great Republican leader. What I have not seen reported is the tremendous and decisive role he played in the development of the Republican Party in the South, which led to the development of a two-party system in Mississippi and other southern states.
>
> Few people in Mississippi today realize the magnitude of the effort to bring about a two-party system, which began with a bitterly fought Mississippi Republican Party convention in 1956. It has also been forgotten how fierce the effort on the part of the Democrats was to thwart the advent of a two-party system and the development of the Mississippi Republican Party. The intimidation and persecution of those in the state who led this development would be difficult for most Mississippians today to believe, but I can assure you it was very real. For example, some lost businesses and others lost their jobs or were transferred out of state. You have to realize that Mississippi in the 1950s did not have a single Republican office-holder at any level of government, no county

officials, no legislator, and certainly no federal- or state-elected person.

Barry Goldwater was severely castigated by the liberal establishment in America and by the extremely liberal and biased news media to a degree that would be hard to appreciate even in our day. He courageously stood firm in the face of this and became a true national leader, even writing a best-selling book ... [*The Conscience of Conservative*] articulating his governmental philosophy which was for very limited government and the rights of the individual.

Goldwater, along with William Buckley, publisher of *The National Review,* were the two most outspoken and articulate leaders espousing the conservative cause when almost all the media and elected officials literally scorned the word "conservative."

At a time when most national leaders disdained Mississippi albeit unfairly, Barry Goldwater provided inspirational encouragement to the Mississippi Republican Party more than any other political figure in the country, and certainly even more than President Dwight Eisenhower. Barry Goldwater paid numerous visits to Mississippi when most American leaders would have nothing to do with our state. In fact, Barry Goldwater was the keynote speaker at the Mississippi Republican Party State Convention held in the House of Representatives chamber in the State Capitol in 1960. Later that year in Chicago at the national convention he met with the Mississippi delegation.

Barry Goldwater during that time was such an inspirational leader that after the Nixon defeat by John F. Kennedy in 1960, a movement began, with the active participation of Mississippians, to draft Barry Goldwater to run for president in 1964. While this effort to nominate him was gathering force, he was very reluctant to allow himself to be nominated for president. Although he began to warm up to the idea of running against President

Kennedy. It would have been a classic ideological battle between Kennedy, a Democratic liberal, and Goldwater, a Republican conservative. This changed dramatically Nov. 22, 1963 when Kennedy was assassinated and Lyndon Johnson, his vice-president, took over as President. The assassination and the elevation of Lyndon Johnson as president along with the tremendous media bias, made it almost impossible for Barry Goldwater to be elected. What ensured his defeat was the Republican Eastern liberal establishment led by Nelson Rockefeller of New York, William Scranton of Pennsylvania, and George Romney of Michigan, all governors of the states who bitterly fought Goldwater in the convention and who refused to support him in the election. This liberal group controlled the Republican Party for decades.

In spite of this, Goldwater received the nomination and even though his heart was not entirely in the contest, did run for President. With all of these obstacles he went down to defeat nationally. Nevertheless, Mississippi admired Goldwater and voted overwhelmingly for his election to the presidency by 87.3% of the vote.

One of the great by-products of the Goldwater campaign was the speech Ronald Reagan gave in his behalf. His one-half hour speech was carried on coast-to-coast television the Sunday afternoon before the election. This was implemented 100% with funds contributed by Mississippians. This Reagan speech and the nationwide exposure was a tremendous boost to his success.

As chairman of the Mississippi Republican Party and an active leader in the Draft Goldwater movement, I was privileged to be a very close "political" friend and admirer.

Without his inspirational leadership we might not have elected a governor, two senators and three congressmen as well as numerous other state and local officials. His courage, fortitude, and patriotic leadership were heartfelt and truly genuine.

In my opinion, there is little doubt that had he been elected president in 1964, the 57,000 Americans killed in Vietnam would still be alive because if we had been in that war at all, he would have led us to immediate victory without casualties, or if any, very few casualties.

Barry Goldwater surely ranks as one of the few true statesmen of our time.[143]

I have purposely gone into great detail about the Goldwater years, mainly because of his influence on the growth not only of the Mississippi Republican Party but also the GOP throughout the South and the nation. His campaign was the turning point for the GOP in Mississippi and the nation. His strong conservative principles have been cornerstones of the Republican Party since his presidential campaign and hopefully will remain for years to come. Barry's conservative principles, patriotism, and integrity, as exemplified in his campaign, set the tone for the future of the Republican Party in this country. As America languishes today amid a growth in the size of federal government so similar to those circumstances in the 1960s, where is our new Barry Goldwater? We desperately need such a leader again today.

CONSERVATIVE CHALLENGE   March, 1964

YERGER AND GOLDWATERS — State Republican Chairman Wirt Yerger Jr., extreme right, is shown talking to Sen. Barry Goldwater and members of his family at a meeting of Goldwater state chairmen in Chicago Feb. 16. Mrs. Goldwater is standing next to the Senator and Barry Goldwater Jr. is at far left. Yerger reported that Goldwater is extremely encouraged in his candidacy for the GOP nomination and predicts that he will win with ease.

VOTING FOR BARRY — Mississippi's seven Republican presidential electors cast the state's electoral votes Monday for Sen. Barry Goldwater. Shown are (left to right): front row — G. D. Causey, Canton; Joe Moore, Pascagoula; Victor Mavar, Biloxi. Back row—State GOP Chairman Wirt Yerger; J. W. Whitten, Batesville; R. H. Buchanan, Bruce; Kelsey McKay, McComb; Julius King, Laurel; and Sec. of State Heber Ladner. (UPI Telephoto)

REPUBLICAN STATE CHAIRMEN'S CONFERENCE
Washington, D. C., Jan. 8-9, 1964

BARRY GOLDWATER
ARIZONA

COMMITTEES:
ARMED SERVICES
LABOR AND PUBLIC WELFARE
SPECIAL COMMITTEE ON AGING

United States Senate
WASHINGTON, D.C.

Dictated July 9, 1964, enroute to California
Transcribed July 14, 1964, in Washington, D. C.

Mr. Wirt A. Yerger, Jr.
Southern Association of Republican
   State Chairmen
Post Office Box 1178
Jackson, Mississippi

Dear Wirt:

Unfortunately, I will have seen you before this letter reaches
you because it is being dictated enroute to San Francisco, but
I did want to answer your letter of July 6.

I must admit that Ray has acted in a very peculiar way, particularly towards me, because I promised to stay out of the
state of Ohio and he in turn inferred that the delegates would
be mine - who wanted to be - at the proper moment. So far,
nothing of that nature has occurred so I must feel that he is
playing it with the other side.

If I happen to be the nominee, you can be assured that the subject of National Chairman will receive my immediate and thorough
attention, as I feel that the National Committee is long past due
for an overhaul. This is no reflection on Bill Miller, for whom
I have the utmost respect. It is merely a reflection on a rather
archaic system with a few archaic people involved.

With best wishes,

Barry

Barry Goldwater

Barry Goldwater

UNITED STATES SENATE

ARIZONA

December 9, 1964

Mr. Wirt A. Yerger, Jr.
Mississippi Republican Party
P. O. Box 1178
Jackson, Mississippi

Dear Wirt:

Having been through campaign after campaign, I know
that the sound trouncing your ticket for the Presidency and Vice Presidency, Bill and myself might
leave you and your fellow Republicans in your state
rather despondent. However, I believe as we begin
to look around after the so-called landslide, we can
see one thing emerging very clearly from which we
can operate a base; namely, approximately twenty-
seven million people in this country believe enough
in what I call sound Republican principles to have
expressed themselves by their vote.

The question now is how do we attract in the next
two years enough additional voters to return many,
many Republicans to the Congress, and in the next
four years to assure a Republican President. We
must keep in mind that about sixty-nine million
Americans voted, which was a lower percentage than
in 1960, and we received eighty percent of the votes
needed for victory, and had some seven to eight
million Republicans who defected to the other side
voted for us, the result would have been greatly
changed. I don't mean to suggest that I think we
could have beaten Johnson, but it would have been
much closer.

-2-

The purpose of this letter is to solicit your criticisms, and I want them to be frank as they should be, and your suggestions. I personally feel that we have a great team at the head of the National Committee, and I place no blame at all on any activity on their part. In fact, I thank them for having made it possible to run a campaign in the black and at the same time satisfy every desire of the candidates and their managers.

Please send the suggestions, etc., to me at my Phoenix address, which is noted below, and I promise you that they will be used for my purposes only and for my eyes only, as I, like you, want to see this Party get ahead, and I think we can do it.

Again, my heartfelt thanks to you for all that you did during this past campagin. I know of your hard work and your dedication and I'll be eternally grateful to you for it.

With best personal wishes,

Barry Goldwater

6250 North Hogahn Drive
Phoenix, Arizona

February 24, 1964

AIR MAIL

Honorable Dwight Eisenhower
Gettysburg,
Pennsylvania

Dear General Eisenhower:

As in many cases in the past, you probably won't ever see this
letter personally because it is critical, but I feel so deeply in
my heart the concern that I want to express that I must satisify
my own conscience.

First of all, we were one of the cities with a dinner on January 29,
and when you came on the screen during the closed - circuit portion
of the program, we were looking for a little bit of the fighting
Dwight Eisenhower of 1952, who was concerned about the future of his
country as not only a Republican but an American. Unfortunately,
we were left not only empty handed on this count, but with only the
idea that there should be forums held around the country to explain
the difference between the two parties and that the Republican
Platform Committee should have a suggestion box so that people could
write in suggestions. I find both of these ideas so shocking naive
politically that I dare not comment on them further except to say
that what the Republican Party and the nation needs more than either
of them a hundredfold is a fighting candidate of the type that you
were in 1952.

While you may not agree with him on many issues, just as many of us
haven't always agreed with you on many issues, The only candidate
being considered at this time that comes even close to filling the
bill is Barry Goldwater. He is the only person in recent years, certainly
since your race in 1952, to breath real life into the organization of
the Republican Party from Maine to California. Not only that, he is
the only Republican who can beat LBJ and start this party of ours on
the road to becoming the majority party once again.

Honorable Dwight Eisenhower
February 24, 1964
Page 2

Let us lay aside our personal likes and dislikes and think of what
is best for America. I am praying that God will guide you in
making the decision to do what is best for America, and that is
for you to throw your support to Senator Goldwater.

                        Sincerely,

                        Wirt A. Yerger, Jr.

WAYJr:sa

P. S. Please don't underestimate the genuine enthusiasm in all
       50 states on the part of the Republican leadership from
       the precinct level up for Senator Goldwater. We will
       need this enthusiasm if we are to win.

D D E

GETTYSBURG
PENNSYLVANIA

Palm Desert, California
March 2, 1964

PERSONAL

Dear Mr. Yerger:

I enjoyed reading your observations about Senator
Barry Goldwater.

Concerning my own attitude to leading figures in
our Party, I am persuaded that until after the 1964
convention, I should adhere to a rule of encouragement to all and impartiality toward all, with favor-
itism toward none -- a position which I believe each
of those leaders would agree to be the only proper
one. While I do not want to give even the appearance
of suggesting the importance of my own support, or
non-support, for any seeking the nomination, I do want
to make it clear that after the nomination, I want to be
in a position to support that name, whatever his identity.

I have the rather deep conviction that we should so
function inside our Party as to encourage a multiplicity
of candidates so that, even though one may be clearly
the favorite, the public interest in our proceedings will
be intense, and our Party will demonstrate vitality by
the eagerness of many to carry its banner. In short, I
should regret it a great deal if we should go into the convention period with a political situation that is cut and
dried. Actually, such a situation would be harmful to
Barry Goldwater himself if it developes that he is to be
the Party's choice.

- 2 -

With appreciation for your interest in writing and best wishes,

Sincerely,

Dwight D Eisenhower

Mr. Wirt A. Yerger, Jr.
Chairman
Southern Association of Republican
  State Chairmen
P. O. Box 1178
Jackson, Mississippi

PERSONAL

HAD ENOUGH?

Join other conservative
Mississippians to meet,
hear and support . . .

**SENATOR BARRY
GOLDWATER**

**THURSDAY--NOVEMBER 29-6:30
HOTEL HEIDELBERG--JACKSON**

Every Mississippian genuinely interested in a return to sound constitutional government owes it
to himself, his family, and his state to meet, hear
and support Senator Goldwater. This is your opportunity to take positive action..don't miss it!

WIRT A. YERGER, JR., CHAIRMAN
MISSISSIPPI REPUBLICAN PARTY AND
MISSISSIPPI GOLDWATER FOR PRESIDENT COMMITTEE
JACKSON, MISSISSIPPI

I AM SHOCKED TO LEARN FROM NEWS SOURCES THAT ANYONE WHO INTENDS

TO VOTE FOR ME IN MISSISSIPPI WOULD EVEN CONSIDER SPLITTING THE

VOTE OF MY SUPPORTERS OR CONFUSING THE ISSUE IN ANY MANNER.

I AM A REPUBLICAN AND SOUGHT AND RECEIVED THE REPUBLICAN

NOMINATION FOR PRESIDENT. I CERTAINLY HOPE THAT REPUBLICANS,

DEMOCRATS OR INDEPENDENTS WHO SUPPORT ME AND THE CONSERVATIVE

CAUSE WILL UNITE BEHIND THE DULY CHOSEN REPUBLICAN ELECTORS IN

YOUR STATE. TO DO ANYTHING ELSE WOULD MERELY FURNISH AID AND

COMFORT TO THE OPPOSITION. WE CAN ILL AFFORD ANY DIVISION

OF STRENGTH. PLEASE EXPRESS MY POSITION TO ALL CONCERNED.

LET'S CCARRY THE ENTHUSIASM OF SAN FRANCISCO FORWARD TO VICTORY

IN NOVEMBER

                                BARRY GOLDWATER

204P CST JAN 3 64 NSB124
NS L PFF525 PFZ4   PFZ4 PD PHOENIX ARIZ 3 NFT
WIRT A YERGER, JR (CHAIRMAN)
  BOX 1178 JACKSON MISS *Lamar Life Bldg*
TODAY I ANNOUNCED MY CANDIDACY FOR THE REPUBLICAN PRESIDENTIAL
NOMINATION. I HAVE DECIDED TO DO THIS BECAUSE OF THE
PRINCIPLES IN WHICH I BELIEVE AND BECAUSE I AM CONVINCED THAT
MILLIONS OF AMERICANS SHARE MY BELIEFS AND WANT THE OPPORTUNITY
TO MAKE A REAL CHOICE IN 1964.
  I HOPE THAT I WILL HAVE YOUR SUPPORT IN A DEDICATED
CAMPAIGN TO ASSURE THEM THAT CHOICE
BARRY GOLDWATER.

C O N F I D E N T I A L

MEMORANDUM

TO: ALL KEY LEADERS

The Goldwater tide is still rising, but heavily financed and experienced opposition is going to make every effort to thwart his bid for the nomination. The last report of this nature which I forwarded to you concerned the meeting in Denver and the strong Goldwater sentiment expressed by so many of the other State Chairmen and the National Committee leaders, and this sentiment was even greater this time except that some of those few who previously remained silent are now attempting to downgrade Goldwater and find another candidate which they can all back in an effort to stop Barry.

The left-wing national press seems to be making a deliberate effort to try and convince everyone that Lyndon Johnson can safely carry the South even against Goldwater. I see this was even put forth in this week's issue of the usually reliable United States News and World Report.

In my opinion, and I am sure in yours, they are misjudging the people of the South, but unless we step up our efforts in order to conclusively prove that we will carry Mississippi and the South for Barry Goldwater, we won't have a chance to prove.it. It is of critical importance to Goldwater's nomination and subsequent election that we not waste time now and put forth a maximum effort to make the "GO GOLDWATER" Dinner the smashing success it must be in this all-important presidential election year. The time for us to roll up our sleeves and go to work to nominate this great American is now.

The seven member Review Committee of the National Committee on which I had the pleasure of serving made its report at this National Committee meeting and made a number of excellent suggestions for improvement in the operation of your national headquarters. In addition, it was reported that for the first time in three years your National Party is in the black without a deficit.

The State Chairmen's meeting had an unusually fine program, and one of the highlights was the program put on by the newly elected Republican Mayor of Louisville, Kentucky, stressing the importance of municipal elections. Research on the vote in this past year's general election indicates the municipalities of our state should be our prime objective in the year 1965. As you know, Rubel carried quite a few of our municipalities around the state.

Your state headquarters is operating more efficiently than ever before, and I trust that you will stop by for a visit whenever you are in Jackson.

Sincerely,

Wirt A. Yerger, Jr., Chairman

P. S. Nelson & Happy Rockefeller plus George Romney and Bill Scranton were each at one of the functions in Washington, but no sale.

STATEMENT BY WIRT A. YERGER, JR., CHAIRMAN, SOUTHERN ASSOCIATION OF
REPUBLICAN STATE CHAIRMEN AND CHAIRMAN, MISSISSIPPI REPUBLICAN PARTY.

November 4, 1964

We conservatives throughout this land have just begun to fight.
We would like to serve this notice on Chet Huntley, David Brinkley,
and Walter Cronkite, who, together, with the owners of these networks
and the people who work under them are the most powerful men in America.
The brainwashing that has been engaged in in recent years and particularly in recent months by these gentlemen and the bulk of the national
press corps has been utterly fantastic and in our opinion represents
a national scandal.

These men were the principle culprits in making it appear that
Lyndon Johnson was a saint and Barry Goldwater was the devil himself,
when in fact, more nearly the opposite is true. America has not
rejected conservatism by any stretch of the imagination.

Barry Goldwater would rather be right than President, and
conservatives across this nation feel the same way, and theirs is the
cause that will some day triumph.

History shows that the best man isn't always elected, and
history also shows that those overwhelmingly defeated once can come
back to win later by an overwhelming margin.

In spite of these attempts of the national television and
press media to discount conservative control of the Republican Party
it is in fact a reality. There can be no doubt but that the
Republican Party will remain the conservative party of this nation
for the rest of our lifetime, and we now call on all true conservatives to unite in the Republican Party to help insure conservative
victories in the battles that lie ahead.

Let's face it, Senator Goldwater was bucking overwhelming odds
when he was running not only against an incumbent President and all
the power of the administrative bureaucracy, but also against the
liberal television and news media. When the election is viewed in
this light, and when the great advance that has been made in the
South is considered, conservatives can take heart in the results of
November 3. As an example of the increased Southern influence in
the Republican Party by virture of carrying five deep South states,
31 additional delegates from these states will be at the 1968
Republican National Convention, and the State Chairman of each of
these states will have automatically been made members of the
Republican National Committee.

#

September 25, 1964

Honorable Dwight D. Eisenhower
Gettysburg
Pennsylvania

Dear General Eisenhower:

The program with you and Senator Goldwater at your farm was excellent and most worthwhile. I do wish that you could have been given the opportunity to back up Senator Goldwater's stand on the use of nuclear weapons and that you could have been a little bit more enthusiastic about what Barry Goldwater's election means to the future of freedom and to America's future. I note in Illinois last night you had a good statement along this line.

It must make you sick to see so many people who claimed to be dedicated Republicans during the Eisenhower administration and who served on such high levels, going all out for Lyndon Johnson. I hope that your disappointment in this group of pure phonies will be displayed by an all out effort on your part to insure Barry Goldwater's election. Frankly, I hope that you can make more and more enthusiastic statements about Barry Goldwater and attack Lyndon Johnson for the phoney that he is.

General Eisenhower, in my opinion, an all out effort on your part could be that all important difference between success and failure. There are a lot of us, including my- self, who have been among your most severe critics in the past who would be eternally grateful for not just token support, but all out support.

Trusting you will give this matter your attention, I am

Respectfully,

Wirt A. Yerger, Jr.,
Chairman

WAY; jr/lm

July 2, 1964

Honorable Dwight D. Eisenhower
Gettysburg,
Pennsylvania

Dear General Eisenhower:

The question in the minds of people throughout America,
and particularly in my own mind, is what will folks
think of Dwight Eisenhower thirty days from now? Will
he have been discredited regardless of whether or not
he wins or loses in a last minute attempt to stop
Goldwater's nomination?

There can be no doubt but that Senator Barry Goldwater
is the overwhelming choice of both the organizational
and rank and file Republicans throughout America, and
in view of the press, radio and television bias against
him it is truly amazing that he has held up so wonderfully
well and his popularity remained so high. In my opinion,
even if you came out full force against Senator Goldwater
he would still be nominated, but in doing so you would
seriously damage the Republican Party and our chances for
victory this year.

The campaign of William Scranton for the nomination has
been one of the more pathetic examples in my lifetime of
a national political performance. He is so far away from
being an Eisenhower that it absolutely defies comparison.

General, we hope and pray you will do what is best for
America and the Republican Party, and there can be no
real doubt that that is to get behind Senator Goldwater
with everything at your command so that we can defeat
Lyndon Johnson in November.

Thank you.

                    Sincerely,

                    Wirt A. Yerger, Jr.,
                    Chairman

WAYJr:sa

DENYING A DICTATORSHIP: In the following six-page speech, Wirt boldly challenged Mississippi legislators to stand up for a two-party system and to support the right to free speech.

TESTIMONY OF MISSISSIPPI REPUBLICAN STATE CHAIRMAN, WIRT A. YERGER,JR.
BEFORE REGISTRATION OF ELECTIONS COMMITTEE, MISSISSIPPI: HOUSE OF
REPRESENTATIVES, APRIL 6, 1964.

We would first like to express our appreciation to Mr. Sillers, to Representative Strickland and to Members of the Committee for this opportunity to present our viewpoint on the proposed election law changes.

While these proposals are intended to stamp out the Republican Party in Mississippi, I am sure that many of you by now, realize that they would go far beyond that aim.

These proposals are a vindictive effort to forever bind our state to the National Democrat Party. They would take away the sacred right that our people have held since time immemorial to cast their ballots for an independent, a Democrat, Republican or a Hindu, if they so desired.

Most backers of this proposed legislation have said that these laws are intended to equalize rules for both parties. They say this in spite of the fact that their battle cry only six months ago was "Bury the Republicans for 100 years", "Bury The Scalawags", & Stamp Out Republicanism."

In a bitter election struggle in the face of more personal intimidation than perhaps in any state-wide election in American history, Rubel Phillips, the Republican candidate for Governor, rolled up almost 40% of the total vote or approximately two of every five votes cast.

Now, some of these same forces are attempting to do through legislation what they obviously could not do at the polls. As one newsman has described it, "If you can't lick em, then abolish them."

In the heated debate in the Mississippi Senate just ten days ago the backers of this legislation dropped all pretense concerning the actual intent and effect of this vicious legislation. Senator George Yarbrough, said of one measure, "With this bill, you'll have your election in August and be through with it."

An effort has been made to lead you to believe that Republicans have some special advantage under present election laws. Nothing could be further from the truth.

You have been told that Republicans nominate by convention, while Democratic candidates are forced to run in primaries. Let us put this misconception to rest once and for all.

In the general election of 1959, there was not a single Republican nominee. In 1963, there were 33 Republican candidates for an estimated 2,500 offices in the State of Mississippi.

Yerger P-1

Our party is small and growing, but none of our 33 candidates had opposition or put another way, sought the same office. However, if two or more Republicans had filed for the same office, they would have had to run in a primary election, just as opposed Democrats did.

The Republican Party could not have gotten around holding a primary for the opposed candidates, because there is State Law and applies to us just as it does to Democrats. In fact, we look forward to the day under present law when two or more candidates will file for many offices making Republican primaries a reality. For example, it is very likely that the next Gubernatorial Election (1967) will find at least two and probably more seeking the Republican Gubernatorial nomination.

At this time, I would like to very briefly outline the fundamental objections to five of the bills sent over from the Senate.

First, let me again re-emphasize that we operate under exactly the same laws that the Majority Party does, except that our primaries are not paid for by the Taxpayers as are those of the Democrats.

SENATE BILL 1764

Senate Bill 1764 makes it a requirement that a properly constituted county convention must have a majority of precincts represented. Even if our precincts in Mississippi were all of relatively the same size in the number of voters, which they are not, this provision would be unfair, because if a man or woman desires to be Republican, Democrat or Independent it should be their "Free Choice" without being told they cannot participate because certain rigid requirements have not been met.

Even if we assume a percentage of precincts would be fair, which it certainly is not, the widely disproportionate number of voters in various precincts makes it possible for a clear majority of voters to be disfranchised. This is true because more than half of Mississippi's voters are in less than ten per cent of the precincts.

Of our state's 1,888 precincts, 323 precincts cast less than 50 votes and 710 precincts, or more than one out of three, cast less than 100 votes in the 1963 General Election.

Let's look at several counties specifically. Take the case of Tunica and Humphreys Counties where half of the voters are in only one precinct. One third of the voters in Coahoma County are in only one of seventeen precincts in the county. Or take the cases of Newton, Noxubee and Montgomery Counties where half the precincts contain only 10% of the voters.

Whether an individual chooses to be an active Democrat, Republican or Independent, he should not be restrained by law from

Yerger P-2

participating or running as a candidate and this is exactly what the
effect of this bill would be: A basic denial of individual freedom
and personal liberty.

SENATE BILL 1768

Senate Bill 1768 concerning the providing of primary election
poll books for each party provides that poll books shall not be issued
to any party not organized under the strict and inequitable provisions
of Senate Bill 1764, just discussed. This proposed law is unfair and
unjust because it denys the minority political party access to the poll
book of registered voters which is essential to the conduct of a
statewide party primary for having its candidates names placed on the
General Election Ballot. Such a provision would prevent a party from
holding a statewide primary in every county and thus make it even more
difficult to poll the required ten per cent of the vote in a statewide
primary.

SENATE BILL 1776

Present law states specifically that all three members of the
County Election Commission shall not be members of the same party.
While in the past the elected state Democratic leadership have ignored
this law completely it is of utmost importance and only fair to all
concerned that the minority party have representation on the county
commission which conducts the elections and thereby controls the
counting of the ballots. Senate Bill 1776 strikes out the provision
requiring representation by the minority party and is therefore extremely
unfair and not in the interest of good and honest government. Who ever
heard of an election being held with only one side allowed to give out
and count the ballots? How would Mississippians feel if whenever our
states football teams played our opponents always provided the game
officials?

SENATE BILL 1766

Present law provides for the declaration by the proper party
executive committee that the sole and only candidate for party nomination
shall be declared the party nominee for the General Election Ballot.
Senate Bill 1766 would do away with this provision. It is under this
provision that all 33 of the Republican candidates in 1963 were declared
the party nominees and placed on the General Election Ballot, while at the
same time well over five hundred Democratic nominees were put on the General
Election ballot in exactly the same manner. In other words for every
unopposed Republican candidate there were better than fifteen unopposed
Democrat candidates also nominated without their name even appearing on

Yerger P-3

the August primary ballot. Less than one per cent of these Democrats so nominated had any opposition, even in the General Election.

Included among this group of unopposed Democrat nominees were 30 members of the legislature or what amounts to better than 17% of the entire state legislature. The highly regarded Mr. Sillers, was one of these, as was Representative Russell Fox of Claiborne County, a member of your Committee, as well as many other outstanding legislators.

As a matter of fact the only two elected Republicans thus far in the state, Representative L. L. (Mac) McAllister of Meridian and County Attorney Joe Sams, Jr., of Lowndes County, defeated Democrat opponents nominated without opposition and therefore without a party primary.

This proposed law also still provides that a candidate must take a loyalty oath even though most state Senators intended to remove this provision. This law sounds like something out of Bobby Kennedy's book, and certainly all freedom loving Mississippians deeply resent political loyalty oaths.

SENATE BILL 1767

Senate Bill 1767 provides that candidates must run in primaries even if they are unopposed. This brings up the question of whether the bill implies that S peaker Sillers, twenty-nine Legislators and the more than 400 other unopposed Democrat nominees were unfairly and improperly nominated or took undue advantage of present law. We don't believe they did, but some backers of this legislation apparently do.

Such a mandatory primary, where there is no opposition within the party, would have absolutely no purpose whatsoever other than wasting the candidates time and his and the taxpayers' money, as it would be a foregone conclusion who the party's nominee would be and the results of such a primary would be absolutely without purpose.

The proposed law also provides that at least ten per cent of all those voting in both party primaries must vote in the minority party's primary in order for any of that party's candidates to be put on the General Election Ballot. This law systematically denies access to the General Election Ballot to the minority party candidates. Less than one out of every one hundred offices filled last year had a Republican candidate. The sponsors of this legislation know this and also realize that for many years to come in most counties 90% or more of the local offices will not be contested by Republican candidates making it virtually impossible for the minority party to attain 10% of those participating in both primaries.

Why place undue and unfair restrictions on candidates? Why not allow the voters their right to a free choice in the General Election?

One provision of this same bill absolutely eliminates the right of a person to seek office as an Independent by requiring a petition by 10% of the registered voters. It also provides none of those signing the petition may vote in any party primary. While we would agree that an Independent should file for office at the same time as party candidates, a person should not be totally and effectively prevented from running as an Independent if that is his desire.

Another very clever and unfair provision provides that all candidates for each party shall be listed separately from the other party candidates and independent candidates. This means a rigged ballot designed to confuse the discriminating voter. The ballot in state elections would be approximately a foot wide and three feet long.

SUMMARY

Impartial observers readily admit that the majority of last year's Republican candidates could have easily won election as Democrats, had they been able to do this in good conscience. However, they put their principles and convictions first and ran as Republicans.

If, as some say, Republicans have an undue advantage over Democrats under the present laws, why did only 33 out of more than 7500 candidates seek office as Republicans?

No public office holder or Democrat candidate in Mississippi has anything to fear from good honest competition with Republicans, as long as he is the most qualified and is doing a competent job. Only those not confident of their abilities or those ashamed of their record have anything to fear from Republican competition, because most Mississippians want to support the "Best Men" regardless of party.

The fact of the matter is that by fundamental beliefs and convictions at least sixty per cent of Mississippi's local and state office holders and the same high percentage of Mississippi voters are Republicans, but some of these don't yet realize that they are. Heretofore, the only way to run for office has been in the Democrat primary, and it is only for this reason that so many officeholders are technically Democrats. The State Democratic Party leadership tries desperately to make those public officials feel allegiance to the Democrat party when in truth they owe the party absolutely nothing.

The young and rapidly growing Mississippi Republican Party is made up largely of disgusted former Democrats who seek only better Government for their state and nation. They have captured the imagination of tens of thousands of independent-minded, conservative Mississippians.

Yerger P-5

and at the same time gained the respect and admiration of political leadership throughout the United States with their willingness to face countless obstacles in order to put principles first rather than expediency.

Mississippi Republicans are mostly native Mississippians, born, reared and educated in Mississippi. We raise children, worship God, support our communities, pay taxes, and have honest convictions just as each of you. We seek no special privileges but only justice and fairness under the law, just as all Mississippians have a right to expect regardless of their political philosophy. We deeply resent, as do all fair minded Mississippians, any attempts through legislation to take away precious freedoms which countless thousands of Mississippians have given their lives to protect.

The net effect of this proposed legislation would be to establish by law in Mississippi a one-party "Police State" such as they now have in Communist Russia and Castro's Cuba.

It would be interesting to learn on what grounds backers of these election law changes would oppose the vicious National Civil Rights Legislation. They could certainly not base their opposition on any "threat to individual freedom."

If our state's election laws are to be revised, it should not be done in haste, but only after deliberate and careful consideration and thorough study by a bi-partisan commission. After all, the next county and statewide races are not until 1967.

It cannot be said that there is any popular demand whatsoever for changes in our present election laws. In fact, it can be said that the overwhelming majority of Mississippians, whether Republicans, Democrat or Independent are deeply concerned over the threat to freedom posed by this legislation.

We are confident you, the Members of the Legislature, will live up to your responsibilities to all Mississippians and to our State's future. May Almighty God guide you in your deliberations.

Yerger P-6

Barry Goldwater may have been an unrelieved disaster for the National Republican Party, but he put the Mississippi GOP back in business for the first time since Reconstruction.

—Time magazine, 1965

The Mississippi Republican Party is moving right along the road to success. ... Mississippi has become in fact a two-party state.

—The Clarion-Ledger, 1965

Nobody seems to know now just what a Democrat is in this Deep South state with its one-party tradition. At present there are three varieties of Democrats.

—The Associated Press, 1965

12

1965

A TWO-PARTY SYSTEM ACHIEVED!

Many Beltway Republican liberals were angry about Goldwater's loss and our conservative takeover. They tried to convince everyone that Goldwater had split the party and that everyone must now move quickly to re-unify. They, however, had split the GOP.

One Southern state chairman offered better wisdom: "Continue the policies of Barry Goldwater. Soon the American people will awaken and find that the 'Great Society' is a costly political promise that will bankrupt the American government."[1]

That wisdom over the decades has proved true.

Nonetheless, GOP liberals ousted Dean Burch as chairman of the Republican National Committee. Dean, in actuality, had been a weak leader. Burch was replaced by Ohio's Ray Bliss, who had been serving as chairman of the National State Chairman's Association. In 1965, the NSCA appointed me vice chairman.[2]

Bidwell Adam said Burch's ouster was a horrible defeat for me. He invited Goldwater voters back into the old-line Democratic Party. "Rockefeller, Scranton, Javits and Romney have now become the four horsemen of the Republican Party," Adam crowed.

I replied: "We are glad to know that Mr. Adam is still alive. ... He can tell his friend Lyndon Johnson that Ray Bliss is a strong conservative."[3]

Our party in Mississippi was very much alive. Prentiss Walker from Mize, Mississippi had won the state's Fourth District U.S. House of Representatives seat, a first for our state GOP. Walker was a solid conservative, winning a perfect rating during the 80th Congress, his first, from the conservative Americans for Constitutional Action.[4]

Prentiss was one of eight new GOP elected officials in Congress as a result of the Goldwater effect. Georgia had one Republican to nine Democrats; Virginia, two to eight; Tennessee, three to six; North Carolina, two to nine; Florida, two to ten; and Mississippi, one to four.[5]

Of the 99 members of the U.S. House of Representatives, 16 were now Republicans from ten Southern states; but 40 Republican congressmen from other parts of the nation had been voted out in 1964.

If our Mississippi GOP had run more candidates in 1964 alongside Goldwater, they would have won. We missed a tremendous opportunity. I had wanted to run more candidates, but others in our state party had not. *Time* magazine noted both our state GOP's success and our missed opportunity: "Barry Goldwater may have been an unrelieved disaster for the National Republican Party, but he put the Mississippi GOP back in business for the first time since Reconstruction. He won an astonishing 87 percent of the state's vote; at the same time, the only Republican who ran for Congress was elected, and Republican officials are still kicking themselves for not having gone after all five Mississippi seats in the House of Representatives."[6]

• • •

Mississippi Democrats in early 1965 quickly saw the political writing on the wall. Consider:

- The effect of the 1964 Civil Rights Act was now sweeping the South. Waves of county-based federal registrars had now moved into Mississippi to register more blacks to vote.

- The introduction of Lyndon Johnson's new Voting Rights Act of 1965 consumed political debate in 1965 before achieving passage in the fall. It would remove any literacy standard as a requirement to vote.

- The new Mississippi Freedom Democratic Party, recognized at the 1964 national convention, was now a player in Mississippi. The group in 1965 called on the U.S. Congress to unseat all of Mississippi's congressmen for opposing them at the 1964 Democratic National Convention. By a 276-148 margin, the House let the old-line Democrat congressmen stay.

Meanwhile, Goldwater had radically altered Mississippi's political landscape. Responding to these changing realities, I told Bill Wilkins to prepare a detailed report on the state's new political voting trends.

Wilkins recalls that report:

"Where do we go from here and how do we get there?" was my mandate from Wirt. Responding, I prepared a detailed report, "Negro Voting Trends—A Mississippi Dilemma," which Wirt presented to the State Central Committee, resulting in much serious deliberation over several long winter nights. Ultimately, the committee directed that we undertake a "Conservative Voter Registration Campaign" which, if I recall correctly, was not especially successful, as it was hard to get much enthusiasm from "the troops" without the more immediate motivation of an election campaign.[7]

Bill Wilkins' report confirmed what most Mississippians intuitively were seeing: a massive shift would be occurring in our state's voting patterns. Wilkins' "Confidential Report Copy No. 1" stated, "Negroes in the South and throughout the nation voted as a solid block for Lyndon Johnson and voted the straight Democratic ticket in the 1964 elections. ... Senator Goldwater ... received as little as one percent of the Negro vote in some southern states. ... Out of a total of 422,256 Negroes of voting age in Mississippi, only about 32,000 are registered to vote. This total has risen steadily over the last few years. From 22,000 in 1954 to 26,000 in 1959, and 28,500 in 1962 to the present figure. At present, only about 7.5 percent of the 422,256 Negroes of voting age in Mississippi are registered to vote. This contrasts sharply with the white voter registration in the state. Out of 748,266 whites of voting age in Mississippi, approximately 568,228 or 76 percent are registered to vote. White voter registration has shown only moderate change during recent years."[8]

The report made it clear that one party was going to receive a massive influx of new voters. "In the South as a whole, a total of 2,164,000 Negroes are now registered to vote. This is an increase of almost 700,000 in the last two years."[9]

Wilkins added: "One could certainly expect an organized drive by civil rights organizations to register Negroes to vote in Mississippi, once the federal government intervenes in the States' voter registration process. ... A conservative estimate would indicate that 130,000 to 150,000 Negroes would be registered to vote in Mississippi by the time of the 1966 congressional election registration deadline and that an additional 75,000 to 100,000 Negroes could be registered prior to the 1967 state elections. ... Negro voter registration would eventually pass the 300,000 mark and 300,000 could possibly be registered by the 1968 presidential election."[10]

The report ultimately concluded: "An increase in Negro voter registration ... can radically change the political picture in Mississippi ... and there will be very little left ... of the regular state Democrat organization. ... It will be extremely hard for Republicans to elect a United States senator if they must spot the Democrat nominee one hundred or one hundred and fifty thousand votes to begin with. ... Mississippi Republicans will not be opposing the traditional Democrat Party in Mississippi as has been done in recent years. ... Mississippi Republicans will have to oppose a Democrat Party with a base constituted similar to that found in Northern and Eastern states. There will be a very clear liberal-conservative division in the state along party lines."[11]

Wilkins was a brilliant political analyst. All of his predictions came true. His analysis showed us that we in the state GOP clearly would not have a chance to gain this massive minority block; plus, any effort to do so would likely require forfeiting our very real conservative tenets of small government and less federal intervention. Even then, the liberal national establishment in the media and Democratic Party—with Lyndon Johnson in power—would continue their unstated goal of stereotyping the word "conservative" as a racist label.

It was not realistic to expect good minority men and women to see past the realities of our state's old-line Democrat "conservatism" and join our more principled conservative ranks, especially when the NAACP and other civil rights groups were bidding them to come into the Democratic Party.

Meanwhile, some decent conservative Democrat leaders in Mississippi were now being punished or kicked out of their party for having supported Barry. Liberal political novices were being elevated for having opposed him.

All of these facts added up to "the irreversible dynamics of the Negro vote," noted top Beltway political writers Rowland Evans and Bob Novak. The media's year-long 1964 slander campaign against Goldwater had caused most blacks to consider Barry a bigot; and by that logic, all conservative Republicans were, too. So black Americans now moved *en masse* into the Democratic Party in 1965. "The Negroes ... were washed" into the Democratic camp "by the Goldwater campaign," claimed Evans and Novak.[12]

Our Republican state leadership made a choice. It was a political choice, as it had to be. The choice was to stage an all-out voter registration of every possible remaining conservative-leaning voter in the state.

In another confidential report by Wilkins titled, "Mississippi Republican Party: 1965 Conservative Voter Registration Campaign Plan," Wilkins rightly surmised: "A way must be found for the Mississippi Republican Party to meet this challenge" of the new political demographics. We set a goal of registering "one hundred and fifty thousand ... new registrants."[13]

• • •

As this played out, the Voting Rights Act of 1965 was coming into being. It would take most of the year to pass. It would outlaw using literacy standards as a voter criteria in key Southern states. But it would still permit literacy tests to be used in other states including California and New York, whose voters had backed Johnson in 1964.

I wrote Lyndon Johnson calling this an "injustice" and act of "discrimination ... against the two million law abiding, tax paying, God fearing, and proud citizens of the State of Mississippi." I added: "The State of Mississippi does not seek special favors" but it did "deserve to be treated fairly, with due consideration being given to the fact that problems of a serious nature exist throughout our country."[14] If the act was to be applied the same throughout the nation, it would have been more reasonable; but national Democrats were not going to do that because it would risk raising their own voting bases' ire in Boston, New York City or Los Angeles, etc.

Our national congressional Republicans put forth an alternative bill to Lyndon Johnson's. The Republican Ford-McCulloch Bill would have certified any citizen with a 6th-grade education level to vote, or anyone who could pass a basic reading test. It would have been applied to every state in the Union where discrimination was proven to occur, not just in the South. No poll tax could be used to discriminate. And voter fraud would be punished as a criminal act.[15]

This was a fair and smart plan. I still believe someone should be able to read in order to vote. Our state GOP called Lyndon Johnson's new bill "punitive, immoral, and hypocritical."

Clarke Reed, our Washington County Republican Chairman and now a state GOP executive committee member, said the proposed law is "designed virtually to punish only Southern states that voted for Barry Goldwater in the presidential election."

Our GOP executive committee adopted a resolution saying, in part, "The Mississippi Republican Party wants to upgrade the electorate of our state and nation by means of voter qualification tests, while this bill would remove all voter qualifications and create a pool of illiterates ... whose vote could be controlled by liberal extremists and demagogues."[16]

About this time, Governor Paul Johnson panicked when faced with President Johnson's new national voting bill. In a complete reversal from any and all policies he had previously held, Gov. Johnson began advocating his own set of state voting-rights bills, the very sort he once professed to hate. If his old-line Democrats couldn't stop Mississippi blacks from voting, then they would pull them into their old-line party and control them.

While furiously engaged in holding onto their raw power, Paul Johnson and his state Democrats were not leading on key issues such as Mississippi's economy. In doing so, they scared off business and industrial growth with their hard-line, racist image. E.J. Palmer, president of the Mississippi Manufacturers Association, said racial violence in our state had cost us new industry. He added, "Nothing can be gained by anyone by a continuation of what has happened in the past."[17]

Charlie Klumb told the Hinds County Junior Bar Association that we needed real leadership in 1965. "Our state and its leaders are going to have to come to grips with the real problems that beset us, rather than being totally preoccupied with the race question as serious as it may be. We are still fiftieth in the nation in per capita income, teachers' salaries and many other important matters which are often overlooked."

Charlie said our leaders should show "more dignity," adding, "Mississippians have a right to expect this in a state where the poorest sharecropper has pride and dignity, if nothing else."[18]

• • •

Lyndon Johnson pushed harder than ever for the Voting Rights Act of 1965 to get through Congress. Meanwhile, Goldwater publicly said more laws were not the solution. "I think we have enough laws," he told a high-school group in Arizona. "If the president and the attorney general don't want to use them [the laws already on the books], I don't think more will help." Removing any literacy requirement for voting was foolish, he said. "I don't want to see us destroy a whole concept of government by writing laws so loose that just anyone would be able to vote, whether qualified or not."[19]

I told Mississippians we needed "sober judgment" and not "emotional panic" regarding voting laws. Our citizens were "strongly opposed to discrimination against any qualified voter," I said, but I also suggested that the new voting rights bills and pressure tactics by civil rights activists had created potential "geographic discrimination" against the South in general.[20]

Our party in 1965 for the first time had enough Republican leaders that we actually had GOP candidates competing within primaries in some of that year's municipal elections.

Two Republicans ran against one another both in Hattiesburg and in Columbus.[21] We had candidates for mayor running in a record eight cities: Hattiesburg, Columbus, Pascagoula, Clarksdale, Long Beach, Moss Point, Laurel, and Vicksburg.[22] In 19 cities statewide, a Republican was seeking some city office. In Pascagoula, our man John Gautier sought the mayor's post, while ten party members were in the race for five city council seats.[23] In Jackson, two in the GOP ran for a commissioner's seat.

After all their years of living life unchallenged, some Democrats actually started whining that our candidates now got too much media coverage. "The Republican in Mississippi has it made," wrote reporter William I. Chaze. "At least, it has it made as far as publicity is concerned. ... Those Republicans, ... when they run, the papers help pick up the ball and carry it. Maybe it's the instinct of rooting for the underdog."[24]

How ironic!

On Tuesday, May 11, the state's municipal election primaries were held. We ran a record 55 Republicans in municipal primaries. Democrat candidates won by a 10-to-1 margin over our Republicans on May 11 in Hattiesburg and Laurel. We were not discouraged, however. The June 8 primary would see 47 of our candidates on the ballot. "People in the cities and towns of Mississippi are ready for two-party government," I declared.[25]

On June 8, we made history.

Republicans Paul E. Grady of Hattiesburg and R.D. Harmond of Columbus won their mayoral races—both were firsts for our state GOP. "These victories were particularly significant because they were at the grass-roots level," I announced. "And this is the greatest source of any party's strength."[26]

Predictably, Paul Johnson tried to downplay our victories. He blamed "voter apathy" and added, "This two-party system is a problem."[27]

The nation took note. *Time* magazine reported,

Last week, in a series of municipal elections, the GOP proved that its 1964 performance was not a flash in the pan. Where the party ran only two candidates in the 1961 municipal elections, this time it put up no fewer than 46—seven for mayor, 39 for lesser posts in 18 towns and cities. Sensing a threat to Democratic rule, Governor Paul Johnson urged Mississippians to the polls for "probably the most important election in this state's recent history."

When the votes were tallied, even the hopeful Republicans were surprised. They elected a city councilman in Columbus, a total of seven aldermen in four other towns. More important, they elected two mayors—the first ever in Mississippi. In Hattiesburg, Lawyer Paul Grady, 41, who lost a runoff election for mayor as a Democrat in 1961, decided he'd rather switch before fighting again, did much better as a Republican. Though Hattiesburg is the Governor's home town, Grady defeated Democratic Incumbent Claude Pittman Jr. 2,429 to 1,827. In Columbus, another Democrat-turned-Republican, City Councilman Robert D. Harmond, 54, beat Democratic Mayor William Propst, 1,394 to 1,191.

In most leagues, nine wins out of 46 would be rated an anemic average, but Mississippi has been a one-team league for so long that GOP officials were elated. To Republican State Chairman Wirt Yerger, Jr., an efficient organizer who has seeded all of Mississippi's 82 counties with GOP workers, the party's victories represented "a history-making breakthrough, particularly because they were at the grass-roots level." Next year, added Yerger, the GOP will try for all of Mississippi's congressional seats, and will even contest veteran Senator James O. Eastland's. Said Yerger: "We think Eastland is vulnerable."[28]

Only weeks later, our Young Republican Federation took 17 members to its national conference, our biggest group ever. Manly Molpus, YRF state director, said it showed "the growing strength of the South and of conservatives in the affairs of the national group."[29]

We were setting our sites on 1966 and our state's senate and congressional races, plus key judgeships. My main concern was "the availability of top-notch candidates," I told the media. "Our big job now is candidate recruitment."[30]

Meanwhile, three groups of Mississippians were trying to claim leadership of the state's Democratic Party.

• • •

Back in 1962, Robert Oswald—then-president of the Young Democrats of Mississippi—had let that group's charter expire. In 1965, a new biracial group called the Young Democratic Clubs of Mississippi applied for the charter, but the group was stalled.

Now a power struggle emerged between those two groups. Members of both the former Young Democrats of Mississippi and the current Young Democratic Clubs met at Tougaloo College on Sunday, May 1, to seek common ground. State AFL-CIO union boss Claude Ramsey, and Lawrence Guyot, executive chairman of the Mississippi Freedom Democratic Party, influenced the meeting.[31]

A second meeting at Tougaloo College of the two Democrat factions also ended without agreement. Some in the Young Democratic Clubs of Mississippi were saying that no one should be accepted into the newly forming Democrat group if they attended, or had attended, a still-segregated college such as the University of Southern Mississippi or Mississippi State University, which integrated on June 25, 1965. Others argued that someone was not a segregationist just because they attended a segregated college.

Whatever the two groups decided ultimately would require approval by the national Democrat leadership. A representative of the national party told the Tougaloo gathering that the national party would insist any new Young Democrats group have a strong pro-civil-rights base.[32]

Even as these two groups battled for control of the Young Democrats of Mississippi charter, the old-line state Democrats played their same old tune. On the one hand, Governor Paul Johnson tried to convince state citizens that he was holding a hard line against new federal civil rights laws; on the other, he was pushing new state civil rights bills through the state legislature to hedge his bets. He wanted the state to have its own set of new voter laws before Lyndon Johnson's Voting Rights Act of 1965 passed the United States Congress.

"Mississippians are anxious to improve our relations with our sister states and the federal government," Johnson said at a special legislative session.[33] Could this be the same man I had had battled in years past?

Paul Johnson's logic was to try to preempt Lyndon Johnson's Voting Rights Act of 1965 by having state legislators approve new state laws letting non-reading citizens vote. The decision still had to be approved by a referendum vote of Mississippi citizens, because it required changing the state's constitution. That vote was to take place on Aug. 17, 1965. Charles

Evers was now field secretary for the state NAACP, the role his brother Medgar once held. He was assembling volunteer registrars to enlist more black voters. Charles, who eventually became a Republican, understood that his workers were setting a tone for our state's future race relations. "We ... have stressed good conduct, being well-dressed and neat, which are major steps in getting people to accept us." He said he wanted to give "anyone the opportunity to show good faith" in this new era of race relations.[34]

Paul Johnson countered Evers by publicly, blatantly, urging all white voters in the state to register to vote and to vote with his group.[35]

The Governor started attacking me again via the media for my efforts to build a two-party system. He said my effort to build the Republican Party in Mississippi was "dangerous and plays right into the hands of a minority, whether it be black, white, labor or industrial." I told the media that our governor was acting just like President Johnson, saying one thing while doing another. The strategy of both Johnsons, I said, "seem[ed] to be to register more Democrats and at the same time legislate conservative opposition out of existence."[36]

The leaders of the Mississippi Freedom Democratic Party saw Paul Johnson's hypocrisy, just as I saw it. They said the governor's plan was to "side step the [upcoming] federal voting regulations."[37]

I had urged state legislators not to pass such laws. I asked them not to get "caught up in the emotional panic which has seized most of our nation's congressmen and senators. We need laws which will serve the present, but we also need legislation that will be good ten years from now."[38] For saying this, Johnson lumped me and his Mississippi Freedom Democratic Party detractors together. He said, "Yerger has thus joined the revolutionary demonstrators of the so-called Freedom Democratic Party in its brazen attempt to discredit and disrupt the present special session of the legislature."[39]

The MFDP leadership and I were, in fact, similar in at least one important way: *we both believed passionately in principles and we stood on them.*

The days of Paul Johnson's populist, power politics were numbered.

• • •

On Sunday, July 18, a gathering of about 125 white and black Mississippians launched the Mississippi Democratic Conference, professing full support for the liberal National Democratic Party line. Leadership from the NAACP and the Mississippi Labor Council factored greatly in its formation. Charles Young, "a wealthy Meridian Negro businessman," was elected vice chairman; Robert Oswald, a white attorney from Pascagoula, was chairman. Hodding Carter III of Greenville helped nominate the group's first board. "This is an historic moment," said Oswald, adding, "It has been in the past that the only words heard in the capitol were 'Never, never,' but that is passing into history."[40] But "conspicuous by their absence" at the Mississippi Democratic Conference's launch "were Negroes and whites connected with the Freedom Democratic Party and the Student Non-Violent Coordinating Committee who" had "been struggling with the NAACP-labor group for control."[41]

This was a sign of things to come. For several more years, these three groups—the Mississippi Democratic Conference, the Mississippi Freedom Democratic Conference, and the Student Non-Violent Coordinating Committee—would fight for control of the state's Democratic Party while also facing off with the old-line Democrat machine led by Bidwell Adam. "This gap will remain for some time," *The Clarion-Ledger* predicted, adding, "Personal animosities are now a primary factor in the split."[42]

The Aug. 17 date inched closer for the state vote to amend the Mississippi Constitution regarding lowering voting standards. I never flinched in my opposition to removing all voter standards. "There is absolutely no reason Mississippi could not have qualifications [to vote] without discrimination," I told the media.[43]

But two weeks before Mississippi citizens could vote on their own state voting standards, on Aug. 4, Lyndon Johnson's historic Voting Rights Bill of 1965 passed Congress, a "proud moment," the President said. It not only removed any literacy tests from the criteria to vote, but it also put state voter registration into federal hands.[44] Again, the power of federal government swelled, despite the fact that states were now attempting decent resolutions on their own.

More than 40 percent of all Americans said race-related issues were going too fast, compared to less than about 35 percent saying it was going "just right."[45] New waves of federal registrars now poured into Mississippi counties to register blacks. More than 1,100 were qualified in their first day in nine counties in Alabama, Louisiana, and Mississippi.

This prompted the Governor's administration to file suit against the federal registrars. And it prompted *yet-another sudden change of heart, or mind,* by Paul Johnson. Johnson in October reconvened the state legislature, saying that Washington D.C. had a "vendetta" against Mississippi. He wanted to try to redraw our congressional districts.[46] He indicated that he regretted his previous decision to change our voter standards.

Johnson estimated that between 15,000 and 20,000 illiterate blacks already had been registered to vote in Mississippi. Speaking to a conference in Sea Island, Georgia, Johnson now vowed that no illiterate person, "black or white," would be permitted to vote in Mississippi. "So long as an illiterate cannot go from our state to New York or California and vote, he will not be allowed to vote in Mississippi," Johnson said.[47]

Johnson had no idea what he really wanted at this point except to keep his power.

Many inflammatory rumors were out there as the federal registrars did their work, including that anyone still opposed to such mass registrations might lose their own voting rights. I called it "a smokescreen of misinformation." Some people "were trying to leave the impression that anyone who opposes [mass registration] because he believes there is a better way is ignorant and prejudiced."[48]

As Mississippi again was being taken to the woodshed, the horrible Watts Riots of Los Angeles broke out. By Aug. 14 twenty people had been killed in four nights of rioting—some white, others black.

President Johnson called the riots "tragic and shocking," adding, "Killing, rioting, and looting are contrary to the best tradition of this country."[49] By Aug. 15, 31 were dead and 762 hurt[50] L.A. Mayor Samuel W. Yorty said the riots were "an attack by Negroes on whites"; Martin Luther King, Jr., after a meeting with Yorty, said L.A. police were to blame, and King kept calling for the resignation of L.A. Police Chief William H. Parker.[51] Meanwhile, in Chicago, the federal government froze more than $34 million in federal funds to the city's public schools, citing racial discrimination.[52]

• • •

As 1965 progressed, Lyndon Johnson was creating even more laws over and above the Voting Rights Act of 1965.

By late July, he had pressed into being Medicare, plus increasing Social Security benefits.[53] Such entitlements all seemed compassionate, except for the fact that my children and grandchildren today face a government debt from it that is crippling, with no cure in sight and with the reality that Social Security will not be there for them.

On our nation's foreign front, Johnson had further led us into a catastrophic Vietnam situation. The undeclared war was out of control. During one 1965 visit to Johnson's Texas ranch, Sen. Dick Russell of Georgia reportedly told the president, "We made a mistake in going in there, but I can't figure any way to get out without scaring the rest of the world."[54] Russell spoke for most Americans.

The military draft in 1965 called up 27,400 more men in September and 33,600 in October—the largest drafted force since 80,000 in the Korean War. Earlier in the year, I had told the media that "any war worth fighting is worth winning and no American serviceman's life should be sacrificed unless this country is willing to make a complete effort to gain victory."[55]

Now Lyndon Johnson was sending more troops, while still insisting that we were fighting a "limited war." I publicly decried such logic. "Until we have bombed and attacked Hanoi and every area of North Vietnam with any war making potential and set up a complete naval blockade to prevent our so called allies from shipping goods to our acknowledged enemies, we cannot say we have taken every step to bring this conflict to an end."[56] By year's end, I had wired President Johnson urging for the resignation of Secretary of Defense Robert McNamara.

Such issues had further thrown Democrats in our state into turmoil. Some of the imported Democrats now running things in Mississippi simply were different than the vast majority of our state's citizens, black or white, when it came to what they considered to be patriotic support for our country. For instance, the Mississippi Freedom Democratic Party had urged state black mothers to keep their sons from registering for the draft. "No Mississippi Negroes should be fighting in Vietnam until all the Negro people are free in Mississippi," the MFDP stated. "Negro boys should not honor the draft. ... Mothers should encourage their sons not to go. We will gain respect and dignity as a race only by forcing the U.S. government to come with guns, dog and trucks to take our sons away to fight."[57]

The spokesman for the MFDP was Charles Horwitz, a leader in the Council of Federated Organizations, a group formed in 1962 to consolidate efforts between groups including the Student Non-Violent Coordinating Committee, the NAACP, the Congress on Racial Equality, and the Southern Christian Leadership Council, among others.

The American Legion in Mississippi called for the indictment of those in the MFDP who supported draft-dodging.[58] No action was taken by Lyndon Johnson. The NAACP's Charles Evers seemed to sense the MFDP was damaging state blacks' cause in Mississippi. When the MFDP denounced the draft, Evers was put in a position of publicly disagreeing with civil rights constituents. Only months after they had worked together on key issues and protests, some of them now were at each other's throats. Similarly, there were now major leadership skirmishes in the Congress on Racial Equality and the Student Non-Violent Coordinating Committee as some leaders in these groups pushed to back a black nationalist movement. "In times of peril it is the duty of every American to give unstinted support to the fight for freedom abroad and step up the pace in the fight for democracy at home," Evers said. He was joined by Aaron Henry, the founder of the Regional Council of Negro Leadership. "Since the beginning of America," said Evers, "Negroes have fought and died honorably to make this country the world's greatest democracy."[59]

So by the end of 1965, a whole range of factions and groups vied to gain control of the Democratic Party in Mississippi.

Said the Associated Press, "Nobody seems to know now just what a Democrat is in this Deep South state with its one-party tradition."[60]

Meanwhile new Republican leadership was emerging within our state GOP. In Meridian, an automobile dealer named Gil Carmichael in August of 1965 was elected chairman of the Lauderdale County Republican Executive Committee. He had previously served as the county party's finance chairman.[61] Gil would eventually run for several state offices, including twice for governor. History shows that Gil had a moderate, somewhat erratic political philosophy, taking positions on gun control and other issues often in unpredictable fashion. But he certainly had the right to assert himself into politics, and my party supported him.

Also, Clarke Reed was becoming more active in our state organization. He had begun to meet national GOP leaders, largely as a result of introductions made by me. In mid-September, Reed was named chairman of our United Republican Fund of Mississippi. Clark replaced my good friend Charlie

Klumb. Reed made one of his first public statements in what would become a decades-long political career. Said Reed: "The only way to stop the extremism of this administration and restore responsible government to the people is through the vehicle of the Republican Party. It is therefore imperative that we keep our state Republican Party financially strong in order to maintain the outstanding conservative influence we now have within our national party. I know there are enough dedicated, patriotic, and conservative people in Mississippi to get this job done and I am counting on their support."[62]

Then I took the podium at our Jackson press conference and plugged Reed. "Financing is vital to any political organization and the growing Mississippi Republican Party is fortunate to have a dedicated conservative of Mr. Reed's qualifications who will serve in this capacity."[63]

I told the media that Reed was "the William Buckley of the Mississippi Republican Party."[64]

In the autumn of 1965 I ended my final term as chairman of the Southern Association of Republican State Chairmen. At my final meeting as chairman, Winthrop Rockefeller, brother of Nelson and then-governor of Arkansas, met the media with me. I forecasted even greater Republican gains in the South in the upcoming 1966 senatorial and congressional elections. "There can and will be dramatic gains," I said.[65]

As the year wound down, the old-line Democrats fell into one of their own traps. They once had passed a law aimed at us, saying no party receiving less than one-third of the vote in a presidential election could get state funding in the next election cycle. Now their own law hit them after Barry Goldwater had taken 87 percent of the vote in 1964. So what did they do? They met to try to pass yet another law to permit their party to get state funding anyway. "Now that the Democrats have trapped themselves with this law which they said was fair and equitable for all, it will be interesting to see what arguments they can come forth with to justify their [new] position," I observed.[66]

Our forces were looking to the future. Our slogan was,

"Take the Hill in '66," and I said we were "tremendously en-thusiastic over chances of winning congressional races."[67] We published a new brochure that began to further define us as the only true conservative party in our state. "The Democratic Party ... is now the party of the ultra-liberal and the welfare state," it read. "Democrats ignore the lessons of history with political and economic ideas that have destroyed nations since the beginning of time ... inflation ... wasteful spending ... crushing taxes ... dictatorial central government. And no mat-ter what Democrat politicians pretend, ... their party is com-pletely controlled by power-mad liberals, whose policies and aims are opposed to everything Mississippians hold dear."

We held a news conference with state media to announce our new brochure. I put our national committeeman, Fred LaRue, at the microphone, as well as Reed. They both did a fine job of clearly stating that we were the state's true conser-vative party.

And then something strange happened. *The Clarion-Ledger* of Jackson, Mississippi, admitted the following in their paper: "Actually, the Mississippi Republican Party is moving right along the road to success. It must be acknowledged, how-ever, that the Mississippi Democratic Party continues to be the dominant party in state politics. The Democrats, more than incidentally, intend to keep it that way. But Mississippi has be-come in fact a two-party state. Only the future will determine whether the Mississippi Republican Party or the Mississippi Democratic Party can deliver the most muscular, conservative appeal to Mississippi voters."[68]

As 1965 drew to a close, our state now had a galvanized Republican Party and a splintered Democratic Party. Our state finally had a two-party system—even *The Clarion-Ledger* had admitted it.

GATHERING LEADERS: Top, Wirt leads the nation's Republican state chairmen during one of their key gatherings. Below, the nation's Republican state chairmen pose for a picture; Wirt is seated on the far front left.

REPUBLICAN STATE CHAIRMEN'S CONFERENCE

CHICAGO, ILL., JAN. 21, 1965

Nobody knows who is the titled, or untitled, head of the Democratic Party in the state.

—Bill Minor, Mississippi liberal
political commentator, 1966

Serving as state chairman has been one of the happiest experiences of my life.

—Wirt A. Yerger, Jr., 1966

13

1966

MY RESIGNATION

I had always believed we needed to run statewide and national candidates whenever possible to build our state party.

Challenging someone as powerful as Eastland, however, was an idea that some of our newer state GOP leaders wished to avoid no matter what. They felt we should bide our time, not upset Eastland or Stennis, and seek the big offices in Washington, D.C. later.

But since 1956, our party had always taken bold moves against big opposition if we were confident in our cause. In 1966, Mississippi once again needed such bold leadership against rising liberalism and the lingering, but still-powerful, old-line Democrats.

I was determined to find someone to run in 1966 for the U.S. Senate against James Eastland. And I was still speaking to groups whenever possible, highlighting our need for solid moral leadership in Washington. "Lack of effective leadership is Mississippi's number one problem and if we can overcome this obstacle, the rest of our problems will disappear like dew before the morning sun," I told the West Jackson Civitan Club on Jan. 10. I added: "Mississippi has the most intelligent and highly moral people in the nation and with those qualities there is no reason we should not succeed under proper leadership. We do deserve better leaders and we must have them if we are to achieve our full potential."[1]

Our state's Democrats faced a lack of clear leadership. They had no obvious man to guide their party's factions. They were infighting over whether to rebuild themselves as true liberals. Lamented liberal political commentator Bill Minor in a 1966 column: "Nobody knows who is the titled, or untitled head, of the Democratic Party in the state."[2]

Senator Eastland was seeking reelection for the first time in six years. The last time he had run for the Senate was in 1960—pre-Goldwater days. His previous races had not required any real organization or funding. This year would prove to be different. A Republican was about to run against Eastland, and that would anger the old gentleman.

In 1966 Eastland started taking control of his state party leadership, skirting Governor Paul Johnson. He pushed again to open a real state Democrat campaign office, to be located in Jackson. It would be "established with an experienced campaign director to back all Democratic nominees next year," crowed Minor.[3] Minor, who would become Mississippi's best-known liberal columnist, added: "This is not supposed to be any mere token gesture."

No doubt our success running a real party in the state had finally inspired even Minor.

Minor continued: "The people who are behind it are saying that real money is going to be poured into a Democratic war chest to back every Democratic candidate down the line who gets Republican opposition in 1967."[4]

The fact that Senator Eastland would actually be challenged in his coming reelection race spurred Mississippi Democrats to organize into a real party operation. Back-room meetings alone would not cut it any more. Eastland and old-liners also feared the human power of the Mississippi Freedom Democratic Party, and Eastland surely felt organizing would help avoid any internal takeover by such new factions.

Minor even admitted that "all of this [new organization] will further scramble the present proliferation of Democratic organizations of various hues which exist in the state. There are already the Young Democrats, formally reorganized by the national organization; the 'Mississippi Freedom Democratic Party,' the Negro-Civil rights dominated group; the Mississippi Democratic Conference, an abortive effort of organized labor and the NAACP to provide some national party base in the state; and then, what is loosely known as the Mississippi Democratic Party."[5]

As the state's Democrats and their media backers worried about rudimentary organizational questions, I spent my time trying to lead Mississippians. I decried racial violence, both in our state and elsewhere. From the cowardly Klan to the race riots nationally, I emphasized that the battle for good government should be waged in the realm of ideas. "Those who commit acts of violence deserve the condemnation of all people," I told the citizens of our state and nation.

Ruffians in Mississippi were only "promoting the interests of left-wing radicals" by using violence. "Without incidents of violence, the punitive civil rights bill [of 1965], which is now the law of the land, would never have been passed," I said, adding, "It is true that only a small misguided minority commit these acts and it is also true that the number of violent crimes in Mississippi during any one year would probably not equal those in New York City in one week. However, all the people of our state are forced to suffer when these acts occur here."[6]

I served notice to Jim Eastland in early January that he could "rest assured that he will have Republican opposition in his bid to return to the U.S. Senate."[7]

I added, "Our senior senator is back in the state campaigning after making himself scarce for six years except for the time he spent campaigning for presidents Kennedy and Johnson and Gov. Paul Johnson."

• • •

There was going to be a serious, well-funded Republican senatorial candidate for the first time since Reconstruction. If I could not find a qualified one, I was considering stepping forward myself. Someone needed to contest Eastland; this kept running through my mind and coming out in conversations with others.

I felt that I had what it took not only to be an electable senatorial candidate, but also to be an effective United States senator. I knew well the national party leadership. I knew how Washington, D.C. worked. And no Mississippi Republican was better acquainted with our grass-roots constituency in all 82 counties. A study by the Dallas-based Louis and Bowles Research Consultants had shown that, prior to Rubel Phillips running for governor, my name was better known than any Republican's in our state. I had traveled the state for years meeting people. We had corresponded. We had fought in the trenches.

Together, we could defeat Eastland.

I was contemplating all of this in early 1966.

I felt a civic responsibility to consider running. If it was possible for me to defeat Eastland, shouldn't I put my hat in the ring? Even still, I kept my eye out for other possible candidates.

I respected anyone willing to put himself out there and run as a Republican. Rumors were that Dr. M. Ney Williams, Jr.—a Jackson anesthesiologist and first cousin of John Bell Williams—might run against Eastland, either as an independent or Republican.

I knew I had a better chance of winning than Williams. Williams eventually did get elected Hinds County coroner, a major win for our fledgling party.

But there were other important concerns in my life in early 1966: *my wife and children were extremely important to me and already had been very patient and supportive as I spent long hours working for the state party.*

A campaign for election to the United States Senate would take me away from home more; and if I won, we all would have to move to Washington. The idea of raising our children anywhere but Jackson was not appealing.

Also, my business needed my attention.

I had been working with my aging father for ten years. He had consistently backed my political efforts. But Ross & Yerger Insurance needed me. The rigors of the senate would have curtailed my helping to foster growth in our company.

• • •

By early February, my deliberations were increasing. It was very difficult, but I finally decided that the senate would have to wait if, in fact, I would ever run. Moreover, I decided that it was time for me to step down as chairman of our state party. Fresh blood was emerging in the state party, and they were ready for more responsibility.

So I called a press conference for Feb. 7, 1966.

At the time, I still had two years remaining in my current term as chairman of the Mississippi Republican Party.

When I scheduled the press conference, most people thought it was to announce my candidacy for the United States Senate. Scheduling that press conference quickly set into action a chain of events. Almost immediately Mississippi U.S. Rep. Prentiss Walker called his own press conference for the same day as mine—Monday, Feb. 7. Bill Wilkins later would tell me that Walker had, in fact, thought I was going to announce my candidacy for the United States Senate and that he wanted to beat me to the punch with his own announcement.

Wilkins recalls: "Yerger was the obvious candidate for the Eastland senate seat and the near unanimous first choice of the party leadership. And he was certainly the most qualified person for the job. Much effort in the party by many people went into his recruitment. We were all completely blindsided by Prentiss Walker's announcement."[8]

Prentiss Walker had good qualities, but he did not look

like, act like, or talk like a guy that most would want as a senator. He had no chance against Eastland. He made a hasty, bad
decision that seemed, in part, spurred by a faulty fear that I
was about to announce for the senate.

The conservative cause was in my heart; it ran to the core
of my being. When you get wrapped up in a cause such as I
had while starting the modern Mississippi Republican Party, it
is almost like holding a tiger by the tail—you're unable to let
go even if it's clawing at you. But I knew it was time for me to
do just that.

On Monday, Feb. 7—hours prior to Walker's press conference that same day—I met with the press at the Mississippi
Republican headquarters.

I looked out through the media lights and cameras and
saw many friends and foes. I'd grown to appreciate all of
them over the past ten years. As many awaited, thinking I
might announce a run for the U.S. Senate, I stepped to the
podium and said the exact opposite ... I was retiring from
state GOP leadership.

The following article ran in *The Clarion-Ledger* on Feb. 7,
1966:

Wirt Yerger Quits Post As GOP Chairman

Wirt A. Yerger Jr. resigned today as chairman of the
Mississippi Republican Patry (sic) and said his present
plans don't include a race for the U.S. Senate.

Yerger's successor will be elected at an Executive
Committee meeting Thursday night when his resignation becomes effective.

"After serving as state chairman for 10 years and seeing the development of Mississippi as a two-party state,"
he told a news conference, "I feel that I owe it to my family
and my insurance business to devote more time to them."

There has been speculation that Yerger might seek
the Senate seat now held by Senator James O. Eastland.

But, the retiring chairman said, that "is not in my
present plans."

He declined to elaborate but told a questioner: "We will have a candidate or candidates, and we will be victorious. I believe he [Eastland] is in his last term."

Yerger also declined to disclose whether he had a personal choice as his replacement.

"We have a number of well-qualified men to serve," he said. "However, I don't anticipate any ideological shift."

... The new chairman will be elected from the 15-member Executive Committee.

Clarke Reed of Greenville, the party's state Finance Committee Chairman, is considered a strong candidate for the post.

Reed's supporters point out that his business affairs would enable him to spend the time necessary in directing the affairs of the party.

Yerger said he will remain a member of the Executive Committee. He said he doesn't anticipate any immediate resignations on the committee.

Fred LaRue was ruled out as a possible chairman since he is the party's national committeeman and, consequently, isn't a member of the Executive Committee, although he does serve on the Central Committee.

A year ago, Charles Klumb of Crystal Springs was believed to be Yerger's heir apparent. Since then, however, he has resigned from the Executive Committee.

Klumb was replaced by W.D. Mounger, a Jackson banker also considered a possible successor to Yerger.

Yerger recounted the growth of the Mississippi Republican Party during the past 10 years.

"When we held our 1956 state convention in Jackson," he said in a prepared statement read to reporters, "the crowd was so small that a prominent Democrat remarked that we could have held our convention in a telephone booth."

"He was right," he added.

"But we matured. He should have been around for our state convention in 1964, when we had hundreds of people and delegates from practically every county in the state."

In 1964, the state shattered a 92-year-old tradition by voting Republican in a presidential election. Goldwater garnered 87 percent of the total vote in Mississippi.

"The conservative cause in this nation will rise or fall with the Republican Party," Yerger said, "and the same is true in Mississippi."

"I believe that it will be victorious because of the inherent love of individual freedom and the free enterprise system which we all value."

Yerger founded the Mississippi Young Republicans in 1956, the same year he was first elected chairman of the Executive Committee.

He has held a number of important posts within the National Republican Party and served as chairman of the Southern Association of Republican State Chairmen from 1961 until September of 1965.

Yerger became a member of the Republican National Committee in 1964.

He was chairman of the Mississippi delegations to the Republican National Conventions in 1956, 1960 and 1964.

Yerger told his news conference today that the state GOP "is on the verge of electing officials throughout the state."

"Soon," he predicted, "well (sic) will be the dominant party in the state."

The retiring chairman believes the party will also control the Mississippi House of Representatives within five years.

Yerger cited Mississippians' "desire for a two-party system in the state" for the party's growth. Additionally, he said, Mississippians wish to be affiliated with a national political party.

The Mississippi Democratic Party claims it isn't associated with its national counterpart.[9]

For my successor as state party chairman, I had first considered Buddy Klumb, an ideal choice. Then I had looked at Billy Mounger. In early January of 1966, Mounger, a Jackson banker and oilman, had accepted my invitation to get involved in the party apparatus. I had originally invited Billy to attend the 1963 Republican National Convention. In upcoming years, he would provide a lot of energy in fund-raising in his own inimitable fashion.

Neither Klumb nor Mounger, however, was able to serve in 1966 as state party chairman, for different reasons.

So at a Feb. 10 meeting of our state executive committee, I virtually handed the state party to Clarke Reed. Reed was 37 years old, a Greenville resident who ran a river transport business and an agricultural equipment manufacturing business. Billy Mounger took over Reed's former position as state fund-raising chairman.

I now went to bat for Reed in the media. "Reed is well-grounded in conservative doctrine and is one of the most well rounded people in conservative thinking I know," I told a press conference. "I am confident he will lead the Republican cause to new heights."

I appreciate the recent kind words of Bill Wilkins, who with my resignation became Reed's top employee. Wilkins recently noted: "I must say that it [the transition from Yerger to Reed] went much smoother than I had expected. Yerger had the good grace to immediately pull way back and let Reed have his show. But knowing Yerger as I do, I can imagine how hard this much have sometimes been for him."[10]

It was, indeed.

I had felt a deep responsibility as state party chairman to the people of Mississippi.

"In my opinion Mississippians in their convictions are far ahead of the politicians," I told the media in my farewell address, adding: "Abraham Lincoln once said, 'The people are always nearer the truth than politicians suppose.'"[11]

Lincoln was right.

People should have a chance to govern themselves; that belief had led me to fight for a two-party system in our state. It was this belief that had led me to join forces nationally to help form a new, truly conservative movement that now swept through the Republican Party nationwide and would culminate with the presidential years of Ronald Reagan.

We had "seen the Mississippi Republican Party come from the days when we had slightly about fifty people at our state convention to a position of prominence and respect with elected officials from congressman to school board member."[12]

I had stood on principle over the past ten years, including a belief in small government, low taxes, and a strong defense. I had fought racism, Communism, and big government. I had applied my principles in the political realm.

In the end, a man standing on solid principle will remain, but all politics is temporal. Because I always had made decisions based on principle, I had endured even the toughest times during my leadership of the state Republican Party, and I had even enjoyed them. "Serving as state chairman has been one of the happiest experiences of my life," I told the media upon my resignation.[13]

As I looked out at the media, I knew Mississippi was changing, and I felt for the better. A great team of people had worked so hard to achieve this goal. "My heart will always go out to the unselfish and dedicated men and women who were in the first waves of citizens to bravely storm the bastions of the one-party system," I told the press, adding that "endearing friendships" had been my reward.

It is now 2010, and my heart still goes out to these great people—those who successfully took up our courageous cause.

FAREWELL: "The conservative cause in this nation will rise or fall with the Republican Party," Wirt said, "and the same is true in Mississippi." The photo above was taken at the press conference where Wirt resigned from his state GOP chairman post.

WORDS OF THANKS: When Wirt announced his resignation as chairman of the Mississippi Republican Party, words of thanks and commendation flowed into him from hundreds of leaders around the nation. What follows is a small sample.

MISSISSIPPI REPUBLICAN PARTY

P. O. BOX 1178   •   JACKSON, MISSISSIPPI   •   948-5191

February 5, 1966

Mr. Julius W. King
7 Pineridge Road
Laurel, Mississippi

Dear Judy:

    This is to advise you that I will resign as State Chairman February 10, at which time a new chairman will be elected by the party's Executive Committee.

    After serving as Chairman for ten years, I feel that a two party system is now a reality in our state and that we are on the verge of electing Republicans to all levels of government.

    One of the things I shall miss most after stepping down will be the constant association with our key leadership, such as you. Surely, no other State Chairman has ever been blessed with the cooperation and support given me and I want you to know how deeply it is appreciated.

    It is my intention to remain a member of the State Central Committee and to be as active in party ranks as possible.

    Again, let me thank you for the effort you have put forth in behalf of the party. I am confident that the new State Chairman will be able to lead us on to greater victories for the GOP with your continued help.

Sincerely,

Wirt A. Yerger, Jr.,
Chairman

WAYJr:sa

Dear Wirt,

I'm upset because I don't know who can step in to your big shoes — Being Chairman is part + parcel of you now so why not stay Mon with it — Will call you soon —

Fighting for Mississippi and America!

Regards,
Rudy

REPUBLICAN NATIONAL COMMITTEE

1625 EYE STREET NORTHWEST ● WASHINGTON, D. C. 20006 ● NAtional 8-6800

J. WILLIAM MIDDENDORF II
TREASURER
80 BROAD STREET
NEW YORK, NEW YORK

RAY C. BLISS
CHAIRMAN

March 15, 1966

Mr. Wirt A. Yerger, Jr.
Mississippi Republican Party
P. O. Box 1178
Jackson, Mississippi

Dear Wirt:

Please pardon my very late reply to your kind letter of February 5, but I have been all over the country and in Europe. When the history books are written about the growth of the two party system in the South, you will be one of the heroes. I don't know of anybody that could have done the job you've done.

I have always enjoyed our close association and I am delighted to hear that you are going to continue to be active in the party ranks in Mississippi.

With every best wish, I am,

Very sincerely yours,

Bill

J. William Middendorf II
Treasurer

JWM/pm

McCARTY ENTERPRISES

FEED MILL — HATCHERIES — POULTRY FARMS

TELEPHONE 466-3351 & 466-3352

MAGEE, MISSISSIPPI   39111

February 8, 1966

Mr. Wirt A. Yerger, Jr.
Mississippi Republican Party
P. O. Box 1178
Jackson, Mississippi

Dear Wirt:

I was somewhat surprised to receive your letter yesterday indicating that you had definitely decided to resign as State Chairman February 10. I knew that you had considered this course of action previously but did not realize that you had definitely made up your mind. I am sure though that your business, family and your private affairs deserve more attention than you have been able to give them during the past ten years.

I wish to express my personal appreciation for the unselfish service which you have rendered for the cause of the Mississippi Republican Party. I am sure thousands of us must realize that a great deal of our progress for the two-party system in Mississippi is the direct result of your personal effort and sacrifice. For this we say thank you.

We are pleased to note that you will remain as a member of the State Central Committee. Those of us who have seen you in action during the past several years can hardly conceive of you retiring from the services now or ever. I am sure that the new chairman, whoever he may be, will be anxious to have all of the help which you find yourself able to give.

Stop by to visit when you are passing through Magee.

Sincerely,

Mac

H. F. McCarty, Jr.

HFMJr:gf

The Republican Party of Georgia

P. O. BOX 96   PHONE (912) 788-4641   MACON, GEORGIA

G. PAUL JONES, JR.
Chairman   February 14, 1966

Mr. Wirt A. Yerger, Jr., Chairman
Mississippi Republican Party
P. O. Box 1178
Jackson, Mississippi

Dear Wirt:

Thank you for your letter dated February 5. I of course saw Clarke Reed
in Washington at the recent meeting of the National Committee, and he
indicated that you were preparing to resign.

Certainly Mississippi and the Republican Party will forever be in your
debt for the untiring efforts and hard work that you have given on behalf
of competitive government in the state of Mississippi and in the South.
I am sure that your inspiration and your tireless efforts have encouraged
many of us to work harder in our own states, and when the history of the
Republican Party in the South is written, you certainly shall play an
important part in its development and in its progress.

I of course met you long before becoming actively involved in Republican
politics, but knowing you and knowing of your involvements certainly
influenced my decision to become active in this vital effort.

If you or any of your friends ever get over to Macon, please do not hesitate
to let me know. I shall always look forward with pleasure to seeing you.

Sincerely,

G. Paul Jones, Jr.

GPJJr:af

REPUBLICAN NATIONAL COMMITTEE

1625 EYE STREET NORTHWEST ● WASHINGTON, D. C. 20006 ● NAtional 8-6800

ALBERT B. HERMANN
SPECIAL ASSISTANT TO THE CHAIRMAN

RAY C. BLISS
CHAIRMAN

February 11, 1966

Mr. Wirt A. Yerger, Jr.
1936 Bellewood Road
Jackson, Mississippi

Dear Wirt:

I have your letter advising that you have resigned as Mississippi State Chairman on February 10th.

While through the years you and I have held different views on issues; nevertheless, I do not believe anyone is more aware than I of the tremendous job you faced in giving life to the Republican Party in Mississippi.

I can well remember when I first joined the National Committee in 1949, the organization which was the so-called Republican Party in your state. Your courage and dedication to our Party in bringing into actual existence a Party which now has every possibility of becoming a major factor in the State of Mississippi deserves the utmost commendation.

You, Wirt, remind me of the "Mountain Men" who opened the West in the early history of our country. You, like they, faced grave dangers and many responsibilities. Behind the "Mountain Men" came the planners and the reapers. As in the case history of our "Mountain Men" of the early West, their names are sometimes forgotten but their deeds – never.

I do hope that if the Republicans in Mississippi should hold a Testimonial Dinner for one Wirt Yerger, they will allow me the privilege and honor of coming to the affair to express publicly the sincere admiration I hold for you -- a truly great Republican warrior.

Cordially yours,

AB Hermann

ABH:pgc

JOHN E. GRENIER
1500 BROWN-MARX BUILDING
BIRMINGHAM, ALABAMA

February 21, 1966

Mr. Wirt A. Yerger, Jr.
P.O. Box 1178
Jackson, Mississippi

Dear Wirt:

I learned only a few days ago of your recent resignation
as State Chairman and I received the news with very mixed
emotions. You were the first in the south to lead the so
called "new breed" and your resignation undoubtedly signals
the end of the first phase of the revolution in southern
politics which you did so much to start. Certainly your
leadership almost assures the ultimate of success with this
political upheaval. Accordingly I cannot help but mark
your resignation with some regret.

On the other hand, I know that it has been a very long and
very hard road and that this move will permit you to enjoy
your own life and your friends and family more than you have
in the past. And after all, that's worth something.

So, I extend my deep personal appreciation for all you have
done to lead the way and offer my sincere best wishes for
a successful future. I trust you will give my best regards
to Mary.

With warm personal regards,

Sincerely,

John E. Grenier

JEG/gh

909 RING BUILDING, 18TH AND M STREETS, N.W., WASHINGTON, D.C. 20036, FEderal 8-1350 (Area Code 202

Calcium Chloride Institute

March 1, 1966

Mr. Wirt A. Yerger, Jr.
c/o Box 1178
Jackson, Mississippi

Dear Wirt:

I was surprised to learn today of your resignation
as chairman of the Mississippi Republican Party.

You are almost singly responsible for the establishment of an increasingly vital second party in a state that so
desperately needs a two-party system. All Mississippians, and all
Americans, owe you a great debt.

It is to your credit that, in the space of ten years,
you were able to have found a movement that will so greatly
enhance the futures of millions of present and future citizens.

Sincerely,

Roger Coleman
Director of Public Relations

RC:1

ENGINEERING, RESEARCH AND DISTRIBUTION OF INFORMATION RELATIVE TO THE USES OF CALCIUM CHLORIDE

If you stand on principle, you will always be able to sleep at night and you won't have to worry about remembering what you said because you will always have told the truth.

—Wirt A. Yerger, Jr., 2010

Be strong and of good courage; be not afraid, neither be thou dismayed: for the Lord thy God is with thee wherever thou goest.

—Joshua 1:9

14

2010

CLOSING ADVICE

In the spring of 2008, more than a thousand people gathered at a downtown Jackson hotel for an event given by the Mississippi Republican Party honoring my GOP efforts. I was both humbled and reluctant, but I truly appreciated it. Miss. Gov. Haley Barbour and my old GOP partner Buddy Klumb spoke, among others; then I addressed the gathering. That speech seems an appropriate way to conclude this book. But first, let me thank some of the key people in my life, as I did that night in 2008.

My deepest thanks go to my wife Mary, who married me in spite of her uncle asking her the day before our wedding if she was sure she wanted to marry a Republican. Also, thanks to our sons Wirt and Frank, and our daughter Mary, and their spouses Linda, Jane, and Tom Dunbar, respectively. Our wonderful grandchildren mean the world to me: Adams and wife, Jordan, David, Richard, John, Thomas, Wirt, Mary, Frank Jr., Sarah Jane, and Harlan. For more than seventy years, I've been blessed with the company of my sister Rivers Lurate and my brothers Swan and wife Gingia, and Ivan and wife Pate. Much gratitude to my brother-in-law Frank Montague and his wife Mary for their support and encouragement.

Lastly, thanks to those friends who supported Mary and me through the ups and downs of those early GOP days in Mississippi, and beyond. Now here is my speech from that special night.

It has been quite a while—about 40 years—since I've stood at the podium of a Mississippi Republican Party function, but I must say tonight will be the most memorable of all.

As you have heard tonight, incredible progress has been made in the Mississippi Republican Party since the 1950s when there was effectively only one party. At that time there was little room in the Democrat Party for my conservative views. The Democrats believed in massive government spending in areas previously reserved for free market and private enterprise, and in the redistribution of wealth by unfair taxation. The media was totally infatuated with the Democrat leaders and all they stood for. Does this sound familiar?

The Republican Party was the place to make a difference in our state and nation then, as it is today. Challenging the status quo in our state wasn't easy. All of the business interests and political power were vested in the Democratic Party. I am sure some of my early stalwart supporters wondered what I had gotten them into.

Harassment, ridicule, and misunderstanding were experienced by all of us in the early GOP, as well as gratification in seeing the establishment of a viable Republican Party in Mississippi.

How refreshing it is to see all of the Republican elected officials here tonight: Legislators, mayors, and statewide officials. In 1956 we had no Republican elected officials. We didn't even have candidates.

The honor you have given to me tonight goes to all of the young, courageous individuals of the fifties and sixties who provided such tremendous leadership and enthusiasm and worked so tirelessly and sacrificially throughout the state. I may have been a pioneer, but it is all of you and many who are no longer with us who were the trailblazers and early settlers of the Mississippi Republican Party.

Coinciding with the establishment of Republicanism in Mississippi, the party was witnessing phenomenal growth all over the South. We learned much from each other, achieved many accomplishments as a strong voice, and established many political and personal friendships that have been enjoyed through the years.

I have sat with Dwight Eisenhower, Ronald Reagan, Barry Goldwater, Richard Nixon, senators, and business leaders. They have heard my advice and I have heard theirs. My life is richer for it.

Seeing the reality of the two-party system in Mississippi has been one of the greatest blessings of my life. It is imperative for today's generation, and for tomorrow's, that we remain committed to the principles upon which it was founded. Today we are facing a battle not only with a liberal, biased media, but also with many institutions and individuals determined to destroy the morals, individual freedoms, conservative ideals, and Christian beliefs that we take for granted today.

The battle can be won, but only with our resolve to be active in the grass-roots efforts of the Republican Party and doing all we can to elect officials who will continue to attempt to get our nation back on the right course and away from the socialistic spiral we are presently experiencing.

Under the leadership and hard work of the Republican elected officials, led by Governor Haley Barbour and the dedication of Mississippi Republican Party Chairman Brad White and his capable staff, the future of the Mississippi Republican Party looks very promising and exciting. Our party is in good hands, and they deserve and need support from all of us here tonight.

How gratifying and encouraging it is for all of us with white hair—and some with no hair!—to see so many young people here. The best advice I can give to you is to always choose principles over pragmatism or power.

Keep these other thoughts in mind:

- Standing on principle is not easy. You get tired and discouraged, but the satisfaction of accomplishing all you can for a better nation is worth it all.

- Everybody wants to be recognized and appreciated, that's just human nature, but when push comes to shove, some are just willing to give up too many of their principles for power. I have not ever been able to do that, and I hope you younger people among us won't compromise, either.

- If you stand on principle, you will always be able to sleep at night and you won't have to worry about remembering what you said because you will always have told the truth.

My thanks to Brad and his staff for all of their preparation for this memorable event and to all of you for being here tonight for this very special occasion. And much appreciation goes to you in this audience for your service and commitment to the future of our country.

May God bless America and our great State of Mississippi.

Appendix

Correspondence with U.S. presidents
Ronald Reagan, George Bush, and
George W. Bush, as well as Pat Buchanan,
Dick Cheney, Barry Goldwater, and others.

August 27, 1970

Mr. Wirt A. Yerger, Jr.
Ross & Yerger, Inc.
P.O. Box 1139
Jackson, Mississippi 39205

Dear Mr. Yerger:

This is just a note to thank you for your support
for my reelection.

We have made significant progress in improving and
streamlining state government these past four years,
but there is a sizeable job yet to be done.

You may be sure I will do my best to merit your
continued confidence.

Sincerely,

RONALD REAGAN
Governor

EMG:bh   (incoming retained for pol. office)

ROSS & YERGER   *"The House of Insurance since 1860"*

January 10, 1972

Honorable Barry Goldwater
United States Senator
Senate Office Building
Washington, D. C.

"Conscience of a Conservative"
Real or Imaginary

Dear Barry:

You are well aware in what high regard millions of conservatives hold you,
and I trust you know that I am among that group. Nevertheless, I did
find it hard to take a couple of years ago when on two occasions you
apparently refused to take a phone call from a former ally and compatriot.

That, however, is not the purpose of this letter. What I am seriously
concerned about is your apparent opposition to any Republican, whether
its John R. Ashbrook or anyone else taking serious public issue with
Richard Nixon. In my judgment when he does something in direct contra-
diction to one's own principles or what history has indeed taught us then
anyone has a moral obligation to speak out loud and clear.

Barry, you know as well as I do that if the policies Richard Nixon has been
pursuing both domestic and foreign were pursued by a Democrat many of the
now mute Republicans would be screeming at the top of their lungs in protest.
Let's be honest with ourselves and with the people of our country. Without
it, our freedom is in serious jeopardy.

With warmest best wishes and personal regards always, I am

Sincerely,

Wirt A. Yerger, Jr.

ROSS & YERGER, INC. • P. O. BOX 1139 • SUITE 523 FIRST NATIONAL BANK BUILDING • JACKSON, MISSISSIPPI 39205 • TELEPHONE 948-2900

January 21, 1972

Mr. Wirt A. Yerger, Jr.
Ross & Yerger, Inc.
Post Office Box 1139
Suite 523
First National Bank Building
Jackson, Mississippi 39205

Dear Wirt:

If I oppose "any Republican who takes serious public issue
with Richard Nixon" I would have to oppose myself. Long
before John Ashbrook took an unrealistic and unfortunate
course in New Hampshire, I have made many critical
statements about the Nixon Administration. For example,
I opposed the admission of Red China to the United Nations--
under any circumstances, whether it be by a "two-China
policy" or something else. I also opposed the expulsion
of Taiwan and suggested that if this happened the United
States should withdraw from the United Nations. The day
after it happened, I made that flat recommendation.

What's more as a politician, I am inclined to understand,
as you must, that the place to complain effectively is
within the confines of the party. It serves no purpose
to run around issuing ultimatums which you can't back up.

For your information, I am enclosing a copy of a letter I
recently wrote to Bill Buckley pointing out that he, as well
as several other conservative writers, have been flagrantly
misquoting me on the basis of something they read in the
public press and without checking to discover whether the
ever wayward press was correct.

In closing, let me tell you that I am being completely
honest with myself and with the people of this country
when I say the surest way to wreck the U.S. is to
perform in any way that would contribute to the defeat
of Richard Nixon by a Democrat in this year's election.

Your letter is the first I had known you made a phone call
to me at any time and I have to apologize for that kind of
a slip on the part of my staff.

Sincerely,

Barry Goldwater

WIRT A. YERGER, JR.
JACKSON, MISSISSIPPI

January 24, 1974

PERSONAL AND CONFIDENTIAL

Where and what is your limit?

Dear Barry:

With the almost total forfeiture by Dick Nixon on his promises
and the mandate he received in both 1968 and 1972 as evidenced
by so many actions including the recent stand on the Rhodesian
chrome, the backing down on meaningful welfare reforms, and the
failure to shake some sanity into the radical bureaucrats in
the office of the HEW, you must be deeply concerned.

Your support more than ever before is critical to his survival,
and it is for this reason I cannot understand the kick in the teeth
which he has continued to give conservatives and those who espouse
our philosophy, on which he was twice elected.

Barry, as you know, I have never completely trusted the gentlemen
since he went over to Rockfeller's apartment in 1960 in the middle
of the night. This was my turning point, and I was just wondering
if you are nearing yours. At the very least, it seems you
could insist he fulfil a few of his fundamental commitments
to the people of America.

Sincerely,

Wirt A. Yerger, Jr.

WAY,Jr.:da

Honorable Barry Goldwater
United States Senator
Senate Office Building
Washington, D. C.

February 1, 1974

Mr. Wirt A. Yerger, Jr.
Jackson, Mississippi

Dear Wirt:

Naturally I am not happy with many of the things that
President Nixon has done, but he is our President and
I am going to stand behind him unless he is proven to
be dishonest and deceitful.

Why he has taken some of the liberal routes that he has
I can't tell you, but I can tell you a few of us are trying to change him.

With best wishes,

Barry Goldwater

BG/judy

WIRT A. YERGER, JR.
JACKSON, MISSISSIPPI

January 24, 1980

STRICTLY PERSONAL AND CONFIDENTIAL

Dear Ronnie,

You may recall that when you called me early last March asking me
to serve on your Campaign Committee, I spent nearly three-fourths of th
time telling you why I felt John Sears should not be involved in any wa
whatsoever in your 1980 campaign. You will also remember that I said
that I was strongly convinced that had any number of other people,
including even myself, managed your campaign in 1976, you would have
been nominated and elected.

Your files will reveal that I wrote you in the strongest possible
terms in the fall of 1975, urging you to come out swinging rather than
taking a soft approach to Gerald Ford's presidency. You followed John
Sears' advice, lost the New Hampshire primary, and what ultimately woulc
have been the presidency. You have again been following his advice, anc
you did not even appear in Iowa for the debate. I think that in terms
of political judgment, this was incredibly stupid. This is not hindsight, but rather exercising foresight.

If you are going to fall under the hypnotic spell of John Sears
again, or for that matter already are, how can you possibly ask us to
support you blindly for President when you would have this same man or
someone like him helping steer the ship of state? To be an effective
President, you have absolutely got to face the facts and take decisive
action. Please give this your utmost prayerful consideration. Having a
person such as yourself in the White House is far more important than
the personal feelings of John Sears or anybody else.

Ronnie, I will be glad to meet with you anywhere you choose to
discuss this face to face and to help you in getting someone who can
take charge and see that this, your last shot at the presidency and the
most important for all of us, is not forfeited. Please give this your
immediate consideration, as it is absolutely imperative. Thank you and
may God bless you.

Sincerely,

WAYjr:jw

Governor Ronald Reagan
c/o Mr. Kenny Kling
1828 L. Street, N. W.
Washington, D. C. 20036

RONALD REAGAN

February 13, 1980

Mr. Wirt A. Yerger, Jr.
P.O. Box 1139
Jackson, Miss. 39205

Dear Wirt:

Paul forwarded your letter and I appreciate your concern.

I have to be honest and tell you that not debating in Iowa was my decision just as not attacking Ford in New Hampshire in '76 was my decision.

I've spent so many years preaching to Republicans that we should campaign against the Democrats, not each other, that I truly felt a debate could be divisive. In '76 I was striving mightily to keep our 11th commandment and not split the party so that the nomination would be worthless.

Well, I believe I was right in New Hampshire but wrong in Iowa. The debate did not prove divisive so I've agreed to debate in New Hampshire, February 20th. Maybe the difference is - this time we have a Democrat incumbent to deal with.

Wirt, there was no way I could match Bush in Iowa, as to time and effort spent there. He took a home in Iowa last March - 8 months before I even announced. My strategy has to be aimed at the long haul - 35 primaries. George zeroed in on a few early states to make a breakthrough. One of those was Iowa - another is New Hampshire. I'm campaigning in New Hampshire as the underdog because he has spent as much time there as he did in Iowa.

I'm not under any spell. I think I know John's shortcomings as well as his abilities and I'm in charge this time. I hope I'll have your continued support because I need it.

Again thanks, and

Best Regards,

Ron

RONALD REAGAN

9841 AIRPORT BOULEVARD, SUITE 1430, LOS ANGELES, CALIFORNIA 90045

WIRT A. YERGER, JR.
JACKSON, MISSISSIPPI

July 11, 1980

Dear Ronnie,

Bush is acceptable, but Laxalt would be an outstanding choice.
Geographical or ideological balance, as in my letter previously, means
little to the final outcome.

Please don't make any absolute commitments on cabinet positions
until after the election. Feel free to call on me for any help at any
time. You're doing great!

Warmest regards always,

WAYjr:jw

Governor Ronald Reagan
Republican Convention Headquarters
Detroit, Michigan

cc: Reagan for President Headquarters
    9841 Airport Boulevard
    Suite 1430
    Los Angeles, California 90045

bc: Senator Paul Laxalt
    326 Russell Senate Office Building
    Washington, D. C. 20515

WIRT A. YERGER, JR.
JACKSON, MISSISSIPPI

July 18, 1980

A Brush With Catastrophe –
New Campaign Leadership A Must

Dear Ronnie,

The fact that the news media joined forces with Ford, Kissinger, Brock, and many others within our party who have fought you every step of the way to stampede you and your staff into selecting Gerald Ford as a running mate was absolutely shocking. You should have personally stopped them in their tracks. Before going to bed, I finally, after several desperate attempts, got a call in to your headquarters suite and left a message, which I hope you received, saying the selection of Ford would be a monumental catastrophe for both you and the nation. Mary and I were so disgusted that we cut off our television and went to bed to try to sleep, which we couldn't. When Swan, my brother, called at 11:00 p.m. and said you had selected Bush, I really felt you had, by some miracle, been saved from disaster.

You will recall that I had at least one short face to face meeting with you in which we discussed very briefly some of the many mistakes in the Goldwater campaign in 1964 where, up until the Arizona crowd took over, I was a major participant as chairman of the Southern Republican State Chairmen and one of the original group which drafted Goldwater. You will also recall that I have sent you, over the years, very pointed letters with succinct and well thought out advice which has proven remarkably (100%) correct all the way from 1968 and including my first warnings about the necessity to drop John Sears in the fall of 1975, when I also urged you to come out swinging in opposition to Gerald Ford in order to win the New Hampshire primary, the lack of which ended up costing you the nomination. I also volunteered to serve as your campaign director in the state of Mississippi or any other capacity, and I can assure you that if I had been given this responsibility, Clarke Reed who, as I warned your staff, was weak and undependable, would not even have been in the delegation. Again, you will recall when you called me in March last year to serve on your national campaign committee, I spent most of the conversation begging you not to get John Sears or anyone like him in charge of your campaign.

Those on your staff presently who were pushing you to take Gerald Ford as a running mate, making even a single concession regarding your powers as President, displayed an incredible lack of judgment and foresight. They should either be quietly dismissed or their judgment for the campaign ahead questioned or sidetracked completely. The Ford matter made you appear weak and indecisive.

You made quite a point about wanting some fresh leadership in your administration and cabinet positions composed of persons with proven records of success who would be making a sacrifice to take the positions, and who are not looking for a career in Washington or with the federal government. I submit that I fit your description exactly, and since I have had a tremendous amount of political experience as indicated on the attached resume, I am offering my services, without pay, to move into the top echelon of your campaign staff for the balance of the campaign. I need to either be totally in charge of the campaign or, at the very least, in the position at the top where I have complete access to you.

Ronnie, as you know from our previous correspondence and contact, I will pull no punches in the suggestions and advice I give. I also want you to know that I would not be saying the things about myself and my experience, which surely sounds ambitious and egotistical, were it not for the critical importance I attach to your election. I believe the Lord has blessed me with certain gifts and a vast amount of political experience that can be of decisive value to you. I hope you will glance at my resume, reflect and pray on this. I would welcome a call from you to set up a visit at which you can make your own evaluation. I would be delighted to bring Mary along. Just as you, I was lucky in love, and I know she and Nancy would really hit it off.

On this and any other matter in your campaign, I hope you will follow your basic instincts, and for all decisions, rely on advice and counsel of those who have been consistently with you and steady supporters of your conservative ideology. May God bless, protect, and lead you. I will continue to pray for you.

Sincerely,

WAYjr:jw

Enclosure
cc: Senator Paul Laxalt

Governor Ronald Reagan
Republican Presidential Candidate
9841 Airport Blvd. - Suite 1430
Los Angeles, California 90045

WIRT A. YERGER, JR.
JACKSON, MISSISSIPPI

September 2, 1980

Dear Ronnie,

Your slide in the polls is largely the result of some incredibly bad judgment and advice, but thankfully there is time to recover.

The issue in this campaign is the ineptitude of Jimmy Carter in domestic and foreign policy, and the thrust of the campaign must never let up from carrying the attack to him and his record. Please don't get bogged down in explanations, and never appear to be weakening in your own instincts. For example, you could have simply said that the United States government reserves the right to have diplomatic relationships on whatever basis it desires with whomever it chooses.

Ronnie, one problem you have already had and one that you are going to continue to be plagued with is that you have some advisors on your staff who have been, as recently as four months ago, for anybody but Reagan, and an incredibly large number who were strongly opposed to you four years ago. I am not saying these people should be left on the platform or even have to ride the rear of the train, but I do say letting them ride in the engine of the train with you, calling the signals, is extremely dangerous. You got where you are with your own conservative instincts, and you shouldn't for a moment forget this. Any of the advisors who have been picked up should either get in step with your philosophy completely, or get out. I can't put it any clearer than that.

The biggest danger you face is letting a staff literally kidnap you and cut you off from any comment or advice from those with whom you have communicated in the past. You may recall I stressed this when you were in Jackson several years ago. This is exactly what happened in the Goldwater campaign with distressing results.

Thanks for giving these thoughts your attention, and I would appreciate hearing from you at your earliest convenience. I am praying for you and Nancy and all those involved in your campaign.

Warmest personal wishes,

WAYjr:jw

Enclosures

Governor Ronald Reagan
September ?, 1980
Page 2

cc: William E. Simon
    Senator Paul Laxalt

P.S. Ronnie, I don't believe you personally saw the last letter I
sent you, and I would appreciate your looking at it, a copy of
which is attached, as well as this letter, and giving me a call
either at my office, 601/948-2900, or at my residence, 601/982-2582.

Governor Ronald Reagan
9841 Airport Boulevard
Suite 1430
Los Angeles, California 90045

WIRT A. YERGER, JR.
JACKSON, MISSISSIPPI

January 15, 1981

The Steel Curtain -
"Presidential Kidnapping"

Dear Ronnie,

You and I have exchanged personal correspondence from time to time
over a sixteen year period. You may even recall my telling you, after a
speech you gave here a number of years ago, that when a man is nominated
or elected President, a very jealous group surrounds him and does not
wish him to have any communication that they don't carefully screen. It
matters not to them that they are cutting off many far more deserving
than they are based on past support, experience, and wisdom in giving
advice and constructive criticism. This is a very bad situation, and I
would conclude by the fact that I have not so much as received an acknow-
ledgement to any of the attached four letters that I have sent you since
the election, this is painfully true. I hope you will forcefully move
to correct this. You need to hear the pros and cons of the policies
that you and your Transition Team and Cabinet appointees have been
expressing.

Furthermore, it is human nature for those who have joined in your
support recently, such as those who clamored aboard the Reagan team in
the spring and fall of 1980, to bear considerable resentment toward
those who supported you in 1968 and 1976, and in my case, even in 1964.
There are notable examples of this from my own state. They themselves
thought you were some sort of nut at the time.

Frankly, your Cabinet selection process must have been so flawed
from the very start that the results were predictable, but I do remain
hopeful that you will exert forceful leadership in directing these
appointees to carry out with the fullest intensity the commitments that
you have expressed for years, including your most recent campaign. You
need Cabinet appointees who will literally wade into each department of
government with machetes, vigorously eliminating waste, but the sound-
ings we have heard so far are grievously disappointing. For you to
express that it will be 1983 before the budget is balanced and to hear
the Treasurer appointee say 1984 is an outrage. The budget should be
balanced immediately through a massive cutback in government spending in
every department, with the possible exception of the Defense Department,
and that department should move strenuously to eliminate the waste. If
you don't have people in your Cabinet who are willing to forcefully move
on this, then I would suggest that you withdraw their names or make the

changes now, rather than later. The American people are frustrated with having their hopes dashed by those who were elected based on solemn pledges, and I frankly think they are not in a mood to take it anymore. Louis Rukeyser spoke in Jackson just yesterday dealing with these matters, and I hope you will ask your staff to get a recording of this so that you can listen to it immediately, preferably even before your inauguration speech.

So far, it appears that you have allowed your administration to be far too much influenced by the Eastern establishment crowd who fought you so bitterly in 1976, and for the most part in 1980. Surely there are many qualified people for these positions who did not go to Harvard. For the moment, you have missed a glorious opportunity to get energetic, new leadership for the positions of responsibility with a sense of urgency for the task at hand. Nevertheless, I hope that yours is the best Cabinet in America's history.

Attached are two articles from last night's newspaper, one of which is quoting Richards, whom you have recommended as Chairman of the Republican Party, as saying, "I'm not an idealogue. I don't take positions on issues. I believe that they (the conservatives) since the campaign, have overstated their role in the last campaign." If your appointee actually uttered these words, then I would urge you to move immediately to withdraw his name and substitute someone who would take a stand on issues. I find this statement incredible.

Also, your nominee for the Secretary of Education has made some strong pro busing statements as quoted in Bill Buckley's column. This name should also be withdrawn.

Ronnie, this is no time for timid, weak leadership, and I would urge that you move forcefully to take charge without delay. The early indications are most disturbing, and would appear to indicate that the American people could find themselves disappointed again. The hour is late for our nation and for our freedom. I trust and pray that you would move immediately to make the corrections necessary in terms of your appointees and access from those of us who have had communication with you in the past. Where mistakes have been made, admit them now, rather than try to live with them. We simply cannot afford it, and the success of your Presidency hangs in the balance.

May God bless you and all of your associates. You certainly have our prayers, but we've got to keep communication open.

Warmest personal regards,

WAYjr:jw
Enclosures

President-Elect Ronald Reagan
1726 M Street, N. W.
Washington, D. C. 20036

WIRT A. YERGER, JR.
JACKSON, MISSISSIPPI

May 18, 1981

The Honorable Ronald Reagan
President of the United States
The White House
Washington, D. C.   20515

Fulfilling the Mandate

Dear Ronnie:

Congratulations on your big budget victory. When I was in
Washington a few days ago I had the privilege of speaking briefly
with Dave Stockman, and the most encouraging thing that he said
was that these spending cuts were just the beginning. I truly
feel with regard to every federal agency that rather than a
scalpel, the meat ax or machete needs to be applied vigorously
and, in many cases, the agencies need to be simply abolished.

The purpose of this letter is to urge you to move vigorously
while your popularity remains quite high, as I trust it always
will, to repair better than 25 years of severe damage to the
quality of our education and to the individual freedoms quaranteed
by the Constitution. What I have reference to is the need for
you to assert aggressive, positive leadership on the following:

1.   You should call for the enactment of a Constitutional
amendment forbidding school busing for the purpose of any
racial percentages. Even the proponents of school busing many
years ago now admit that it has been a colossal failure, and
I feel that you not only owe it to the millions of Americans
who voted for you because of your strong stand on this issue
in the past, but even more you owe it to the children in
America who are having their lives ruined by failing to receive
the quality education they deserve due to all the havoc this
has brought about and the great amount of time and money spent
unduly riding on buses. The children have really been the pawns
of the revolutionaries and liberal sociologists, and it is
high time you took the lead in this matter.

2.   There is no continued justification whatsoever for
the extension of the Voting Rights Act, which in all fairness
should be immediately repealed. I would urge you to make the
simple statement that there are adequate laws presently
assuring qualified voters the right to vote which you will vigorously support, but if Congress does not repeal the Voting Rights
Act then any bill to extend it sent to your desk will be promptly

vetoed. It is much better for the entire country that your position be stated unequivocally at this point so that needless time will not be wasted in debating this matter which has reached the point of absurdity. You know it, and the overwhelming majority of the Congress know it. The very idea of continued punitive legislation aimed at a few states is absolutely nonsense. This should be one of the easiest decisions you have ever made, and I would urge that it be made immediately.

3. Attached is a newspaper story indicating that the Justice Department has asked the Federal Court to declare the form of government in Mobile, Alabama unconstitutional. This is the type of action by the Department of Justice which is totally unwarranted and action which we have come to expect from previous Democratic administrations and even some Republican administrations. This is absolutely outrageous and it strongly indicates that your attorney General does not yet have control over the staff working under him. Whoever is responsible for this should be dismissed. It is long past time when the civil rights activists should be calling the tune in the Department of Justice, and I would urge that you call in the Attorney General to insist that this be changed immediately. Why don't we encourage these individuals to spend their energies fighting crime and drugs?

Ronnie, I believe that what I have suggested above is completely consistent with the positions that you have taken in the past and with the thrust of what you have advocated doing. There is simply no time to delay acting upon important matters which need strong decisive leadership. You received a strong mandate for this type of leadership, and I would urge that action be taken immediately. Thank you for your consideration.

Sincerely,

WAYjr:dn

Enclosure

cc: The Honorable Lynn Nofziger   bcc: Mr. Frank Montague
        The Honorable Jesse Helms   Mr. W. D. Mounger
        The Honorable Thad Cochran   Mr. Buddy Klumb
        The Honorable Paul Laxalt   Mr. Howard Phillips
                                                 Mr. Ed Feulner

P.S.:   If any of your advisors are telling you that these
        steps cannot be taken, then I would suggest that you
        have the wrong advisors. Any advisors who are pragma-
        tists rather than conservative ideologues should be
        eased out or put in some other position.

WIRT A. YERGER, JR.
JACKSON, MISSISSIPPI

August 5, 1981

The Honorable Ronald Reagan
President of the United States
The White House
Washington, D. C. 20515

Decisive Leadership

Dear Ron:

Congratulations to you and Drew Lewis on the superb job you
are doing with regard to the air controllers' strike. People
who strike against the government deserve to lose their jobs,
and the overwhelming majority of the citizens of America are
wholeheartedly behind you. When you follow your heart and
your conscience as to what is really right, you come out on
top every time.

It is tragic that you allowed your pragmatic advisors to prevent
your exercise of strong leadership on the Voting Rights extension
issue. If you have ever taken the time to read this act, you
would agree that it should not be extended, and if you had
taken a strong leadership early on as I wrote and begged
you to do better than six months ago, the issue would have
been greatly diminished. Instead, it was allowed to dangle
in the wind, and now you have been put in a weak position
on this and, incidentally, it is one of several factors that
by itself caused Liles Williams to lose the Congressional
seat.

Ron, shortly after you took office you made the statement that
you were going to do what is right for our nation regardless of
the political consequences. I urge you to eliminate from your
staff your advisors, including your innermost circle of advisors,

The Honorable Ronald Reagan   -2-   August 5, 1981

anyone who is not in total agreement with this. The effectiveness
of your Presidency and its overall success ultimately could be
decided by what you do on this one point. Thank you for giving
these thoughts your consideration.

          Respectfully,

WAYjr:dn

cc: Senator Paul Laxalt   bcc: Mr. Billy Mounger
     Senator Jesse Helms   Mr. Buddy Klumb
     Senator Thad Cochran
     Congressman Trent Lott

P. S.: I was appalled to see where you had given audience
        to Harry Dent. If Harry Dent is allowed even two
        minutes in the Oval Office with you, then folks
        like Billy Mounger and myself ought to have an
        uninterrupted seventy-two hours at Camp David. I
        would hope that you would agree. Thank you.

Ross & Yerger

INSURANCE SINCE 1860

January 5, 1982

PERSONAL AND CONFIDENTIAL

The Honorable Ronald Reagan
President of the United States
The White House
Washington, D. C.

Dear Ron:

This month you will have completed one year in the Presidency. As one
who has supported you actively since 1964, I would appreciate the
opportunity of visiting with you for no more than fifteen minutes to
give you my own insight as one very much experienced in politics but
some distance from Washington. As you know, you are often accused
of not being in touch with the folks, and I do think it would be very
healthy for you on occasion to hear from some of us who have been your
most fervent supporters on a one to one basis. We have had brief visits
in the past, and I have always admired your willingness to listen.

My daughter, Mary, and I will be arriving in Washington this Saturday,
January 9, as Mary is planning to find a job in government and moving
to Washington. We will be staying at the Holiday Inn in Alexandria,
and I would appreciate a member of your staff calling me and letting
me know a time convenient to your schedule for us to chat for just a
few minutes.

Ron, I am most grateful that you are in the office of the Presidency
and most enthusiastic about you're being one of the greatest presidents
in the history of our nation.

Warmest wishes always,

Wirt A. Yerger, Jr.

P.S. I am enclosing my daughter's resume. I thought that perhaps a
member of your staff might have need of a loyal and dedicated
staff member. If Nancy has an opening in her staff of any type,
Mary would be highly qualified and a real asset to her.

WIRT A. YERGER, JR.
JACKSON, MISSISSIPPI

February 22, 1982

PERSONAL

The Honorable Ronald Reagan
President of the United States
The White House
Washington, D. C.   20515

"Keeping the Faith"

Dear Ron:

When you were elected President, the primary reason was people's
confidence in you and the ideology that you represented. They
did not choose to have a blend with what any other individual
or faction represented.

It is precisely because of the fact you have allowed the appointment of nonideological pragmatists to critical positions, nearly
all of whom fought you bitterly in 1976 and 1980, that a great
proportion of the mandate which you received in 1980 has not only
been unfulfilled but rather not even seriously considered. This
applies to both domestic and foreign affairs.

In some ways your first year was a good start, but the long term
picture looks bleak unless you can move vigorously to replace
ALL of those within your administration who do not share explicitly
your views and instincts on the correct course for America. This
would surely include replacing immediately Jim Baker and
Alexander Haig as it has been apparent from the beginning that
neither of these is in step with the ideology which you've
espoused for twenty years. The issues are far too fundamental
and the consequences for America are far too serious for you to
hesitate due to your concern for the personal feelings of these
two or any others.

There are quite a number of fervent Reagan supporters with
business, professional, civic, and political accomplishments
whose credentials will more than match Baker's and Haig's and
who, because of their ideological understanding of the issues
we face, will do a far superior job. The lack of proper leadership around you has caused you far too much embarrassment--
and our nation simply cannot afford for you to fail.

The Honorable Ronald Reagan
Page 2
February 22, 1982

What it boils down to is that those in charge of your
administration absolutely must be firmly committed, not
only to you, but to the policies which you have championed.
This is absolutely not the case at present, and you need to
recognize it and act decisively. There have been several
very pertinent articles dealing with my feeling in Human Events
and in the editorial column of the Wall Street Journal for the
last several months. It would be great just to know that you
read, without screening or deletion, every single issue of these
publications. It would also be nice to know you occasionally
read critical letters from those of us who yearned for a
Reagan Presidency as far back as 1964. I've sent several which
I doubt ever penetrated the "steel curtain" around you.

Ron, let's face it, how many Reagan supporters would there have
been in a Bush Administration or in a Ford Administration? The
answer is obviously zero. For those who have supported you and
what you stood for these years to be left in the position of
begging and being tossed nothing more than a few bones is an
outrage. If it is allowed to continue, you will have most
definitely failed to "keep the faith," which so many of us
placed in you.

Please think it over seriously and prayerfully before it is too
late. Thank you.

                    Warmest wishes always,

WAYjr:gcs
cc: Congressman Trent Lott
     Honorable Jesse Helms
     Honorable Paul Laxalt
     Honorable Strom Thurmond

BCC: Editor, Human Events
     Editor, Wall Street Journal
     Mr. Ed Feulner, American Heritage Foundation
     Mr. Howard Phillips, Conservative Caucus
     Mr. Billy Mounger
     Mr. Buddy Klumb

WIRT A. YERGER, JR.
JACKSON, MISSISSIPPI

April 6, 1982

Honorable Ronald Reagan
President of the United States
The White House
Washington, D. C. 20515

William French Smith –
Back to California

Dear Ron:

From the very first I thought it was incredible to automatically
put your own personal attorney in as the United States Attorney
General. Since then I have seen very few signs that don't make
me feel my original instincts concerning this appointment were
correct. The Justice Department's ruling regarding the
Mississippi Congressional Districting as well as their stance
from the beginning of last year with regard to the Voting Rights
Act lead me to recommend that William French Smith be dismissed
immediately. You expect nonsense such as this from a Democratic
administration, but I'll be doggoned if we expect it from a
supposedly conservative Republican administration.

Ron, you've got to face up to your mistakes and this is definitely
one of them. Please be sure that the next Attorney General you
appoint is a conservative who will grab hold of that department
with both hands, shake it, and get it on its proper course. We
can afford to do no less. Thank you.

Sincerely,

WAYjr:gcs
cc: Honorable Trent Lott
     Honorable Paul Laxalt
     Mr. Lee Atwater
     Mr. Ed Rollins
P. S. Virtually none of the several letters I've sent since
       you assumed office have been acknowledged much less
       specifically answered.
BCC: Mr. Buddy Klumb
      Mr. Billy Mounger
      Honorable Ellis B. Bodron

THE WHITE HOUSE

WASHINGTON

May 5, 1982

Dear Wirt:

Thank you for your letter and your concern.
I know how much you care about the progress
of the Administration and I value your
advice -- even though I don't always take
it. You have been one of my most faithful
supporters and I am grateful for that. I
hope that I will continue to have your
confidence and your trust. And keep the
advice coming!

With best wishes,

                    Sincerely,

                    Ron

Mr. Wirt A. Yerger, Jr.
Ross and Yerger, Inc.
Post Office Box 1139
Jackson, Mississippi 39205

WIRT A. YERGER, JR.
JACKSON, MISSISSIPPI

May 27, 1982

Honorable Ronald Reagan
President of the United States
The White House
Washington, D. C. 20515

Dear Ron:

Thanks for your recent personal letter, and I am delighted
to know that at least some of my correspondence is getting
through to you personally.

If you read the attached by James Kilpatrick and glance at
the Voting Rights Act, I have no doubt that you will agree
this is very bad legislation for our nation. One thing
that folks in politics need to learn to do is reserve the
right to change their mind and admit when they have been
wrong. Whoever suggested to you that you should take a
position saying you would sign whatever Voting Rights Act
that Congress passed needs to be replaced.

Ron, I would respectfully urge you to give most serious
reconsideration to your position on this matter. In no
way is this in keeping with the position that you have
taken in political life for better than 20 years. Thank
you.

Sincerely,

WAYjr:gcs
Enclosure

P.S. In spite of your
publicized statement on
Baker needs to return
to Houston. His pragmatism
has cost you dearly.

WIRT A. YERGER, JR.
JACKSON, MISSISSIPPI

August 24, 1982

Honorable Ronald Reagan
President of the United States
The White House
Washington, D. C.   20515

Dear Ron:

It should make you feel a little bit queasy when
you have to call on Tip O'Neill and Ted Kennedy to
pass any type of legislation, much less a tax hike
bill three months before an election, which goes
against everything you have ever stood for in the
past. As per the attached, I would hope that you
would fire Jim Baker if he doesn't tender his
resignation voluntarily. This man, as I have said
many times in the past, is responsible in large
measure for convincing you to break your sacred
commitments to the people of America, plus assembling
a White House staff composed of over 75 percent who
were opposed to you in the past.

Ron, I hope you would also rethink the tactics that
were used against Republican Congressmen to try to
get their vote for the tax bill. These seem to be
against every sense of decency and fair play that I
would have thought you would have held dear.

You asked me in correspondence a few months ago to
keep my letters coming and you indicated that you
would see them. I continue to hope and pray that you
are reading the editorial pages of the Wall Street
Journal and Human Events. While I would love for you
to read my letters, I would settle for that, and I
would appreciate your advising me accordingly.

May God be with you.

Sincerely,

WAYjr:gcs
Enclosure
cc: Honorable Ed Meese

WIRT A. YERGER, JR.
JACKSON, MISSISSIPPI

November 1, 1982

Honorable Ronald Reagan
President of the United States
The White House
Washington, D. C. 20515

Keeping the Mandate

Dear Ron:

Your Presidency has been a vast improvement over
that of your predecessor, but compared to your
potential when you assumed office and the impera-
tives of the mess you inherited, it has been
significantly short of my expectations and fondest
hopes. I am writing you this letter before the
election, the outcome of which I trust will not be
as bad as feared, but which certainly could have
been significantly better with the kind of leadership you had the opportunity to provide.

You were advised by a number of us to declare an
"economic emergency" from the moment of your
inauguration and to seek immediate and massive
cuts in federal expenditures significant enough
to bring the budget into balance in a matter of
months. Unfortunately, you didn't.

You are an excellent communicator and a number of
us have advised you from the beginning to have
prime time "fireside chats" with the people of
America on a regular basis leading and educating
on the problems our nation faces on specific
domestic and foreign affairs subjects. You
didn't, although this was the only way you could
have successfully combatted the vicious attacks
from the media that have dogged every move you
have made.

Honorable Ronald Reagan
Page 2
November 1, 1982

By far your most significant failing has been
allowing yourself to be virtually kidnapped
by a group of appointees who have no instinct for
or comprehension of the philosophy of government
you have espoused for the last 25 years and who,
until the time of your nomination, considered you
a menace. You may recall me writing you when you
were campaigning in New Hampshire concerning your
needing to discharge John Sears. I promptly
received the attached personal letter from you.
Less than 24 hours after writing that letter, you
dismissed him proving to me that, painful as it
is, you can take decisive action on a change of
personnel.

There are a number of conservatives throughout the
country who do comprehend the principles you have
championed who would be glad to assist you in
making these mid-term corrective changes.

Ron, the hour was late in New Hampshire, and the
hour is late now. I trust and pray that you will
show us the leadership and resolve of which you
are capable, and on the strength of which you
were elected.

                    Respectfully,

WAYjr:gcs
Enclosure
cc: Honorable Ed Meese
     Honorable Paul Laxalt
     Honorable Trent Lott

WIRT A. YERGER, JR.
JACKSON, MISSISSIPPI

November 23, 1982

Honorable Ronald Reagan
President of the United States
The White House
Washington, D. C. 20515

Dear Ron:

My Sunday School teacher passed out the attached, entitled "Thank you, Lord", and I thought it contained some ideas that you would appreciate.

Ron, don't know whether any of the letters I have sent you for the last two years have ever reached you personally, but I do think it is most important to keep the lines of communication open with those who have been among your most staunch supporters for better than two decades. If we cannot visit together personally, perhaps we could by telephone and I hope you will call soon.

Regards always,

WAYjr:gcs

Enclosure

THE WHITE HOUSE

WASHINGTON

December 16, 1982

Dear Wirt:

Thanks for writing and, as usual, for your
advice and counsel. I have not, nor do I
intend to, abandon those principles or that
philosophy which brought me to this office.
What I am doing, is making my decisions based
on what I believe is good for our country and
the American people. Someone once called
politics "the art of the possible." I believe
that the Presidency might be termed "the art
of possibilities, probabilities and imponder-
ables." You have been one of my most faithful
and steadfast supporters over the years. I
have always been able to count on you and I
hope you know that you can still count on me.

Nancy joins me in wishing you and your family
the blessings and joys of the Christmas season.

Sincerely,

Ron

Mr. Wirt A. Yerger, Jr.
Post Office Box 1139
Jackson, Mississippi 39205

WIRT A. YERGER, JR.
JACKSON, MISSISSIPPI

April 13, 1983

The Honorable Ronald Reagan
President of the United States
The White House
Washington, D. C. 20515

Raping Small Corporation Pensions

Dear Ronnie:

Monday I signed the papers terminating our Corporation's
pension plan, not due to the fact of being unable to fund
it but rather being unable to live with the obnoxious
provisions that you allowed Bob Dole, Jim Baker and others
to con you into supporting when you pushed for the TEFRA
legislation. Surely, nobody told you the full impact of
this legislation or bothered to inform you that the provision
of it are so bad for small corporations that the liberals
never dreamed they could get this enacted.

I would have never thought that this type of legislation
would have been vigorously supported by a Republican
President, much less one that was identified as a Conservativ
Ronnie, to say the least, by many of your actions you have
severely dampened the enthusiasm of those of us who formed
the bedrock of your support in 1976 and 1980. This is
something that Jim Baker, try as he might, would never
understand.

How you can live with yourself on the number of key issues
you have waffled and cratered on that were critical to
those who were your strongest supporters, I frankly don't
know. Sorry to be so blunt about it, but that is the way it
is.

Sincerely,

WAYjr:cdh

WIRT A. YERGER, JR.
JACKSON, MISSISSIPPI

May 23, 1983

The Honorable Ronald Reagan
President of the United States
The White House
Washington, D. C.   20515

> Further Congressional Insanity -
> "Non-Discrimination in Insurance Act"
> (H.R. 100) and (S.372)

Dear Ronnie:

This is one of the most clear examples recently of further
absurd legislation where the effect will ultimately penalize
the very ones it supporters claim it will assist.

It is also a further example of legislation that will tend
to make businesses "ice cold" with regard to pension plans.
It is time to end the Congressional tampering and rectify
the grievous mistakes that were made under TEFRA.

Ronnie, please think through the impact of this.
Thank you.

Sincerely,

WAYjr:cdh

THE WHITE HOUSE

WASHINGTON

July 6, 1983

Dear Wirt:

Don't ever worry about being blunt. I
wouldn't have you any other way. Thanks
for continuing to write with your thoughts
and believe me, I am trying not to let you
down.

Sincerely,

Ron

Mr. Wirt A. Yerger, Jr.
Post Office Box 1139
Jackson, Mississippi 39205

P.S. I'm asking that a Fact Sheet on
      TEFRA be included with this letter.

WIRT A. YERGER, JR.
JACKSON, MISSISSIPPI

PERSONAL & CONFIDENTIAL

October 12, 1983

The Honorable Ronald Reagan
President of the United States
The White House
Washington, D.C. 20515

Your 1984 Candidacy

Dear Ronnie:

Recently, in answering a strongly worded letter I
forwarded to you, you sent me a very nice personal
reply, quite obviously written by you, in which you
stated I should never apologize for speaking plainly.
I guess I have a reputation for shooting straight and
pulling no punches, and certainly this letter will be
no exception.

I have noted speculation about whether you will or
won't run for reelection in 1984, and it is on that
subject I wish to make some very pointed comments.
First of all, I think you should ask yourself whether
the ideology you espoused for 20 years was deeply felt
and absolutely genuine. If the answer is yes, and I
still hold that that is the correct answer, then ask
yourself why your core support, which is not some small
minority, but rather many millions of God fearing,
tax paying citizens, who for years have pinned their
hopes and faith in you, have been brushed aside in
your administration right from the start.

Ask yourself why you have allowed your administration,
including the White House specifically, to be staffed
over 85% with personnel who did not support you for
the Republican nomination in either 1976 or 1980,
with most feeling so strongly they thought you to be
a dangerous menace.

Please ask yourself the specifics of where the
actions of your administration have been different
than those of Nixon, Ford, Bush, or Baker
administrations would have been. I would love to
know your answer to that one.

The Honorable Ronald Reagan
Page Two
October 12, 1983

Then I would suggest you ask yourself very honestly
how much more conservative in action, not rhetoric,
which is always nice to hear, your administration has
been than a Bush or Baker administration would have
been.

Ronnie, what I am saying is that compared with what
you had promised to give us in terms of conservative
leadership, your administration has been not only
disappointing, but really heart breaking. No wonder
so many rank and file citizens who work their hearts
out ringing doorbells and contributing money to
leaders in the naive belief that they mean what they
say become cynical and frustrated.

My heartfelt conclusion is that unless you can get
the ship back on the course you espoused as essential
for the 20 years previous to 1980's election, which
would necessitate a massive housecleaning, including
Jim Baker and all of the non-ideological pragmatists,
I would respectfully suggest you had just as well
retire to California, write your memoirs and serve on
various corporate boards, bask in the limelight of
being a former President, reaping millions of dollars
and enjoying life's pleasures. Quite honestly, as
one who has begged you periodically in correspondence
for the last four years to alter your course, I still
hope you will resolve to do it forthrightly and
immediately, but if you feel that you have let things
get out of control so far that you can't do this, the
retirement option is, in my judgment, the right one.

Respectfully,

WAYJr:jmt

371

WIRT A. YERGER, JR.
JACKSON, MISSISSIPPI

February 28, 1984

PERSONAL

The Honorable Ronald Reagan
President of the United States
The White House
Washington, D.C. 20515

"Aid For Afghan Freedom Fighters"

Dear Ronnie:

Attached is a memorandum from The Heritage Foundation concerning the situation in Afghanistan which has troubled me for some time.

Thousands of American lives were lost in Vietnam due to the unrestrained supplying of weapons and ammunition by the Russians. This was not a parallel situation because The United States was not invading as the Russians have done in Afghanistan. I would certainly expect restraint from a Carter Administration, but from the Reagan Administration, when fundamental freedoms and lives are at stake, it is shocking and embarrassing.

Alexander Solzhenitsen and Winston Churchill are unquestionably the greatest spokesmen for freedom in this century. When are we going to start listening to what they have said and following the high road of truth, honor, freedom, spiritual commitment, and recognizing the total absence of these in our adversaries?

Ronnie, you and you alone are in the critically important position of having the football in your hand. May God grant you the courage and wisdom to act accordingly.

Warmest personal regards,

WAYJr:jmt
Enclosure

THE WHITE HOUSE

WASHINGTON

April 16, 1984

Dear Wirt:

Thank you for your letter of February 28 about the
situation in Afghanistan. As always, I was very pleased
to hear from you and to have the benefit of your frank
comments. I am glad to tell you how my Administration
views this important world issue.

The United States strongly opposes the Soviet occupation
of Afghanistan. We are seeking the removal of Soviet
troops from that war-torn land. Apart from our very
real concern about the tragic plight of the Afghans
themselves, we view the Soviet invasion and continuing
occupation in a broad strategic context. It is a disturbing example of Soviet willingness to use its ever-growing
military might beyond its borders in ways that not only
threaten American interests but peace, stability, and
freedom in the Central-South Asian region and throughout
the world. For this reason, we believe it is absolutely
essential that Soviet aggression in Afghanistan not
succeed.

The United States is committed to seeking a negotiated
political settlement for Afghanistan. This settlement must
be based upon the principles spelled out in five United
Nations General Assembly resolutions on Afghanistan.
These resolutions call for the immediate withdrawal of
foreign troops from Afghanistan; reaffirm the right of the
Afghan people to determine their own form of government
and to choose their economic, political and social system;
reiterate that the preservation of the sovereignty, terri-
torial integrity, political independence and non-aligned

2

character of Afghanistan is essential for a peaceful solution of the problem; and call for the creation of conditions which would enable the Afghan refugees to return voluntarily to their homes in safety and honor.

Unfortunately, the prospects for an early political settlement for Afghanistan do not appear bright. We have seen no signs that the Soviet Union is willing to negotiate meaningfully the withdrawal of its forces, the root cause of the problem. The Soviets seem prepared for a long struggle. With their policy of increasingly brutal reprisal tactics against civilians and civilian areas of strategic importance, the Soviets apparently believe that they can wear down the resistance and wait them out, and that the world will forget Afghanistan.

But this does not take into account the incredible will of the Afghan people and their determination to resist. The entire world, including the Soviet Union, has been surprised by what the Afghan resistance has been able to accomplish and by what it has done to complicate Soviet plans for Afghanistan. In general, the Afghan resistance did very well in 1983. They were better armed and trained than ever before, and have displayed more cooperation in military engagements with the Soviet/Democratic Republic of Afghanistan forces. This was particularly evident in campaigns in the eastern part of Afghanistan, in Paktia and Paktika provinces, in the early fall, and in the southern Shomali area in late November and early December. At Guldara, in the first days of December, a large body of mujahidin from different groups made a stand against a large Soviet force of 2,500 men. Although taking heavy casualties themselves, they were described as jubilant with the losses they inflicted on the Soviets. The mujahidin have also displayed increased proficiency in ambushing Soviet/Democratic Republic of Afghanistan supply convoys. Moreover, Soviet helicopter and fixed wing aircraft losses in 1983 were significantly higher than losses in 1982.

As the normal winter lull in fighting ends soon, and as more clement weather brings a resumption of the sporadic but intense fighting that usually occurs from spring to fall, we expect to hear more stories of valor and success from the Afghan resistance, and that they will continue to hold the Soviet/Democratic Republic of Afghanistan forces at bay.

3

You may be sure that the question of how we can
further bring home to the Soviet Union the full cost of its
aggression remains under constant review. In proclaiming
March 21, the Afghan New Year, as Afghanistan Day, I
said, "We stand in admiration of the indomitable will and
courage of the Afghan people who continue their resistance to tyranny. All freedom-loving people around the
globe should be inspired by the Afghan people's struggle
to be free and the heavy sacrifices they bear for
liberty."

Wirt, I'm proud to have your friendship and support, and
I appreciate all that you've done on behalf of the goals
we share.

With my best wishes,

                    Sincerely,

                    Ronald Reagan

Mr. Wirt A. Yerger, Jr.
Post Office Box 1139
Jackson, Mississippi 39205

WIRT A. YERGER, JR.
JACKSON, MISSISSIPPI

August 16, 1984

The Honorable Ronald Reagan
President of the United States
The White House
Washington, D.C.

Dear Ron:

As you know from many of my past letters to you, even
before your inauguration, I have viewed Jim Baker as
a very, very serious mistake as a member of your
staff, much less Chief of Staff. His latest known
move in persuading you to do a flip-flop on the
"no-tax increase" issue should prove, if any other
proof were needed, that he either needs to be
immediately dismissed, put somewhere else, or at the
very least, shoved off in a corner and not listened
to until after the election, when you could allow him
to gracefully go his own way.

What you have failed to understand in this
appointment and in so many others is the fact that if
a person does not possess the ideological
understanding and commitment in tune with that which
you have expressed so eloquently for these many
years, their advise and counsel will be totally
pragmatic and lead us to disaster, both politically,
as well as our nation itself. It is not that people
like Jim Baker do not mean well; they simply do not
have the instincts to stand in the heat of the battle
and to understand the real issues.

Ron, I know what I am suggesting you do is possible,
because you did manage to get rid of John Sears, and
may I respectfully submit that you are four years
overdue in doing the same with Jim Baker. So very
much depends on it that just having him around is a
risk that you nor the nation can ill afford. Please,
please, I beg you to face up to and surgically remove
this very serious problem.

Sincerely,

WAYJr:gw

10/12/84

WIRT A. YERGER, JR.
JACKSON, MISSISSIPPI

Dear George,

Congratulations on a truly masterful job last night. Cannot remember when I've witnessed a more one sided debate.

Regardless of what the liberal media, and nothing has proved their bias more than them calling this debate a "draw", have said you literally overwhelmed Geraldine. She was really pathetic and you were outstanding.

Haven't enjoyed a TV program that much in years.

Hoping & praying for you and Ronnie.

Regards, Out

WIRT A. YERGER, JR.
JACKSON, MISSISSIPPI

May 13, 1985

PERSONAL & CONFIDENTIAL

Honorable Ronald Reagan
President of the United States
The White House
Washington, DC 20515

South Africa - Facing the Facts

Dear Ron:

Attached is a letter which I sent to
Dick Lugar concerning the total hippocritical
position that he and some of our other
conservative friends are taking with regard
to South Africa. With the exception of the
one statement that you made, which really
didn't need to be made, your position and
that of your administration has appeared to
be sound.

Nevertheless, what I do feel is necessary is
for you to take a strong stand against the
hippocracy with regard to South Africa so
that the people of this nation will know the
truth about the situation there.

Sincerely,

WAYjr:dr

Enclosure

WIRT A. YERGER, JR.
JACKSON, MISSISSIPPI

May 13, 1985

Honorable Pat Buchanan
The White House
Washington, DC 20515

Dear Pat:

From time to time when I write to the
President, I take the liberty to send a letter
to you and hope that that will increase the
chances of breaking through the steel barrier.
You don't know how much of a relief it is to
know that you are on the White House staff
and have access to the President.

Sincerely,

WAYjr:dr

WIRT A. YERGER, JR.
JACKSON, MISSISSIPPI

June 17, 1985

Honorable Ronald Reagan
President of the United States
The White House
Washington, DC 20515

Dear Ron:

The time is long past when we can temporize with the Shiite terrorists. I would suggest now is the time for you to announce to the American people and to the world that our country will react directly and immediately, recognizing that innocent lives will often be lost, but we are left with no other viable alternative. Furthermore, let it be known that any nation giving aid and comfort to terrorists will be subject to the most massive and direct retaliation, militarily, economically, and in every other way this country can bring to bear.

Why don't you sometime make the assertion, which is totally true, that it was the liberals, coupled with the American media, who were primarily responsible for the crisis involved in causing the change of government in both Iran and Nicaragua. Let's assess this blame where it truly belongs.

Ron, it is far past the time to get tough, real tough. We are dealing with fanatics, and I don't believe there is any other realistic alternative.

Sincerely,

WAYJR:dr

WIRT A. YERGER, JR.
JACKSON, MISSISSIPPI

August 12, 1985

The Honorable Ronald Reagan
President of the United States
The White House
Washington, D.C. 20515

A Time for Statesmanship -
South Africa

Dear Ronnie:

It is high time for you to put an end to the farce
concerning South Africa by announcing you will veto
the legislation making its way toward your desk and
speaking out forcefully. The media, the leftists,
and the Russians who are in this "up to their
eyeballs" can be routed if you will speak out
forcefully and clearly. Unfortunately, this has
been allowed to "dangle in the wind" too long but
better to speak out now than after the grossest
injustice has been done, not only to South Africa
but to future generations of Americans as well.

While stressing that you do not condone apartheid,
you can point out to the people of America what
tremendous progress has been made, and the standard
of living that blacks enjoy in South Africa are by
far higher than any blacks on the continent of
Africa. You can also point out the total absurdity
of the so called "one man, one vote" on the
continent of Africa, because as the State Department
will verify, there is not a nation on the African
continent that has democratic elections. The "one
man, one vote" has amounted to "one vote, one time,
and then it is over". There are approximately six
million whites in South Africa who do not wish nor
should they be forced to "commit suicide".

As you well know, the Russians are slaughtering
people in Afghanistan every day, and nearly half the
people in the world are enslaved by communist
tyranny. Where is the call for sanctions against
those in the nations involved? Did you know there
are more blacks in South Africa that own a private
automobile than there are Russians that own a
private automobile?

The Honorable Ronald Reagan
Page Two
August 12, 1985

Ronnie, you need to have Pat Buchanan or some clear thinkers to arm you with the full facts and draft a speech that will knock the media and the liberals back on their heels, because the strategic and geographical position and vital minerals involved are simply too much, aside from all the other factors, to allow another fall into the Russian orbit, as has taken place in Zimbabwe and many other areas of Africa. The American people are thirsting for leadership, and it is clearly your call to provide it. Thank you for giving this message your very careful and prayerful consideration.

Sincerely,

WAYJR:dr

WIRT A. YERGER, JR.
JACKSON, MISSISSIPPI

August 13, 1985

Honorable Pat Buchanan
Assistant to the President
The White House
Washington, D.C. 20515

Dear Pat:

A lot more could be said and said better than
what I have put in this short letter to
Ronnie, and I hope you will pass it on to him
if you think it might help.

Sincerely,

WAYJR:dr

Enclosure

WIRT A. YERGER, JR.
JACKSON, MISSISSIPPI

November 21, 1985

PERSONAL AND CONFIDENTIAL

Honorable Ronald Reagan
President of the United States
The White House
Washington, DC 20515

"The Medvid Case: American Honor Lost"

Dear Ron:

Since you are out of the country with your summit
conference, I thought I would enclose to you the
above-captioned article from today's The Wall Street
Journal by Congressman Fred Eckert. I want you to
know that I agree totally with his position, and you
should be ashamed as our President to have allowed
something such as this to happen.

Surely you can pick up the telephone and contact
Gorbachev and explain to him that he should allow
this young seaman, if by chance he is still alive,
to leave the Soviet Union. Their most notable
defector just returned; therefore, it would cause
them no loss of face and would be a very strong
gesture on the Russians' part.

Ron, furthermore, I would hope that you would
dismiss all of the U.S. customs and immigrations
officials involved, as well as those in the State
Department, for their gross insensitivity. It is my
hope and prayer that you will personally intervene
with compassion and sensitivity.

Sincerely,

WAYJR:dr

cc: Honorable Fred Eckert
    Honorable Pat Buchanan

WIRT A. YERGER, JR.
JACKSON, MISSISSIPPI

December 19, 1985

PERSONAL AND CONFIDENTIAL

The Honorable Pat Buchanan
Assistant to the President
The White House
Washington, D.C. 20515

Dear Pat:

Hope you can transmit the attached to the Oval
Office. Maybe if Schultz won't take a polygraph
test, Ron can send him back to California and get
someone who thinks like he has said he has felt for
the last 25 years as the secretary of state.
Wouldn't that be a breath of fresh air?

                            Regards always,

WAYJR:dr

WIRT A. YERGER, JR.
JACKSON, MISSISSIPPI

December 19, 1985

PERSONAL AND CONFIDENTIAL

The Honorable Ronald Reagan
President of the United States
The White House
Washington, D.C. 20515

"Their Fight Is Our Fight"

Dear Ron:

Attached is an editorial from Forbes, and I am
frankly amazed that the the Ronald Reagan some of us
have supported for as long as 25 years vacillates on
a matter such as this when the moral, ideological,
and strategic considerations are so overwhelmingly
obvious.

In the name of everyone who has fought for freedom
and those whose very lives are at stake now, please
act forcefully without another moment's delay.
There have been too few times in our history when we
have had a popular, conservative president with the
means and the ability to strike such a blow of
freedom.

Ron, as one of your most fervent, long-time
supporters, I would appreciate a personal note from
you specifically in response to this concern.

Best wishes always,

WAYJR:dr

THE WHITE HOUSE

WASHINGTON

Received S.S

'='00 JAN 32 10001

January 31, 1986

ACTION

MEMORANDUM FOR THE PRESIDENT

FROM: JOHN M. POINDEXTER

SUBJECT: Reply to Yerger on Medvid Case

Issue

How to reply to Wirt Yerger's letter on the Medvid case.

Facts

Yerger's letter to you is based on a Wall Street Journal
article which contains numerous inaccuracies. The reply
acknowledges the initial mishandling of the case, but sets the
record straight on subsequent treatment of Medvid.

Discussion

I recommend that you not sign the reply to Yerger, but have it
signed by the appropriate White House official, in order to
maintain your distance from the mishandling of the case and to
avoid stimulating renewed media interest in the Medvid affair.
However, should you desire to reply personally to Yerger, a
letter for your signature is at Tab II.

Recommendation

OK   No

        _____   That you agree to have the attached letter
                            signed by an appropriate White House official

Attachments

Tab A   Reply for Appropriate White House official's
           signature
Tab B   Alternative Reply for your Signature

                          Prepared by:
                          Judyt Mandel

cc Vice President

NATIONAL SECURITY COUNCIL   10001 add on
WASHINGTON. D.C. 20506

February 5, 1986

MEMORANDUM FOR ANNE HIGGINS

FROM: RODNEY B. MCDANIEL

SUBJECT: Reply to Wirt Yerger

The President has decided (memo attached) not to reply directly
to a letter from Wirt Yerger concerning the Soviet Seaman who
jumped ship, but to have a reply signed by the appropriate
White House official. I am, therefore, attaching for your
consideration a draft reply to Yerger.

Attachments

Tab A   President's Memo

Tab B   Draft Reply

note on incoming.

SUGGESTED REPLY FOR APPROPRIATE
WHITE HOUSE OFFICIAL

Dear Mr. Yerger:

I regret the delay in responding to your November 21 letter to
President Reagan in which you expressed concern about the case
of Soviet Seaman Miroslav Medvid. I want you to know that we
share your outrage that the local Border Patrol officials/who
first interviewed Seaman Medvid on October 24, returned him to
his ship without consulting with officials in Washington, or
following other standard procedures established to ensure that
asylum claims made in such circumstances are given full and
expedited consideration. The Commissioner of the U.S. Immigration and Naturalization Service (INS) has already acknowledged this error and the Attorney General is conducting an
investigation of INS handling of this incident. Several INS
officials have already been disciplined.

While we all greatly regret the initial mistake, the U.S. did
make a concerted effort to ensure that Seaman Medvid subsequently had an opportunity to decide whether he wished to
remain in the United States or to return to the Soviet Union.
Seaman Medvid was removed from the Soviet ship and interviewed
in an environment under U.S. control, first aboard the U.S.
Coast Guard Cutter Salvia and again at a U.S. Navy shore
facility near New Orleans. Scrupulous care was taken to
establish his identity through documents, photos and an
eye-witness. He was examined by U.S. medical doctors, and
remained in U.S. custody for twenty-four hours. As a matter of
policy, we allow Soviet consular officials to be present when
their citizens are interviewed to promote reciprocal treatment
of our own citizens. The U.S. officials present, however, made
sure that no coercion or intimidation took place during the
time Medvid was in U.S. custody. U.S. officials took pains to
ensure that Seaman Medvid understood that he was free to remain
in the United States if he wanted to do so.

Seaman Medvid was questioned extensively, including about why
he first jumped from the Soviet ship and what happened after he
was returned to the ship. In response, he repeatedly expressed
his desire to return to the USSR. There was no doubt on the
part of the two U.S. military doctors who examined him that he
was physically and mentally competent to make such a decision.
Further, despite some press accounts, there was also no doubt
about our ability to communicate with Seaman Medvid. The
professional interpreter engaged by the Department of State was
himself of Ukrainian origin, and was able to communicate with
Seaman Medvid in both Ukrainian and Russian. It was the
interpreter's assessment that Seaman Medvid was more fluent in
Russian than Ukrainian.

Unfortunately, during these interviews it was impossible to recreate Seaman Medvid's original frame of mind of October 24. We will never know what pressures may have been exerted on him while he was on the Soviet ship. Nor did we ever discount the possibility that such pressures may have influenced his final decision. We are under no illusions about the repressive nature of the Soviet Government and its willingness to use coercion and threats to control its people. There was always the possibility that Seaman Medvid would decide to return to the USSR and that we would have to respect that choice. In cases such as this, only the individual involved can decide what action to take in light of the risks and personal costs involved for himself or for others. It was not a decision we could make for him.

Despite the initial mistakes, we made a strong effort to give Seaman Medvid a chance to remain in the U.S., if he so chose. As a result of this tragic case, the U.S. Government has reviewed and tightened procedures to avoid any recurrence of such incidents.

Sincerely,

WIRT A. YERGER, JR.
JACKSON, MISSISSIPPI

February 17, 1986

Honorable Pat Buchanan
Assistant to the President
The White House
Washington, D.C. 20515

Dear Pat:

I hope something can be done concerning the
enclosed. Thanks for all your attempts to pass my
letters on. One of these days, one may penetrate
the "iron curtain".

Sincerely,

WAYJR:dr

Enclosures

WIRT A. YERGER, JR.
JACKSON, MISSISSIPPI

February 17, 1986

Honorable Ronald Reagan
President of the United States
The White House
Washington, D.C. 20515

The Price of Pride

Dear Ron:

R. C. Sproul, Presbyterian preacher and writer, to a
packed sanctuary at the Mid-South Men's Prayer
Conference spoke glowingly of how proud he was to
know that you would not allow politics or the
political implications of anything to be discussed
in a Cabinet meeting. I was very much impressed to
know this, but either at separate conferences with
you or your staff separately, quite to the contrary,
on numerous occasions have justified actions which
they really knew to be wrong as warranted simply by
the political aspects.

It would appear that your staff or you particularly,
once you have yourself out on a position as
committed, will pay any price whatsoever rather than
tighten up the belt, swallow pride and say, "We made
a mistake." or "It has not turned out like we
thought it would, and we are changing course."

A classic example of this is the situation you find
yourself in on tax reform. Your advisors' and your
own judgment have you in a position where
politically they think you will have to sign any tax
bill which is presented to you, and without a doubt
the house bill should have been allowed to die.
Please look at the enclosed articles from Business
Week and The Wall Street Journal with Paul Craig
Roberts and Martin Feldstein bearing out precisely
the situation.

Ron, as Paul Craig Roberts put it, "Reagan has been
outmaneuvered by the bureaucracy, which has
substituted its agenda for his. The current tax
reform is just the latest in a string of tax
increases on business that began in 1982."

Honorable Ronald Reagan
Page Two
February 17, 1986

The "price of your pride" in 1982 (TEFRA) was that a small company like ours had to terminate its pension plan which we had for many years, and thousands of others had to do the same. Please, I beg you to look carefully at the enclosed and consider this matter so you can take a strong position on it now, telling the Congress to go back to square one. If you really felt sincerely about the desire for tax reform (and I know you did), this is the only realistic alternative at this point, and you will have kept faith with your constituency as well as your own position. Thank you for your consideration.

Sincerely,

WAYJR:dr

Enclosures

3661
1 M

February 18, 1986

Dear Mr. Yerger:

I regret the delay in responding to your November 21 letter to
President Reagan in which you expressed concern about the case
of Soviet Seaman Miroslav Medvid. We share your outrage that
the local Border Patrol officials who first interviewed Seaman
Medvid on October 24 not only returned him to his ship without
consulting with officials in Washington, but also did not follow
other standard procedures established to ensure that asylum
claims made in such circumstances are given full and expedited
consideration. The Commissioner of the U.S. Immigration and
Naturalization Service (INS) has already acknowledged this error
and the Attorney General is conducting an investigation of INS
handling of this incident. Several INS officials have already
been disciplined as a result.

While we all greatly regret the initial mistake, the United
States did make a concerted effort to ensure that Seaman Medvid
subsequently had an opportunity to decide whether he wished to
remain in the United States or to return to the Soviet Union.
Seaman Medvid was removed from the Soviet ship and interviewed
in an environment under U.S. control, first aboard the U.S.
Coast Guard Cutter Salvia and again at a U.S. Navy shore facility near New Orleans. Scrupulous care was taken to establish
his identity through documents, photos and an eyewitness. He
was examined by U.S. medical doctors, and remained in U.S.
custody for twenty-four hours. As a matter of policy, we allow
Soviet consular officials to be present when their citizens are
interviewed to promote reciprocal treatment of our own citizens.
The U.S. officials present, however, made sure that no coercion
or intimidation took place during the time Seaman Medvid was
in U.S. custody. U.S. officials took pains to ensure that
Seaman Medvid understood that he was free to remain in the
United States if he wanted to do so.

Seaman Medvid was questioned extensively, including about why
he first jumped from the Soviet ship and what happened after he
was returned to the ship. In response, he repeatedly expressed
his desire to return to the U.S.S.R. There was no doubt on the
part of the two U.S. military doctors who examined him that he
was physically and mentally competent to make such a decision.

2

Further, despite some press accounts, there was also no doubt about our ability to communicate with Seaman Medvid. The professional interpreter engaged by the Department of State was himself of Ukrainian origin, and was able to communicate with Seaman Medvid in both Ukrainian and Russian. It was the interpreter's assessment that Seaman Medvid was more fluent in Russian than Ukrainian.

Unfortunately, during these interviews it was impossible to recreate Seaman Medvid's original frame of mind on October 24. We will never know what pressures may have been exerted on him while he was on the Soviet ship. Nor did we ever discount the possibility that such pressures may have influenced his final decision. We are under no illusions about the repressive nature of the Soviet Government and its willingness to use coercion and threats to control its people. There was always the possibility that Seaman Medvid would decide to return to the U.S.S.R. and that we would have to respect that choice. In cases such as this, only the individual involved can decide what action to take in light of the risks and personal costs involved for himself or for others. It was not a decision we could make for him.

Despite the initial mistakes, we made a strong effort to give Seaman Medvid a chance to remain in the United States, if he so chose. As a result of this tragic case, the U.S. Government has reviewed and tightened procedures to avoid any recurrence of such incidents.

With the President's best wishes,

Sincerely,

Anne Higgins
Special Assistant to the President
and Director of Correspondence

Mr. Wirt A. Yerger, Jr.

Jackson, MS 39205

AVH/NSC/CAD/ddb   (2AVHA)

THE WHITE HOUSE

WASHINGTON

February 28, 1986

Dear Wirt:

Pat gives me all your letters. I know I
don't always answer myself, but believe me,
you give me food for thought and action.
I often ask others for comments and that
also stirs the pot. So continue keeping
me posted.

With best wishes,

Sincerely,

R̲n̲

Mr. Wirt A. Yerger, Jr.
Post Office Box 1139
Jackson, Mississippi 39205

WIRT A. YERGER, JR.
JACKSON, MISSISSIPPI

May 8, 1986

Honorable Ronald Reagan
President of the United States
The White House
Washington, D.C. 20515

Dear Ron:

Enclosed is a copy of my letter to Strom Thurmond.
Frankly, I do not care if Michael Deaver or anyone
else is involved, but something needs to be done to
curb the abuse of privileges which is the result of
using government positions and personal
relationships for individual economic bonanzas. I
trust you will give this very careful thought before
getting too far out on a limb. Surely you also will
find it repugnant.

Glad you had a most successful trip to Japan.

Sincerely,

WAYJR:dr

Enclosure

WIRT A. YERGER, JR.
JACKSON, MISSISSIPPI

June 23, 1986

Honorable Ronald Reagan
President of the United States
The White House
Washington, D.C. 20515

Maintaining Sanity Regarding South Africa

Dear Ron:

The left wing media and the so-called "world
opinion" are in a mindless lynch mob with South
Africa as their target. They have not stopped to
realize that there is not one single country on the
continent of Africa which has even a semblance of
democracy nor have they recognized that the average
South African will not be better off but rather far
worse off with a totalitarian regime such as those
which exist throughout that continent and many parts
of the world.

Have you ever asked yourself what position you would
take if you were the head of the South African
government? How would you like it if a despicable
person such as Chester Crocker were telling us what
type of laws we needed to govern our country. I
have corresponded with you several times in the past
about so many of your personnel who have nothing but
contempt and disdain for the values and principles
you have stood for over the last 30 years, and
Crocker is the epitome of this. I would hope you
will direct Shultz to fire him or reassign him to
other duties without another moments delay.

Furthermore, I must say that I remember all too well
your position in Detroit when Walter Cronkite and
Dan Rather, along with the rest of the media, were
trying to set Jerry Ford up as your "co-president"
with one of the conditions being that
Henry Kissinger be named secretary of state. You
flinched at this, as well you should have, but I
would like to ask you what the distinguishable
difference is between Henry Kissinger and
George Schultz. It would appear to me that they are

Honorable Ronald Reagan
Page Two
June 23, 1986

cut off the exact same piece of cloth with Kissinger
maybe even being closer to your views and those of
your supporters than Schultz.

Schultz's calling a news conference and condemning
your announced position on polygraph tests was, in
itself, enough insubordination and lack of respect
to insure his discharge. You have two precious
years left in your administration, and I can only
think how great it would be to have someone truly
representative of your foreign policy views as the
secretary of state. As you know, the State
Department has not been thoroughly cleaned out in 50
years, and you yourself have said many times how
critically important this is.

Ron, congratulations to you on the moves you have
made with the Supreme Court. I am deeply heartened
by this, and I hope you will move just as decisively
on Crocker and Schultz. Let's get some Reaganites
on board where it counts while there is still time.

Best wishes always,

WAYJR:dt

Enclosure

P.S. Enclosed is a copy of a great speech that was
given at Hillsdale College which so well expresses
the concerns that millions of us who have supported
you for so many years have felt. As stated above,
there is still time, but you must move swiftly and
with total determination. I would welcome the
chance to visit with you personally to discuss any
aspect of these concerns.

WIRT A. YERGER, JR.
JACKSON, MISSISSIPPI

June 23, 1986

Honorable Pat Buchanan
Assistant to the President
The White House
Washington, D.C. 20515

Dear Pat:

Just a note to tell you how much I will always
appreciate the tremendous opportunity you have made
possible for my son, Frank. He is excited to be
where he is and to be working for your people and is
thoroughly enjoying spending the summer in
Washington.

Enjoyed the opportunity to visit with you briefly,
and I deeply appreciate the sacrifice you are making
to be where you are. Having to continually battle
with a staff that never should have been appointed
in the first place over philosophical and
ideological priorities is really heartbreaking.

Many of us have dreamed of what it could have been
like if one of us who was completely attuned to
Ronald Reagan and his philosophy had been chief of
staff from the beginning. Just walking through the
White House for a few seconds to visit you gave me
the same impression I have always received in the
past that the "eastern establishment" prevails.

Pat, thanks for passing my expressed concerns to
Ron. It is gratifying to feel that at least some of
my correspondence reaches its target.

Continued best wishes to you.

Sincerely,

WAYJR:dt

WIRT A. YERGER, JR.
JACKSON, MISSISSIPPI

September 29, 1986

Honorable Pat Buchanan
Assistant to the President
The White House
Washington, D.C. 20515

Dear Pat:

In my view, this is surely one of the most shocking
positions I have seen the leadership of our country
take, and I know it has to be a moment of tremendous
discouragement for you. You certainly are in my
thoughts and prayers.

                    Sincerely,

WAYJR:dt

Enclosure

WIRT A. YERGER, JR.
JACKSON, MISSISSIPPI

September 29, 1986

Honorable Ronald Reagan
President of the United States
The White House
Washington, D.C. 20515

                          Daniloff - Lost Compass

Dear Ronnie:

The actions of your administration in allowing the
Russians to completely dominate and intimidate you
and your advisors are simply shocking beyond words.
It has to be one of the greatest moral setbacks your
administration has ever had and must be completely
devastating to the morale of all of our country's
law enforcement personnel.

Those who advise you to allow such a swap are not
your friends, and I would give 100 to 1 odds not a
single one who advised you in such a fashion cast a
vote for you for the Republican nomination in either
1976 or 1980. By staffing your administration and
your White House staff over 90 percent with people
who did not vote for you in either of those primary
contests and who had nothing but smug contempt for
the ideological positions you espoused for decades,
you have effectively forfeited considerable
ideological and moral ground.

It is my hope you can someday tell me specifically
in what way George Schultz is more conservative or
more palatable to conservatives than
Henry Kissinger.

Ronnie, there is no conference or relationship that
is worth sacrificing your ideological and moral
compass. I do hope you will reflect deeply and
prayerfully on this matter. Furthermore, I
respectfully suggest that every single person in
your administration, whether on the White House
staff or in the State Department, who has urged
accommodations to the Russians in this blatant and

Honorable Ronald Reagan
Page Two
September 29, 1986

totally immoral act be dismissed without delay. The
people who have fought hard for what you stood for
and elected you deserve no less.

Sincerely,

WAYJR:dt

P.S. Congratulations on your veto of the totally
absurd sanctions legislation. How about
reminding Americans very strongly concerning
what is at stake, the progress that has been
made and the absurdity of telling others they
must conform to our standards of democracy.
In my judgment, your punches on this entire
matter have been late and pulled.

WIRT A. YERGER, JR.
JACKSON, MISSISSIPPI

December 1, 1986

PERSONAL AND CONFIDENTIAL

Honorable Pat Buchanan
Assistant to the President
The White House
Washington, D.C. 20515

Dear Pat:

Enclosed is an envelope with a letter per the
attached to Ron. This may seem like a totally
far-fetched idea to you and everyone else, but
I am 1000 percent confident that I could have
done the job from the beginning, and I can do
it now if a change is contemplated. It would
certainly appear to me that a fresh
perspective from someone who has seasoned
political savvy and a proven business
leadership background would be precisely what
is needed.

Best regards,

WAYJR:dt

Enclosures

WIRT A. YERGER, JR.
JACKSON, MISSISSIPPI

December 1, 1986

CONFIDENTIAL

Honorable Ronald Reagan
President of the United States
The White House
Washington, D.C. 20515

Fresh Leadership - Proven
Capacity - Unquestioned Loyalty and Commitment

Dear Ron:

In recent days you have undoubtedly been feeling
totally besieged, and my prayers have been with you.
To get right to the point, if you feel the
circumstances are such that you are forced to name a
new Chief of Staff, I want you to know I have a
genuine interest and, in fact, a real calling to
serve or at the least make you aware of my
availability.

Before you or anyone instinctively reacts with the
question of lack of Washington experience, I feel a
most compelling argument can be made for precisely
the opposite, that is, someone who does not carry
any of those past liabilities but rather possesses a
fresh vitality, a keen mind, proven political
instincts and sound judgment. Let's face it, nearly
all your problems can be directly traced to the lack
of clear ideological commitment and proven ability
in the staffing of your administration from the very
beginning. As I stated in my letter to you a few
months ago, there is still time to rectify this and
make the last two years highly productive ones.

With the exception of Nancy and possibly one or two
others, I do not know of anyone on your White House
staff who has been inspired by your leadership and
committed to your policies longer than I have. As
you may recall, I served as Chairman of the
Mississippi Republican Party during its most
formative years from 1956 to 1966, starting
virtually from scratch, and I served as the Southern
Association Republican State Chairman from 1962 to

Honorable Ronald Reagan
Page Two
December 1, 1986

1966. As you are well aware, your speech in behalf of Barry Goldwater was the most inspiring thing to come out of that entire campaign, and with money donated by my fellow Mississippians, I personally put your speech on coast-to-coast television.

In other words, when many around you, including several individuals on your present staff, thought you were a screw ball and a right wing fanatic, my support never waivered. In fact, if I had been given the job of Reagan Chairman in Mississippi as was originally contemplated in 1976 rather than being blocked by my successor, Clarke Reed, I believe you would have been nominated and elected then. That would have insured entirely different outcomes in Iran and Nicaragua, not to mention far better domestic conditions, and you and Nancy would now be enjoying your retirement after eight very successful years in the White House. Never once during my tenure in active politics and service in managing campaigns did I have any problem in dealing with the media or "put my foot in my mouth". I feel I have a real gift in being able to handle situations involving the media, because I have been on the political battlefield many times.

So much for the political history, but what about my business and administrative ability? While I run and own a small business, it has been one of the most successful insurance agencies in America, and a most dramatic growth has occurred under my leadership these last 25 years. The Lord has blessed us with people who have great talent and commitment, and I have been blessed with the ability to select and recruit this talent. A national consulting firm, after performing a study of our agency this year, made the following statement: "Based on our observation of several hundred insurance agencies throughout America, yours has by far the highest employee morale, the greatest professionalism and the highest productivity." These results need to be achieved at the White House in the last two years of your administration.

Honorable Ronald Reagan
Page Three
December 1, 1986

My family is grown; my youngest is a senior in college, and I am in a position to make such a move. Furthermore, I have been blessed with a wife who has the charm and grace to be a tremendous asset and who would impress you and Nancy from the first moment; I have been well blessed in this way just as you have. Obviously, this would represent a considerable economic sacrifice on my part, but I am fully able to handle this since I have been successful for many years well beyond my fondest expectations. The change, if it is made, is of such importance I hope you will move very carefully and be willing to interview me and other possibilities directly, with no obligation whatsoever. I would love to come up with Mary and visit with you and Nancy regarding this. I truly feel I am presenting you with an idea that is deserving of your careful consideration. Regardless, you will continue to be in my thoughts and prayers.

Ron, if you can find someone better qualified and more committed to you, then by all means bring them aboard, but I hope you will take my offer to serve and provide leadership insuring the success of your administration these last two years quite seriously.

Continued best wishes,

WAYJR:dt

WIRT A. YERGER, JR.
JACKSON, MISSISSIPPI

December 29, 1986

PERSONAL

Honorable Pat Buchanan
Assistant to the President
The White House
Washington, D.C. 20515

Dear Pat:

Enclosed is a letter from me to the President,
and I continue to be amazed at how, in a
supposedly conservative administration,
schemes such as catastrophic health coverage
for the elderly can be born and pushed by
Reagan appointees. As you and I both know,
there is more legislation of this type than we
can presently afford to pay for as it is.

Pat, best wishes for a most successful 1987.

Sincerely,

WAYJR:dt

Enclosure

WIRT A. YERGER, JR.
JACKSON, MISSISSIPPI

December 29, 1986

Honorable Ronald Reagan
President of the United States
The White House
Washington, D.C. 20515

Catastrophic Health Coverage for
the Elderly - Economic Catastrophe for America

Dear Ron:

Never in my wildest dreams could I have imagined a
member of your cabinet, Health and Human Services
Secretary Otis Bowen, proposing such a fiscal
disaster and dangerous step toward a full-blown,
government-run national health insurance scheme. We
have only to look at what has happened in
Great Britain to see how truly catastrophic this
will be for America.

Ron, with all due respect, if you have someone in
the cabinet proposing a scheme such as this, he
should be replaced immediately for lack of foresight
and lack of savvy and intelligence to do the type of
job you need done. Please do not let this go one
inch further, and I hope Bowen will be replaced.
Obviously, his appointment was simply a mistake.

Thank you for giving this important matter and my
concern your careful attention.

Sincerely,

WAYJR:dt

THE WHITE HOUSE
WASHINGTON

March 16, 1987

Dear Wirt:

Pat passed your note along to me. I'm sorry I
haven't gotten back to you sooner, but my side-trip
to Bethesda and work on the State of the Union kept
me away from my mail.

As you know, I am asking the Congress to help give
Americans protection from the devastating effects of a
catastrophic illness. The legislation I am proposing
provides health insurance for those who suffer from
such an illness. Specifically, our plan would furnish
acute care coverage to those over 65 through restruc-
turing the Medicare program and by charging a small
additional Medicare premium.

I am confident this proposal is fully consistent with
the principles of limited government and compassion for
the truly needy. As the coverage is financed through
premiums, the legislation I have proposed is budget
neutral and does not represent a new entitlement.

I remain strongly committed to reducing the size and
cost of government. Best regards,

Sincerely,

Ron

Mr. Wirt A. Yerger, Jr.
Post Office Box 1139
Jackson, Mississippi 39205-1139

WIRT A. YERGER, JR.
JACKSON, MISSISSIPPI

September 9, 1987

Honorable Ronald Reagan
President of the United States
The White House
Washington, D.C. 20515

Dear Ron:

As you know from all my past correspondence, there
is probably no one in America who is more
disappointed than I am in your selection of
personnel and staff these last seven years. In my
judgment personnel are policy, and this very
fundamental fact was overlooked from the beginning.
There is probably no more glaring example of this
than George Schultz who would fit comfortably in any
democratic administration and by no means shares the
concern that you and millions of us have held for
many years about the United States State Department.

I must admit to great reservations about signing a
treaty of any type with someone who has repeatedly
shown that they do not abide by treaties, and what
else could we expect from atheistic communists who
have no moral or theological mooring whatsoever.
With them the means justify the ends no matter what.

Much has been said about you wanting to establish
your reputation for historical purposes as being an
advocate of peace, and I am afraid that Nancy, the
media and others have pushed you way beyond where
you should be in this regard. Let me just say that
if you will follow your heart and your conscience in
doing what is right for America and pay no attention
whatsoever to how history may regard Ronald Reagan,
you will indeed be way ahead both presently and in a
historical context.

You only have a few months of your administration
left, and I continue to plead with you to make
whatever staff changes you can to bring in those who
fought for you when it counted rather than those who
have scorned everything you have ever championed.
You know who they are, and they are all around you
with Howard Baker at the top of the list.

Honorable Ronald Reagan
Page Two
September 9, 1987

Furthermore, I share with many the concern expressed
regarding your capitulation to the so-called Jim
Wright peace plan in Central America. This
certainly appears to have been a cave-in, and I
would strongly suspect that Howard Baker is involved
in this right up to his eyeballs.

Ron, I will, as always, look forward to hearing from
you, and now that Pat is gone, I would appreciate
your letting me know who I should direct
correspondence to so I can be assured, as in the
past, that you see it personally.

Sincerely,

WAYJR:dt

THE WHITE HOUSE

WASHINGTON

October 28, 1987

Dear Wirt:

I'm a little late in getting back to you, but your letter has just
reached my desk.

I can understand your misgivings about the proposed intermediate-
range nuclear force (INF) agreements with the Soviet Union.
However, I would not have made these proposals if I thought they
weakened our own security or that of our allies. Our INF policy has
been developed as a result of extensive and intensive consultation
with the governments of our NATO allies. The Joint Chiefs of Staff,
representatives of the Office of the Secretary of Defense, and NATO
military authorities have fully participated in every stage of the
process. NATO defense ministers have regularly endorsed the
United States' INF position.

I also share your concerns about Soviet compliance with arms control
agreements. That's why we have insisted on strict, effective verification procedures so we can ensure that the Soviet Union is
complying with the terms of any agreement. In our negotiations with
the Soviets on INF, we have proposed procedures that will constitute
the most extensive and stringent verification standards in the
history of arms control.

With regard to peace efforts in Central America, we must not forget
that there already exists a negotiated settlement with the Sandinistas
that pre-dates President Arias' plan -- the OAS agreement of 1979.
As part of that settlement, the Sandinistas agreed to implement
genuine democracy, with free elections and full civil liberties. Full,
free, and fair elections, including full human rights and expulsion of
all Soviet and Cuban forces -- these must be the bedrock conditions
upon which any further agreement with the Sandinistas is built. We
will not tolerate communist colonialism on the American mainland.
I've made a personal commitment to the Nicaraguan freedom fighters,
and I will not walk away.

Again, thanks for your candid views, Wirt, and God bless you.

Sincerely,

Ronald Reagan

Mr. Wirt A. Yerger, Jr.
Post Office Box 1139
Jackson, Mississippi 39205

WIRT A. YERGER, JR.
JACKSON, MISSISSIPPI

March 18, 1988

PERSONAL AND CONFIDENTIAL

Honorable Ronald Reagan
President of the United States
The White House
Washington, D.C. 20515

Dear Ronnie:

While I was visiting in Pat Buchanan's office when
he was on your staff some time ago, I told him that
in my view since you have been President there has
never been a speech given in which the "punches were
not pulled". I still believe this, and I think that
it is high time this was corrected and that you
exert the dynamic leadership you were elected to
provide in such a forceful, honest and soundly
correct manner so the left wing media and
congressional critics will know in unmistakable
terms that you are not going to put up with anymore
of their nit-picking and carping.

Enclosed are copies of two editorials that were in
today's The Wall Street Journal which I hope you
have seen. As I have written you in the past, I
would appreciate knowing that you see these
editorials on a daily basis, because it would just
be a godsend if your advisers were in tune with the
thinking and position they have displayed
consistently for years.

You were right to send the troops into Honduras, but
they are absolutely correct in that no one in your
administration should make any apology for it or
tell anyone that they are not there to shot. This
is another example of "pulling punches".

On the matter of North, Poindexter and Secord, I
would suggest that you read the indictments
carefully, check into the facts and then swiftly and
forcefully, if this editorial commentary is anywhere
near correct, issue a pardon for any crimes they may
have committed and accept full responsibility for
everything that happened yourself, simply saying
that obviously mistakes were made which you have
said in the past, but if you did not know what was

Honorable Ronald Reagan
Page Two
March 18, 1988

going on, you should have known. You should
announce that it is high time this country recognize
the perils it faces against communist conspiracies
and revolutions in Latin America and throughout the
world. In my judgment, while there will be a
political storm and a media bashing storm as well,
the American people will rally to this sort of
leadership to a degree beyond anything previously
imagined.

Ronnie, after you have read this letter, I would
appreciate your calling me so we can discuss these
suggestions. My office number is (601) 948-2900,
and my residence number is (601) 982-2582. I truly
believe when you think this through and weigh this
matter, you will find that this represents sound
judgment.

Sincerely,

WAYJR:dt

Enclosures

P.S. I have your letter dated February 28, 1986, in
      my desk, and I just want you to know how much
      it has meant to me to know that you do
      personally see my correspondence.

THE WHITE HOUSE

WASHINGTON

April 13, 1988

Dear Wirt:

I'm sorry to be so late getting back to you, but I do want you to know I appreciated once more your candid letter and enclosures. Actually, I try to read The Wall Street Journal as often as possible. In addition to the stacks of reading I get from the regular sources here at the White House, I do my best to keep up with all the advice of our gifted friends in the Fourth Estate. And I often find The Wall Street Journal right on target.

Thanks, again, and I'm sorry not to have written sooner.

Sincerely,

Ron

Mr. Wirt A. Yerger, Jr.
Post Office Box 1139
Jackson, Mississippi 39205

WIRT A. YERGER, JR.
JACKSON, MISSISSIPPI

January 16, 1989

Dear Barry:

I just finished your new book, and I must say that
once I got into it, I really could not put it down.
The contribution you have made toward extending
freedom and helping preserve our nation is almost
indescribable. From the first moment during the
1950s I have truly revered you and regarded you as
not only my hero but an answer to prayer.

Your courage along with your candor and gift for
"telling it like it is" was and is truly a godsend
to our nation. I do not know whether historians
will give you the credit you truly deserve, but if
they do not, they will have missed a real story of
how it happened. You are so right about
Robert McNamara, Bill Moyers, Richard Nixon and many
others, and I must say that your feelings and
comments about the media, considering the hatchet
job they have performed on you, represent the truest
sense of understanding and forgiveness I can
imagine.

Your comments concerning Dennison Kitchel and the
so-called "Arizona Mafia" at least bring up the
subject of what I have wanted to tell you for almost
25 years but truly could not bring myself to state
since it was "water under the bridge". In fact,
that evening in 1966 when you were making a speech
in Jackson and spent the night with us, I still
could not bring myself to tell you how I felt about
the 1964 campaign.

In my opinion, your appointment of Kitchel instead
of a professional with political experience was so
disastrous that I feel we will never know how close
you truly could have come or whether you may have
even been able to win. In fact, in my judgment it
was so bad that I suspected sabotage in the highest
echelons of the campaign.

As I guess you know, those of us who had for years
been your staunchest allies were completely walled

Honorable Barry Goldwater
Page Two
January 16, 1989

off by Kitchel and company to a degree beyond
anything you could imagine. Kitchel at least knew
how disgusted I was with the conduct of the
campaign. When Stets Coleman had arranged for
Buddy Klumb and I to go on your campaign plane and
tour for a couple of days during the final days of
the campaign, I spoke with Denny during the short
flight from Washington to New York where you were to
attend the Hoover funeral. He said, "I understand
you are not real pleased with the conduct of the
campaign." My answer was, "Denny, I'd say that is
the understatement of the year." Denny's response
was, "Wirt, what you've got to understand is we want
to portray Barry as subdued and low-key and down
play the emotional aspect." I replied, "You have
been amazingly successful at accomplishing just this
while our opposition is portraying Barry as tearing
up social security cards and blowing up people with
atomic weapons."

When you had a tremendous rally in Milwaukee with
thousands of people screaming with enthusiasm, they
wanted to cut it short and not let the nation's TV
audience see the wild enthusiasm which people were
displaying for you.

I remember the speech you gave in Balboa Stadium
when we were privileged to ride your whistle stop
train at the close of the campaign, and Buddy Klumb
and I both were thrilled at what a wonderful speech
you gave. We both said, "Where has this speech been
throughout the campaign?" Why was the message so
diluted and the punches so pulled?

One last point in this regard was the only good
speech given and shown on television in your behalf,
including your own, was that given by Ronald Reagan.
We had raised, as I recall, over 1,700 percent of
our state's quota in your fund-raising effort and
still had some more money to spend that had been
given in your behalf. I remember calling the media
people in New York who were handling your campaign,
and I talked to a man to see whether or not we could
underwrite the cost of a coast-to-coast broadcast
with these funds. I learned that the plans for the
Sunday afternoon before the election were to once

Honorable Barry Goldwater
Page Three
January 16, 1989

again show a 30-minute program billed as "Brunch
With Barry" which I thought was the most subdued,
dullest 30-minute program imaginable, and the man in
New York I was talking to agreed with me
wholeheartedly; however, he was powerless to do
anything about it. I asked him what it would cost
for us to put Ronald Reagan's speech on TV
coast-to-coast that same Sunday afternoon. As I
recall, the figure was something like $185,000. In
short, he made the arrangements with the Mississippi
funds paying the tab. I hope this will at least
help you understand the depth of the frustration
that many of your most fervent supporters felt.

Kitchel, Burch, Grenier and the whole crowd not only
shut the rest of us off but displayed unparalleled
arrogance in the process, and I knew that there was
no possible way you could be fully aware of just how
they were treating us.

Barry, I shall never forget what a great inspiration
you were to all of us, and with the glaring
exception of the campaign itself after you were
nominated, you have been true to your philosophy and
convictions. You are the greatest, and I will
always appreciate you for what you have meant to
America and the inspiration you have provided so
many millions of us.

                    Sincerely,

WAYJR:dt

Honorable Barry Goldwater
U.S. Senator, Retired
6250 North Hogahn Drive
Scottsdale, AZ 85252

Barry Goldwater

P. O. BOX 1601
SCOTTSDALE, ARIZONA 85252

January 26, 1989

Mr. Wirt A. Yerger, Jr.
P.O. Box 1139
Jackson, Mississippi 39205-1139

Dear Wirt:

You letter of January 16th, was on my desk when I returned from a short visit with my youngest daughter in California

Instead of being upset with what you said, I'm very happy to finally get your comments. I knew all through the campaign, that you, and quite a few others of my original backers, did not approve of what became known as the Arizona Mafia. I don't want to put down in writing some of the things that did happen, but when you and I see each other again, I'll give you word for word just what came about.

I have known Denny Kitchel all of my life. I knew him first when he came to Arizona as a young lawyer, particularly bent to the left, and I watched through the years as he became a great Constitutionalist, and a very devoted conservative. He would be the first one to agree that he did not know a whole lot about running a campaign. On the other hand Wirt, and I don't offer this as an excuse, from the time the Convention was over, and the nomination was ours, to the time we started working, was not more than a few weeks, trying to put together a fine, productive team in that length of time was impossible. I must tell you though, that no Republican, I don't care what his name was, could ever have won the election in 1964. The country was not ready for three presidents in two and a half years. I will admit that I probably could have done better, but I have to confess something to you, that you probably already know, I never had the real "fire in my belly" to conduct that campaign. I just did the best I could. You will probably remember that the speech that Ron Reagan made, that got him started, was a speech that I was supposed to have made in Milwaukee, but when I received it, and read it, I said this is not for me. It doesn't sound like me, I don't have the fluency to do it, so I said send it to Ron Reagan and let him use it, and that's what we did.

I can never tell you, and the other friends I have, how greatly I cherish the memories of working with you, getting to know you, in fact, it created a fondness for you all that will be there for the rest of my life. Thanks for your letter.

Sincerely,

Barry Goldwater

THE WHITE HOUSE

WASHINGTON

Kennebunkport

August 23, 1989

Dear Wirt:

Just a brief note to thank you for writing
and to assure you that any decisions I make
as President will continue to be based on my
conviction that they are right for the country,
not on how they will affect my standing in some
poll.

Best wishes and thanks for your thoughtfulness
and your prayers.

Sincerely,

G Bush

Mr. Wirt A. Yerger, Jr.
Post Office Box 1139
Jackson, Mississippi 39205-1139

WIRT A. YERGER, JR.
JACKSON, MISSISSIPPI

October 29, 1990

Honorable George Bush
President
The White House
Washington, DC 20515

Dear George:

Almost ten years ago I wrote you a personal letter
suggesting you go off to the top of a mountain by
yourself, away from all the advisors and opinion
polls, and not come down until you decided what
course you thought America should follow. What has
happened during the last few weeks and months has
convinced me that you never went, and belatedly, I
truly hope, for the sake of America, you will.

To see a President of the United States break with
his own party and those who were the bedrock of his
support is disgusting. Your indecisiveness and
ineptitude in this situation has truly rivaled that
of Jimmy Carter.

Surely you realize there is not a single department
of government that could not slash its spending
25 percent if it had to operate on a business-like
basis. Why couldn't you have held the congressional
feet to the fire instead?

You have managed to surrender to the Democrats in
Congress, aided and abetted by the national media,
and received nothing in return but a kick in the
face for yourself and, more importantly, for the
hardworking candidates of your party throughout
America. This is one election for which I would not
like to be around to hear the results, because I
fear a tremendous disaster for which you bear almost
the entire responsibility.

I am grateful for your veto of the so-called "civil
rights" bill, but the votes to sustain a veto due to
the election debacle will probably be lost.

Honorable George Bush
Page Two
October 26, 1990

George, I desperately hope my fear of the outcome
and criticism of your role is misplaced, but in my
heart and soul I know it is on target. I wrote you
several months ago begging you to reverse your
course regarding an increase in taxes and suggested
you fire Darman. Brady and Sununu should also
depart.

At this point I hope you will apologize to your
supporters and all Americans with enough genuine
remorse to help in the regrouping and healing
process so America can go forward.

Sincerely,

WAVJR:dt

WIRT A. YERGER, JR.
JACKSON, MISSISSIPPI

November 15, 1990

Honorable George Bush
President of the United States
The White House
Washington, DC 20515

Dear George:

The more I see of the provisions of the Budget
Reconciliation Act of 1990, the more shocked I am as
to the damage you have allowed to be done to
America. It is really tragic that you have allowed
the debate to degenerate into class warfare when the
truth of the matter is that just a few years ago the
tax rates were made more equitable, recognizing the
fact that what made America is individuals who have
the opportunity to grow and spend the money they
have earned.

It is easy for someone like Ted Kennedy, who has
never earned a nickel in his life and inherited a
trust fund well in excess of $10,000,000, to talk
about taxing the wealthy, but the matter overlooked
is, What about the ones who are not in that position
who are trying, through hard work, initiative and
imagination, to earn a sufficient income to allow
them to save and accumulate assets.

The latest thing I noted in what has just been
passed is the limitation on itemized deductions,
reducing the deduction by 3 percent of income in
excess of $100,000. The very sick people who wrote
this legislation put this in at a time when you and
I are trying to get people in America to give
generously on a voluntary basis to charitable,
educational and religious institutions.

Honorable George Bush
Page Two
November 15, 1990

George, whenever you have an opportunity to realize
what is taking place in this and other matters, I
would love to know what you really think.

Sincerely,

WAYJR:dt

P.S. Now I see you are contemplating hitting the
affluent again by eliminating or reducing their
benefits from social security, but I am sure
you are not going to be proposing, reducing or
eliminating their taxes paid into that fund.
When will someone up there wake up and realize
that you do not benefit the country by
attacking the successful?

WIRT A. YERGER, JR.
JACKSON, MISSISSIPPI

January 22, 1991

Honorable George Bush
The White House
Washington, D.C. 20500

Dear George:

Congratulations on the successful war effort up to
this point. I would remind you I wrote you on
August 3, 1990 that there should be <u>no</u>
<u>restrictions</u> on the military in terms of use of
weapons when it comes to saving American lives.

Furthermore, I am appalled at the statements that
have come out of the military to try to satisfy
the insatiable appetite of the media. Why
broadcast to the enemy that we are going to
concentrate on the attacking of the Republican
Guards? Why broadcast the fact that when the scud
missiles are fired it makes it easy for us to find
where they are to try to knock them out? Either
of these statements, while true, could even
further alert the anti-aircraft forces and make it
more dangerous for the american pilots.

It is quite obvious that torture and intimidation
must have been used on the pilots to make the
statements they did, and this was so obvious that
I believe people of the world will recognize it
for what it is just as they did Saddam's
intimidating interview with the small British boy
several months ago.

George, whatever is necessary to conclude this war
quickly, and hopefully from the air, should be
done. May God bless you and the others and give
you wisdom to see it through without worrying

Honorable George Bush
January 22, 1991
Page 2

about "world opinion" or the "media". Frankly, I
am amazed that the people in CNN seem to take
pride in claiming that they are neutral between
Iraq and America. I would hope that you would
publicly take them to task.

Sincerely,

cc: Vice President Dan Quayle
      Honorable Thad Cochran
      Honorable Trent Lott

P.S.   Please use your office to strongly attack
those who in time of war fail to support the
effort.   There is simply no substitute for
standing 100% united.   I trust you will publicly
condemn those who dissent, as at this point they
are traitors to their country.

THE VICE PRESIDENT
WASHINGTON

January 29, 1991

Mr. Wirt A. Yerger, Jr.
P.O. Box 1139
Jackson, Mississippi 39216

Dear Wirt:

Thank you for taking the time to share your words of
support.

With the first year behind us, Marilyn and I have reflected
on our travels in the United States, Central America and in the
Far East. We are amazed at having seen the beginning of a war
against drugs, free elections in countries where many thought it
not possible and the collapse of the Berlin Wall. It has never
been more appropriate to say a new breeze is blowing.

With so many exciting events taking place, your sentiments
are deeply appreciated. Our nation may well be facing greater
challenges than any yet encountered. Marilyn joins me in
thanking you for your thoughtful letter of encouragement.

Sincerely,

Dan Quayle

WIRT A. YERGER, JR.
JACKSON, MISSISSIPPI

February 4, 1991

PERSONAL & CONFIDENTIAL

Honorable George Bush
President of the United States
The White House
Washington, D. C. 20500

Dear George:

On August 5, 1990, I wrote you personally urging
that if it came to fighting with U.S. lives at
stake to not place any restrictions whatsoever on
the military in terms of weapons and I would also
say targets. With Jim Baker and the world media
deeply involved I should also have said, "let's
finish the job completely" with the total
elimination of Saddam Hussein in either his death
or trial for war crimes.

The column that Paul Gigot wrote last week about
Brady being a good friend but a bad advisor can
certainly also apply to Jim Baker, who is the very
definition of a pragmatist and deal maker without
ideology. As you know, you and I corresponded on
this situation some time ago.

With the media led by CNN claiming they are so
independent they have no allegiance to their own
country I say it is time to terminate briefing for
the press, and let the generals get on with
winning the war. After victory, there will be
plenty of time for them to tell us how they won it
without informing the enemy what is happening
while the war is in progress.

The insatiable appetite of the media should be
resisted if the life of one American soldier is at
stake, and it obviously is.

George, I continue to pray daily for you and those
engaged in battle. Let's face it, with media such
as CNN and Congress with the likes of Sam Nunn and
many others Adolph Hitler could well have been
still reigning in Europe. This is outrageous!

Sincerely,

WIRT A. YERGER, JR.
JACKSON, MISSISSIPPI

February 27, 1991

Honorable George Bush
President
The White House
Washington, D.C.   20500

Dear George:

Thank you for your excellent leadership on the war
effort.

The attached article from yesterday's Wall Street
Journal entitled "Don't Sell the Patriot to Moscow" is
indeed shocking, and I hope you will act immediately in
the next hours to put a stop to this. As a further
background article, I am also enclosing from the same
editorial page and article outlining severe problems
with Mikhail Gorbachev's Russia. Frankly, I would have
to feel that he has tested your patience about trying
to come in to play the role of peace maker without
having one single soldier's life at stake.

George, I am anxious to learn what you are going to do
about the Patriot technology. Please act immediately
before it is too late.

Thank you.

Very sincerely,

WIRT A. YERGER, JR.
JACKSON, MISSISSIPPI

April 12, 1991

The Honorable George Bush
President of the United States
The White House
Washington, D. C.   20500

Dear George:

  After your great leadership earlier, you should hang
your head over the lack of will in allowing the slaughter
of the Kurds in Iraq. At the blink of an eye, all of this
could have been prevented, but you and Jim Baker showed a
deplorable lack of foresight.

  Consequently, I would suggest at the very minimum that
you fire Jim Baker and clean house in the State Department,
as I'm sure most of this advice came from them as opposed
to the U.S. military forces, who obviously wanted to finish
the job. As you know, I have written you before; and you
and I have corresponded previously about Jim Baker's lack of
ideological feelings. Seeing him visiting the Kurds knowing
he was the likely cause, was simply too much.

  George, I hope you will apologize for the mistake on
your part for encouraging the revolt and then sitting idly
by while the slaughter took place. You have truly managed
to stain the great victory which was achieved by the U.S.
military by your own unwillingness to hang tough at the
end. Incidentally, I thought at the time your should have
battle that you should have demanded they capitulate totally.
This would have solved this problem as well as probably
guaranteeing the removal of Saddam. For you to hang a
sign out saying "gone fishing" while this has been taking
place is simply disgusting and an embarrassment to our nation.
Sorry, but that is the way it is, and I must tell you
forthrightly.

          Sincerely,

          Wirt A. Yerger, Jr.

Barry Goldwater

P. O. BOX 1601
SCOTTSDALE, ARIZONA 85252

June 5, 1991

Mr. Wirt A. Yerger, Jr.
P.O. Box 1139
Jackson, Miss.   39215-1139

Dear Wirt:

What a pleasant surprise it was to have your card delivered
to me the other day.

It's been a long, long time since we've been together, and I
miss seeing you. I don't get out of Arizona much anymore, I
just say home and enjoy my home and my beautiful desert.

If you ever get out this way, be sure and give me a call.

Sincerely,

Barry Goldwater

WIRT A. YERGER, JR.
JACKSON, MISSISSIPPI

August 29, 1991

The Honorable George Bush
President of the United States
The White House
Washington, D. C. 20224

Dear George:

The August 19th issue of <u>Backgrounder</u> published
by The Heritage Foundation appears to be very well
researched, and I would hope that you will reverse
your position on this just as you needed to and
apparently are reversing your position on Boris
Yeltsin.

George, if you recall, I continue to have the deepest
reservations on Jim Baker because he simply does
not appear to have an ideology and thereby doesn't
comprehend the issues he often faces. Also, the
position he took on Yugoslavia a few months ago
was both ridiculous and embarrassing. Friends are
fine, but often better leadership and advice are
obtainable.

                    Sincerely,

WAYjr/sgr

Enclosure

REDRAFT

February 3, 1992

PERSONAL AND CONFIDENTIAL

The Honorable George Bush
President of the United States
The White House
Washington, D. C. 20224

Dear George:

After all your ballyhooing about your upcoming "State of the Union" address, it had all the impact of a bomb whose fuse never went off. You and your advisers don't seem to realize just how vulnerable your reelection is; and at this point, it rests almost solely on the weakness and frailties of the opposition. The American people deserve far better; and even though I have grieved many times in the past over your lack of an ideology, I really believe you are capable of doing much better than you have done. To put it bluntly, because of the weaknesses of your presidency, with the exception of Desert Storm (until ending it several days too soon), you deserve to lose; but the American people and our future make it imperative as the Republican nominee that you win.

In my judgment, you desperately need someone to give you some very pointed and candid advice on how to correct the course you are following; but for that to have any impact whatsoever, you need to recognize the situation and be willing to do something that is rare on the American political scene, and that is be willing to admit error.

Either you are not getting the correct advice or you are not paying attention and willing to change course; but in case you are receptive to a new, straight-talking adviser, I am volunteering for that mission, and I feel I have a perception of what you need to do. However, I am not going to bother unless you personally call and invite me to come up and speak with you directly, for several hours, if need be, and including Dan Quayle and possibly Sam Skinner or one of your other advisers.

George, if you are not totally receptive to this suggestion, willing to listen, and willing to acknowledge mistakes in the past, it would be a meaningless exercise and I wouldn't even want to expend the time to come. I fully recognize the audacity of what I am suggesting; but in the remote possibility it would strike a chord with you, I feel constrained to send you this message.

I didn't attend Phillips, Andover, or Yale, but I do have considerable political savvy and a better touch with what moves mainstream America than most. For example, my support for Ronald Reagan began in 1964, when most Republican leaders thought he was a radical extremist.

Sincerely,

WAYjr/sgr

P.S. Simply by way of identification, I am attaching a resume
      showing my background. My present position is president
      and owner of one of America's most successful insurance
      brokerage firms.

DRAFT

March 2, 1992

The Honorable George Bush
President of the United States
The White House
Washington, D. C. 20224

Dear George:

Enclosed is a redraft which I dictated to you about six
weeks ago ~~and~~ I feel ~~to be~~ worthy of your ~~attention~~. Since the
time it was dictated, it appears the need for you to be willing
to listen and for somebody to give you some solid ideas to
correct the course you have been following is greater than ever.

You may recall that you and I have corresponded in the past
regarding your apparent lack of ideological direction. For you
to succeed this year, this situation has got to be fixed
immediately; and, frankly, from all I can see, you don't have a
single adviser on board now who can tell you what you need to
~~hear and listen to.~~

In the outside possibility that you are willing to listen
and change course, I am sending you this letter. I hope my fears
for your electability in your present course are exaggerated.

                              Sincerely,

WAYjr/sgr

WIRT A. YERGER, JR.
JACKSON, MISSISSIPPI

June 11, 1992

The Honorable George Bush
President of the United States
The White House
Washington, D. C.   20224

COURAGE AND FORESIGHT

Dear George:

'You've had an illustrious career in many top
governmental positions, culminating with your
.election to President of the United States.   In
my judgment, at this time you should prayerfully
consider enjoying your retirement years with your
family and writing your memoirs, simply announcing
that you plan to withdraw from seeking the Republican
nomination and to allow the Republican Convention on a
fully wide-open-basis to-make a choice for President
and Vice President. Realistically, I honestly feel
you don't have any other viable alternative, and I do
feel this is the best course of action for you, your
family, and the nation.

George, rightly or wrongly, the risk of your being
defeated is overwhelming, and I honestly do not feel
the situation can be turned around. Please give
this your deepest, most prayerful consideration; and
I know what I'm asking you to do is to make one of the
most courageous decisions you've ever made, but I do
feel it's the only correct course open at this moment.
Thank you for your consideration.

Sincerely,

WAYjr/sgr

THE WHITE HOUSE

WASHINGTON

June 30, 1992

Dear Wirt:

Thank your for your letter. I appreciate your
views, particularly your comments about courage.
I believe that the more courageous decision is
to continue the fight for the policies that the
American people elected me to put in place and
for the principles that we all cherish, but that
are under siege. The people sent me here to
accomplish certain things -- to reform education,
to toughen crime laws, to create jobs and opportunities, and, yes, to stand up for what's right.

We're working hard against the odds with the
Democratic-controlled Congress, but I'm determined
to bring about positive change. I am quietly
confident that I will be reelected, and I hope
that I can count on your support.

Best wishes.

Sincerely,

G. Bush

Mr. Wirt A. Yerger, Jr.
Post Office Box 1139
Jackson, Mississippi 39205-1139

P.S. Wirt, you're not a quitter —
nor am I

WIRT A. YERGER, JR.
JACKSON, MISSISSIPPI

July 20, 1992

The Honorable Dan Quayle
Vice President of the United States
Washington, D. C. 20224

COURAGE AND PATRIOTISM

Dear Dan:

For quite some time, I have told many friends that I
would much rather have you as President of the United
States than George Bush, and I still feel that way
very strongly because I have been woefully disappointed
in George's performance as President.

Nevertheless, the hatchet job that the media did on
you four years ago and has continued to do has been
very thorough, and the perception in America counts
more at the ballot box than the facts; and I know that
you have got to admit that this is a political fact of
life. In my judgment, under the circumstances, you
need to show the courage and foresight to withdraw
from another term as Vice President to help improve
the chance of keeping Clinton and Gore from being
elected. Let's face it: As you and I both know, they
are both liberals whose leadership would be devastating
to the future of our nation.

This is not an easy letter to write because I've
admired you and Marilyn both, but I don't think you
want to take the chance of failing to do anything that
would help forestall the election of Clinton and Gore
and all the crowd that would come with them.

The Honorable Dan Quayle
Page Two
July 20, 1992

Dan, the step I'm recommending needs to be taken
within the next few days, and I believe it will
insure for you an important place in the future of
our nation and will always be thought of as an act
of courage and statesmanship, almost without parallel.
Please think about it and pray about it because the
time is critically short.

                         Sincerely,

WAYjr/sgr

Enclosures

cc: The Honorable George Bush
     President of the United States

 bcc: Mr. William D. Mounger
       Mr. Swan Yerger
       Mr. James B. Furrh, Jr.

WIRT A. YERGER, JR.
JACKSON, MISSISSIPPI

July 31, 1992

<u>URGENT</u>

<u>PERSONAL AND CONFIDENTIAL</u>

The Honorable George Bush
President of the United States
The White House
Washington, D. C.   20224

Dear George:

As you will recall, I wrote you in June and suggested
you withdraw, and I appreciate getting that very
personal note from you in response. Nevertheless,
it is even more obvious now unless there is a major
bombshell that is going to knock Clinton out, you
will have a very difficult time in surviving this
election. It is also quite obvious that the people
of the nation, while not in love with Clinton, prefer
somebody other than George Bush, considering the
economy and other domestic issues.

As you well know, if it was a fair and open convention,
there is no way in the world the convention would
pick you now under these circumstances; therefore, you
should withdraw immediately so that in the next days
before the convention, the delegates can consider
other alternatives. I know you love and cherish this
country as much as you say you do; therefore, you would
want to do everything in your power to insure that
Clinton and Gore are not elected. Quite obviously, the
most significant thing you can do is to withdraw and
let another candidate emerge whom the people can support.

The Honorable George Bush
July 31, 1992
Page Two

George, for you to survive, it will take a miracle
turnaround; and with the media-bashing that you and
Dan are taking now coupled with the economy and people's
desire for a change, you simply must show the courage
and foresight necessary to withdraw. Please give this
your immediate and prayerful consideration. Our
nation will have a very perilous future domestically
and internationally with Clinton and Gore, and you
should realize that more than anyone.

Sincerely,

WAYjr/sgr

WIRT A. YERGER, JR.
JACKSON, MISSISSIPPI
October 1, 1992

PERSONAL & CONFIDENTIAL

The Honorable George Bush
President of the United States
The White House
Washington, DC   20224

    Your last and only hope for re-election--regaining
    the trust of the American people by genuine contrition
    and seizing the initiative with clear action

Dear George:

At this moment you are bound to feel that my advice of my
letter in early June to announce your retirement was some of
the best you have ever received, but since you did not take
heed at that moment, I believe what I am suggesting now is
your one and only hope to be re-elected to a second term.

Your personal note and response at the time was very much
appreciated.

As it stands now, you are entering the last quarter behind
by at least two touchdowns and unless you do something very
dramatic, your bid for re-election is going to be rejected
overwhelmingly. After the election, the media is going to
work you over as such an inept President, that even Jimmy
Carter is going to look like a great President in
comparison. Many feel you have screwed up so badly as
President that you deserve to lose, but the people of
America do not deserve Bill Clinton and Al Gore. You are
the only other alternative we, the American people, have at
this moment.

By now it should be painfully obvious, George, that most
have a greatly diminished trust in you. As a matter of
fact, you have crisscrossed on so many issues and have been
back and forth, that I wonder how you can even trust
yourself. In my judgement, the only way you will ever gain
the trust of the American people is by a genuine act of
contrition starting with an apology to the people of America
for not listening as well to their real concerns as you
should have and for not being the decisive leader whom they
had a right to expect. In order to stand a chance of being
believed, this conversion has got to be real, and you have
got to do it completely by yourself--on your knees.

The Honorable George Bush
October 1, 1992
Page Two

After you have done this, you must demonstrate forcefully
your sincerity by decisive action. For openers, I would
suggest you need to name Jack Kemp as Secretary of the
Treasury and Vin Webber as Director of the Budget. You
should also issue an Executive Order indexing capital gains
for inflation, suspend the Davis-Baker Act and introduce
legislation to repeal the tax increase you mistakenly
signed. You should also announce you are going to trim the
bloated Federal payroll by at least 250,000 (more than twice
Clinton's figure).

There are probably several other major and much-needed moves
such as this which should be announced as well. The
Heritage Foundation could probably give you some immediate
suggestions at this point.

If you find it within yourself to do what I am suggesting
and praying you will do, you need to announce that you will
give a Presidential address to the people of America,
reserving at least 15 minutes of air time, and make
the speech of your lifetime and, hopefully, one which will
be etched in the memory of the people of America beyond any
they have heard in many a day. As you well know, to
accomplish what I am suggesting, it must be done in the next
few hours or few days and cannot be done on the eve of the
election.

Attached are some of my thoughts on what you could say if
you mean it, and those of an insightful good friend.
Obviously, your speech needs to approach the Gettysburg
Address in its content and its impact. If you feel that my
thoughts and ideas have merit, I would be willing to visit
directly with you and your speech writers, and I realize
there are many who can do better, but you need somebody that
understands and truly comprehends the problem, and it needs
to be done immediately.

George, it is my hope and prayer that you will take this to
heart, as your present disastrous course will ensure a
Clinton Presidency, which America cannot afford to endure.

Prayerful wishes,

Enclosure
cc: Jim Baker, White House Chief of Staff

SUGGESTED THOUGHTS FOR SPEECH
TO THE AMERICAN PEOPLE

My Fellow Americans, I come to you tonight with the full
realization that I have disappointed many of you who have
put your trust and faith in me. I now realize this more
than ever, and I want you to know that I have come to the
full realization to a point that I have been disappointed in
myself. One thing that has been clear in this campaign is
that the people of America are seeking a genuine and
meaningful change.

What I want to demonstrate to you tonight through words and
action is that the George Bush who is speaking to you is not
the George Bush you have known, but a new George Bush. The
old George Bush was not as good a listener as he should have
been, nor was he the decisive leader he should have been.
The new George Bush will be decisive and trustworthy to such
a degree that he intends to be one of the very best
Presidents America has ever known. I am willing to swallow
my pride and take a large dose of humility, which I truly
deserve. As you well know, it is very rare for any of us in
political office to admit and fully acknowledge error.

I know that there will be great skepticism and some who
feel that what I am saying is simply to get re-elected. Of
course, I am hoping to be re-elected, but I intend to earn
your trust and your respect such as seldom seen in the
political arena. I know that because I have not been the
President I should have been, that many of you have been so
committed to change that out of frustration thought about
voting for Bill Clinton or Ross Perot, but what I want to
assure you tonight is that the new George Bush is far more
committed to change and forceful leadership.

As simply a beginning, I am tonight announcing that I have
asked Jack Kemp to take over as Secretary of the Treasury
and Vin Webber to take over as Director of the Budget.
There will be other very significant personnel changes
announced so that you will have absolutely no doubt that you
are voting for a reshuffled and totally new team of
leadership.

I have also issued today an Executive Order indexing capital
gains for inflation as a significant step to improve our
economy and bring about the dynamic growth in newly created
jobs. Furthermore, I am asking the Congress to repeal the
tax increase I mistakenly signed. I am also seeking to
eliminate a minimum of 250,000 Federal jobs. For us as a
Nation to reach our potential, we must have greater
productivity and the Government has to do this as well.

My friends, I hope you will appreciate my sincerity, and I promise you that the new George Bush will be a truly decisive leader and one who is a keen listener to the concerns and frustrations of the people of America. We as a Nation have a great future, but we can only achieve it by working together and with the leadership totally committed to the ideals and principals that have made America great, preserving the freedom of the individual and the entrepreneur spirit that has made our country the greatest in the world.

Thank you. Goodnight.

THE WHITE HOUSE

WASHINGTON

October 19, 1992

Dear Mr. Yerger:

On behalf of the President, thank you for your letter of
September 16. I apologize for the delayed response.

In this first term, the President has surrounded himself with
people of outstanding talent, and Nick Brady and Dick Darman are
a part of that team. The President feels that their efforts have
contributed directly to the Administration's success. Through
their hard work and loyalty, they have done an excellent job
serving the President and the United States.

Again, thank you for taking the time to write. We have noted
your comments, and forwarded them to the appropriate Bush-Quayle
Campaign Committee. I hope the President and his administration
may count on your support.

Sincerely,

Ronald C. Kaufman
Deputy Assistant to the President
for Political Affairs

Mr. Wirt A. Yerger, Jr.
P.O. Box 1139
Jackson, Mississippi

WIRT A. YERGER, JR.
JACKSON, MISSISSIPPI

December 21, 1992

The Honorable George Bush
President of the United States
The White House
Washington, D.C. 20224

Dear George:

You and I have corresponded several times over the last four
years, and you have never once taken my advice, but the
record will show that every time I have made a suggestion it
has been correct, and the course you have been following has
been dead wrong, including your decision to run for
re-election.

While you are still President, you do have an opportunity to
strike a blow for what is right and for the American
taxpayer as well, and that is simply to fire Larry Walsh and
pardon Elliot Abrams, Casper Weinberger, Oliver North, and
everybody involved.

George, you will send 30,000 American troops to Somalia, but
will you take this decisive action now?

Sincerely,

P. S. — After you have done this, how about directing the
        Justice Department to launch an investigation of
        Larry Walsh and every single facet of his operation?
        Everybody knows this has been a total farce from
        start to finish. Quit worrying about the media, as
        you have done for four years, and act while you can.

WIRT A. YERGER, JR.
JACKSON, MISSISSIPPI

September 22, 2000

Honorable George W. Bush
PO Box 1902
Austin, TX 98767

"Winning vs. Losing"

Dear George:

It is quite obvious to everyone and I hope by now is totally obvious to you that Al Gore and the Democrats will never be accused of playing kinder and gentler on any issue whether it is personal or a campaign issue. You cannot wait many hours, much less days or weeks to launch a full-scale assault on Al Gore and his "spin" machine with constant lies and misrepresentations.

You should be able to literally "eat Al Gore alive" on almost every major issue. You have a strong background in what you've done for public education in Texas. Appeal to those mothers and fathers of the public school children to make a vote for the future of their children. Gore and his tie-in with the NEA will lead to complete failure. Hang this around his neck thoroughly. It could make a major difference.

Secondly, crime is still a major issue in this country and you need to emphasize that you will appoint judges who will uphold the law as it is written rather than seek ways to change the law so that criminals go free. Emphasize that you will appoint to the judiciary only those qualified who will uphold the Constitution and laws holding criminals accountable for their crimes.

You had a good idea in opening Social Security to private investment and in tax cuts to help prolong our economic expansion. You should make a stand against Internet taxes, making the point that Gore's antibusiness strategy is out of date. Emphasize that Gore's economic program, which includes massive government spending, as well as ideas on public financing of campaigns (welfare for politicians) would threaten our economic expansion. Point out that the Kyoto global-warming accord Gore favors would raise taxes on middle class Americans and make cars more expensive. Go after Gore tooth and toenail with the fact that his economic plan does not maximize retirement plan benefits for Americans.

You are never going to out-promise Gore in the areas of medical coverage and drug programs. Label him a Socialist, and point out that nations have rejected this as a failed idea time and time again. Why reinstate the failed Hillary Clinton medical programs?

Gore and the Democrats have been careful to give respect to the role that religious faith plays in the lives of individuals and the community. However, when asked about abortion, for example, Senator Lieberman says he is personally opposed but doesn't want his understanding of what a fetus is to impinge on anyone else. This is all-talk, no action. Religion's importance should include taking a firm stand on issues of morality. How is the Presidential order issued in June this year prohibiting government agencies from cooperating with groups that discriminate against homosexuals going to be adhered to when Gore allows the Boy Scouts to use federal lands as he has promised? Gore is making promises he can't keep, just to appeal to religious groups.

You and Dick Cheney need to mount a relentless attack on the lack of military preparedness, morale and recruitment problems in the armed forces. If you can emotionalize this issue properly you should receive tremendous support.

On the issue of Strategic Defense Initiative, point out that rogue states could lob missiles at our cities threatening every American. It is totally inconceivable to take the position we do not want to protect ourselves. You will remember in the 1964 Goldwater campaign the Democrats ran ads showing an atomic explosion, which was used effectively against Barry Goldwater. You could do likewise saying that without SDI this could happen to American cities, and dramatically show it.

Your pitch to the electorate must be specific, and I trust you can take the offensive and wear Al Gore out on the issues I've mentioned. Never forget elections are won on emotion, not logic.

Best wishes and God bless you and yours,

October 16, 2000

Mr. Wirt A. Yerger, Jr.
P.O. Box 1139
Jackson, MS 39215

Dear Wirt,

Thanks for your kind words and for your ideas and suggestions. I appreciate having the benefit of your views.

The remaining weeks will be tough, but I welcome the contest and take nothing for granted.

Laura and I are grateful to have you on the team.

On to victory,

George W. Bush

www.GeorgeWBush.com
Post Office Box 1902, Austin, Texas 78767-1902 **OFFICE** 512-637-2000 **FAX** 512-637-8800

Paid for by Bush/Cheney 2000, Inc.

January 24, 2001

Honorable George W. Bush
President of the United States
The White House
Washington, DC 20224

Dear Mr. President:

Congratulations on being elected to serve as our President. We are truly excited over what your leadership will mean to our nation.

Your inauguration was extremely well done with the exception of the truly outrageous behavior of Bill Clinton. Whoever allowed him to have a Marine band at Andrew's Air Force Base to send him away on Air Force I made a serious mistake. With Bill Clinton, there is simply no reason to yield one inch because you know as well as anyone that he is a scoundrel.

Enclosed is a column by David Bowen, a former Democratic congressman from our state, and I would beg you to read this column because it speaks directly to the problem we have with regard to the very illusive and unattainable black vote. It is past time for all of us to wake up and be realistic about this issue.

Whoever told you to accept a phone call from Jesse Jackson, a man who was trying to lead a revolution against your election, should be replaced on your staff. I was also dismayed to see that you called Jesse Jackson within the last few days. You could call him twice a day from now on and see no positive effect.

Also enclosed is a short paper that I prepared two months ago to pass on to Morton Blackwell's Leadership Institute, Ed Feulner's Heritage Foundation, and Brent Bozelle's Media Research, all of which I have been privileged to support for many years. In order to be sure that we do well in the congressional election two years from now and your re-election in 2004, we must get busy immediately and show a lot more savvy and determination than we have demonstrated in the past. It is only by God's grace that Ralph Nader was on the ballot to enable you to win the election and serve as our President. You are in my prayers and I will be happy to support and assist you in any way I possibly can.

Sincerely,

P.S. I knew your father and have visited him several times over the years, but since I have never had the privilege to know you I am enclosing a biography to show my involvement in the political process going back to Eisenhower, Barry Goldwater, Richard Nixon and Ronald Reagan.

October 23, 2001

Honorable George W. Bush
White House
Washington, DC 20001

"Moment of Truth"

Dear Mr. President:

You have proven yourself to be a truly great President in our moment
of greatest need. We are most thankful for this, and are praying for
your complete success as a leader of our nation.

As you well know, your own father and Colin Powell made a grievous
mistake twelve years ago in not completing the conquest of Iraq. To
make matters much worse, the Clinton administration weakened us
militarily and in the intelligence area. They did not persist in making
Saddam Hussein comply with the agreement to allow inspection of his
war-making ability including germ warfare.

In view of this, my strongest suggestion is that we give Saddam
Hussein and any other similar regimes 72 hours to turn over all germ
warfare material and allow complete and thorough inspection. If they
do not do this, we have no alternative but to blow them away and
conquer what is left so that the world will not live in fear of attack
from these evil forces.

You have done an excellent job of building a coalition against those
who have destroyed us, but I truly feel that we are at a critical juncture
in history where we must be forthright and do what is right for
ourselves and the free world not being cowed by the fear so often in
the last hundred years shown by the state department of "World
Opinion".

Mr. President, we are at a decisive point in history. I trust you are
ready to meet the challenge. All of our lives and those who cherish
freedom hang in the balance.

Sincerely,

Cc: Honorable Thad Cochran, US Senator
Honorable Trent Lott, US Senator
Honorable Donald Rumsfeld, US Secretary of Defense

February 26, 2002

Honorable George W. Bush
President of the United States
White House
Washington, DC 20002

"Judge Charles Pickering"

Dear Mr. President:

There is no better and more clear-cut time to mount the "bully pulpit'
in the strongest possible manner than the Pickering nomination.
Leftists are making a total farce out of this, and if you don't step into it
and capitalize on your own popularity, they will get away with it. This
would be a disaster for our nation.

What I am suggesting is that you, in the strongest possible way, go to
the people of America literally "letting the leftists have it" for how
they are destroying the fabric of our nation so well laid out in the U.S.
Constitution. They are the ones who have argued for years that there
shouldn't be a litmus test, and now they are the ones doing just that.
If a nominee of yours is dishonest or does not have strong integrity,
then that would be reason for opposition but otherwise they should
cease and desist what they are doing and apologize to the people of
America for what they have said and done.

Mr. President, please jump into this with both feet. I am enclosing
columns from our newspaper from some who are certainly not friends
of Republicans to help you gauge what these leftists are really doing.
They have proven themselves "racists" and I think you should use that
term when you get in the fray.

As you well know, when you do what is right, it will turn out
politically right in the final analysis every time. You have surely
demonstrated you have the right instincts, and please don't be
dissuaded.

Sincerely,

P.S. When I recently read that in the war effort, lawyers attached to
combat units are making decisions on what should and should not be
done, I find this totally shocking, and I hope this policy will be
reversed. Our military should be given the opportunity to win the war,
not hamstrung by lawyers attached to our command staff.

May 20, 2002

Honorable Richard Cheney
Vice President of the United States
Washington, DC
VIA E-Mail—vice.president@whitehouse.gov

"Cynicism—Lack of Trust in Government"

Dear Dick:

Yesterday I watched you on "Face the Nation" and as usual you did a superb job of communicating. I consider you in the position of Vice President at this time a tremendous blessing for our nation.

Nevertheless, I must tell you that I feel that the Administration should have been far more forthcoming with the information that was received prior to the September 11 attack. This is just another example of what had done on for decades, where the government refuses to have faith in the judgment of the American people. I cite, for example, when Jeremiah Denton was a prisoner for the North Vietnamese and he blinked out in Morse code the word "torture." The US State Department felt that the American people should not be told this information when a man risked his life to reveal it. The US State Department has not made a significant correct decision in over fifty years.

I just finished the book "SPY CATCHER" by Peter Wright, a senior intelligence director of M15 in Britain. When you see the penetration that the Russians had with all of the spies in Britain, such as Burgess, McLean, and many others such as the FBI man just recently, you have every reason to wonder, "What else is going on?" The fact that the FBI was not polygraphing everyone in the name of protecting someone's civil rights is simply deplorable.

Dick, it is high time that the Administration showed more candor with the American people and that the fact that this has not been done in the past is the reason everyone is so cynical of the government. Many elected and appointed government officials are too desperate to protect their own turf and cover their own inept decisions.

What I am suggesting is forming a committee of citizens from across this nation to delve into the entire matter of security and make a report to the people. I would like to serve on this committee, and would be thrilled with a role in helping spearhead this vital project. It could help to reassure a nation that has been left in doubt on this and other related issues.

If Ashcroft and Mueller didn't feel the Phoenix memo was important enough to tell the President, they should both be replaced immediately. We as a nation must wake up and dramatically change our ways and not worry about the ACLU thinks about everything. This is now at the point of having attorneys in the field with our fighting forces.

Another example of extremely bad judgment, in my opinion and that of many others, is no allowing pilots to carry weapons in the cockpit. This does not make sense when pilots have control of the lives of all on board.

Furthermore, we should immediately profile people coming into this country in any way whatsoever and should not apologize for it. Not doing this is insane as I'm sure you will agree. Let's concentrate on what is right for the survival of this nation first and foremost.

May God grant you the wisdom and courage to do what is best for America.

Sincerely,

Cc: Honorable George W. Bush
        Honorable Thad Cochran
        Honorable Trent Lott
        Honorable Chip Pickering

September 30, 2002

Honorable George W. Bush
White House
Washington, DC 20001

Dear Mr. President:

You have been in our thoughts and prayers during this critical time in our nation's history. I firmly believe that you will stay the course and not back away from Saddam as has been done in the past. It would prove to be the right course for America and save lives rather than cause lives to be lost.

The book Tuxedo Park by Jennet Conant is most fascinating, and shows how one man and his physicist colleague changed the course of World War II. I came across a quote in the book by Henry Stimson, Secretary of War under Franklin Roosevelt, which is as follows:

"I am not one of those who think that the priceless freedom of our country can be saved without sacrifice. It can not. That has not been the way by which during millions of years humanity has slowly and painfully toiled upwards towards a better and more human civilization. The men who suffered at Valley Forge and won Yorktown gave more than money to the cause of freedom. Today a small group of evil leaders have taught the young men of Germany that the freedom of other men and nations must be destroyed. Today those young me are ready to die for that perverted conviction. Unless we on our side are ready to sacrifice and, if need be, die for the conviction that the freedom of America must be saved, it will not be saved. Only by a readiness for the same sacrifice can that freedom be preserved."

Mr. President, history repeats itself, and this admonition years ago is very much needed now. It is amazing how so called European allies, with certain exceptions, are so prone to appeasement.

Sincerely,

January 26, 2004

Vice President Dick Cheney

Washington, D.C.

"Stop Bleeding Coalition Lives"

Dear Dick:

Some months ago I sent the attached letter to the President with a copy to Donald Rumsfeld and our two Senators. Now that we have dramatically won the war and have captured Saddham, why can't we base our troops in safe areas, totally away from the Iraqi population and let them become totally responsible for policing their country?

The only other alternative is to withdraw, which I really don't recommend or crack down security so hard that you temporarily create a "police" state.

Why continue to expose coalition lives to danger?

Dick, with the present course you risk losing the election.

We need to dramatically change tactics to allow troops to be deployed more safely than they are now.

Sincerely,

Wirt A. Yerger, Jr.
129 Woodland Circle
Jackson, MS 39216

December 2, 2004

Honorable George W. Bush
President of the United States
1600 Pennsylvania Ave NW
Washington, DC 20500

"Facing Facts"

Dear Mr. President:

It is high time to swallow our pride and recognize that going into Iraq was a horrific mistake. It would be one thing if the people were willing to work for freedom and give their lives for it. It is obvious now that that is just not the case. Therefore, no matter what these elections hold, I would suggest we make plans to immediately remove all American personnel from the cities and on the highways.

As you will note from the enclosed correspondence I sent previously, I've been begging you to get the American personnel where they can be fully protected, but this suggestion has been ignored and we've ended up with hundreds of Americans killed and severely wounded.

It is amazing that you were able to win re-election in view of this tragic situation. Before declaring a mandate of any kind, you need to realize you were running against one of the weakest candidates the Democrats could have run. We are desperate for leadership, and I fully believe that you can do much better in this term than the last. I pray you will.

Your idea of sacrificing American lives in order to bring Democracy to Muslim nations is simply absurd and I hope that you will realize this and quit talking about this like it is doable.

Thank you,

Cc: Senator Trent Lott
     Senator Thad Cochran
     Honorable Donald Rumsfeld, Secretary of Defense

Wirt A. Yerger, Jr.
129 Woodland Circle
Jackson, MS 39216

January 5, 2005

Honorable George W. Bush
President of the United States
White House
Washington, D.C.

"Facing Reality"

Dear Mr. President:

The preparation for normal inaugural ceremonies sickens me when U.S. troops are on the battlefield risking their lives.

Without the Swift Boat Veterans we would not even be celebrating the inauguration of George W. Bush. If we are having an inaugural parade, John O'Neal should be the head of it. He is the principal reason, far more than Karl Rove, you will be sworn in as President.

The situation in Iraq grows worse every day, and it is past time for you and all of us to swallow our pride and get out completely before risking another American life. If the Iraqis are not willing to appreciate all we've done by fighting for their independence and freedom, we do not need to use our resources and certainly not lives.

Sincerely,

BARRY M. GOLDWATER, JR.

February 7, 2005

Wirt A. Yerger, Jr.
129 Woodland Circle
Jackson, MS 39216

Dear Wirt,

Thank you for your kind letter. I hope this finds you well. I am writing to let you know that I am unable to assist you with copies of correspondence between you and my father. I have never actually had control of documents of that nature.

You may be able to find some help from the Arizona Historical Foundation. Contact information for them is:

Arizona Historical Foundation
Hayden Library, ASU
Box 871006
Tempe, AZ 85287
(480) 966-8331

I hope this information will be of help to you, and I wish you well.

The best always,

Barry M. Goldwater Jr.

BMG/dd

3104 E. Camelback Road, Suite 274, Phoenix, Arizona 85016
602- 840 3510 (Phone)   602-840-2505 (Fax)   602-499-6399 (Mobile)
BGOLDWATERJR@COX.NET

Wirt A. Yerger, Jr.
129 Woodland Circle
Jackson, MS 39216

October 11, 2005

Honorable George W. Bush
President of the United States
White House
Washington, DC

"Facing Facts in Iraq"

Dear Mr. President:

Your decision to invade Iraq was, in my opinion, the correct decision under the circumstances and based upon the facts that were known at the time.

The initial invasion was tremendously successful and a most impressive demonstration of military bravery and technology.

Nevertheless, the decision to stay in Iraq and use American military to police the country was a grievous mistake which you must be willing to acknowledge and do what is necessary to correct before more American lives are lost.

If we can not accomplish a complete withdrawal of our forces, we should at least place all of our forces in protected places around the country rather than where the people of Iraq who obviously want us out of there are in close proximity to our troops.

For more than three years I have been pleading with you and the Vice President and the Secretary of Defense and Congressmen to face up to this problem. After demonstrating tremendous courage in the face of adversity, it is high time you have the courage to face up to the dilemma we are in and change the course.

The end game in Iraq does not have to be another Vietnam. I hope and pray that you will have the courage to make a dramatic change. We have suffered a substantial number of casualties but not one more American life should be sacrificed at this point. We need to realize that we are in a no-win situation.

Sincerely,

Cc: Vice President Richard Cheney
     Donald Rumsfeld, Secretary of Defense
     Honorable Thad Cochran
     Honorable Trent Lott
     Honorable Chip Pickering
     Secretary of State Condoleezza Rice

OFFICE OF THE VICE PRESIDENT
WASHINGTON

November 9, 2005

Dear Mr. Yerger:

The Vice President has asked me to reply to your letter expressing your thoughts on the Supreme Court nomination. Your comments have been carefully noted.

Vice President Cheney was pleased that you let him know of your views. Thank you for taking the time to write.

Sincerely,

Cecelia Boyer

Cecelia Boyer
Special Assistant to the Vice President
For Correspondence

Mr. Wirt A. Yerger, Jr.
129 Woodland Circle
Jackson, Mississippi 39216-4194

Wirt A. Yerger, Jr.
129 Woodland Circle
Jackson, MS 39216

December 17, 2008

Honorable George W. Bush
White House
Washington, DC 20001

Dear George:

Honestly, I've been grievously disappointed in your leadership for the most part. Nevertheless, thank you for the tireless hours in service to our country. May the Lord bless you and your family in your future endeavors.

Please consider reducing Bernie Ebbers' sentence to no more than ten years. In light of recent events, it is clearly evident that he was over sentenced. And I'm saying this as one who lost quite a bit of net worth in Worldcom stock. In all honesty I feel it is the fair thing to do.

Sincerely,

Notes

Introduction

1 James Ewing, "Wright Blames Truman Committee; Warns Dems State May Bolt Party,' *The Jackson Daily News,* 20 January 1948.

2 Barry Goldwater, "Barry Goldwater Warns: Philosophy of Superstate Threatens Human Liberties," *The Clarion-Ledger, 9* March 1961, 3.

Chapter 1
1880s-1950s: Ancestors, Strange Republicans, & the Need for Change

1 *Jackson Daily News, 21* April 1860, as quoted by Mr. Carl André, *Yerger History*, unpublished manuscript, no date, p. 21.

2 *The Papers of Jefferson Davis, Vol. 2, June 1841-July 1846* (Baton Rouge: Louisiana State University Press, 1974) 50-51.

3 Neil R. McMillen, "Perry W. Howard, Boss of Black-and-Tan Republicanism," 1924-1960," *The Journal of Southern History, Vol. 48, No. 2*, May 1982, 205-224.

4 All citations in this paragraph are from McMillen, 205-224.

5 McMillen, 205-224.

6 McMillen, 209-210.

7 McMillen, 210.

8 McMillen, 211.

9 McMillen, 213, 214.

10 McMillen, 217.

11 McMillen, 214.

12 McMillen, 219.

13 McMillen, 216.

14 McMillen, 221.

15 *The Daily Clarion-Ledger,* "Marriage of Miss Mae Rivers Applewhite and Mr. Wirt Yerger Beautifully Solemnized," 18 October 1928, 6.

Chapter 2
1952-1956: New Republicans vs. Dated Democrats

1 Carl Walters, "Republicans No Longer Rare—And Apparently 'Human,' Too," *The Clarion-Ledger/Jackson Daily News,* 10 February 1957, 17.

2 James Edward Cliatt, III, "The Republican Party in Mississippi: 1952-1960," Thesis submitted to the faculty of Mississippi State University, August 1964, 36.

3 Joseph Crespino, *In Search of Another Country: Mississippi and the Conservative Counterrevolution,* (Princeton: Princeton University Press, 2007) 4.

4 Crespino, 7.

5 Crespino, 211.

6 Arch Puddington, *The National Review,* 8 April 1996; 30 October 2009 www.thefreelibrary.com.

7 Crespino, 52.

8 Neil R. McMillen, "Development of Civil Rights: 1956-1970," *A History of Mississippi, Vol. ii* ed. Richard Aubrey McClemore, (Hattiesburg, Miss.: University and College Press of Mississippi, 1973) 167.

9 Crespino, 53.

10 *The Clarion-Ledger,* January 29, 1956, 8.

11 "Battle for Segregation, Racial Incidents Marked Year," Editorial, *The Clarion-Ledger 1* January 1956, 4.

12 "Battle for Segregation, Racial Incidents Marked Year," 4.

13 "Young Republicans Hear McWhorter," *The Clarion-Ledger,* 25 May 1956, 1.

14 *The Clarion-Ledger,* 4 January 1956, 1.

15 *The Clarion-Ledger,* 4 January 1956, 1.

16 "Ired NAACP Says Eastland Just a 'Stinking Albatross': Civil Rights Session Hits at Senator; Asserts Their Vote Will Say Goodbye to The Democrats," *The Clarion-Ledger,* 5 March 1956, 1.

17 John M. Fenton, "The South and 'Mixin' In'—Will the Day Ever Come? Whites Hoping Time's Far Off," *The Clarion-Ledger,* 1 March 1956, 10.

18 *The Clarion-Ledger,* 10 January 1956, 8.

Chapter 3
1956: Miss. GOP Galvanizes in San Francisco

1 "Spencer Again Heads 'Citizens for Ike' in Mississippi Area," *The Clarion-Ledger,* 19 February 1956, 1.

2 "Spencer Again Heads 'Citizens for Ike' in Mississippi Area," 14.

3 "Citizens for Eisenhower Out To Carry State: Got 40 Percent of Mississippi Votes in 1952," *The Clarion-Ledger,* 11 March 1956, 2.

4 "Hinds Lily White Convention Called," *The Clarion-Ledger,* 11 March 1956, 1.

5 Lamar Falkner, "No Longer Just Lily White GOPs," *The Clarion-Ledger,* 25 March 1956, 3.

6 "Black-Tan Group Plans Convention," *The Clarion-Ledger,* 3 May 1956, 4.

7 Quotes in this paragraph are from Fred Sullens, "Howard Tosses Load of Fear Into Minds of Lily Whites," *The Clarion-Ledger,* 17 June 1956, 1-2.

8 "State GOP Factions Argue Their Merits," *The Clarion-Ledger,* 19 April 1956, 1.

9 Howard Suttle, "State GOP Contest Is Top Controversy for '56 Convention," *The Clarion-Ledger,* 13 May 1956, 1.

10 Gene Wirth, "State's White GOP Faction Optimistic," *The Clarion-Ledger,* 20 April 1956, 1.

11 *The Jackson Daily News,* April 18, 1956, cited in James Edward Cliatt, III, "The Republican Party in Mississippi: 1952-1960," Thesis submitted to the faculty of Mississippi State University, August 1964.

12 "Spencer Confident of GOP Recognition: Says Convention to Seat All-Whites," *The Clarion-Ledger,* 19 May 1956, 1.

13 "Howard Blithely Expecting GOP Will Seat His Faction," *The Clarion-Ledger,* 19 July 1956, 8.

14 Gene Wirth, "Lily Whites Push Recognition Drive," *The Clarion-Ledger*, 9 August 1956, 1.

15 "Coleman Asks United in Party, Hits NAACP," *The Clarion-Ledger*, 12 August 1956, 2.

16 "Coleman Asks United in Party, Hits NAACP," 2.

17 "States' Righters Will Talk Unpledged Electors on Ticket," *The Clarion-Ledger,* 21 August 1956, 2.

18 Jack K. Russell, "GOP Gives South Delegate Strength," *The Clarion-Ledger*, 6 July 1956, 12.

19 Gene Wirth, "Southerners See Compromise Cut: Spencer GOP Group Loses in Contest To Obtain Seating," *The Clarion-Ledger,* 15 August 1956, 1.

20 Gene Wirth, "Perry Howard Reign as State GOP Boss May Be Near End," *The Clarion-Ledger,* 16 August 1956, 1.

21 "Spencer Invited to Rejoin Demos," *The Clarion-Ledger,* 16 August 1956, 1.

22 "Lily Whites Returning Home: Refuse to Mix with Black & Tans," *The Clarion-Ledger,* 17 August 1956, 1.

23 "Mississippi's Split Vote Is Confusing," *The Clarion-Ledger,* 20 August 1956, 1.

24 James Featherstone, "Yerger Returns: Lily White Head Says Black and Tans Doomed," *The Jackson Daily News,* 23 August 1956, 1.

25 "Gradual Racial Change Favored," *The Clarion-Ledger,* 9 May 1956, 5.

26 Russell Bruce, "Segregationists Threaten Dynamiting: White Mothers Report Having Telephone Calls," *The Clarion-Ledger,* 6 September 1956, 1.

27 "Mansfield Integration Efforts Are Abandoned: Young Priest Rescued from Angry Texas Mob," *The Clarion-Ledger*, 5 September 1956, 1.

28 B. F. Kellum, "NAACP Pledged to Pay $11,000 to Negro Boy," *The Clarion-Ledger*, 30 September1956, 1.

29 "Bus Officials To Ignore Edict of Supreme Court: No New Instructions Are Given to Drivers," *The Clarion-Ledger*, 17 November 1956, 1.

30 "Integration and Communism," *The Clarion-Ledger*, 9 September 1956, 38.

31 "Integration and Communism," 38.

32 "Sovereignty Board Organizes to Fight,"*The Clarion-Ledger*, 16 May 1956, 1.

33 Ed Goins, "Lily Whites Assert Group Reorganized," *The Clarion-Ledger*, 4 September 1956, 1.

34 "Yerger Blasts Gov. Coleman for Statement," *The Clarion-Ledger*, 30 October 1956, 9.

35 Howard Suttle, "Spencer-Yerger Faction's GOP Leadership Going Up," *The Clarion-Ledger*, 11 November 1956, 6.

Chapter 4
1957: Out-Organizing the Dusty Democrats

1 Elson C. Fay, "AP Military Affairs Reporter," *The Clarion-Ledger/Jackson Daily News*, 14 January 1957, 4.

2 Purser Hewitt, "Spencer Gets Close Spot for Inaugural," *The Clarion-Ledger*, 21 January 1957, 1.

3 "Predict Republican Gains in the South," *The Clarion-Ledger/Jackson Daily News,* 13 January 1957, 2.

4 George Gallup, "Democrats Gaining in Voter Confidence," *The Clarion-Ledger*, 14 June 1957, 3.

5 Tom Ethridge, "State Solons Making Fun of 'Modern Republicanism,'" *The Clarion-Ledger*, 14 April 1957, 7.

6 "Pictures Clash With 'New Republicans," *The Clarion-Ledger*, 4 June 1957, 8.

7 "Potter Will Address GOP Officials," *The Clarion-Ledger*, 11 July 1957, 8.

8 Kay Ray, "Republicans' Top Donors Beat Demos: Committee Report Lists Contributors From Mississippi," *The Jackson Daily News*, 3 February 1957, 1.

9 *The State Times,* Jackson, Mississippi, 14 February 1957, 6-A.

10 Jack Bell, "Demos Predict South to Reject Ike's GOP," *The Clarion-Ledger*, 2 June 1957, 1.

11 Jack Bell, 1.

12 "Ike & GOP Will Press Civil Rights," by J.W. Davis; and, "Another Integrated City Bus Ambushed By Pistol Wielder," *The Clarion-Ledger*, 1 January 1957, 1.

13 Ralph McDill, "Hope for Two-Party System: Dixie GOP Leaders Urge Right to Vote Legislation," *The Clarion-Ledger*, 26 July 1957, 6.

14 "State's GOP Disapprove of CR-Bill," *The Clarion-Ledger*, 2 August 1957, 1.

15 Ralph McDill, "Hope for Two-Party System: Dixie GOP Leaders Urge Right to Vote Legislation," *The Clarion-Ledger*, 26 July 1957, 6.

16 "Police Nab 33 Negroes in Rioting," *The Clarion-Ledger*, 2 January 1957, 1.

17 "Negroes Start Melee Injuring 3 Detectives," *The Clarion-Ledger*, 9 January 1957, 1.

18 *The Clarion-Ledger*, 3 January 1957, 11.

19 Greene, like Piney Woods founder/president Laurence Jones, began to be labeled by civil rights activists as being paid by the white power system; this was a smear on their good names by groups vested in discrediting their voices; the same groups smeared Booker T. Washington; claims were that Greene's travel expenses were paid once by the state's Citizens' Council to speak in Memphis at a national gathering; but Greene had long written as a black conservative, and his views were not coerced.

20 "Evolution, not Revolution: No Bus Boycott Needed Here, Negro Editor Says," *The Clarion-Ledger*, 6 January 1957, 1, 10.

21 Caryl A. Cooper, "Percy Greene and *The Jackson Advocate*," *The Press and Race: Mississippi Journalists Confront the Movement*, ed. David R. Davies (Mississippi: University of Mississippi Press, 2001) 45.

22 "Evolution, not Revolution: No Bus Boycott Needed Here, Negro Editor Says," *The Clarion-Ledger*, 6 January 1957, 1, 10.

23 "Uncle Toms Needed, Says Negro," *The Clarion-Ledger*, 24 January 1957, 1.

24 "Uncle Toms Needed, Says Negro," 1.

25 Charles M. Hills, "Affairs of State," *The Clarion-Ledger*, 12 February 1957, 8.

26 "Says Reds to Infiltrate Negroes' Organizations," *The Clarion-Ledger*, 21 February 1957, 1.

27 "Expert Assistance in Racial Agitation," *The Clarion-Ledger*, 21 February 1957, 12.

28 "McClendon Heads Young Republicans in State," *The Clarion-Ledger/Jackson Daily News,* 7 April 1957, 11.

29 "State Republican Women's Club Head to Attend Meet," *The Clarion-Ledger*, 27 April 1957, 5.

30 "The Gallup Poll: John Q. Public Is Looking Optimistically Toward '57," *The Clarion-Ledger*, 6 January 1957, 6.

31 "Republicans Boast of Gains in South," *The Clarion-Ledger*, 1 June 1957, 6.

32 "GOP Planning to Enter State Political Races," *The Clarion-Ledger*, 14 May 1957, 1.

33 "GOP Planning to Enter State Political Races," *The Clarion-Ledger*, 14 May 1957, 1.

34 "Young GOP Hears Ike," *The Clarion-Ledger*, 21 June 1957, 1.

35 *The Clarion-Ledger*, 15 September 1957, 10-D.

36 Ed Goins, "Segregation Battle Rages: Jackson Remains a Fortress," *The Clarion-Ledger,* 29 September 1957, 13.

37 Jere Nash and Andy Taggart, *Mississippi Politics: The Struggle for Power, 1976-2006,* (Jackson, Mississippi: University Press of Mississippi, 2006) 39.

38 "E.O. Spencer Quits GOP Patronage Post Over Use of Troops," and, "Yerger Says He'll Stay Within GOP Framework, *The Clarion-Ledger,* 2 October 1957, 1.

39 Joseph Crespino, *In Search of Another Country: Mississippi and the Conservative Counterrevolution* (Princeton: Princeton University Press, 2007) 85.

40 "Dixie GOP Members Quitting in Numbers," *The Clarion-Ledger*, 4 October 1957, 1.

41 "E.O. Spencer Quits GOP Patronage Post Over Use of Troops," and, "Yerger Says He'll Stay Within GOP Framework," *The Clarion-Ledger*, 2 October 1957, 1.

42 "[Mayo] Reed Blasts Republicans," *The Clarion-Ledger*, 27 October 1957, 9.

43 "Democrats: Through the Roadblock," *Time* magazine, 28 October 1957, 23.

44 "Our New Political Leonidas," *The Clarion-Ledger,* 20 October 1957, 2-D.

Chapter 5
1958: Confronting Eisenhower and Kennedy

1 Earl Black and Merle Black, *The Rise of Southern Republicans,* (Cambridge: The Belknap Press of Harvard University Press, 2003) 66.

2 Nash and Taggart, 40.

3 "If America Re-Registered Republicans Would Lose," *The Clarion-Ledger/ Jackson Daily News, 23* May 1958, 3.

4 " 'Defeatism' Is Major Problem Facing The GOP," American Institute of Public Opinion, *The Clarion-Ledger/Jackson Daily News,* 8 June 1958, 2-A.

5 *The Clarion-Ledger*, "Integration Can Destroy Nation' Kiwanians Told," 13 March 1958, 14.

6 Charles M. Hills, "State's Young GOP Blasts at Kennedy," *The Clarion-Ledger/Jackson Daily News*, 15 April 1958, 10.

7 Hills, 10.

8 Charles M. Hills, "Affairs of State, *The Clarion-Ledger/Jackson Daily News*, 18 April 14-A.

9 "Jackson Young GOPs Ask Representation," *The Clarion-Ledger/Jackson Daily News*, 27 April 1958, 2-A.

10 "Jackson Young GOPs Ask Representation," 2-A.

11 "State GOP Chief In Washington," *The Clarion-Ledger/Jackson Daily News*, 17 June 1958, 3.

12 Vernon Louviere, "Republicans Don't Want Questioning," *The Clarion-Ledger/Jackson Daily News*, 26 June 1958, 8.

13 Louviere, 8.

14 Gardner L. Bridge, "GOP Puts Out Fresh Oust Adams Demands," *The Clarion-Ledger/Jackson Daily News*, 22 June 1958, 1.

15 "Ike, Negro Panel Plan Conference," *The Clarion-Ledger/Jackson Daily News*, 20 June 1958, 1.

16 "Negro's Vote Case Set Today: Federal Judges Will Hear Darby's Challenge of Laws," *The Clarion-Ledger/Jackson Daily News*, 22 July 1958. 1

17 "Hurrah, The Yanks Are Coming," *The Clarion-Ledger/Jackson Daily News*, 3 August 1958, 2-D.

18 "6 of 10 Southerners See Violence Possible," *The Clarion-Ledger/Jackson Daily News*, 31 August 1958, 2-A.

19 "State GOP Scores Unfair Tax Laws," *The Clarion-Ledger/Jackson Daily News*, 10 August 1958, 2.

20 "Business Magazine Cites City's Status," *The Clarion-Ledger/Jackson Daily News*, 26 August 1958, 4.

21 "All of Mississippi Joins With Brandon in Loving Miss America," *The Clarion-Ledger/Jackson Daily News*, 8 September 1958, 6.

22 Cliatt, 56.

23 "State GOP Launches Fund Drive," *The Clarion-Ledger/Jackson Daily News*, 3 October 1958, 1.

24 "State GOP Launches Fund Drive," 1.

25 "State GOP Launches Fund Drive," *The Clarion-Ledger/Jackson Daily News*, 3 October 1958, 1.

26 "State Republicans Sponsor Fair Booth," *The Clarion-Ledger/Jackson Daily News*, 3 October 1958, 20.

27 Charles M. Hills, "Dollars for Democrats New Project Within the Party," *The Clarion-Ledger/Jackson Daily News*, 7 September 1958, 3-D.

Chapter 6
1959: Setting Up Headquarters

1 "1959—A Year To Trumpet About," *The Mississippi Republican News*, Vol. 3, No. 1, January 1960, 4.

2 "Russian Rocket Heads for Orbit Around Sun: Reds Boast of First Manmade Solar Planet," *The Clarion-Ledger/Jackson Daily News*, 4 January 1959, 1.

3 "Barnett Puts Hat In Ring," *The Clarion-Ledger/Jackson Daily News*, 11 January 1959, 1.

4 "By Adam: Butler Invited To Make Personal Apology Here," *The Clarion-Ledger/Jackson Daily News,* 11 January 1959, 1.

5 *Mississippi Republican Newsletter: Devoted to a Two-Party System,* Vol. 2, No. 1. January 1959.

6 *Mississippi Republican Newsletter: Devoted to a Two-Party System,* Vol. 2, No. 7. July 1959.

7 *Mississippi Republican Newsletter: Devoted to a Two-Party System,* Vol. 2, No. 7. July 1959.

8 "Adam to *The Clarion-Ledger*: NAACP Aim Is Colored Nation," *The Clarion-Ledger,* 24 February 1959, 1.

9 James Saggus, "J.P. Agrees With Adam," *The Clarion-Ledger/Jackson Daily News,* 17 January 1959, 1.

10 *Mississippi Republican Newsletter: Devoted to a Two-Party System,* Vol. 2. No. 9, September 1959.

11 *Mississippi Republican Newsletter: Devoted to a Two-Party System,* Vol. 2. No. 9, September 1959.

12 Charles M. Hills, "Affairs of State," *The Clarion-Ledger/Jackson Daily News,* 18 March 1959, 10.

13 "Political Plum: State Republicans Eye Census Job," *The Clarion-Ledger/Jackson Daily News,* 22 January 1959, 9.

14 "State GOP To Hold Seminar Here Today," *The Clarion-Ledger/Jackson Daily News,* 1 June 1959, 2.

15 "State GOP Announces Fund Drive," *The Clarion-Ledger/Jackson Daily News,* 2 June 1959, 10.

16 "Yerger Attends GOP Conference," *The Clarion-Ledger/Jackson Daily News,* 9 April 1959, 12.

17 "The Gallup Poll: Nixon Out In Front As GOP Voters' '60 Choice," *The Clarion-Ledger/Jackson Daily News,* 10 April 1959, 12.

18 "Congress Members Top MEC Final Day," *The Clarion-Ledger,* 17 April 1959, 1, 4.

19 *Mississippi Republican Newsletter: Devoted to a Two-Party System,* Vol. 2. No. 7, July 1959,

20 *Mississippi Republican Newsletter: Devoted to a Two-Party System,* Vol. 2. No. 10, October 1959,

21 *Mississippi Republican Newsletter: Devoted to a Two-Party System,* Vol. 2. No. 7, July 1959.

22 *Mississippi Republican Newsletter: Devoted to a Two-Party System,* Vol. 2. No. 7, July 1959.

23 "Ross Barnett Is Our Choice," *The Clarion-Ledger,* 13 July 1959, 1.

24 "Democrats Defeat GOP," *The Clarion-Ledger,* 4 November 1959, 1.

25 *Mississippi Republican Newsletter: Devoted to a Two-Party System,* Vol. 2. No. 10, October 1959.

26 *Mississippi Republican Newsletter: Devoted to a Two-Party System,* Vol. 2. No. 10, October 1959.

27 *Mississippi Republican Newsletter: Devoted to a Two-Party System,* Vol. 2. No. 10, October 1959.

28 *Mississippi Republican Newsletter: Devoted to a Two-Party System*, Vol. 2. No. 10, October 1959.

29 "Democrats Defeat GOP Attempt At County Level: Campbell is Winner Over Westbrook, 6 to 1," *The Clarion-Ledger,* 4 November 1959, 1.

30 Charles M. Hills, "Democrats Face Test In Hinds Voting Today," *The Clarion-Ledger*, 3 November 1959, 1.

31 "Democrats Defeat GOP Attempt At County Level: Campbell is Winner Over Westbrook, 6 to 1," *The Clarion-Ledger,* 4 November 1959, 1.

32 *Mississippi Republican Newsletter: Devoted to a Two-Party System*, Vol. 2. No. 11, November 1959.

Chapter 7
1960: Nixon and Goldwater Storm Mississippi

1 James Saggus, "Coleman Urges Care In Racial Problems," *The Clarion-Ledger*, 7 January 1960, 1.

2 "Text of Inaugural Address By Barnett," *The Clarion-Ledger*, 20 January 1960, 3.

3 "Mississippi GOP to D.C.," *The Mississippi Republican News*, Vol. 3, No. 2, February 1960, 3.

4 "Nixon Leads Kennedy In South," *The Mississippi Republican News,* Vol. 3, No. 2, February 1960, 3.

5 "Ross Speaks In S.C.; Asks for Demos Unity," *The Clarion-Ledger*, 30 January 1960, 1.

6 John Herbers, "Sovereignty Group May Get New Life," *The Clarion-Ledger*, 6 March 1960, 10.

7 Charles M. Hills, *The Clarion-Ledger*, 25 May 1960, 1.

8 "Barnett Urges South To Launch Offensive," *The Clarion-Ledger*, 8 March 1960, 5.

9 "GOP State Chairman To Orleans," *The Clarion-Ledger*, 18 March 1960, 4.

10 "1960 Goals Set High for State GOP," *The Mississippi Republican News,* Vol. 3, No. 2, February 1960, 1.

11 "Goldwater to Keynote State Convention," *The Mississippi Republican News,* Vol. 3, No. 4, April 1960, 1.

12 "'Goldwater for President,' Say South Carolinians," *The Mississippi Republican News,* Vol. 3, No. 4, April 1960, 4.

13 "Warren County," *The Mississippi Republican News,* Vol. 3, No. 4, April 1960, 2.

14 "Congressional Races Get GOP Candidates," *The Clarion-Ledger*, 8 April 1960, 1.

15 "Meet Your GOP Candidates," *The Mississippi Republican News*, Vol. 3, No. 5, May 1960, 3.

16 "Attend Your May 14 Precinct Meets," *The Mississippi Republican News,* Vol. 3, No. 5, May 1960, 1.

17 "Westbrook To Head Hinds Republicans," *The Clarion-Ledger*, 15 May 1960, 2-A.

18 "Attend Your May 14 Precinct Meets," *The Mississippi Republican News,* Vol. 3, No. 5, May 1960, 1.

19 "Nixon-Goldwater Pledged Support," The Mississippi Republican News, Vol. 3, No. 6, July 1960, 2.

20 "Nixon-Goldwater Pledged Support," 2.

21 "Nixon-Goldwater Pledged Support," 2.

22 "Nixon-Goldwater Pledged Support," 2.

23 "Nixon-Goldwater Pledged Support," 2.

24 "Code words of county fair platitudes? Reagan Speech Autopsy," in *The Clarion-Ledger,* 25 November 2007, 1-G.

25 "Code words of county fair platitudes? Reagan Speech Autopsy," 1-G.

26 Barry Goldwater, *The Conscience of a Conservative* (Shepherdsville, Kentucky: Victor Publishing Company, Inc., 1960) 37.

27 John Herbers, "Republican Laying Foundation in State," *The Clarion-Ledger,* 12 June 1960, 10.

28 Herbers, 10.

29 "Mississippi Republican Party Platform," *The Mississippi Republican News,* Vol. 3, No. 7, July 1960, 1.

30 "Quotes On The Convention," *The Mississippi Republican News*, Vol. 3, No. 7, July 1960, 3.

31 "The Positive Approach Of A Mississippi Republican," *The Mississippi Republican News*, Vol. 3, No. 8, August 1960, 2.

32 "GOP Predicted To Win State: Who Knows How The Democrats Stand?" *The Mississippi Republican News,* Vol. 3, No. 7, July 1960, 1.

33 "GOP Predicted To Win State: Who Knows How The Democrats Stand?", 1.

34 "Whoa, Donkey! Make Up Your Mind!" *The Mississippi Republican News*, Vol. 3, No. 6, June 1960, 3.

35 Gene Wirth, "Jack Wins On First; State for Barnett," *The Clarion-Ledger*, 14 July 1960, 1.

36 Gene Wirth, "Southern States' Rights Revolt Is Taking Shape: Protest Will Be More Than Talk, Ross Says," *The Clarion-Ledger*, 17 July 1960, 1.

37 "The Dawning Of A New Era," *The Mississippi Republican News*, Vol. 3, No. 8, August 1960, 3.

38 Gene Wirth, "Thurmond May Head New Southern Revolt," *The Clarion-Ledger*, 18 July 1960, 1.

39 "GOP Calls Splinter Move Waste of Time," *The Clarion-Ledger*, 20 July 1960, 5.

40 "Mississippi Republicans Hear Rocky, Goldwater," *The Clarion-Ledger*, 20 July 1960, 2.

41 "Douglas Cornell, "Rocky-Nixon Platform Pact Rocks Dixie GOP: Agreement Gives Party Shove to Liberal Side," *The Clarion-Ledger*, 24 July 1960, 1.

42 Purser Hewitt, "Platform Battles Loom As GOP Opens Meeting: State Delegation Eyes Support For Goldwater," *The Clarion-Ledger,* 25 July 1960, 1.

43 Purser Hewitt, "Nixon Takes Command Of Right For Tough CR: State GOP Group Told Can Support Goldwater," *The Clarion-Ledger*, 26 July 1960, 1.

44 Purser Hewitt, "Republican Banner Is handed to Nixon: State Group Joins Show For Goldwater," *The Clarion-Ledger,* 28 July 1960, 1, 4.

45 "GOP Backs Individual Initiative; Democrat Party Deserts Its Members, Nixon Says," *The Mississippi Republican News,* Vol. 3, Nos. 9 & 10, September-October 1960.

46 Charles M. Hills, "Yerger Is Encouraged By Support For GOP In State," *The Clarion-Ledger*, 31 July 1960, 1.

47 "Republican Goal Of 2-Party State Will Be Exceeded Now," *The Clarion-Ledger*, 1 August 1960, 6-A.

48 Charles M. Hills, "Put Principle Ahead of Expediency—Williams," *The Clarion-Ledger*, 11 August 1960, 1.

49 Hills, "Put Principle Ahead of Expediency—Williams," 1.

50 Hills, "Put Principle Ahead of Expediency—Williams," 1.

51 Hills, "Put Principle Ahead of Expediency—Williams," 1.

52 "MRP Offers the Ostrich As—Symbol of Independent Electors: What Would Be Accomplished?" *The Mississippi Republican News,* Vol. 3, No. 8, August 1960, 1.

53 Bob Pittman, "Southern GOP Chiefs Here To Map Strategy," *The Clarion-Ledger/Jackson Daily News*, 28 August 1960, 2-A.

54 Jerry DeLaughter, "Nixon Slates Speech In Jackson September 7," *The Clarion-Ledger*, 29 August 1960, 1.

55 "We Choose Our Course: An Editorial," *The Clarion-Ledger*, 16 September 1960, 1.

56 "The Dawning Of A New Era," 3.

57 "The Dawning Of A New Era," 3.

58 "Louisiana and Wirt Yerger," *The Jackson Daily News,* 22 August 1960, 8.

59 Robert Webb, "GOP Nets $60,000 As 600 Buy Tickets," *State Times,* 30 September 1960, 1.

60 Webb, 1.

61 Webb, 1.

62 Wikipedia, March 22, 2008, http://en.wikipedia.org/wiki/James_Eastland.

63 " 'How Can Mississippi Senators Support Kennedy?'—Moore," *The Mississippi Republican News,* Vol. 3, No. 9 & 10, September-October 1960.

64 "Let Our Voice Be Heard," *The Clarion-Ledger*, 14 October 1960, 1.

65 "Supreme Effort By U.S. Requested By Kennedy: Senator Wins Popular Vote By Thin Edge," *The Clarion-Ledger,* 10 November 1960, 1.

66 "The Mississippi Vote, *The Clarion-Ledger,* 10 November 1960, 1.

67 *The Clarion-Ledger*, 9 November 1960, 8.

Chapter 8
1961: "Two-Party Air Blitz" Yields Our First Win

1 "Kennedy Program Boosts Welfare State," *The Mississippi Republican News,* Vol. 4, No. 1, February-March 1961, 1.

2 "Kennedy Program Boosts Welfare State," 1.

3 "Kennedy Orders Boost In U.S. Military Power: Asks Russians To Join In Science, Space Push," *The Clarion-Ledger,* 31 January 1961, 1.

4 "Kennedy Program Boosts Welfare State," 1.

5 "Kennedy Program Boosts Welfare State," 1.

6 "Kennedy Program Boosts Welfare State," 1.

7 "Big Stories of 1960: Political News Tops Listing In Old Year," *The Clarion-Ledger/Jackson Daily News,* 1 January 1961, 1.

8 "Big Stories of 1960: Political News Tops Listing In Old Year," 1.

9 "Yerger Gets Service Award a Second Time," *The Mississippi Republican News,* Vol. 4, No. 1, February-March 1961, 2.

10 "Fair Question: What Are State GOP Activities?" *The Mississippi Republican News,* Vol. 5, No. 5, November-December 1961, 3-4.

11 "Minutes Meeting Mississippi Republican Party State Executive Committee, January 12, 1961;" Special Collections, Mitchell Memorial Library, Mississippi State University.

12 "Minutes Meeting Mississippi Republican Party State Executive Committee, January 12, 1961;" Special Collections, Mitchell Memorial Library, Mississippi State University.

13 "Fair Question: What Are State GOP Activities?" *The Mississippi Republican News,* Vol. 5, No. 5, November-December 1961, 3-4.

14 As told to Wirt A. Yerger, Jr., by Robert E. Enlow.

15 As told to Wirt A. Yerger, Jr., by Robert E. Enlow.

16 "Klumb Named Chairman of State Finance," *The Mississippi Republican News,* Vol. 4, No. 1, February-March 1961, 1.

17 "Plan Governor Race: GOP Names State Executive Director," *The Clarion-Ledger,* 23 April 1961, 6-A.

18 "County Executive Committee," Mississippi Republican Party papers, Mitchell Memorial Library Special Collections, Mississippi State University.

19 "Republicans Announce For Meridian Offices," *The Clarion-Ledger,* 7 April 1961, 3.

20 "Seven GOP Candidates Speed Two-Party Era," *The Mississippi Republican News,* Vol. 4, No. 2, April-May 1961, 1.

21 Press Release by John D. Gautier, May 13, 1961, from the Mississippi Republican Party papers, Mitchell Memorial Library Special Collections, Mississippi State University.

22 Press Release by John D. Gautier, May 13, 1961, from the Mississippi Republican Party papers, Mitchell Memorial Library Special Collections, Mississippi State University.

23 "Remember When?" *The Mississippi Republican News,* Vol. 4, No. 2, April-May 1961, 3.

24 Mississippi Republican Party Press Release, May 17, 1961, from the Mississippi Republican Party papers, Mitchell Memorial Library Special Collections, Mississippi State University.

25 "Capitolization: Vote All Over State," *The Clarion-Ledger/Jackson Daily News,* 7 May 1961, 15-A.

26 "A Strong Two-Party Government Assures Aggressive Leadership," *The Mississippi Republican News,* Vol. 5, No. 3, June-July 1961, 3.

27 "Republicans Lose in 3 State Cities," *The Clarion-Ledger,/Jackson Daily News,* 7 June 1961, 1.

28 Barry Goldwater, "Barry Goldwater Warns: Philosophy of Superstate Threatens Human Liberties," *The Clarion-Ledger/Jackson Daily News,* 9 March 1961, 3.

29 Barry Goldwater, "Barry Goldwater Warns: Philosophy of Superstate Threatens Human Liberties," *The Clarion-Ledger/Jackson Daily News,* 9 March 1961, 3.

30 "Democrat Aim: Total Control of Medical Care," *The Mississippi Republican News,* Vol. 4, No. 2, April-May 1961, 4.

31 "Kennedy Club of Mississippi Remains Silent: Why? Yerger Asks," *The Mississippi Republican News,* Vol. 5, No. 3, June-July 1961, 1.

32 Cliff Sessions, "United Press International, "GOP Is Happy Adam Worries: Republicans See Gains In Recognition By Foe," *The Clarion-Ledger/Jackson Daily News,* 21 May 1961, 3-A.

33 Sessions, 3-A.

34 Charles M. Hills, "Affairs Of State: Adam Hits GOP Push *The Clarion-Ledger,* 21 May 1961.

35 Hills, 21 May 1961.

36 Sessions, 3-A.

37 "GOP Ovations Given Barry, John, and Ike," *The Mississippi Republican News,* Vol. 5, No. 3, June-July 1961, 2.

38 "Alternate Route Sought, Southern Vote Shows," *The Mississippi Republican News,* Vol. 5, No. 3, June-July 1961, 4.

39 Letter from Robert E. Enlow to Clarke Reed, July 1, 1961, from the Mississippi Republican Party papers, Mitchell Memorial Library Special Collections, Mississippi State University.

40 "Frontier Budget Increased Daily by $49,000,000 Through August 15," *The Mississippi Republican News,* Vol. 5, No. 4, August-September 1961, 1.

41 "GOP On The Move In Southland: National Chairman Tells Of Progress, Defines Activities," *The Mississippi Republican News,* Vol. 5, No. 4, August-September 1961, 1.

42 "Diplomats Report Nikita Will Give JFK Breather," *The Clarion-Ledger,* 16 January 1961, 1.

43 "No Rest Until World Is Red: Khrushchev Tells Soviets They're Overtaking U.S.," *The Clarion-Ledger,* 22 March 1961, 1.

44 "Nuclear Test Renewal Ordered By President: Will Curtail Fallout; Third Blast By Reds, 1

45 "Nikita Warns West Pushing Near To War: Calls for Negotiations; Threatens Mobilization," *The Clarion-Ledger/Jackson Daily News,* 8 August 1961, 1.

46 "Angry Berliners Clash With Communist Cops: Tanks, Troops Seal Off Refugee Escape Points," *The Clarion-Ledger/Jackson Daily News,* 14 August 1961, 1.

47 Charles M. Hills, "Face Slow Death Without One: Fallout Shelters Favored By Civil Defense Officials," *The Clarion-Ledger,* 6 October 1961, 1.

48 "President Warns Of Peril," *The Clarion-Ledger,* 13 October 1961, 1.

49 "Red H-Bomb Fallout due Over U.S. Soon," *The Clarion-Ledger,* 25 October 1961, 1.

50 "U.S. And Soviet Tanks Square Off; Guns Aimed: 6,500 U.S. Troops No Longer On Alert," *The Clarion-Ledger,* 28 October 1961, 1.

51 "Russia Explodes Two More A-Bombs," *The Clarion-Ledger,* 1 November 1961, 1.

52 "Another Atomic Device Is Exploded By Soviet," *The Clarion-Ledger,* 5 November 1961, 1.

53 "Red Party Is Indicted By U.S. Grand Jury," *The Clarion-Ledger,* 2 December 1961, 1.

54 United Press International, *The Clarion-Ledger,* 7 March 1961, 4.

55 Cliff Sessions, "Citizens Council Contributions Not Yet Deductible: Internal Revenue Department Has Not Put Group On List," *The Clarion-Ledger/Jackson Daily News,* 22 January 1991, 7-A.

56 Cliff Sessions, "It's Mississippi: Expect Fireworks in '61 In Most Segregated State," *The Clarion-Ledger/Jackson Daily News,* 1 January 1961, 2.

57 Gene Wirth, "NAACP Mobilizes For State Campaign," *The Clarion-Ledger,* 7 April 1961, 1.

58 "Negro President Possible Within 40 Years, Says RFK," *The Clarion-Ledger,* 27 May 1961, 1.

59 "To Avoid Trouble: More Education, Faulkner Advises," *The Clarion-Ledger/ Jackson Daily News,* 28 May 1961, 12-A.

60 Tommy Herrington, "Negro Brings suit To Enter Ole Miss," *The Clarion-Ledger,* 1 June 1961, 1.

61 "Troublemaker King Is Dangerous Leader: An Editorial," *The Clarion-Ledger,* 6 July 1961, 1.

62 Bob Pittman, "Mississippi Under Full Attack By Integrationists," *The Clarion-Ledger/Jackson Daily News,* 9 July 1961, 2-A.

63 Press Release: "Lumberman Criticizes Kennedy Administration's Action on Hiring Workers," May 8, 1961, from the Mississippi Republican Party papers, Mitchell Memorial Library Special Collections, Mississippi State University.

64 "The Gallup Poll: Public Fears Racial Status Will Worsen In The South," *The Clarion-Ledger/Jackson Daily News,* 26 June 1961, 4-A.

65 "Gallup Poll: Public Thinks 'Riders' Hurting Negro's Chances," *The Clarion-Ledger/Jackson Daily News,* 26 June 1961, 1.

66 Tommy Herrington, "Negro Loses In bid To Enter Ole Miss," *The Clarion-Ledger,* 13 December 1961, 1.

67 Caption, *The Mississippi Republican News,* Vol. 5, No. 5, November-December 1961, 3.

68 Caption, *The Mississippi Republican News,* Vol. 5, No. 5, November-December 1961, 3.

69 "Republican Post Goes To Yerger," *The Clarion-Ledger,* 18 November 1961, 1.

70 "Cheering 500 Hear National Chairman: Miller Speaks Our Strongly For States Rights—Against One Party Corruptness," *The Mississippi Republican News,* Vol. 6, No. 1, January-February 1962, 2.

71 "Republican Is Elected In Lowndes," *The Clarion-Ledger,* 6 December 1961, 1.

72 Edmund Noel," GOP Winner Says Party Lineup Was Indistinct," *The Clarion-Ledger,* 8 December 1961, 9.

73 "Warren A. Hood Named Chairman Of URF Dinner," *The Mississippi Republican News,* Vol. 5, No. 5, November-December 1961, 2.

Chapter 9
1962: "Southern Strategy" at a Minnesota Lodge, Goldwater Gala in Mississippi

1 "A Spirited Fighter: Yerger Named To Top Southern Post At Atlanta Meet," *The Mississippi Republican News,* Vol. 6, No. 1, January-February 1962, 2.

2 Letter from Charles Thone of Lincoln, Nebraska, to F. Clifton White, New York, New York, 19 April 1962 (Personal Papers of Wirt A. Yerger, Jr.).

3 "Barry M. Goldwater, "How Do You Stand, Sir?" *The Clarion-Ledger,* 23 January 1962, 5.

4 "Barry M. Goldwater, "How Do You Stand, Sir?" 5.

5 Letter from F. Clifton White to Wirt A. Yerger, Jr., 7 April 1962 (Personal Papers of Wirt A. Yerger, Jr.).

6 "Can A Conservative Republican Win?" attached to letter from F. Clifton White to Wirt A. Yerger, Jr., 7 April 1962 (Personal Papers of Wirt A. Yerger, Jr.).

7 Letter from Wirt A. Yerger, Jr., to William Miller, 19 July 1962 (Personal Papers of Wirt A. Yerger, Jr.)

8 Letter from William E. Miller to Wirt A. Yerger, Jr., 15 August 1962 (Personal Papers of Wirt A. Yerger, Jr.)

9 Letter from Wirt A. Yerger, Jr., to Barry Goldwater, 18 July 1962 (Personal Papers of Wirt A. Yerger, Jr.).

10 Letter from Wirt A. Yerger, Jr., to Barry Goldwater, 18 July 1962 (Personal Papers of Wirt A. Yerger, Jr.),

11 "The New Breed," *Time* magazine, 13 July 1962, 12.

12 "The New Breed," 12.

13 "The New Breed," 12.

14 "The New Breed," 12.

15 "Attend 'Tower Workshop' on August 4: Senator John Tower To Highlight Day-Long Workshop-Dinner," *The Mississippi Republican News,* Vol. 6, No. 4, July-August 1962, 1, 3.

16 Letter from John G. Tower to Wirt A. Yerger, Jr., 15 August 1962 (Personal Papers of Wirt A. Yerger, Jr.).

17 Letter from Wirt A. Yerger, Jr., to F. Clifton White, 7 August 1962 (Personal Papers of Wirt A. Yerger, Jr.).

18 Letter from Tad Smith, State Chairman, Republican Party of Texas, to Wirt A. Yerger, Jr., 14 August 1962 (Personal Papers of Wirt A. Yerger, Jr.).

19 Letter from Wirt A. Yerger, Jr., to Barry Goldwater, 17 September 1962 (Personal Papers of Wirt A. Yerger, Jr.).

20 Letter from F. Clifton White to Wirt A. Yerger, Jr., 21 August 1962 (Personal Papers of Wirt A. Yerger, Jr.).

21 Letter from I. Lee Potter to Wirt A. Yerger, Jr., 14 August 1962 (Personal Papers of Wirt A. Yerger, Jr.).

22 Letter from Wirt A. Yerger, Jr., to the Honorable William Miller, 2 November 1962 (Personal Papers of Wirt A. Yerger, Jr.).

23 Letter from Wirt A. Yerger, Jr., to William E. Miller, 20 December 1962 (Personal Papers of Wirt A. Yerger, Jr.).

24 "Convict's Story Dips Into State Politics," *The Clarion-Ledger*, 6 January 1962, 1.

25 James Saggus, "Gov. Barnett Questions Report On Penitentiary: Investigation Conclusion Branded Misleading," *The Clarion-Ledger*, 31 March 1962, 1.

26 "Fraud Seen In Release Of Berry," *The Clarion-Ledger*, 4 April 1962, 1, 14.

27 "Jones Says Paroles Offered For Payoffs," *The Clarion-Ledger*, 28 April 1962, 1.

28 "Barnett Criticized For Latest Vetoes," *The Clarion-Ledger*, 2 June 1962, 1.

29 "Civics Classes Use GOP News Release On 'Smoke Signals'," *The Mississippi Republican News*, Vol. 6, No. 2, March-April 1962, 4.

30 "Law Demands It, But Sheriffs Fail To Report Incomes," *The Mississippi Republican News,* Vol. 6, No. 2, March-April 1962, 1, 2.

31 Gene Wirth, "State Senate Okays Probe of Kickbacks," *The Clarion-Ledger*, 5 January 1962, 1.

32 "Why Permit Payoffs, Graft, Kickbacks, To Blacken Mississippi's Good Name? An Editorial," *The Mississippi Republican News,* Vol. 6, No. 3, May-June 1963, 2.

33 "Law Demands It, But Sheriffs Fail To Report Incomes," *The Mississippi Republican News,* Vol. 6, No. 2, March-April 1962, 1, 2.

34 "Law Enforcement Fails In County Kickback Graft," *The Mississippi Republican News,* Vol. 6, No. 1, January-February 1962, 4.

35 "Political Dynamite Brewing," *The Clarion-Ledger*, 29 January 1962, 1.

36 "President Proposes Tough Farm Policy," *The Clarion-Ledger*. 1 February 1962, 1, 5.

37 "JFK's Tractor Driver Deal Backfires In Smith's Face," *The Mississippi Republican News*, Vol. 6, No. 1, January-February , 1962, 3.

38 "State Farm Bureau Backs Same Plan As GOP House Members," *The Mississippi Republican News,* Vol. 6, No. 2, March-April 1962, 3.

39 "President Presents Public Welfare Plan," *The Clarion-Ledger*, 2 February 1962, 1.

40 "Hard-Hitting Speech: Eisenhower Says Kennedy Is Floundering Aimlessly," *The Clarion-Ledger*, 23 June 1962, 1.

41 "New Frontier Is Lambasted," *The Clarion-Ledger*, 1 July 1962, 1.

42 "The Gallup Poll: Increase In View JFK Will Veer Left," *The Clarion-Ledger*, 24 June 1962, 4-A.

43 "Disarmament Moves Urged By President;" "Ted Kennedy Will Seek Brother's Seat," *The Clarion-Ledger*, 15 March 1962, 1.

44 "JFK Strongly Supports Home, Church Prayers: Urges All Americans to Back Court Decisions," *The Clarion-Ledger,* 28 June 1962, 1.

45 "Kennedy Says Talks On Berlin To Go On," *The Clarion-Ledger*, 10 May 1962, 1.

46 "Laotian Reds Push Offense," *The Clarion-Ledger*, 9 May 1962, 1.

47 "Kennedy Summons Congress Leaders: Landing of Marines In Thailand Expected," *The Clarion-Ledger*, 15 May 1962, 1.

48 "Combat-Ready Marines Go Ashore In Thailand: Americans To Back Up Pledge To Aid Nation," *The Clarion-Ledger*, 17 May 1962, 1.

49 James Saggus, "NAACP Plans To Fight Mixing Battle In Court: White School Enrollment Won't Be Sought Now," *The Clarion-LedgerR*, 1 September 1962, 1.

50 "Little JFK Support In State, Ross Says," *The Clarion-Ledger*, 7 September 1962, 1.

51 "Governor Vows Negro Won't Enter Ole Miss," *The Clarion-Ledger*, 11 September 1962, 1.

52 "Gov. Barnett, Officials, Discuss Meredith Case: Report College Board Will Block Admission," *The Clarion-Ledger*, 12 September 1962, 1.

53 "Gov. Barnett, Officials, Discuss Meredith Case: Report College Board Will Block Admission," 1.

54 "Gov. Barnett, Officials, Discuss Meredith Case: Report College Board Will Block Admission," 1.

55 Gene Wirth, "Gov. Barnett Interposes Self Against Federals: Calls on Officials To 'Stand or Quit'," *The Clarion-Ledger*, 14 September 1962, 1.

56 "All But Smith Support Ross," *The Clarion-Ledger*, 15 September 1962, 1.

57 "J.P. Coleman Backs Barnett;" "On Ole Miss: Senate Asks Board To Support Barnett," *The Clarion-Ledger*, 19 September 1962, 1.

58 "Supervisors Back Barnett," *The Clarion-Ledger*, 20 September 1962, 12.

59 Charles M. Hills, "Board of Trustees Spilt On Meredith: Minority Unwilling to Go All The Way," *The Clarion-Ledger*, 16 September 1962, 1.

60 Hills, 18-A.

61 Edmund Noel, "Governor Barnett Rejects Meredith: Keeps His Word to State Citizens," *The Clarion-Ledger*, 21 September 1962, 1.

62 Noel, 12.

63 Letter from Bidwell Adam to Wirt A. Yerger, Jr., 21 September 1962 (Personal Papers of Wirt A. Yerger, Jr.).

64 Letter from Wirt A. Yerger, Jr., to Bidwell Adam, 24 September 1962. (Personal Papers of Wirt A. Yerger, Jr.).

65 "NAACP Asks JFK To Arrest Barnett," *The Clarion-Ledger*, 24 September 1962, 1.

66 Charles M. Hills, "Ross Halts Negro For Second Time: And Stands Ready to Halt 3rd Time" *The Clarion-Ledger*, 26 September 1962, 1.

67 "Democratic Chairman Is Quitting With Protests," *The Clarion-Ledger*, 28 September 1962, 3-B.

68 Edmund Noel, "600 U.S. Marshals Group At Memphis: U.S. Changes Mind On Fourth Attempt" ; "May Use Troops: Bobby Vows Integration," *The Clarion-Ledger*, 28 September 1962, 1.

69 Noel, 1.

70 Noel, 1.

71 "At Oxford: Gun Battle 'Possible'," *The Clarion-Ledger*, 28 September 1962, 3.

72 "Gov. Barnett Convicted of U.S. Court Contempt: 3 Judges Vote," *The Clarion-Ledger,* 29 September 1962, 1.

73 "JFK Takes Over Guard As Army Enters Crisis: Schedules Video Address To U.S.," *The Clarion-Ledger/Jackson Daily News*, 30 September 1962, 1.

74 "Fall Day Is Lovely In Oxford," *The Clarion-Ledger/Jackson Daily News*, 30 September 1962, 1.

75 "In The Chancellor's Box," *The Clarion-Ledger/Jackson Daily News*, 30 September 1962, 6.

76 "Negro At Ole Miss; Campus in Uproar: Two Killed During Outburst of Rioting;" "Governor Releases Statement on Case," *The Clarion-Ledger*, 1 October 1962, 1.

77 "Negro At Ole Miss; Campus in Uproar: Two Killed During Outburst of Rioting;" "Governor Releases Statement on Case," *The Clarion-Ledger*, 1 October 1962, 1.

78 "Say Violence Is Regrettable," *The Clarion-Ledger*, 3 October 1962, 1.

79 Letter from Wirt A. Yerger, Jr., to Owens Alexander, 29 September 1962 (Personal Papers of Wirt A. Yerger, Jr.).

80 Letter from Wirt A. Yerger, Jr., to the Honorable Barry Goldwater, 2 October 1962 (Personal Papers of Wirt A. Yerger, Jr.).

81 Letter from James F. Hooper to Wirt A. Yerger, Jr., 13 October 1962 (Personal Papers of Wirt A. Yerger, Jr.).

82 Bill Simmons, Untitled Essay, c. 10 October 1962 (Personal Papers of Wirt A. Yerger, Jr.).

83 Bill Simmons, Untitled Essay.

84 "Goldwater Committees Named By State GOP," *The Clarion-Ledger*, 17 November 1962, 3.

85 Letter from Wirt A. Yerger, Jr., to Mr. H. L. Hunt, 3 November 1962.

86 Letter from C.C. Alexander to Wirt A. Yerger, Jr., 31 October 1962.

87 Press release from Wirt A. Yerger, Jr., November 1962.

88 Press release from Wirt A. Yerger, Jr., November 1962.

89 Letter from Wirt A. Yerger, Jr., to the Honorable Barry M. Goldwater, 21 November 1962.

90 As told to Wirt A. Yerger Jr., and Joe Maxwell by Robert E. Enlow.

91 Jerry DeLaughter, "Sen. Goldwater Invites State Into Republican Party's Fold," *The Clarion-Ledger*, 30 November 1962, 1.

92 DeLaughter, 1.

93 Letter from Wirt A. Yerger, Jr., to Barry Goldwater, 4 December 1962.

Chapter 10
1963: Outlawing Our GOP?

1 "Phillips' Words Used To Label Him A Moderate," *The Clarion-Ledger*, 15 October 1963, 3.

2 Jerry DeLaughter, "Tops In Other Ways, Too: Jackson Among Four 'Best Educated' Cities in U.S.," *The Clarion-Ledger*, 20 January 1963, F-1.

3 Letter from William T. Wilkins to Wirt A. Yerger, Jr., 7 May 2008 (Personal Papers of Wirt A. Yerger, Jr.).

4 Wilkins letter.

5 "The Gallup Poll: Rocky No. 1, Goldie Next Among GOP's," *The Clarion-Ledger*, 15 February 1963, 8.

6 "Paul Harvey News: GOP May Be Making 'Same Old Mistake," *The Clarion-Ledger*, 20 February 1963, 5.

7 "Meredith To Return; Publicity Restricted," *The Clarion-Ledger*, 31 January 1963, 1.

8 "Before Destroying School: Phillips Says He Would Enroll Negro In College," *The Clarion-Ledger*, 31 January 1963, 3.

9 Bill Simpson, "State Gubernatorial Candidates Speak," *The Clarion-Ledger*, 1 February 1963, 1, 14.

10 Charles M. Hills, "Before Harvard Audience: Barnett Sidesteps Pickets To Discuss States' Rights," *The Clarion-Ledger*, 5 February 1963, 1.

11 "GOP Split Proves Our State Should Defeat Current Drive," *The Clarion-Ledger*, 21 October 1963, 6.

12 Voters' Attitudes in Mississippi: Confidential Report of a Sample Survey Conducted February 1963, Louis and Bowles Research Consultants, Dallas, Texas (Private Papers of William T. Wilkins).

13 Voters' Attitudes in Mississippi: Confidential Report of a Sample Survey Conducted February 1963, Louis and Bowles Research Consultants, Dallas, Texas (Private Papers of William T. Wilkins).

14 Voters' Attitudes in Mississippi: Confidential Report of a Sample Survey Conducted February 1963, Louis and Bowles Research Consultants, Dallas, Texas (Private Papers of William T. Wilkins).

15 Voters' Attitudes in Mississippi: Confidential Report of a Sample Survey Conducted February 1963, Louis and Bowles Research Consultants, Dallas, Texas (Private Papers of William T. Wilkins).

16 Voters' Attitudes in Mississippi: Confidential Report of a Sample Survey Conducted February 1963, Louis and Bowles Research Consultants, Dallas, Texas (Private Papers of William T. Wilkins).

17 "Citizens' Council Raps Activity of Moderates," *The Clarion-Ledger*, 25 January 1963, 1.

18 Bill Simpson, "With Rockefeller As Leader: State GOP Faces Hard Task Trying to Construct Party," *The Clarion-Ledger*, 28 March 1963, 12.

19 "North and South: RFK Sees 10 Years of U.S. Race Strife," *The Clarion-Ledger*, 22 April 963, 1.

20 Letter from Wirt A. Yerger, Jr., to Ab Hermann, 17 September 1963 (Personal Papers of Wirt A. Yerger, Jr.).

21 Charles M. Hills, "Gov. Barnett Opposes State Playing In NCAA: Feels Mixed Tourney Not 'In Best Interests'," *The Clarion-Ledger*, 7 March 1963, 1.

22 Letter from Harry L. Marsalis to Rubel Phillips, 27 February 1963 (Personal Papers of Wirt A. Yerger, Jr.).

23 Letter from William L. Spicer to Wirt A. Yerger, Jr., 10 March 1963 (Personal Papers of Wirt A. Yerger, Jr.).

24 Letter entitled, "Important & Confidential: Southern GOP Conference," from Wirt A. Yerger, Jr., to Southern State Chairmen, 1963 (Personal Papers of Wirt A. Yerger, Jr.).

25 Letter entitled, "Important & Confidential: Southern GOP Conference," from Wirt A. Yerger, Jr., to Southern State Chairmen, 1963 (Personal Papers of Wirt A. Yerger, Jr.).

26 Jerry DeLaughter, "State GOP Runs Morse for Lt. Gov.," *The Clarion-Ledger*, 28 March 1963, 1.

27 Letter from I. Lee Potter to Wirt A. Yerger, Jr., 1 February 1963 (Personal Papers of Wirt A. Yerger, Jr.).

28 "Republican Is Winner In Meridian: Mack McAllister Runs Ahead of Demo Opposition," *The Clarion-Ledger*, 20 February 1963, 1.

29 "Republican Is Winner In Meridian: Mack McAllister Runs Ahead of Demo Opponents," 1.

30 "Republican Is Winner In Meridian: Mack McAllister Runs Ahead of Demo Opponents," 1.

31 Bill Simpson, "Barnett Urges electors Plan To Baffle Parties: Would Solidify State's Democrats, Harass GOP," *The Clarion-Ledger*, 1 March 1963, 1.

32 Bill Simpson, 1.

33 Bill Simpson, "GOP Crying 'Foul' Over Elector Plan," *The Clarion-Ledger*, 6 March 1963, 3.

34 "Lt. Gov. Johnson Asking Promotion to Governor," *The Clarion-Ledger*, 18 April 1963, 1, 14.

35 Letter from Earl Cuevas to Wirt A. Yerger, Jr., 19 March 1964 (Personal Papers of Wirt A. Yerger, Jr.).

36 Letter from M. W. Swartz to Wirt A. Yerger, Jr., 8 February 1963 (Personal Papers of Wirt A. Yerger, Jr.).

37 Letter from Wirt A. Yerger, Jr., to M. W. Swartz, 25 February 1963 (Personal Papers of Wirt A. Yerger, Jr.).

38 "Yerger Says Loyalty Oath Un-American," *The Clarion-Ledger*, 25 April 1963, 6.

39 "Phillips Says Demo Loyalty Pledge Is Insult To Voters," *The Clarion-Ledger*, 8 May 1963, 3.

40 Raymond Moley, "The GOP in Mississippi," *Newsweek,* 13 May 1963, 112. More of the *Newsweek* article follows:

An advantage possessed by the Republicans is the absence of party registration in Mississippi. This enables conservative Democrats to support Republican candidates without too much soul-searching.

Republican strategy in 1963 is to concentrate on the governorship and to win as many seats in the legislature as possible. Perhaps later, county and local Republican candidates will be in the field.

The state committee is placing great emphasis upon effective precinct work. Yerger's aim is to have a statewide organization with every precinct staffed with workers.

The Democratic Party in the state is genuinely alarmed. The State Democratic Executive Committee is seeking to exact a loyalty oath from all candidates to support all other candidates. Two Democratic candidates for the nomination for governor have made this pledge. But the third, so far, refused.

One portent of what may come has been the election of a Republican to the legislature in the by-election in Meridian. The man elected is the former head of the state Young Republican organization. Everywhere here in Mississippi, as well as over the South, accent is on youth. I hear constantly from these party workers that it is about time to end the long captivity in the Democratic Party. Women, too, are finding that political loyalty should mean something far more than the memory of what the Republican Party inflicted upon the South in the Reconstruction years.

As we drove over from Louisiana we passed through the beautiful battleground at Vicksburg. That battle began exactly a century ago this month and ended on July 4. It is a cherished memory of brave men there. But it is only a memory now for another generation. Those young people who are fighting for a two-party system in the South have work to do in their time.

41 "Renewed Race Turmoil Hits South's Steel City: Snarling Police Dogs Chase Mobs of Negroes," *The Clarion-Ledger*, 4 May 1963, 1.

42 "Negro Area Isolated After Night Rioting," *The Clarion-Ledger*, 13 May 1963, 1.

43 "Wallace Gives In To Federal Might: 2 Negroes Register As Alabama Students," *The Clarion-Ledger*, 12 June 1963, 1.

44 Bill Simpson, "Negro Leaders Refuse To Talk Over Demands: Reject Mayor's Please, Quit Racial Meeting," and, "To Negro Leaders: Full Text of Speech," *The Clarion-Ledger*, 28 May 1963, 1.

45 Bill Simpson, "Negroes' Claim Refuted In Violence Wake Here: Lunch Counter Shut in Walgreen Store," *The Clarion-Ledger*, 29 May 1963, 1.

46 Bill Simpson, "19 Persons Are Jailed In City Demonstrations: 3 Negro Youths Held After Rock-Throwing Incidents," *The Clarion-Ledger*, 30 May 1963, 1.

47 "Agitators Seek Troops, Mayor Thompson Says: Operation At Columbus Is Rumored In Jackson," *The Clarion-Ledger*, May 31, 1963, 1. "On Race Issue: Bobby Sees North As Most Explosive," *The Clarion-Ledger*, 9 June 1963, 10-A.

48 "Suspect eyed In Evers Case: Reward of $22,350 Offered To Tipsters," *The Clarion-Ledger*, 13 June 1963, 1.

49 "Funeral March Finished In White-Led Agitation: Minority of Mourners At Evers Rites Jailed," *The Clarion-Ledger*, 16 June 1963, 1.

50 "FBI Nabs Greenwood Man In Evers Murder: Indicate Others May Be Implicated in Plot," *The Clarion-Ledger*, 22 June 1963, 1.

51 "Beckwith Is Indicted In Slaying of Evers," *The Clarion-Ledger*, 3 July 1963, 1.

52 "The Gallup Poll: Integration Now Pushed Too Fast," *The Clarion-Ledger*, 14 July 1963, 5-A.

53 "U.S. Army Leaving Quarters At Oxford," *The Clarion-Ledger*, 24 July 1963, 1.

54 "Dedicated Zealot: Martin Luther Admits Link Between SLC, Former Red," *The Clarion-Ledger*, 26 July 1963, 1.

55 "JFK Admits CR Stand Hurts Him Politically: But Says He Must Press On To Meet Obligations," *The Clarion-Ledger*, 2 August 1963, 1.

56 "Meredith Receives Degree At Ole Miss," *The Clarion-Ledger*, 19 August 1963, 1.

57 "March On Washington Is Staged By 200,000: Demonstrations Orderly, Group Disperses Quietly," *The Clarion-Ledger*, 29 August 1963, 1.

58 "Four Children Dead In Church Bombing: Two Others Slain In Birmingham Violence," *The Clarion-Ledger*, 16 September 1963, 1.

59 Charles M. Hills, "Affairs of State: Campaigns Warm Up," *The Clarion-Ledger*, 16 June 1963.

60 Jerry DeLaughter, "But No Promises: Candidates Pledge 'Try' For Teachers," *The Clarion-Ledger*, 18 June 1963, 3.

61 DeLaughter, 3.

62 Charles Hills, "Affairs of State: Getting On With Races," *The Clarion-Ledger/Jackson Daily News*, 12 May 1963, 3-F.

63 "Rubel Raps State's 'Big Government'," *The Clarion-Ledger*, 13 July 1963, 5.

64 "Time and Circumstance Point To Paul Johnson As Governor: An Editorial," *The Clarion-Ledger*, 5 July 1963, 1.

65 J. P. Coleman Full-Page Ad, *The Clarion-Ledger*, 14 August 1963, 14-A.

66 Jack Shearer, Jr., "Coleman Tells His Account of Oxford," *The Clarion-Ledger*, 23 August 1963, 1.

67 "Not Interested In 'Veep' Post: Goldwater Against Proposal for Split-Personality Ticket," *The Clarion-Ledger*, 5 March 1963, 1.

68 "Goldwater On Local TV Thursday PM," *The Clarion-Ledger*, 8 March 1962, 7-A.

69 "The Gallup Poll: Goldwater Gains Ground On Rockefeller With GOP Voters," *The Clarion-Ledger*, 9 March 1962, 7.

70 "Senator Won't Help: 'Draft Goldwater' Movement Opens," *The Clarion-Ledger*, 9 April 1963, 1.

71 Letter from Bidwell Adam to Wirt A. Yerger, Jr., 10 May 1963 (Personal Papers of Wirt A. Yerger, Jr.).

72 Letter from Wirt A. Yerger, Jr., to Bidwell Adam, 15 May 1963 (Personal Papers of Wirt A. Yerger, Jr.).

73 Memo of the Republican State Chairman's Conference, 20 June 1963 (Personal Papers of Wirt A. Yerger, Jr.).

74 "Liberals Bankrupt, Goldwater Declares," *The Clarion-Ledger*, 23 June 1963, 10.

75 "Old Fuddy-Duddies Take Over Young GOP," *Political Memo from COPE: Committee on Political Education,* AFL-CIO, No. 14–63, 15 July 1963, 3.

76 "Old Fuddy-Duddies Take Over Young GOP," 3.

77 "Goldwater Pace Scares Liberal Faction of GOP," *The Clarion-Ledger*, 1 July 1963, 2.

78 "Rocky Opens Attack On Goldwater Drive," *The Clarion-Ledger*, 16 July 1963, 1.

79 Paul Harvey, "Goldwater Boom In Grass Roots Growing," *The Clarion-Ledger*, 26 July 1963, 8.

80 George Gallup, "Goldwater Leading Rocky In Late Poll," *The Clarion-Ledger*, 14 August 1963, 5.

81 George Gallup, "Goldie Wins Easily Over Kennedy In Solid South," *The Clarion-Ledger*, 18 August 1963, 3-A.

82 "Demo Rallies Set In Every County," *The Clarion-Ledger*, 28 September 1963, 5.

83 Mississippi Republican Party State Executive Committee meeting, 8 June 1963 (Personal Papers of Wirt A. Yerger, Jr.).

84 Letter from Charles Klumb to Wirt A. Yerger, Jr., 7 August 1963 (Personal Papers of Wirt A. Yerger, Jr.).

85 Telegram from John E. Grenier to Wirt A. Yerger, Jr., 30 August 1963 (Personal Papers of Wirt A. Yerger, Jr.).

86 Letter from Mrs. Arthur Goodsell to Wirt A. Yerger, Jr., 20 August 1963 (Personal Papers of Wirt A. Yerger, Jr.).

87 "Oppose GOP Efforts: Supervisors Pledge Support To Johnson," *The Clarion-Ledger*, 10 September 1963, 1.

88 "United Democrat Party Urged For Mississippi: Destruction of Whites' Majority Much Feared," *The Clarion-Ledger*, 21 September 1963, 1, 10.

89 Letter from Rubel Phillips to Wirt A. Yerger, Jr., 27 February 1964 (Personal Papers of Wirt A. Yerger, Jr.).

90 Letter from Bill Wilkins to Wirt A. Yerger, Jr., February 1964 (Personal Papers of Wirt A. Yerger, Jr.).

91 Phillips letter, 27, February 1964.

92 Memo to Rubel Phillips, Stanford Morse, Dave Maddox, and Sam DuVall, from Wirt A. Yerger, Jr., 19 September 1963 (Personal Papers of Wirt A. Yerger, Jr.).

93 "State Demos Rally Force," *The Clarion-Ledger*, 4 September 1963, 1.

94 Memorandum from Wirt A. Yerger, Jr., to "Key Leadership," 7 October 1963 (Personal Papers of Wirt A. Yerger, Jr.).

95 Letter from Francis G. Davis to Wirt A. Yerger, Jr., 9 October 1963 (Personal Papers of Wirt A. Yerger, Jr.).

96 Notes taken by Mrs. Mitchell, contained in Letter from Lowry Tims to Wirt A. Yerger, Jr., 9 October 1963 (Personal Papers of Wirt A. Yerger, Jr.).

97 Letter from Janet B. Givens to Wirt A. Yerger, Jr., 9 October 1963 (Personal Papers of Wirt A. Yerger, Jr.).

98 Digest of Speech by Charley Jacobs, state rep. from Bolivar County, in "Summary of Democratic Election Rally, Washington County Courthouse," 8 October 1963 (Personal Papers of Wirt A. Yerger, Jr.).

99 "Rubel Charges Deal Was Made At University," *The Clarion-Ledger*, 8 October 1963, 10.

100 "Rubel Says Article Did Not Tell All," *The Clarion-Ledger*, 10 October 1963, 10.

101 "Rubel Claims Barry Would Keep Customs," *The Clarion-Ledger*, 12 October 1963.

102 "Barnett, Johnson Reply To Article In Magazine," *The Clarion-Ledger*, 10 October 1963, 11.

103 "GOP Win 'Threatens' Segregation," *The Clarion-Ledger*, 12 October 1963, 12-A.

104 "Rubel Raps Newspapers, Democrats," *The Clarion-Ledger*, 13 October 1963, 16-A.

105 "Johnson Lashes At Phillips In Speech At Natchez," *The Clarion-Ledger*, 24 October 1963, 4.

106 "Johnson Lashes At Phillips In Speech At Natchez," 4.

107 "Yerger Gives Pre-Vote Statement for Voters," *The Clarion-Ledger*, 3 November 1963, 11-A.

108 "Yerger Gives Pre-Vote Statement for Voters," 11-A.

109 Letter from William T. Wilkins to Wirt A. Yerger, Jr., 7 May 2008 (Personal Papers of Wirt A. Yerger, Jr.).

110 "Election Results Are Setback for 2-Party System Proposal," *The Clarion-Ledger*, 7 November 1963, 8-A.

111 "GOP's Yerger Hails Campaign As Successful," *Franklin Advocate,* Meadville, MS, 21 November 1983.

112 "GOP's Yerger Hails Campaign As Successful," 21 November 1983.

113 " 'Draft Goldwater' Drive Is Begun In Mississippi," *The Clarion-Ledger*, 11 September 1963, 3.

114 " 'Draft Goldwater' Drive Is Begun In Mississippi," 3.

115 "Slates Speeches In 10 States: Goldwater Going On Tour; May Decide Future Plans," *The Clarion-Ledger*, 2 September 1963, 1.

116 "Would He Like To Try? Goldy Thinks GOP Can Win If Clear Choice Is Offered," *The Clarion-Ledger*, 14 September 1963, 1.

117 Letter from Lew Heilbroner to Wirt A. Yerger, Jr., 13 September 1963 (Personal Papers of Wirt A. Yerger, Jr.).

118 "Would He Like To Try? Goldy Thinks GOP Can Win If Clear Choice Is Offered," 1.

119 "The Gallup Poll: Goldy Increases Lead Over Other Hopefuls," *The Clarion-Ledger*, 6 October 1963, 1.

120 "Hodding Says Barry Would Carry South," *The Clarion-Ledger*, 1 November 1963, 1.

121 "The Gallup Poll: JFK's Appeal To Women Voters Bests Goldwater's," *The Clarion-Ledger*, 17 November 1963, 4-A.

122 Paul Harvey, " 'Time for a Choice' in U.S. Campaigns," *The Clarion-Ledger*, 21 November 1963, 9.

123 "Governor Sets Mourning, Expresses Personal Grief," *The Clarion-Ledger*, 24 November 1963, 1.

124 Bob Howie, "For Guidance," *The Clarion-Ledger*, 24 November 1963, 2-F.

125 Letter from Richard H. Poff to Wirt A. Yerger, Jr., 10 December 1963 (Personal Papers of Wirt A. Yerger, Jr.).

126 Wirt A. Yerger, Jr., Press Release, 27 December 1963 (Personal Papers of Wirt A. Yerger, Jr.).

Chapter 11
1964: Jousting with Johnsons for Goldwater and Mississippi

1 Press Release, Mississippi Republican Party, 11 December 1963 (Personal Papers of Wirt A. Yerger, Jr.).

2 Stephen Shadegg, *What Happened to Goldwater: The Inside Story of the 1964 Republican Campaign,* Holt, Rinehart and Winston, 1965, 17.

3 Confidential Results of Survey of White Mississippi Voters, conducted September, 1964, (Special Collections, Mitchell Memorial Library, Mississippi State University).

4 Jerry Delaughter, "Michigan Governor Romney Says He's State's Righter: Tale of 2 Jacksons-North and South," *The Clarion-Ledger*, 21 February 1964, 1.

5 Wirt A. Yerger, Jr., Speech to the Mississippi Republican Convention, 30 May 1964 (Personal Papers of Wirt A. Yerger, Jr.).

6 Wirt A. Yerger, Jr., Speech to the Mississippi Republican Convention, 30 May 1964 (Personal Papers of Wirt A. Yerger, Jr.).

7 Letter from Newton I. Steers, Jr. to Wirt A. Yerger, Jr., The 1964 Presidential Election, c. January 1965 (Personal Papers of Wirt A. Yerger, Jr.).

8 "Think Goldy Will Enter 1964 Race," *The Clarion-Ledger,* 1 January 1964, 1.

9 Shadegg, 59.

10 Russell Kirk, "To the Point: Presidency Costs Money," *Fort Smith Times Record,* January 21, 1964, 4-A, quoted in letter from Bill Spicer to "Friends," 21 January 1964 (Personal Papers of Wirt A. Yerger, Jr.).

11 Kirk quote in Spicer, 4-A.

12 Shadegg, 58.

13 *Tulsa Daily World,* "The Hokum Merchants," January 20, 1964, 4.

14 "The Hokum Merchants," 4.

15 Shedegg, 54, 55, 64.

16 Shedegg, 65.

17 Jay D. Hartz, "The Impact of the Draft Goldwater Committee on the Republican Party," *Continuity: A Journal of History, Fall 2000,* 9 February 2010, http://www.ashbrook.org/articles/hartz-draftgoldwater.html.

18 Hartz.

19 Hartz.

20 "Goldwater Declares Himself Candidate For Nomination: Begins Fight Monday Night," *The Clarion-Ledger, 4* January 1964, 1.

21 Letter from William L. Spicer to Wirt A. Yerger, Jr., 26 December 1963 (Personal Papers of Wirt A. Yerger, Jr.).

22 Letter from Wirt A. Yerger, Jr., to Craig Truax, 24 February 1964 (Personal Papers of Wirt A. Yerger, Jr.).

23 Wirt A. Yerger, Press Release, 13 January 1964 (Personal Papers of Wirt A. Yerger, Jr.).

24 Wirt A. Yerger, Jr., Speech to the Mississippi State Legislature, Special Collections, Mitchell Memorial Library, Mississippi State University, 1964 files.

25 Wirt A. Yerger, Jr., Speech to the Mississippi State Legislature, Special Collections, Mitchell Memorial Library, Mississippi State University, 1964 files.

26 Charles M. Hills, "Shoe Fits 2 Parties," *The Clarion-Ledger*, 5 April 1964, 3-F.

27 Letter from Wirt A. Yerger, Jr., to Jack Reed, president of the Mississippi Economic Council, 11 April 1964 (Personal Papers of Wirt A. Yerger, Jr.).

28 Wirt A. Yerger, Jr., Press Release, 13 March 1964 (Personal Papers of Wirt A. Yerger, Jr.).

29 Wirt A. Yerger, Jr., Press Release, 13 March 1964 (Personal Papers of Wirt A. Yerger, Jr.).

30 "Adam Charges Yerger Has Dictatorial Power," *The Clarion-Ledger*, 15 March 1964, 11-A.

31 "Leaders Agree To Ask State Sales Tax Boost: Senate Unit For Change In Elections," *The Clarion-Ledger*, 18 March 1964, 1, 14.

32 Bill Simpson, "18 Voting Law Bills Approved By Senate," *The Clarion-Ledger*, 27 March 1964, 1, 16-A

33 Bill Simpson, "Vote Changes Go To House," *The Clarion-Ledger*, 26 March 1964, 1, 16.

34 "Vote Bills Lambasted By Yerger," *The Clarion-Ledger*, 29 March 1964, 6-A.

35 "Our Vote Laws Are Lambasted," *The Clarion-Ledger*, 22 April 1964, 2.

36 Charles M. Hills, "House Rejects Action On Election Changes," *The Clarion-Ledger*, 30 April 1964, 1.

37 "Election Bills Are Defeated," *The Clarion-Ledger*, 13 May 1964, 1.

38 Wirt A. Yerger, Jr., Speech to the Mississippi Republican Party Convention, 30 May 1964 (Personal Papers of Wirt A. Yerger, Jr.).

39 "Goldy Is Favorite of GOP Grass Roots," *The Clarion-Ledger*, 29 March 1964, 3-F.

40 "Barry, Connally Win Big In Texas," *The Clarion-Ledger*, 3 May 1964, 1.

41 Wirt A. Yerger, Jr., Press Release 4 July 1964 (Personal Papers of Wirt A. Yerger, Jr.).

42 "Goldy Shifts School Stand, Urges Mixing," *The Clarion-Ledger*, 25 May 1964, 1.

43 "Rocky Admits Barry Won; Still in Fight: Other Results Reported From Primary Elections," 4 June 1964, 1.

44 "Survey Shows Goldy Almost Has It Made," *The Clarion-Ledger*, 5 June 1964, 1.

45 "Block-Goldwater Move Fizzles At Conference: Governors' Meet Fails To Touch Off Backfire," *The Clarion-Ledger*, 9 June 1964, 1.

46 "Scranton Takes Aim At Barry Goldwater," *The Clarion-Ledger*, 13 June 1964, 1.

47 Letter from Dwight D. Eisenhower to Wirt A. Yerger, Jr., 2 March 1964 (Personal Papers of Wirt A. Yerger, Jr.).

48 I again wrote on September 25, 1964, to Dwight D. Eisenhower, appealing for him to work hard down the stretch for Barry. I wrote Ike asking for his "all-out support," adding, "It must make you sick to see so many people who claimed to be dedicated Republicans during the Eisenhower administration and who served on such high levels, going all out for Lyndon Johnson."

49 "Gov. Scranton Begins His Last-Ditch Battle: Politics of Goldwater Called 'Outlandish'," *The Clarion-Ledger*, 14 June 1964, 1.

50 "Wirt Yerger Speaks Out," 10 June 1964, 3, (Personal Papers of Wirt A. Yerger, Jr.).

51 "Lodge Backers Throw Scranton Full Support: Pennsylvania Governor Sure He Can Beat Barry," *The Clarion-Ledger*, 15 June 1964, 1.

52 "Rockefeller Quits Race; Will Support Scranton: Goldwater Heads West Seeking More Delegates," *The Clarion-Ledger*, 15 June 1964, 1.

53 "Rockefeller Quits Race; Will Support Scranton: Goldwater Heads West Seeking More Delegates," 1.

54 "Goldwater Still Wavers On How To Vote On CR," *The Clarion-Ledger*, 18 June 1964, 1.

55 "Scranton Hits Goldy Stand," *The Clarion-Ledger*, 19 June 1964, 1.

56 "Goldwater Reluctantly Planting CR Bill 'No': But Still Unalterably Opposes Discrimination," 19 June 1964, 1.

57 "LBJ Orders Dulles Into Hunt for Trio: To Meet Governor, Youths' Auto Found," *The Clarion-Ledger*, 24 June 1964, 1.

58 William Peart, "Growing Mississippi Group Believes Goldwater Can Win," *The Clarion-Ledger*, 5 July 1964, 3-F.

59 "Barry's Platform Aide Avoids CR Showdown: Spokesman Okays Plan To Cut Southern Solons," *The Clarion-Ledger*, 6 July 1964, 1.

60 "GOP Studies Plan on CR," *The Clarion-Ledger*, 8 July 1964, 1.

61 "Goldwater Arrives For Frisco Meeting," *The Clarion-Ledger*, 10 July 1964, 1.

62 "A Moderate Alternative: A Guest Editorial," *The Wall Street Journal* in *The Clarion-Ledger*, 22 July 1964, 9.

63 "Lead By Goldwater Thought Unbeatable," *The Clarion-Ledger*, 12 July 1964, 1.

64 William Peart, "State GOP Can Live With Expected Plank," *The Clarion-Ledger*, 12 July 1964, 13-A.

65 Bascom E. Timmons, "Those Eastern Kingmakers Are Losing Their Powers," *The Clarion-Ledger*, 14 July 1964, 3.

66 "State GOP Delegates Hail Scranton Defeat," *The Clarion-Ledger*, 13 July 1964, 6.

67 Drew Pearson, "Right-Wing Neanderthals' Push Barry Off On Unwitting Citizenry," *The Clarion-Ledger*, 15 July 1964, 10.

68 "833 To Goldwater Is Republican Vote: Scranton Withdraw After Tally Is Cast," *The Clarion-Ledger,* 16 July 1964, 1,

69 Arthur Edson, "Political Observers Agree Republican Era Has Ended," *The Clarion-Ledger*, 16 July 1964, 1.

70 Jay D. Hartz, "The Impact of the Draft Goldwater Committee on the Republican Party," *Continuity: A Journal of History, Fall, 2000,* 9 February 2010, http://www.ashbrook.org/articles/hartz-draftgoldwater.html.

71 Letter from William T. Wilkins to Joseph L. Maxwell, III and Wirt A. Yerger, Jr., 7 May 2008 (Personal Papers of Wirt A. Yerger, Jr.).

72 William L. Chaze, "Yerger Predicts Goldwater Victory: Manpower Needed," *The Clarion-Ledger*, 22 July 1964, 2.

73 Letter to F. Clifton White from Harry V. Jaffa, August 16, 1992, papers of F. Clifton White, Box 9, Ashland University Archives, quoted by Jay D. Hartz in "The Impact of the Draft Goldwater Committee on the Republican Party," *Continuity: A Journal of History, Fall, 2000,* 9 February 2010, http://www.ashbrook.org/articles/hartz-draftgoldwater.html.

74 "Goldwater Explains Use of 'Extremism'," *The Clarion-Ledger*, 10 August 1964, 1.

75 Jack Bell, "Barry Takes Firm Control," *The Clarion-Ledger*, 18 July 1964, 1.

76 Paul Harvey, "Extremist Label Can Be Misleading," *The Clarion-Ledger*, 17 September 1964, 10-A.

77 "A Moderate Alternative: A Guest Editorial," *The Wall Street Journal* in *The Clarion-Ledger,* 22 July 1964, 9.

78 Paul Harvey, "Will Goldwater Try To Fit Party Image?" *The Clarion-Ledger,* 18 June 1964, 14-A.

79 Drew Pearson, " 'White Protestant Country Club' Set Displaces Liberals in GOP," *The Clarion-Ledger,* 18 July 1964, 4.

80 "An Ugly Campaign," Editorial in *The Arizona Republic*, in *The Clarion-Ledger,* 17, September 1964, 10-A.

81 "An Ugly Campaign," 10-A.

82 "An Ugly Campaign," 10-A.

83 "Daisy," January 8, 2008, wikipedia, http://en.wikipedia.org/wiki/Daisy.

84 "Daisy."

85 "An Ugly Campaign," 10-A.

86 "Report of the Resolutions Committee of the 1964 Mississippi Republican Party State Convention," Special Collections, Mitchell Memorial Library, Mississippi State University.

87 "In Mississippi Today," in *The Dallas Morning News*, Guest Editorial in *The Clarion-Ledger,* 9 July 1964, 8-A.

88 "In Mississippi Today," 8-A.

89 Drew Pearson, "South Should Be Given Time To Adjust," *The Clarion-Ledger,* 10 July, 1964, 8-A.

90 "Rev. King May Ask Marshals," *The Clarion-Ledger,* 23 July 1964, 1.

91 "Violence, Disorder Deplored By LBJ: 'Too Much At Stake'," *The Clarion-Ledger,* 24, July 1964, 1.

92 "King Tells Pool Hall Crowd Trio Dead Now," and, "Charges Face Café Owners, Registrars," and, "Harlem Is Braced for 'Hot Weekend'," *The Clarion-Ledger,* 25 July 1964, 1.

93 Charles M. Hills, "May Ask State Democrats For Recessed Convention," *The Clarion-Ledger/Jackson Daily News,* 26 July 1964, 1,

94 "Rev. King Promises To Return," *The Clarion-Ledger/Jackson Daily News,* 26 July 1964, 6-A.

95 "Race Riots Become Small War In NY: Arrest Communist To Check Demonstration," *The Clarion-Ledger/Jackson Daily News,* 26 July 1964, 1.

96 "Rocky Says State To Help In Riots," *The Clarion-Ledger/Jackson Daily News,* 26 July 1964, 6-A.

97 Bernard Gavzer, "Harlem Afire Is Result of Decades of Racism," *The Clarion-Ledger/Jackson Daily News,* 26 July 1964, 3-C.

98 "New York's Responsibility: A Guest Editorial," *Richmond News-Leader* in *The Clarion-Ledger,* 29 July 1964, 10.

99 Charles M. Hills, " 'Freedom Party' Fails To Meet Requirements," *The Clarion-Ledger,* 24 July 1964, 10.

100 James Saggus, "State's Democrats Keep Silent Guard," *The Clarion-Ledger,* 30 July 1964, 7.

101 " 'Freedom Demo' Party Leaders Are Enjoined: State Fights Name Use; CR Suit Attacks 16 Laws," *The Clarion-Ledger,* 13 August 1964, 1.

102 "State Demo Delegates Refuse To Compromise: Decline to Share Seats With 'Freedom' Group," and, "Governor Won't Meet with LBJ," *The Clarion-Ledger,* 19 August 1964, 1.

103 William Theis and Purser Hewitt, "Alabama Delegation Rejects Loyalty Pledge for Seating: No Ruling On State but May Face Oath," *The Clarion-Ledger,* 24 August 1964, 1.

104 Purser Hewitt, "State Delegates Boycott Democratic Convention: Give Hotel Staff Tickets; No Decision on Seating," *The Clarion-Ledger,* 25 August 1964, 1.

105 Charles M. Hills, "Demo Rift Won't Heal," *The Clarion-Ledger,* 26 August 1964, 1.

106 William L. Chaze, "National Demos Rapped By Brady," *The Clarion-Ledger,* 27 August 1964, 4.

107 Letter from William T. Wilkins to Joseph L. Maxwell, III and Wirt A. Yerger, Jr., 7 May 2008 (Personal Papers of Wirt A. Yerger, Jr.).

108 "GOP, Demo Chairmen Air Views," *The Clarion-Ledger,* 27 August 1964, 1.

109 "GOP, Demo Chairmen Air Views," 1.

110 "Separate But United Goldwater Vote Urged: Sillers Asks Same Electors Be Used," *The Clarion-Ledger/Jackson Daily News,* 30 August 1964, 1.

111 "State Voters Wait Decision: No World On Special Session To Consider United Electors," *The Clarion-Ledger,* 1 September 1964, 1.

112 "Democrats-For-Goldwater Makes Sense In Forthcoming Election," *The Clarion-Ledger,* 1 September 1964, 6.

113 William Peart, "Mississippi Party Meets To Decide On Dems or GOP," *The Clarion-Ledger/Jackson Daily News,* 6 September 1964, 3-D.

114 "Yerger Urges 'Clean' Ballot," *The Clarion-Ledger,* 9 September 1964, 3.

115 George Gallup, "2-Party Support Is High In South," *The Clarion-Ledger,* 9 September 1964, 8.

116 Charles M. Hills, "Governor Predicts Barry Win in State," *The Clarion-Ledger,* 10 September 1964, 1.

117 William Peart, "Demo Party Could Finance Own Primaries Next Time," *The Clarion-Ledger,* 20 September 1964, 1.

118 George Gallup, "GOP Is Working At 'Grass Roots'," *The Clarion-Ledger,* 8 October 1964, 1-B.

119 "LBJ Has 65%; Barry Has 29%," *The Clarion-Ledger,* 16 September 1964, 2.

120 Letter from Wirt A. Yerger, Jr., to Dean Burch, 6 October 1964 (Personal Papers of Wirt A. Yerger, Jr.).

121 "LBJ Cabinet's Effort In Campaign Is Rapped: Goldwater In Texas; President Is Harsh," *The Clarion-Ledger,* 24 September 1964, 1.

122 "States' Power Gets Goldwater Backing," and, "Thurmond Goes Republican With Blast at Democrats," *The Clarion-Ledger,* 17 September 1964, 1.

123 Tom Ethridge, "Mississippi Notebook: It's Goldwater, By A Country Mile," *The Clarion-Ledger,* 22 September 1964, 6.

124 "Adam Blasts GOP Leader On Wallace," *The Clarion-Ledger,* 18 May 1964, 1.

125 Ed McCusker, "Chairmen Divided On 2-Party Role," *The Clarion-Ledger,* 22 September 1964, 6.

126 Letter from Charles W. Pickering to Wirt A. Yerger, Jr., 1 October 1964 (Personal Papers of Wirt A. Yerger, Jr.).

127 Wirt A. Yerger, Jr., Press Release, 22 October 1964 (Personal Papers of Wirt A. Yerger, Jr.).

128 Wirt A. Yerger, Jr., Press Release, 22 October 1964 (Personal Papers of Wirt A. Yerger, Jr.).

129 "Yerger Says Feds 'Soft' On Commies," *The Clarion-Ledger,* 11 October 1964, 11-A.

130 George Gallup, "Cold War Tops Race Issue As Greatest Voter Worry," 11 October 1964, 7-A.

131 "Big Showdown Looming Over South Viet Nam: President Meets Again With His Top Assistants," *The Clarion-Ledger,* 17 May 1964, 1.

132 "Big Showdown Looming Over South Viet Nam: President Meets Again With His Top Assistants," 1.

133 "Grim New Warnings Given On Red Cuba," *The Clarion-Ledger,* 17 May 1964, 1.

134 "The Worker," in The *Jackson Daily News*, 19 October 1964, 8.

135 For the full transcript of Barry's letter and Wirt A. Yerger, Jr.'s letter to him, see Appendix. (Personal Papers of Wirt A. Yerger, Jr.).

136 For full contents of Barry Goldwater's January 26, 1989 letter to Wirt A. Yerger, Jr., see Appendix. (Personal Papers of Wirt A. Yerger, Jr.).

137 For full contents of Barry Goldwater's January 26, 1989 letter to Wirt A. Yerger, Jr., see Appendix. (Personal Papers of Wirt A. Yerger, Jr.).

138 "Mississippi: Goldwater for President Committee," Press Release, 23 October 1964 (Personal Papers of Wirt A. Yerger, Jr.).

139 Letter from Wirt A. Yerger, Jr., to Dean Burch, 27 October 1964 (Personal Papers of Wirt A. Yerger, Jr.).

140 Wirt A. Yerger, Jr., Press Release, 29 October 1964 (Personal Papers of Wirt A. Yerger, Jr.).

141 Wirt A. Yerger, Jr., Press Release, 29 October 1964 (Personal Papers of Wirt A. Yerger, Jr.).

142 "Statement by Wirt A. Yerger, Jr., Chairman, Southern Association of Republican State Chairmen and Chairman, Mississippi Republican Party," 4 November 1964 (Personal Papers of Wirt A. Yerger, Jr.).

143 Wirt A. Yerger, Jr., "Barry Goldwater did much to help," *The Clarion-Ledger,* 8 June 1998, 7-A.

Chapter 12
1965: A Two-Party System Achieved!

1 "GOP County Leaders Offer Their Blueprint," *The Clarion-Ledger,* 20 January 1965, 3.

2 "Yerger Chosen As Officer In National Group," *Mississippi Conservative Challenge,* Vol. 3, No. 8, August 1965, 1.

3 "Adam Invitation Prompts Yerger To Offer Reminder," *The Clarion-Ledger,* 14 January 1965, 5.

4 "Top Conservative Rank Is Won By Rep. Walker," *Mississippi Conservative Challenge,* Vol. 3, No. 9, September 1965, 4.

5 Mary Ann Pardue, "Walker, Other GOP Frosh To Meet Press Corps Today," *The Clarion-Ledger,* 14 January 1965, 6.

6 "A Two-Team League," *Time* magazine, 18 June 1965.

7 Letter from William T. Wilkins to Joseph L. Maxwell, III and Wirt A. Yerger, Jr., 7 May 2008 (Personal Papers of Wirt A. Yerger, Jr.).

8 "Negro Voting Trends—A Mississippi Dilemma," Confidential Copy No. 1, January 1965 (Personal Papers of William T. Wilkins).

9 "Negro Voting Trends—A Mississippi Dilemma."

10 "Negro Voting Trends—A Mississippi Dilemma."

11 "Negro Voting Trends—A Mississippi Dilemma."

12 Rowland Evans and Robert Novak, "Moderate Republicans Plotting Comeback Attempt in Georgia: Switch In Negro Votes To Democrats Key Reason," *The Clarion-Ledger,* 4 January 1965, 8.

13 "Mississippi Republican Party: 1965 Conservative Voter Registration Campaignn Plan," Confidential Copy No. 24, January 1965; (Personal Papers of William T. Wilkins).

14 A letter from Wirt A. Yerger, Jr., to "The President" (i.e. Lyndon Johnson), 8 February 1965 (Personal Papers of Wirt A. Yerger, Jr.).

15 "GOP Voting Rights Bill is Better," *The Conservative Challenge,* June 1965, 4.

16 Press Release by the State Executive Committee of the Mississippi Republican Party, 16 April 1965.

17 W.C. Shoemaker, "State Leaders Say Changes Are Coming," *The Clarion-Ledger,* 21 February 1965, 20.

18 "Klumb Urges State To Take Initiative," *The Clarion-Ledger,* 6 February 1965, 3.

19 "Goldwater Opposed Voting Bill," *The Clarion-Ledger*, 19 March 1965, 14.

20 "Yerger Urges 'Judgement' In Legislation," *The Clarion-Ledger,* 17 March 1965, 6.

21 "Republicans Now Face Primary In Election," *The Clarion-Ledger, 12* April 1965, 12.

22 "Republicans Now Face Primary In Election," 12.

23 "GOP Primaries Seen in Two State Cities," *The Clarion-Ledger,* 16 April 1965, 6.

24 William I. Chaze, "Republicans Have It Made When It Comes To Publicity," *The Clarion-Ledger,* 18 April 1965, 3-F.

25 "GOP Leaders Aim for June," *The Clarion-Ledger, 12* May 1965, 9.

26 "Yerger Calls GOP Wins Historic Breakthrough," *The Clarion-Ledger, 9* June 1965, 10.

27 "Johnson Doubts GOP Making Great Gains," *The Clarion-Ledger,* 10 June 1965, 4.

28 "A Two-Team League," *Time* magazine, 18 June 1965.

29 "17-Member State Group To Young GOP Confab," *The Clarion-Ledger/ Jackson Daily News,* 13 June 1965, 12-A.

30 "State GOP Hoping for Primaries," *The Clarion-Ledger, 20* June 1965, 6.

31 "Biracial Group Studies Capturing Young Demos," *The Clarion-Ledger,* 3 May 1965, 1, 12.

32 Bessie Ford, "Biracial Group Fails to Agree," *The Clarion-Ledger*, 5 June 1965, 3.

33 Charles M. Hills, "PBJ Hopeful on Vote Plan," *The Clarion-Ledger*, 10 July 1965, 1.

34 "Voting Laws Too Late, Evers Says," *The Clarion-Ledger*, 8 July 1965, 12.

35 Don McKee, "Negro Vote Power Growing in South," *The Clarion-Ledger*, 12 July 1965, 6.

36 "Yerger Hits at Johnson," *The Clarion-Ledger*, 5 June 1965, 3.

37 "State Senator Raps Yerger," *The Clarion-Ledger*, 18 June 1965, 3.

38 Press Release from Wirt A. Yerger, Jr., to Mississippi media, 16 June 1965.

39 William Peart, "Incongruity of Protests and Yerger About Session," *The Clarion-Ledger*, 29 June 1965, 3-F.

40 John Hall, "Negroes, Whites Organize National Democratic Group," *The Clarion-Ledger*, 19 July 1965, 1.

41 Hall, 1.

42 William L. Chaze, "Democratic Party In State Heading Toward New Split," *The Clarion-Ledger/Jackson Daily News*, 25 July 1965, 3-F.

43 Press Release from Wirt A. Yerger, Jr., to Mississippi media, August 8, 1965 (Personal Papers of Wirt A. Yerger, Jr.).

44 "Voting Rights Bill Gets Senate Okay: LBJ Hails Action as 'Proud Moment'," *The Clarion-Ledger*, 5 August 1965, 1.

45 "Many People Dissatisfied With Speed of Integration," *The Clarion-Ledger*, 8 August 1965, 2.

46 Charles M. Hills, "Governor Sees U.S. Vendetta: 'Most Likely' Will Call Meet of Solons in Early December," *The Clarion-Ledger*, 1 October 1965, 1.

47 Charles M. Hills, PBJ Asserts Illiterates To Be Kept From Polls: Charges Discrimination By U.S. Against State," *The Clarion-Ledger*, 14 September 1965, 1.

48 "Yerger Proposes Session to Set Up Qualifications," *The Clarion-Ledger*, 13 August 1965, 12.

49 "L.A. Guardsmen Curb Violence, Pillage, Ruin," *The Clarion-Ledger*, 15 August 1965, 1.

50 "Police, Guardsmen Battle L.A. Snipers," *The Clarion-Ledger,* 16 August 1965, 1.

51 "Martin Luther Says Police Responsible," *The Clarion-Ledger*, 20 August 1965, 1.

52 "Chicago's School Aid Frozen By Government: Racial Discrimination Evidence is Claimed," *The Clarion-Ledger*, 2 October 1965, 1.

53 "Historic Medicare Bill Awaits LBJ Signature: Senate Vote 70-24 On Aid to Elderly," *The Clarion-Ledger*, 29 July 1965, 1. 3.

54 Drew Pearson, "United States Should Find Way To Get Out of South Vietnam," *The Clarion-Ledger*, 27 February 1965, 4.

55 "Yerger Blasts 'Limited War' On Viet Cong," *Mississippi Conservative Challenge,"* Vol. 3, No. 6, June 1965.

56 Press Release from Wirt A. Yerger, Jr., 29 December 1965 (Personal Papers of Wirt A. Yerger, Jr.).

57 "Draft Calls Up Sharply for September, October," *The Clarion-Ledger*, August 4, 1965, 1; and, James E. Bonney, "FDP Urges State's Negroes To Ignore Their Uncle Sam," *The Clarion-Ledger*, 31 July 1965, 1.

58 "Legion Urges U.S. Act on FDP Defy-Draft Call: Asks Probe, Indictment, Prosecution of Charges," *The Clarion-Ledger*, 2 August 1965, 1.

59 "Freedom Democrats Rapped by NAACP," *The Clarion-Ledger/Jackson Daily News*, 1 August 1965, 7-A.

60 James Saggus, "State Democrats Face Quandary; No Solution Seen: No Agreement Likely Between Three Factions," in *The Clarion-Ledger/Jackson Daily News*, 22 August 1965, 12-A.

61 "Carmichael Lauderdale GOP Chief," *The Clarion-Ledger*, 21 August 1965, 3.

62 "Clarke Reed Named GOP Fund Chairman For State," *The Clarion Ledger*, 21 September 1965, 6.

63 "Clarke Reed Named GOP Fund Chairman For State," 6.

64 "Clarke Reed Named GOP Fund Chairman For State," 6.

65 "Republican Gains Are Forecast," *The Clarion-Ledger*, 26 September 1965, 10-A.

66 Wirt A. Yerger, Jr., Press Release from Wirt A. Yerger, Jr., to Mississippi media, 21 October 1965 (Personal Papers of Wirt A. Yerger, Jr.).

67 "Republican Leaders Plan State Meeting," *The Clarion-Ledger*, 4 October 1965, 2.

68 William Peart, "Republicans Seek To Prove Party of the Conservatives," *The Clarion-Ledger/Jackson Daily News*, 17 October 1965, 3-F.

Chapter 13
1966: My Resignation

1 "State's Lack of Leadership Hit by Yerger," *Mississippi Conservative Challenge*, Vol. 4, Number 1, January 1966, 3.

2 W.F. Minor, "Democrats Take Aim At GOP Once Again," *Mississippi Conservative Challenge*, Vol. 4, Number 12, December 1966.

3 W.F. Minor, "Democrats Take Aim At GOP Once Again," *Mississippi Conservative Challenge,* Vol. 4, Number 12, December 1966.

4 W.F. Minor, "Democrats Take Aim At GOP Once Again," *Mississippi Conservative Challenge,* Vol. 4, Number 12, December 1966.

5 W.F. Minor, "Democrats Take Aim At GOP Once Again," *Mississippi Conservative Challenge,* Vol. 4, Number 12, December 1966.

6 "Yerger Says Violence Aids Left Wingers," *The Clarion-Ledger*, 14 January 1966, 3.

7 "Yerger Says GOP Candidate Will Oppose Eastland," *The Clarion-Ledger*, 25 January 1966, 6.

8 Letter from William T. Wilkins to Joseph L. Maxwell, III and Wirt A. Yerger, Jr., 7 May 2008 (Personal Papers of Wirt A. Yerger, Jr.).

9 "Wirt Yerger Quits Post As GOP Chairman," by William Peart, *The Jackson Daily News,* Monday, 7 February 1966, A-1.

10 Letter from William T. Wilkins to Joseph L. Maxwell, III and Wirt A. Yerger, Jr., 7 May 2008 (Personal Papers of Wirt A. Yerger, Jr.).

11 "Yerger Says Farewell; Brings Forth Memories," *Mississippi Conservative Challenge*, February 1966, 2.

12 "Yerger Says Farewell; Brings Forth Memories," 2.

13 "Yerger Says Farewell; Brings Forth Memories," 2.

Index